THE HARMONISATION OF EUROPEAN PRIVATE LAW

The Harmonisation of European Private Law

Edited by

MARK VAN HOECKE

and

FRANÇOIS OST

• HART •
PUBLISHING

OXFORD – PORTLAND OREGON

2000

Hart Publishing
Oxford and Portland, Oregon

Published in North America (US and Canada) by
Hart Publishing c/o
International Specialized Book Services
5804 NE Hassalo Street
Portland, Oregon
97213-3644
USA

Distributed in the Netherlands, Belgium and Luxembourg by
Intersentia, Churchilllaan 108
B2900 Schoten
Antwerpen
Belgium

Hart Publishing Ltd is a specialist legal publisher based in Oxford, England. To order further copies of this book or to request a list of other publications please write to:

Hart Publishing Ltd, Salter's Boatyard,
Folly Bridge, Abingdon Road, Oxford OX1 4LB
Telephone: +44 (0)1865 245533 or Fax: +44 (0)1865 794882
e-mail: mail@hartpub.co.uk
www.hartpub.co.uk

British Library Cataloguing in Publication Data
Data Available
ISBN 1 84113–137–7 (cloth)

Typeset by Hope Services (Abingdon) Ltd.
Printed in Great Britain on acid-free paper
by Biddles Ltd, Guildford and King's Lynn.

EUROPEAN ACADEMY OF LEGAL THEORY MONOGRAPH SERIES

General Editors

Professor Mark Van Hoecke
Professor François Ost
Professor Luc Wintgens

Titles in this Series

Moral Conflict and Legal Reasoning *by Scott Veitch*

The Harmonisation of European Private Law
by Mark Van Hoecke and François Ost

Contents

Contributors

Zenon Bankowski is professor of Legal Theory at the *University of Edinburgh*. He teaches courses in jurisprudence and the philosophy of private law. Among his research interests are law and legality considered in the perspective of social theory and theology and the impact of the European Union on conceptions of legal theory.

(e-mail: Z.Bankowski@ed.ac.uk)

Anthony Chamboredon is a doctoral researcher at the *European University Institute* in Florence. He obtained the master's degree in legal theory from the *European Academy of Legal Theory* in 1995. He is currently preparing a doctoral thesis on the progressive formation of contracts.

(e-mail: Chambore@datacomm.iue.it)

María Elósegui is Professor at the *Universidad de Zaragoza*, where she teaches Legal Theory, Philosophy of Law and Human Rights. In 1994 she obtained the master's degree in legal theory from the *European Academy of Legal Theory*. Her current research focuses on legal aspects of equal opportunities between women and men and on legal implications of interculturalism.

(e-mail: Elosegui@posta.unizar.es)

José García Añón is professor of Legal Philosophy at the *Universitat de València*. He teaches Legal Theory, Legal Philosophy, and Human Rights. As a doctoral student he took part in an intensive *Erasmus seminar on legal theory*, organised by the *European Academy of Legal Theory*, in 1991. He has published some works on utilitarianism and rights, especially focused on John Stuart Mill. His current research focuses mainly on human rights and rights of minorities.

(e-mail: Jose.Garcia@uv.es)

Fritz Jost is Professor of Private Law, Procedural Law and Legal Sociology at the *Universität Bielefeld*. He is a member of the board of directors of the *Institut für Anwalts- und Notarrecht der Universität Bielefeld*.

(e-mail: Jostmail@uni-bielefeld.de)

Ireneusz C. Kaminski is Associate Professor (*adiunkt*) at the *Polish Academy of Sciences*, Chair for International and European Law, in Warsaw. He also teaches several courses at the *Jagiellonian University* in Cracow. He obtained the master's degree in legal theory at the *European Academy of Legal Theory*, in 1997. His recent interests focus on media law issues and legal cultures in

Europe. Currently, he is working on a project related to media standards, which is financed by the Open Society Institute (New York/Budapest).

(e-mail: Kaminski@if.uj.edu.pl)

Basil S. Markesinis, QC, DCL., Dr.Iur. h.c. mult., is Clifford Chance Professor of Comparative Law at the *University of Oxford*, where he is a Fellow of Brasenose College. He is a Fellow of the British Academy and the Founder/Director of the Oxford Institute of European and Comparative Law. His research focuses on the comparative law of obligations.

Paolisa Nebbia is lecturer in law at the *University of Southampton*. She obtained her law degree from the *Università degli studi di Torino*, in 1994, and the master's degree in legal theory from the *European Academy of Legal Theory*, in 1996. She is preparing a doctoral thesis on Unfair Contract Terms and Consumer Law in a comparative perspective.

(e-mail: P.E.Nebbia@soton.ac.uk)

Giorgio Pino is lecturer at the *Università degli Studi di Palermo*. He obtained the master's degree in legal theory at the *European Academy of Legal Theory* in 1997. His research focuses on legal interpretation, legal theory and fundamental rights. He is completing his PhD thesis on privacy rights, which will be studied from both a philosophical and a comparative perspective.

(e-mail: gPino@unipa.it)

François Rigaux is emeritus Professor of the *Université Catholique de Louvain* (Louvain-la-Neuve) and Professor at the *European Academy of Legal Theory*, where he is conducting a seminar on *Constitutional and International Justice*, after having taught the course on *Theory of European Legal Integration*, from 1992 till 1999.

Geoffrey Samuel is Professor of Law at the Kent Law School (*University of Kent* at Canterbury) and, in 1999–2000, *professeur associé* at the *Université de Paris II*. He teaches (part of) a course on *Theory of Comparative Law* in the master's course in legal theory at the *European Academy of Legal Theory*.

(e-mail: G.H.Samuel@ukc.ac.uk)

Burkhard Schäfer has been a lecturer at the *Edinburgh University* Law School since 1996. His main research interest is the transfer of formal methods from comparative linguistics, epistemology and cognitive science to comparative law and ultimately a "Chomsky Programme" for legal comparison. He also works on computer support systems for comparative and international private law.

(e-mail: B.Schafer@ed.ac.uk)

Mark van Hoecke is professor of law at the *Katholieke Universiteit Brussel* and (with François Ost) founder and co-director of the *European Academy of Legal Theory*. In the master's course in legal theory, he teaches, with F.Ost, the course on *Jurisprudence*. His current research focuses mainly on theory of comparative law.

(e-mail: Mark.VanHoecke@kubrussel.ac.be)

Alain Wijffels is Professor of Legal History and Comparative Law and affiliated to the Universities of *Leiden* and *Louvain-la-Neuve*. At the *European Academy of Legal Theory* he teaches the course on *European Legal History*. His current research focuses on early-modern European *ius commune* and the history of public international law.

Foreword

This volume contains a selection of papers presented at the Conference *European Private Law in Context*, organised in Brussels, by the Katholieke Universiteit Brussel and the European Academy of Legal Theory, on the 5th and 6th of February 1999, at the occasion of the 10th anniversary of the Academy and with the financial support of the Fund for Scientific Research, Flanders (Belgium). The first activity organised by the European Academy of Legal Theory has been the *First Erasmus Seminar on Legal Theory*, which took place from the 6th to the 10th of February 1989. In the following years, five more such seminars have been set up, the latest having been held in March 1994. As from October 1992, a Master's Course in Legal Theory (LL.M.) has been organised. From the very start, an important part of this programme has been devoted to problems of comparative law and European legal integration. This is demonstrated by the fact that one of the three compulsory main courses in this programme is entitled Theory of Comparative Law and of European Legal Integration. However, many of the other courses and seminars discuss these problems, or to some extent pay attention to them. This area has also been, since 1994, a major field of research within the Centrum voor Rechtstheorie at the Katholieke Universiteit Brussel.

The interest of legal theorists in European legal integration is, of course, partly due to the paramount importance of the topic in present day legal practice and political, sociological and economic developments. But, this is not the only reason. The discussions on European legal integration, and, more generally, on the methodology of comparative law, show the limits of traditional legal doctrine. Once one begins to *compare*, to *harmonise* and to *integrate* legal systems, it transpires that a broader approach is needed.

Firstly, when such a project is carried out, one needs to *define* and delimitate "legal systems". What must we compare: statutory rules, case law, legal history, law's political, sociological and economical environment, the ideological background of the lawyers, legal techniques, legal traditions, legal cultures, etc.? This question is at the core of many current debates and will, at least to some extent, be discussed in most of the papers in this volume. Without knowing *what* we should compare, harmonise or integrate, no fruitful work could be done in the field of comparative law and European legal integration. Today, nobody doubts that limiting oneself to statutory law and case law cannot suffice. Studying positive law, in terms of legal doctrine, is not enough. One has to leave this level of pure positive law and to locate the law in its context. By doing so, one automatically reaches a more theoretical and interdisciplinary approach.

This is the second point where legal theory comes into play: *interdisciplinarity*. Even within positive law there is already a pluralism of partly intertwined legal systems: (at least) fifteen national legal systems, EU law, and European Human Rights law. However, this does not lead to "interdisciplinarity" in a strict sense, but rather to some kind of "intersystemicity" and to the creation of a new kind of "European legal doctrine". Once one leaves the level of pure positive law and accepts that law has to be understood by locating it in its context, it should be obvious that the relevant context is not just history, or just politics, or just economics. Law cannot be fully explained by its historical background only, or by current economic developments alone, for instance. *All* such societal elements and developments have to be taken into account when one aims at offering a true picture of law, in view of its comparison with other legal systems, and, even more so, when the aim is their harmonisation or integration. This means that, here, almost all human sciences may, potentially, be relevant: history, politics, economics, sociology, psychology, and so on. Moreover, it should be noted that these disciplines are broader than just *legal* history, or *legal* sociology, etc. Of course, depending on the branch of law and the concrete topic, some disciplines may be more relevant than others, and some may prove not to be relevant at all in that specific case, but at least to *some* extent an interdisciplinary approach will be needed. In its most modest form, this means looking at our current law from the point of view of one non legal discipline, with an eye on at least some other elements of this law's background. This is the approach which is mostly to be found, and also in this volume: notably legal history (most prominently Wijffels, but also Samuel and Kami_ski), and legal sociology (especially with regard to the debate on "legal culture": Van Hoecke, Chamboredon, Schäfer & Bankowski, who also draw an analogy with linguistics).

Thirdly, legal theory has not only a role to play as a kind of catalyst and coordinator of interdisciplinary legal research, it has also its own results of legal analysis to offer. Examples offered in this volume are: legal epistemology (Samuel, Schäfer & Bankowski, Van Hoecke), (pluralist or monist) conceptions of a "legal system" (Rigaux), legal methodology (the methodology of law making, more specifically the use of open concepts: Chamboredon, García Añón; the methodology of legal doctrine: Jost, Van Hoecke, García Añón; judicial legal reasoning: Van Hoecke, Markesinis) theory of legal sources (Chamboredon); the analysis of concepts such as "equality", "rights" or "legal principles" (Elósegui), "personal rights" or "personal identity" (Pino).

One of the most useful elements in legal theoretical research is certainly the uncovering of hidden ideological assumptions, which may be found in law and legal reasoning. Originally inspired by leftist movements in the 1960's and used, most prominently by the Critical Legal Studies Movement in America, within the frame of a critique of law and society, it now turns out to be of utmost importance for any comparative research. In this volume, examples are to be found, most prominently, in the papers by Nebbia, García Añón, Elósegui, Pino and Kamiński, but to some extent in most of the other papers too.

It is not only legal theory which has something to offer to comparative law. High level research in comparative law almost always offers an important contribution to legal theory. An example in this volume is Markesinis' analysis of the ways of reasoning by judges in Britain and in Germany. Markesinis shows the difference between the judges' legal reasoning and the way this reasoning is presented, and, moreover, offers empirical evidence for the viewpoint according to which judicial reasoning is always a mixture of inductive and deductive reasoning.

This volume, thus, hopes to create a bridge, not only between two centuries and millennia (written and orally presented in 1999 and published in 2000), but also, and, of course, in the first place, between comparative law and legal theory, and, by this, between (national or European) legal doctrine and legal theory too.

Mark Van Hoecke & François Ost
Brussels, January 2000

1

The Harmonisation of Private Law in Europe: Some Misunderstandings[1]

MARK VAN HOECKE

1. INTRODUCTION

The unification, harmonisation or convergence of private law in Europe is a typical topic of the nineties. There were almost no publications on this topic until the end of the eighties, but over the last decade there has been a constantly increasing number of publications, including several new journals, which have been created partly, or even mainly, for this purpose. They include: *Zeitschrift für Europäisches Privatrecht* (1993), *European Review of Private Law* (1993), *Maastricht Journal of European and Comparative Law* (1994). Today, in many journals on comparative law, and even in some more traditional national law journals, there is hardly any volume in which the topic is not discussed, directly or indirectly.

As a symbolic starting point we may take the 1989 call by the European Parliament for the elaboration of a European civil code.[2] At the same time it has been the most ambitious proposal in the field. In the common enthusiasm for the building of Europe, beyond the pure economic level, as a political, social, and even military union, encompassing within a near future the whole European continent, the discussion has not been about the question of the desirability or possibility of such a unification or harmonisation, but about the most appropriate ways to reach this aim and, sometimes, about the limits of a short term unification. Drafting and enacting a European civil code was one of the possible ways. Several alternative, or simply concurring, proposals, of which some already have been realised, were proposed, such as:

(1) a *"private" code* of private law, not issued by European authorities, but drafted by representants of all, or most, countries of the European Union and offered as a set of rules to which parties to an international contract may refer, if they want so;[3]

[1] With many thanks to Geoffrey Samuel for his comments on a first draft of this paper.

[2] *Official Journal of the European Communities* 1989, no C 158/400.

[3] Most notably: the *Principles of European Contract Law*, drafted by the Commission on European Contract Law, commonly known as the "*Lando Commission*" (Lando, O., & Beale, H.,

(2) the publication of *case books*, in which court decisions from different European legal systems on concrete similar cases are discussed in a comparative perspective,[4] or of
(3) *text books* offering an overview of some field of private law in a similar comparative European perspective;[5]
(4) *combined study programmes*, in which students receive part of their legal education in another European country,[6]
(5) the creation of a *common European legal doctrine* for all fields of national private law, a common conceptual framework, or a "legal epistemology", as Samuel calls it.[7]

It is striking that the only radical attack against the idea of a "European civil code" came from a non European scholar, Pierre Legrand, a French Canadian who has been working at the University of Lancaster for several years, after that as a professor of "Comparative Legal Cultures" at the University of Tilburg, and who is currently teaching at the University of Lille 2.[8] Partly under his influence some more critical approaches to the possible unification of private law in Europe have emerged recently. Until then, the division was obvious: opponents of any form of legal harmonisation in Europe did not publish on the subject, only the proponents did. Now however, the shortcomings of some rather naive and precipitated approaches have been exposed. Overly simplifying models have been criticised. Attention has been drawn to theoretical and practical elements which sometimes were neglected, or at least underestimated, when dicussing the unification problem. As a result, even advocates of a unification of law have become more careful and are reducing their ambitions, at least in their writings.[9] This is also visible in the wording used: today, 'unification' seems to be less appropriate, as it suggests a complete integration of legal

(eds.) *Principles of European Contract Law, Part I: Performance, Non-Performance and Remedies* (Dordrecht, Martinus Nijhoff, 1995).

[4] E.g. the series *Ius Commune Casebooks for the Common Law of Europe*, launched by the University of Maastricht and directed by professor Walter van Gerven, in which a first volume has been published in 1998: van Gerven, W., e.a., *Cases, Materials and Text on National, Supranational and International Tort Law. Scope of Protection* (Oxford, Hart Publishing).

[5] E.g., as for contract law: Kötz, H. & Flessner, A., *European Contract Law. Volume 1. Formation, Validity and Content of Contracts; Contract and Third Parties*, transl. from German by T. Weir (Oxford, Clarendon Press, 1997).

[6] The most advanced examples are the integrated bi-national law degrees, such as the one offered by the universities of Paris 2 and London (King's College): students attend courses for a period of two years at each of these universities. The most widespread and very successful formula are the Erasmus exchanges, financially supported by the European Union.

[7] Van Hoecke, M., & Ost, F., "Legal doctrine in crisis: towards a European legal science", 18 *Legal Studies* 1998, 197–215; Samuel, G., "Comparative Law and Jurisprudence", 47 *ICLQ* 1998, 817–836.

[8] Legrand, P., "Against a European Civil Code", 60 *Modern Law Review* 1997, 44; Legrand, P. "European Legal Systems are Not Converging", 45 *ICLQ*, 1996, 52.

[9] A most striking example is Walter van Gerven's *Foreword* to his *Tort Law* case book (see fn. 3), in which he anticipates possible criticism by writing: "The objective of this casebook and of the whole series is to help uncover the common roots of the different legal systems, not to unify them. In other words, to strengthen the common legal heritage of Europe, not to strangle its diversity." (p. v).

concepts, rules and cultures, which is hardly advocated nowadays. The word 'harmonisation' is now preferred, as it leaves room for a large scale of possible differences left. Some will prefer the term 'convergence', as it suggest rather a natural development, whereas 'harmonisation' suggests a more active process through which some degree of unification is reached.

All this is as it should be: it is from a critical scrutiny and discussion that the best ideas and practical solutions arise. Nevertheless, the discussion often seems to be unfruitful in that one, or even both parties start from erroneous assumptions, from misunderstandings about what law is and/or about the position taken by the criticised opponent. It is these misunderstandings that I want to discuss in this paper, basically starting from Pierre Legrand's critique. It is my belief that legal theory may be very helpful to elucidate some of the problems which traditional legal doctrine and comparative law are facing, sometimes consciously, but often without being aware of them. This revealing of common misunderstandings amongst proponents and opponents of a unification of law in Europe is also a main concern in the paper, in this volume, by Burkhard Schäfer and Zenon Bankowski, and in which they criticize the assumption that a unification of private law in Europe would destroy particular forms of life. This was also the aim of the conference at which the papers of this volume were presented: by putting private law in its broad theoretical and interdisciplinary context we should be able to improve the discussion on topics such as the unification or harmonisation of private law in Europe, not because legal theory could offer some ready made solutions, but because it may eliminate false discussions; it may exclude some alternatives and expose some new possibilities.

2. LAW AND ITS UNDERLYING LEGAL CULTURE

It has been argued that European legal systems will never converge, because of fundamental differences amongst their underlying (legal) cultures.[10] It is, of course, correct to point to the importance of these cultures for understanding how law works in practice. There is a whole set of common understandings, traditions, habits, ways of life, shared ideological assumptions and views on men and society, which are considerably influencing and determining how law is perceived in a society. Legrand describes (legal) culture as "frameworks of intangibles within which interpretive (legal) communities operate and which have normative force for these communities".[11] One should, indeed, be aware of such cultural differences and commonalities when comparing legal systems. Harmonisation of law is only conceivable within a sufficiently homogeneous legal culture. As suggested in previous writings,[12] such a common legal culture

[10] Legrand, P., "European Legal Systems are not Converging", 45 *ICLQ*, 1996, 52–81.

[11] *Op. cit.*, 56.

[12] Van Hoecke, M., "Unifikácia práva v Európe", *Právny Obzor* 1998, 127–137; Van Hoecke, M., & Warrington, M., "Legal Cultures, Legal Paradigms and Legal Doctrine: Towards a New Model for Comparative Law", 47 *ICLQ* 1998, 495–536.

within some legal community includes shared understandings on, at least, the following points: a concept of law, a theory of valid legal sources, a methodology of law, a theory of argumentation, a theory of legitimation of the law, and a common basic ideology. Legrand sees differences between (European) common law and civil law on most of these points.

As regards the *concept of law*, the common law is, in contrast to the civil law, not perceived as a set of rules, but merely a series of judicial decisions. The common law is preoccupied with the apprehension of regularities rather than the knowledge of rules.[13] The concept of natural rights, with which each citizen is endowed, independently of a concrete action awarded by the legal system, is typical for the continental legal culture, but alien to the common law: "one has no 'rights' unless one is protected by a cause of action".[14]

As regards the *theory of legal sources* the common law is essentially based on court decisions, in contrast to the civil law which is, at least in theory, based entirely on legislation. But, according to Legrand there is more: the common law is perceived as an unchanged and unchangable whole. The common law is not "created" by judges, but only "found". It is custom rather than judge made law. This very static approach to law contrasts with the dynamic continental view, in which law has been made by a legislator at a very precise date, changing by this the previous law and making it subject to new changes in the future. From this Legrand concludes: "The common law and civilian perspectives on historical time are thus seen to be incommensurable."[15]

As regards the *methodology of law* and the *theory of argumentation*, Legrand points to the inductive character of English legal reasoning, as opposed to the deductive way of reasoning on the Continent.[16] In the Common Law legal knowledge emerges from facts rather than from rules, as it is the case on the Continent.[17] Systematisation of the law and its codification seem to be typical for civil law systems, whereas "the common law was never systematised nor has it ever aspired to be".[18] Finally, Legrand sees an *epistemological impossibility* for a convergence between legal systems such as the common law and the civilian ones. Just as an adult, who learns a foreign language, never will be able to speak that language *like a native speaker*, even if he would be fluent in that language, a civilian lawyer may be able to understand English law to a large extent, but never will be able to "understand the English legal experience *like an English lawyer*".[19]

For opponents of convergence, harmonisation or unification of private law in Europe these arguments must sound very convincing, and might easily be

[13] *Op. cit.*, 67–68.
[14] *Op. cit.*, 70.
[15] *Op. cit.*, 74.
[16] *Op. cit.*, 64–65.
[17] *Op. cit.*, 68–70.
[18] *Op. cit.*, 65.
[19] *Op. cit.*, 78.

accepted without much critical appraisal. Those in favour of some form of convergence will probably have the feeling that all this is wrong, or at least exaggerated, so allowing the argument to be easily discarded. However, one is under an obligation to accept Legrand's arguments, unless one is able to indicate where and how they are mistaken. In what follows I will try to show the weak points in Legrand's reasoning.

2.1. The impossible internal point of view

Let us start with the epistemological argument: that is, the impossibility of a really full understanding of foreign legal systems. Another comparison Legrand makes is this. Men may more or less understand women, but they never will be able to *feel* as a woman. Both this statement and the one about the imposibility for a foreigner to become a native speaker are true. But the queston is (a) to what extent can we make a similar reasoning concerning foreign legal systems, and (b) what consequences must be drawn from it? Pierre Legrand quotes Pierre Legendre:

> "An American, even though very learned, cannot enter inside the institutional discourse in use in Continental Europe without running the risk of all experts; this discourse remains as closed to him as would have been, to colonial ears, the Negro discourse".[20]

The easy answer would be to turn this argument against Pierre Legrand himself: "as a Canadian, even though very learned, he cannot enter inside the legal discourse in use in Europe. If he cannot fully understand it, he should not write about it, and if he does, nobody should take it seriously." This, actually, is the consequence of Legrand's own reasoning. But, I do not accept this reasoning, and so do I neither accept this easy conclusion. But why?

2.1.1. Cultures are changing

Every culture, including legal culture, is an open and dynamic, not a closed and static entity, as Legrand seems to assume. Burkhard Schäfer and Zenon Bankowski, in their paper, discuss this open character of cultures and communities. Here, I would like to emphasise the dynamic, changing character of every culture, which, of course, presupposes a cognitive openness towards the external world, including other cultures. Europeans, for instance, do not understand many elements in American culture. Often, we Europeans feel unable to take the internal point of view. But, at the same time, we are and have been taking over many elements of American culture. Our children are partly educated as little

[20] *Op. cit.*, 77, with reference to: Legendre, P., *Jouir du Pouvoir: Traité de la Bureaucratie Patriote*, 1976, p. 58.

Americans by numerous television series and movies.[21] Europeans are, by this, not becoming Americans, but we are converging.

Today, English is the main second language in the world. To such an extent, that the English native speakers became a minority amongst all those who speak English. As knowledge of, and fluency in, English are increasing amongst the foreigners, they are increasingly influencing the English language. Native speakers do not any longer fully control their language (and, henceforth, their culture). A good example is the word "legal dogmatics", an "anglification" of the continental word, which exists in all continental languages, e.g. in German as *Rechtsdogmatik*, or in French as *dogmatique juridique*. The (more or less) equivalent genuine English word is "legal doctrine".[22] *Legal dogmatics* used to be both a concept and a word which were completely alien to English legal culture. However, slowly the word is getting accepted amongst British scholars and, together with the word, the whole continental conception of legal doctrine. It does not mean that the common law conception of "legal dogmatics" will be identical to the continental one, but it means, undoubtedly, that the legal cultures are converging. If, for instance, the English legal profession has changed more in the last few decades than over, let's say, the last five centuries,[23] why would English legal culture not be able to converge with continental legal culture in the next few decades?

The discussion about "incommensurable (legal) cultures" within the European Union reminds a similar discussion on the future of colonial law in post-colonial Africa. European codes, it is said, do not fit at all with traditional African legal culture. Their import in African countries was wrong and doomed to fail. It is perfectly true that European codes did not fit at all with African culture and tradition. Neither did cars, airplanes, radios, televisions, computers, etc. Today, however, nobody in Africa will propose to throw all these out and to start living again as they did before nineteenth-century colonialisation.

[21] This is mainly the case in smaller countries, with a limited population speaking their language. Here, movies and series are not dubbed, but undertitled, because this is much cheaper. As a result, children easily learn (American) English: the spoken foreign language is supported by a written translation into their mother tongue, on the screen. Moreover, the local production is limited, because of the small potential market, so that even more foreign (and thus mainly American) series and movies are programmed.

[22] But what is genuine? "Legal doctrine" is obviously just law-French, derived from "*doctrine juridique*", a French synonym for "*dogmatique juridique*".

[23] Fundamental changes have occured as to: the access to the legal profession (university law degree required, or another university degree supplemented with a conversion course degree; post-graduate education required when preparing for the bar entry), the structure of the bar (abolition of the monopoly of the Inns of Court as the place where the barrister until recently had to practice, and abolition of the monopoly of the barristers vis-à-vis the solicitors for pleading before the higher courts), continuing education (compulsory for all solicitors since 1998), the role and influence of legal academics (legal doctrine now being more and more frequently cited in court decisions, see, e.g., the discussion, on the proper use of academic literature, in *Hunter v. Canary Wharf Ltd* [1997] 2 All ER 426; see, more generally, on this development: Birks, P., "The academic and the practitioner", 18 *Legal Studies*, 1998, 397–414). It is very likely that the next few decades will show even more important changes, such as, probably, the merger of the two professions "barristers" and "solicitors" into one single profession of "advocates".

African culture is not any longer comparable to that of their ancestors. They have to a large extent taken over parts of the culture of the European colonisators. They do not, nowadays, consider cars, computers, codes, and the like, to be alien to their culture. They may use them somewhat differently. Their position towards them may differ, on the basis of specific features of their culture in general. But they certainly do not reject them.

Sometimes, in African countries, rules are imposed by the governing bodies which aim to restore original traditions that disappeared under colonialism. However, they often fail, just because these traditions *have* disappeared and are not any longer felt by the citizens to be part of their culture. A typical example is the introduction by the Mobutu regime of the name "*Zaire*" which had to replace Belgian "*Congo*". One of the first decisions of the Kabila regime, when taking over the power from Mobutu, was restoring the name of *Congo*. In a similar vein, the Mobutu regime forced people to give their children traditional, genuine African names, and not any longer European christian names.[24] This did not work in practice. Although only such names were used in official documents, the citizen went on using the "European" christian name,[25] because it to be part of their identity, obviously to a larger extent than the (first) names of their ancestors.

(European) codes also are still in force in many African countries. They remained largely unchanged and are daily interpreted and applied by courts. Very often recent and older decisions of European courts are used as references in this interpretation process and those foreign decisions and scholarly publications are extensively cited as authoritative sources.[26]

There are many such examples. Eventually, when we take out from English law everything which ever came from the Romans, the French or other Europeans, not much, if anything, will be left of the common law.[27] What, according to Legrand, seems impossible has happened more than once. It is neither "frightening" nor "sad" "to imagine a Europe in which there would be something like a European civil code", as he posits,[28] as long as such a code would not simply be imposed by one part of Europe on another part, but be the outcome of a natural process of the development of law and legal science throughout Europe.[29] It is likely that in such a process, whether it ever will lead

[24] Art. 16 of Act n° 022/73 of 20 July 1973: "Tout zaïrois qui, avant l'entrée en vigueur de la présente loi, porte un nom d'origine étrangère, doit y renoncer. Il est tenu de renoncer à son (ses) prénom(s)."

[25] See Kanglulumba Mbambi, V., "Quelques considérations théoriques et pratiques sur le nom des personnes physiques en Afrique subsaharienne: le danger et le piège de l'uniformité", *Revue de Droit Africain* 1998, 426–452, at 442. One notices that most, if not all, authors from Congo, who after 1973 had to take an African first name, are using their christian name in this journal.

[26] See, e.g. "Cour Suprême de Justice, Chambres Réunies (RD Congo) 16 May 1990", *Revue de Droit Africain* 1998, 460–493, esp. at 464–465 and 472–474.

[27] Even the term 'Common law' has continental origins: 'Common' is French (*commun*) and 'law' is Norvegian (*lov*).

[28] Legrand, P., "Are civilians educable?", 18 *Legal Studies* 1998, 216–230, at 226.

[29] A first step towards the development of such a European legal science is suggested by Legrand himself: "An initial step . . . is to encourage the participation of civil law and common law lawyers alike in a genuine intercultural dialogue, . . ." (*op. cit.*, p. 228).

to a kind of European code or not, more elements of the civil law than of the common law will survive. But that as such will not, by future generations, be looked at as "sad". Legrand does not seem take into account the possibility that preparing such a code may lead to a complete rethinking of fundamental structures, distinctions, concepts and principles, not only of the common law, but also, and maybe to a larger extent, of the civil law. That this might well be the case appears from the papers in this volume by Samuel, by Wijffels and by Paroussis.

It would be equally wrong to see the whole process of harmonisation of private law in Europe as an opposition between two opposite, but internally homogeneous legal cultures: continental civil law as opposed to the common law. Dividing lines often run across both "legal families". Harmonisation, unavoidably, means changes for *all* involved legal systems. Daily legal practice in Europe, at all levels, be it within the European institutions, international contracts, law conferences or other meetings and bargainings, clearly shows how lawyers from all over Europe may very well, from the outside, sufficiently understand other legal systems, concepts and constructions and take, to a sufficient extent, an internal point of view from inside other legal systems.[30]

2.1.2. The integration of cultures

Foreign students may become "native speakers". If a foreigner never will become a native speaker, this is only true for an adult. Young children may become perfectly fluent in a foreign language. This is also true for legal education. A student from the University of Leuven, who follows one year of his law studies in Dublin in the frame of an Erasmus exchange, may obtain his Belgian law degree without having learned anything about, e.g., Belgian labour law and/or company law, but with a sound knowledge of Irish labour law and/or Irish company law. As a result, his "native tongue" in these fields will be the common law and he may be a "foreigner" when later on, in a Brussels law firm, he will have to practice them according to Belgian law. Just like immigrants, who at a young age came to their new country and do not anymore feel at home in their native country, when they go there for holidays, the Erasmus graduate will, at least in a first period, feel more at home in Irish than in Belgian labour or company law. In his pessimistic view, Legrand may reply that this is a lost generation, as they are doomed to remain aliens in both cultures. Some immigrants suffer from this problem, indeed, but others succeed in feeling perfectly at home in both cultures, and the large majority feels at home in at least one of both cultures. Moreover, as already suggested, it is not a sheer choice between two incomensurable cultures. Immigrant Italians have perfectly integrated in all European countries, but, at the same time, they taught the whole of Europe to

[30] Joerges, C., "European challenges to private law: on false dichotomies, true conflicts and the need for a constitutional perspective", 18 *Legal Studies* 1998, 146–166, at pp.151–152.

eat pizza, spaghetti, tagliatelle, etc. and to drink Chianti. And this is true for every intercultural contact. Through our former Erasmus students foreign legal concepts, rules, principles, models may enter into our own law and legal practice, once they become legal practitioners in their home country.

When, in legal education, common European textbooks and case books are used

> "the strange ideology shared by so many lawyers all over the world that law is deeply rooted in the culture of each nation and as such unfit for international uniformity will perhaps less easily slip into the minds of future law students, who learn from the very beginning that the mail box theory is not the only explanation for the validity of a contractual acceptance and that specific performance of contractual promises is not a law of nature."[31]

We may conclude that Legrand's view on the (im)possibility of taking an internal point of view from within a foreign legal system is probably mistaken. When law students or young lawyers are studying or working in a foreign legal system they *are* able to take such an internal point of view. One should not underestimate the importance of initiatives like the Erasmus/Socrates scheme. Even if only a few percent of all law students in Europe participate in it, these students are likely to be, later on, amongst the leading legal practitioners and legal scholars in their home country. By the time Legrand will be retiring as a law professor, a majority of the British Law Lords might well have studied or worked on the continent for some months or years. Would that not make the common law rather converging with civil law than diverging?

Finally, even for those who will not succeed in getting the full internal point of view of the "native lawyer", there is no reason why this should prevent them from acting positively in moving towards a convergence. Convergence does not mean unifying everything, it simply means getting closer to each other. This happens, even if the transplant from a foreign legal system is "incorrectly" interpreted or adapted in order to fit with the local (legal) culture. The fact that Italians have taught other Europeans to drink *cappuccino* and *espresso* does not mean that the latter have to renounce their traditional local coffees. It does not mean, either, that the *cappuccino* is the same everywhere. When ordering a *cappuccino* in some Italian restaurants in Brussels, one is asked "a Belgian or an Italian one?". The Belgian "interpretation" of *cappuccino* is coffee with whipped cream (instead of pressured milk). Of course, Belgians are not taking over the entire Italian culture, and this is certainly even less the case the other way around, but food habits have clearly converged over the last decades.[32] And so has private law.

[31] Basedow, J., "The renascence of uniform law: European contract law and its components", 18 *Legal Studies* 1998, 121–145, at 127.

[32] Once, there were a lot of Italian hotels who did not offer more for breakfast than just coffee. Today, everywhere in Italy a full continental breakfast is available, and mostly even a full English breakfast.

2.2. A different concept of law: no "rules", no "rights" in the common law

2.2.1. *"Rules" or "regularities"?*

It may be true that common lawyers have a somewhat different perception of law, compared to civil lawyers. The question is, whether, eventually, it matters in practice. The English concept of an "estate in fee simple absolute in possession" starts from the assumption that the Crown owns all land. Therefore, it is not called "property" or "ownership". But is there any practical difference as regards the concrete rights and powers of the "possessor" in fee simple absolute, when compared with the continental concepts of *propriété* or *Eigentum*? According to *English law*[33] the fact that the "possession" will be terminated once there is nobody left to inherit it, either by will or on intestacy, is considered to be a restriction on the rights of the possessor in fee simple absolute: the "possessor" may only temporarily dispose of the real estate. In *civil law* the actual legal reality is the same, but as a result of rules of inheritance law. According to art. 544 of the *Code Napoléon*, still in force in several European countries, such as France and Belgium, *propriété* is defined as an absolute and illimited power, as long as nothing illegal is done.[34] All rights and powers are with the proprietor, without any limitation, except legislative rules. But, if the proprietor dies without a will and without close family, his property will go to the State (art. 768 *Code Napoléon*).[35] The practical result is exactly the same as in the common law countries.

The same goes for the distinction between "rules" and "regularities". Customary rules are nothing else but regularities with a normative force. As the common law is perceived as a kind of customary law,[36] it is quite normal to see a series of previous decisions as "regularities". Nevertheless such regularities inevitably express rules, whether they are perceived like that or not. Customary rules are also rules. No common lawyer will deny that these "regularities" have some normative force. As a consequence, judicial decisions are the applications of rules, be they explicitly worded or just implicitly present.

2.2.2. *Rights or actions?*

The common law, says Legrand, does not know "rights", but rather "causes of action". But, actually, it does not make much sense to speak about a "right"

[33] Not anymore "common law", but legislation since the *Law of Property Act* of 1925.

[34] "*La propriété est le droit de jouir et disposer des choses de la manière la plus absolue, pourvu qu'on n'en fasse pas un usage prohibé par les lois ou par les règlements.*" The Spanish Civil code contains a very similar definition: "*La propriedad es el derecho de gozar y disponer de una cosa sin más limitaciones que las establecidas en las leyes.*" (art. 348). The same goes for the Civil code of Québec: "Ownership is the right to use, enjoy and dispose of property fully and freely, subject to the limits and conditions for doing so determined by law" (art. 947).

[35] Also still in force in Belgium and in France. A similar article may be found in many other countries, such as the Spanish Civil code (art. 956), or the Civil code of Québec (art. 696).

[36] Legrand, P., *op. cit.*, 71–74.

when one does not have a cause of action and is unable to claim it before court. On the other hand, a cause of action implies an underlying right. The emphasis may be put on one of both concepts, but they are inseparable twins. It is not because one of the twins is emphasised that the other one would not be present. Moreover, the "human rights" concept will gradually change this view of common lawyers. The practical importance of the European Court of Human Rights and the influence of its case law on domestic law, including the common law, cannot be neglected. Even if it may sound somewhat alien to a common lawyer, solicitors and barristers will certainly not be slow in invoking such "rights" before a common law court, whenever it is in favour of their clients. Common law judges will have to reflect before rejecting such an argument, when they know that the United Kingdom could be sued before the European Court and be condemned for not having respected such fundamental "rights". The introduction of a *Human Rights Bill* in the United Kingdom cannot but reinforce this development. So, common lawyers are almost certainly doomed to think more and more in terms of "rights".

There is, of course, not just the European Court of Human Rights, there is the whole European Union, of which the legal approach is, for obvious quantitative reasons, completely dominated by the continental legal culture. This EU law is affecting daily life in the common law countries to such an extent, that it is rapidly and strongly influencing their legal cultures, including legal thinking about "rights" and "causes of action". Even if Britain decided not to join the European currency, in January 1999 already one third of the operations in the London stock exchange was done in Euros. The richer part of British population will learn to "think" in Euros more rapidly than the poorer part of continental population in the transition period between January 1999 and January 2002. What is true for something where the U.K. stayed outside, is, of course, even more the case for something which affects British law directly: European Union law and European human rights law.

2.3. A different "time conception" as regards the sources of law

The common law, we are told, is not "created" by judges, but just "found". The common law does not have a beginning: it dates from time immemorial.[37] Civil law, by contrast is issued at a specific time, by a legislator. As a consequence, argues Legrand, both legal systems have a different and incommensurable historical time conception. First, even if we accept the argument, it is, by definition, only valid for the *common law* in its strict sense, not for equity law, nor for legislation. Equity law has been quite important for many centuries, and the developments over the last few decades show an impressive increase of legislation in common law countries. European Union law is an important part of it,

[37] Legrand, P., *op. cit.*, 71.

but certainly not the only, and not even the main, one. "Common law" covers an ever decreasing part of English, Welsh, and Irish law. In fact, for the majority of the valid law, the time conception of the "common lawyer" as regards his sources of law is exactly the same as the continental one. If there is any difference left, it is certainly not any longer a paradigmatic one.

Secondly, one must distinguish between the rhetorical discourse once used by common law judges and what common lawyers really think. This way of presenting one's own decision as something "which already always had been there", is just a facade for hidening the underlying reasoning and (slight) changes to the previous law. A comparable approach may be found at the other side of the Channel, where judges often present their decision as something which was already present in the legal system: they just "discovered" the solution, which the legislator already had foreseen at the time the code or the statute had been enacted. This has the comfortable advantage for these judges of not having to give *reasons* for the way the law has been interpreted, but it does not necessarily mean that the judge really believes that his reasoning was the result of a simple and undisputable deductive reasoning. It means even less that other lawyers will believe and accept it.

Thirdly, this mistifying approach to the common law has meanwhile explicitly been rejected by the House of Lords itself in *Kleinwort Benson Ltd v. Lincoln City Council*:

> "The theoretical position has been that judges do not make or change law: they discover and declare the law which is throughout the same. According to this theory, when an earlier decision is overruled the law is not changed: its true nature is disclosed, having existed in that form all along. This theoretical position is, as Lord Reid said, a fairy tale in which no-one any longer believes. In truth, judges make and change the law. The whole of the common law is judge-made and only by judicial change in the law is the common law kept relevant in a changing world."[38]

If the House of Lords says that no-one any longer believes in this myth, it does not seem necessary to discuss it further here.

2.4. A different methodology

2.4.1. *Inductive reasoning from facts vs. deductive reasoning from rules*

Most common lawyers and civil lawyers seem to believe that reasoning on one side of the channel is purely inductive and based on facts, not rules, whereas at the other side, every legal reasoning is exclusively deductive and based on rules, without any influence of the facts. However, both statements are completely

[38] Lord Browne-Wilkinson, for the majority, in *Kleinwort Benson Ltd.* v. *Lincoln City Council*, House of Lords 29 October 1998, 3 *WLR*, 1998, 1095–1155, at 1100. See (http://www.parliament.the-stationery-office.co.uk/pa/ld199798/ldjudgmt/jd981029/klein01.htm).

wrong. On both sides of the channel legal reasoning is a dialectical combination of inductive and deductive reasoning in which the result is both influenced by the existing rules and by the concrete facts of the case.

It is not because a reasoning *starts* from facts, that it remains, as a necessary consequence, purely inductive, nor does starting from rules guarantee an exclusively deductive reasoning. In the common law, it is argued, the decision "arises from the facts, not from rules". This is complete nonsense. "Facts" do not lead to any conclusion, unless they are combined with rules. It is true that common law judges often *present* their decision in this way, but this simply means that the applied rules and principles are hidden, not that they are absent. When the House of Lords, in *White v. Jones*,[39] decides that a solicitor is liable for the loss of a legacy towards the daughters of his client, because he did not draw a new will in time, after his client had asked him to do so, it is not because the "facts" offered this result. If the solicitor has done nothing during six weeks, this can only be considered to be a negligent behaviour if one assumes a rule, according to which the solicitor *should* have drafted a new will earlier. As stated by Lord Goff in this case: "As a general rule . . . there is no liability in tortious negligence for an omission, unless the defendant is under some pre-existing duty."

Once this negligence is concluded, the question arises whether the solicitor is liable towards the *daughters* of his client. Now, the Law Lords turn again from the facts to the rules. Some of the mentioned "rules" are: (1) "the general rule that a solicitor acting on behalf of a client owes a duty of care only to his client", (2) "a plaintiff is entitled to damages if, and only if, he can establish a breach of contract by the defendant", (3) "as a general rule, apart from . . . , no action will lie in respect of purely financial loss in the tort of negligence". But, when applying these rules to the facts, the action should be dismissed and the two daughters could not receive anything. Now, the judges look for another rule, a rule of justice, which says that it would be unjust to dismiss the daughters' action. Starting from this *moral* rule the *legal* rules are being interpreted again, and, surprisingly, a "lacuna in the law" is concluded, "which needs to be filled" (again a rule).[40] And this is done "by holding that the assumption of responsibility by the solicitors towards his client should be held in law to extend to the intended beneficiary who (as the solicitor can reasonably foresee) may, as a result of the solicitor's negligence, be deprived of his intended legacy in circumstances in which neither the testator nor his estate will have a remedy against the solicitor." Here, a rule is construed by the House of Lords, for filling in a construed gap.

This example shows clearly how the reasoning is moving constantly from facts to rules and vice versa. It is, moreover, a very striking example of judge made law, which goes far beyond "concluding a regularity" or "finding the law, which was there since time immemorial". On the Continent, facts are

[39] *White* v. *Jones* (1995) 2 AC, 207–295, at 256–258.

[40] What is meant is that it *ought* to be filled, which starts from the assumption that a legal system should be complete, so that there must be a legal rule for every kind of behaviour and for ordering any situation.

presumed to come into play only at the end of the legal reasoning, when the applicable rules are deductively applied to the facts. In practice, however, the facts often play an important role, both in the choice and in the interpretation of the rules which will be considered to apply to them.

A similar reasoning as the one followed in *White v. Jones* may be found in decisions concerning the right of ownership. The already mentioned large definition of "ownership" in several continental civil codes[41] has faced courts in these countries with comparable problems of a conflict between the prima facie meaning of the law on the one hand, and the feeling that it leads to unjust results when applied to the concrete facts, on the other. On the basis of these facts a new rule has been construed: the prohibition of "abuse of law". Examples are: In 1945 a house had been built, erroneously some 20 centimeters on the land of the neighbour. This was discovered by the aggrieved neighbour only 23 years later. Meanwhile, the house had been sold, and the new owners were sued for pulling down the wall, which standed on the neighbour's land. The plaintiff referred to article 544 of the civil code and the absolute rights it gives to the owner on his property. The court, however, declared that nowadays it is not any longer accepted that property rights would be illimited and that the losses the defendants would suffer when pulling down the wall would be out of all proportion to the advantages for the plaintiff.[42]

It is obvious that the deductive resoning from art. 544 of the civil code should have led to the acceptance of the plaintiffs reasoning and to the demolition of the wall built on his land. However, "from the facts" another conclusion has arisen: inductively, the concrete facts have brought the judges to reinterpret the applicable rules. This is, of course, not just done on the basis of the facts, but by combining the elements of the concrete situation with general values and non-legal norms of reasonableness, equity, justice and the like. The obvious disproportion between the advantage of enforcing one's rights, when compared to the disadvantages for the other party, leads to the creation or establishment of a new "general principle of law": the prohibition of the "abuse of law". And such an abuse is defined on the basis of criteria, such as the mentioned disproportionality.[43]

Actually, limits imposed by courts on the scope of proprietary rights are not something new, which would have been introduced in the last decades only. An example as early as from the first half of nineteenth century is a famous French case of 1836: Mr Villard asked his neighbours Mr and Mrs Denys the permission to built a wall at a closer distance from their land than what the civil code

[41] See fn. 24.

[42] Court of first instance Oudenaarde 13 May 1969, confirmed by the court of cassation on 12 September 1971, *Arresten van het Hof van Cassatie* 1972, 31–43 (in French translation: *Pasicrisie* 1972, I, 28–38).

[43] This principle has been repeatedly accepted afterwards by Belgian courts (e.g. Hof van Cassatie, 19 November 1987, *Rechtskundig Weekblad* 1987–88, 1060–1061; *Pasicrisie* 1987, I, 1299; *Journal des Tribunaux* 1987, 156). Similar positions have been taken by courts in many countries on the Continent.

allowed. They refused, as it would diminish the light and sun entering their house through the windows. Mr Villard then built the wall at the legal distance, but took revenge by painting the complete wall in black at the side of his neighbours. Here, the complete absence of any advantage for Mr Villard, combined with the obvious disadvantage for Mr and Mrs Denys, was a sufficient reason for the court for accepting the claim of Mr and Mrs Denys.[44]

These examples show a much stronger similarity between the way of judicial reasoning at both sides of the Channel than is generally accepted. It is true that there is an obvious difference in the *style* of judgments amongst courts in the different European countries, and most notably amongst the style in use on the continent on the one hand, and the way judicial decisions are drafted in Britain and Ireland, on the other. But it is very doubtful whether the underlying way of reasoning is substantially different. There obviously *are* some differences, but not paradigmatical ones. The judicial reasoning is certainly much more convergent than the way in which court decisions are drafted suggests. As will be pointed out by Fritz Jost, this dialectical interplay of facts and norms is guided by external elements, the main one being legal doctrine, including what he calls the "experience" of the legal system.

2.4.2. *(Lack of) systematisation*

Legrand argues that, as opposed to the very systematised codes on the Continent, a lack of systematisation is typical for the Common law. Of all the arguments he adduced against convergence, this is probably the one where the difference between the two legal cultures is the largest, but, again, today not anymore a paradigmatical one. One should not overestimate the systematisation of private law on the continent. Codes generally are more or less perfectly systematising some areas of the law. This was the case with the two main codes in Europe in the field of private law at the time when they were voted: the French *Code civil* in 1804, and the German *Bürgerliches Gesetzbuch* in 1896. But this is not any longer the case today. Many new rules, and even whole new fields of private law, such as labour law, have developed outside the codes. Parts of the codes have been changing, disturbing the coherence of the code, as these changes were based on very different views. This was especially the case in family law. Interpretations in case law have also on occasions completely altered the original intentions of the nineteenth-century legislator. Finally, European law is not only determining substantially the content of domestic commercial law, but also more and more invading the core of private law, e.g. by introducing new concepts and divisions, such as between "consumer" and "professional supplier of

[44] "Attendu qu'il est de principe qu'on ne peut nuire à autrui sans intérêt pour soi-même; que Villard, en appliquant une couleur noire sur le mur désigné, a porté préjudice aux époux Denys sans en retirer aucun avantage pour sa propriété." (Tribunal de Grande Instance Péronne, 2 December 1836, *Répertoire Dalloz*, 1857, v° *Propriété*, nr 56, note I).

goods or services", thus disturbing the traditional divisions between "vendor" and "buyer" and the like.[45]

It would equally be wrong to present the law in the common law countries as a complete chaos of isolated judicial decisions. In fact, because of the binding character of precedents, judicial decisions in the common law are perhaps more systematised than on the continent, where precedents are not binding at all. In the common law, court decisions have to fit with the earlier ones of higher ranking courts. They must be coherent with them. They have to fit into a system which was built over many centuries. Haphazardly built, case by case, but still a system. Lord Goff's opinion, for the majority of the House of Lords, in *White v. Jones*, offers again a clear example of it:

> "As I see it, not only does this conclusion produce practical justice as far as all parties are concerned, but it also has the following beneficial consequences.
> (1) There is no unacceptable circumvention of established principles of the law of contract.
> (2) No problem arises by reason of the loss being of a purely economic character.
> (3) Such assumption of responsibility will of course be subject to any term of the contract between the solicitor and the testator which may exclude or restrict the solicitor's liability to the testator under the principle in *Hedley Byrne* . . .
> (4) Since the *Hedley Byrne* principle is founded upon an assumption of responsibility, the solicitor may be liable for negligent omissions . . .
> (5) I do not consider that damages for loss of an expectation are excluded in cases of negligence arising under the principle in the *Hedley Byrne* case . . . simply because the cause of action is classified as tortious . . ."[46]

Here, the House of Lords is fitting in its new principle within the system of the previously accepted principles of the common law.

It is not because common law judges, from time to time, emphasise the lack of systematicity of the common law as one of its main features, that this would be true. What does it, for instance, mean when it is said that:

> "Arguments based on legal consistency are apt to mislead for the common law is a practical code adapted to deal with the manifold diversities of human life . . ."?[47]

It suggests that other legal systems, notably the civil ones, are more consistent, but, *by this*, less adapted to "deal with the manifold diversities of human life". Now, this is clearly wrong. When preparing the French civil code of 1804 Portalis already emphasised that, once the code would be enacted, the judge

[45] See, for a more elaborated overview of the current problems relating to an increasing lack of systematisation of private law, Van Hoecke, M., & Ost, F., "Legal doctrine in crisis: towards a European legal science", 18 *Legal Studies* 1998, 197–215.

[46] *White* v. *Jones* (1995) 2 AC, 207–295, at 268–269.

[47] House of Lords 18 October 1946, *Read* v. *J.Lyons & Co Ltd* (1947) AC, 156–188, per Lord Macmillan at p. 175. Compare: "The common law is a historical development rather than a logical whole, and the fact that a particular doctrine does not logically accord with another or others is no ground for its rejection." (House of Lords 11 July 1952, *Best* v. *Samuel Fox & Co. Ltd* (1952) AC, 716–736, per Lord Porter at p. 727.

would be confronted with "*mille questions inattendues*",[48] for which he should be able to find a solution on the basis of the code. Courts clearly have done so. Not always, and sometimes not perfectly, but roughly speaking they did, including creative interpretations for adapting the old texts of the code to changed circumstances. The Dutch civil code of 1992, for instance, is perfectly consistent and even better adapted than the common law "to deal with the manifold diversities of human life" because of a general power given to the judges to "adapt" the rule in a concrete case if the result of an application of that rule in its common understanding would lead to unreasonable or unequitable results. In the case at hand, Lord Macmillan simply wanted the precedent of *Rylands v. Fletcher* not to be applicable. He gave reasons for that, with whom one may agree or disagree, but, *not* applying the rule of *Rylands v. Fletcher* in this case did not make or keep the common law *inconsistent*. Our Law Lord could perfectly have answered the argument of the appelant by denying the implication of inconsistency. There certainly was no need in making a statement suggesting the irrelevance of consistency.

One should also distinguish between the systematisation of the legal rules in legislation and case law on the one hand, and the systematisation of legal concepts, principles and rules, as a product of legal science, on the other. In the common law, there is no tradition of legal science, certainly not of a legal doctrine which would have developed outside legal practice, within the universities. All authoritative commentaries were written by judges, such as Blackstone or Coke. This is also the main reason why a codification never could succeed, despite appeals like Bentham's proposal of a *panommion* in the early nineteenth century. It is precisely the scholarly work of adaptation and systematisation of legal concepts, principles and rules by university professors on the continent since the eleventh century, starting from Roman law, which prepared the codes and made them possible. Systematisation of law is a typical product of legal science, not of legal practice. In the common law, because of a lack of such university scholarly work, judges have been forced to take over the job and to develop at least a minimum of systematisation, which is absolutely necessary in order to make the legal system function and to avoid a chaos. The House of Lords, in particular, has always been in a good position to give attention to this kind of work, as they always have selected only a limited number of cases. They could choose those which were of a more general importance, that is to say, those which could affect the *system* of the common law. But, inevitably, this kind of doctrinal analysis of the law is not comparable to the scholarly work which many hundreds or thousands of full time scholars at continental European universities have pursued during almost a millennium. This is the weakest feature of the common law: a poorly developed legal doctrine, compared to Continental legal doctrine. But, here also things are changing, and rather rapidly. Legal education

[48] Portalis, 'Discours préliminaire', in Fenet, *Recueil complet des travaux préparatoires du Code civil*, I, pp. 462 ff.

is moving more and more from legal practice to universities. Since the upgrading of the polytechnic institutes of higher education to universities in the early nineties, the number of law faculties, and, hence of positions for legal scholars, has roughly doubled.[49] Today, it becomes difficult to get a law professorship at an English university without a doctoral thesis, let alone without a universitary law degree, whereas Herbert Hart, one of the most famous law professors at Oxford, had neither, when he was appointed as a law professor half a century ago. Universities in the U.K. receive more, or less, money on the basis of the assessment of the quantity and quality of their research work. This means a direct financial pressure for developing legal doctrine. That this development is clearly under its way, has been nicely expressed by Peter Birks:

> "The last century has seen a total transformation of our law library. That transformation reflects the emergence of a new branch of the legal profession, namely the university jurist. Equally, it reflects the necessity of sharing between judge and jurist the task of interpretative development of the law. That partnership, alien to the common law as it grew up, responds to the much heavier burdens borne by the law in modern conditions, . . . A system which bears these greater burdens must turn out lawyers who are intellectually equipped to understand and manage its complexity. Law has become infinitely more difficult. It has to be taken more seriously. Our attitudes to law schools and legal education must reflect these facts."[50]

Peter Birks is emphasising the task of the legal scholar at the level of the *interpretation* of the law, leaving aside the level of *systematisation*. Apart from diplomatic reasons (if one wants to bring the legal profession closer to the academic world, it is wise not to mention this part of the academic work), there are also practical reasons for not emphasising the most typical work of legal doctrine, the systematisation of the law. Re-ordering, systematising, developing new concepts and principles, is a process which takes time and needs the cooperation of many lawyers, both in legal practice and in legal scholarship. There is still a very long way to go for the common law. There is much to do at the level of interpretation before something meaningfully can be done at the level of systematisation.

Most English lawyers have only a limited knowledge of foreign languages, which makes it difficult to get direct access to civil law, and to use it as a model. But British universities have a very open policy and regularly appoint continental lawyers as a lecturer or a professor in their law faculties. Continental law is being made increasingly available to an international audience by numerous publications in English. Inevitably, English scholarly legal work will be influenced by it.

[49] In the early 1970's in England and Wales there were about 30 universities, polytechnics or colleges of higher education offering undergraduate law degree programmes, but only some of them were also carrying out research (only law faculties at universities, and even there, research was sometimes very limited). There are now over 80 in the United Kingdom as a whole. (De Friend, R., "Legal education and training in Europe. United Kingdom", 2 *International Journal of the Legal Profession*, 1995, 119–146, at 121–122).

[50] Birks, P., "The academic and the practitioner", 18 *Legal Studies*, 1998, 397–414, at 413.

If one can say that the common law is not systematised in a similar way as civil law is, this is certainly less true for U.K. and Irish *legislation*. In fact, every important new Act has been an attempt to resystematise the previous law, including partly the common law. The Law of Property Act of 1825 reduced the number of estates to two, which meant a resystematisation of the field. The Judicature Act of 1872–1875, e.g., restructured the double court structure for equity and for common law into one whole. The Partnership Act of 1890 and the Sale of Goods Act of 1893 (changed in 1979 and 1994) were not meant to change the law, but to systematise it. They were real codifications of the common law, as it was valid at that time.[51] The Torts (Interference with Goods) Act 1977 reduced the number of torts from three to two, by abolishing *Detinue*,[52] and introduced a new, more general concept of "*wrongful interference with goods*".[53] European consumer law has introduced a general principle of *good faith* into the common law.[54] And so on . . . If the common law may be weakly systematised, it is nowadays constantly being more and more systematised. Moreover, through EU law elements of continental doctrinal systematisation work their way into the common law systems. Whilst some try to block the front door for keeping out continental legal culture, it is entering at the back door.

3. CONCLUSION

Legrand's criticism shows that there is still a long way to go, if one thinks of unification or harmonisation of private law in Europe. It is important to be aware

[51] See, for the Sale of Good Act 1890: ". . . the Sale of Goods Act 1893. In the form in which the Bill was originally drafted by Sir MacKenzie Chalmers that Act was intended to state the common law rules relating to the sale of goods as they had been developed by judicial decision up to 1889. Although a number of amendments were made in committee during the passage of the Bill through Parliament, they did not alter the essential character of the Act as expository of the common law of England at the date at which it was passed. . . . Even a *code* whose content is so limited must proceed by classifying promises, both those which are expressed and those to be implied; the circumstances which give rise to implied promises, and how they are to be performed and the consequences of performing each class of promise or of failing to perform it." (House of Lords, Lord Diplock in *Ashington Piggeries Ltd* v. *Christopher Hill Ltd* (1972) AC, 441–514, at 501).

[52] And the Law Reform Committee had even recommended to replace the three existing torts by one new tort (Eighteenth Report, 1971, Cmnd.4774). But this would have been somewhat too much resystematisation at the same time.

[53] Even if it is not a new tort, but "just a new name" (Tony Weir, in his *A Casebook on Tort*, London, Sweet & Maxwell, 1996, 8th ed., 496), it offers a more general concept, which allows to refer to all torts which involve lost or damaged goods.

[54] By Directive 93/13 of 5 April 1993, *OJL 95/29*. Although the scope of this principle was limited to the area of exclusion clauses in contract law, it has stimulated common lawyers to think in more general concepts. For an earlier example of a House of Lords decision, in which an implicit general principle of good faith in the common law has been recognisd, see Lord Bingham in *Interfoto Library Ltd* v. *Stiletto Ltd*: "In many civil law systems, and perhaps in most legal systems outside the common law world, the law of obligations recognises and enforces an overriding principle that in making and carrying out contracts parties should act in good faith . . . English law has, characteristically, commited itself to no such overriding principle but has developed piecemeal solutions in response to demonstrated problems of unfairness. . . . The well known cases on sufficiency of notice are in my view properly to be read in this context." (House of Lords, [1989] Q.B., 433–446, at 439).

of all the discussed differences in legal culture. But it does not prove that convergence between common law and civil law will not take place, let alone that it will be impossible now or in the future. Divergences between the European legal systems are not anymore of a paradigmatical nature. Traditions, including legal traditions, may change and are changing. There will remain, and probably for a very long time, local cultural differences which affect legal thinking, legal methodology, legal language and the like. But there is no reason to think that some common core of European private law could not develop.

What appears from the current discussion on the topic, including several papers in this volume (most prominently those by François Rigaux, by Geoffrey Samuel, and by Burkhard Schäfer and Zenon Bankowski), is that the future outlook of European (private) law will be much more complex than today and different from the (private) law in all current legal systems, including both the civil and common law ones. The discussion does not seem to be about one legal culture "colonialising" another one. We are working towards completely new conceptions of legal systems, in which such basic distinctions as between "national" and "international" law or between "private" and "public" law may largely disappear. Instead of going on asking ourselves whether any convergence of law in Europe might be possible or not, it is now time to ask which kinds of legal systems, legal structures, legal concepts, legal principles, and the like, we need and how to develop them.

2

Mistaken Identities: The Integrative Force of Private Law

BURKHARD SCHÄFER and ZENON BANKOWSKI

1. INTRODUCTION: *CECI N'EST PAS UN ARTICLE*

In this paper we do not aim to present a worked out argument—rather we offer a number of rather loosely connected ideas, which do not so much present an argument as an invitation to reconsider some established ways of thinking about private law in a European context. But part of the reason for this is not merely because of the stage in our thinking that we are at but because of a difficulty which reflects the problems of integration that we discuss in this paper. For how could one present a coherent argument, which reflects the position of its authors, and try to convince its audience that all is well with European legal integration? Trying to do so would indeed mean attempting the impossible. Firstly it would mean developing a shared vocabulary, a shared set of meanings, between its authors. Then, finding a suitable means to communicate this understanding to a more or less arbitrary selection of European lawyers at different stages of their professional formation. But how can a German cognitive scientist with a long-standing love-hate relationship with German law, and a common-lawyer-turned philosopher possibly establish such an accord? How can both overcome the differences in national, legal and occupational culture between them and their audience? It is clearly not straightforward and the result reflects to some extent the difficulties. But is it altogether impossible?

Pierre Legrand has forcefully and consistently argued against the very possibility of such a cross-cultural understanding. Community, for him, ontologically precedes understanding.[1] Only in merging completely with a different culture, in adopting a shared way of living, can we also create shared meaning. Academic articles, with their emphasis on propositional knowledge and decontextualised information, are a most unsuitable channel for such a task. *Joint* articles however are close to a logical contradiction in terms. Only in giving up my own identity, so it seems when reading Legrand, can a shared meaning emerge. This paper then, is written by a mystical being, a *Bankoschäfer* (a new form of sheep dog) and not by two distinct and distinguishable authors. And if

[1] Pierre Legrand, "Against a European Civil Code" (1997) 60 *Modern Law Review*, pp. 44–63.

you, in reading this paper, think you understand at least enough of it to disagree, then you are obviously under an illusion. Take as an example the title of this chapter. Some of you, living in Brussels and, if not Belgians yourself, merged for some time in the Belgian way of life, will understand it instantaneously and immediately. The Scots will understand it as a clever post-modern but ultimately alien reference to a foreign painter. The Italians will think of that article Eco wrote in *La Republica* about Magritte. The Germans will come up with his precise life-dates and an angstridden memory of schooldays. The English—dumbing down of A-levels—won't understand it at all.[2] A shared European culture? Get a (our) life!

But the illusion of a shared frame of reference, however, seems these days to be common enough. It forms the backbone of international private law. It was recognised by the European court[3] when it referred to "legal rules uniformly recognised in all European countries". In fields as diverse as standard contract terms, insolvency law and the law on commercial partnerships, national courts illusionary believe they apply the same law throughout Europe. And, of course, this illusion is also the centrepiece of the "common core project" in European private law, the codification and *ius commune* schools, which will be at the centre of this article.

2. COMPARATIVE LAW GOING MENTAL

At the heart of Legrand's argument is the notion of a "legal mentality" which explains why continuous divergence between legal systems is consistent with the above mentioned prima facie examples of cross-cultural legal understanding. Legal systems might converge on the superficial, propositional level. But, on the level of the underlying mentalities, which provide the interpretative framework within which alone the legal rules acquire meaning, we remain worlds apart. Legal mentalities are an expression of a "way of living", of culturally determined life forms, and hence national boundaries render different legal mentalities referentially opaque for non-members. We might agree that the *symbols* "contract", "*contratto*" and "*Vertrag*" should form an equivalence class in respect of translation, that is, that they can replace each other, say in legislative proposals by the EU. But once I translate *contratto* as *Vertrag*, I transfer the notion into a German legal context and my own mental frame. It truly becomes a German concept and the original meaning the Italian lawyer tried to convey to me is all but lost. On the level of symbols, we have the illusion of understanding and convergence, on the level of underlying mentalities, we have misunderstanding and confusion.

[2] One of the writers apologises. His constant attempt to blend into his background results in the adoption of instant jingoism for whatever country he happens to live in presently.

[3] See for instance ECJ 46/87 and 227/88.

This approach, however, so it seems to us, faces rather severe conceptual problems. For instance, there seems to be, for Legrand, one and only one German mentality, which is at least partly defined by what it excludes, i.e. by not being French or English. But, how then can this approach explain the obvious fact that lawyers within one and the same legal tradition often disagree, sometimes vehemently so? Conversely why should the legal mentalities, and hence agreement, be delimited the way Legrand does. Is it really so counterintuitive to assume that, for example, environmental lawyers of different legal systems share more of a common frame of reference than they do with their compatriots who specialise in commercial law? That German and French defence lawyers have more in common with each other than prosecutors in their own culture? Is it so obviously absurd to assume that young female lawyers in Italy and Scotland, equally attempting to break through the "glass ceiling", share amongst them more common experiences than they do with their middle age upper-class male colleagues? Or will an elderly crofter from the Hebrides really have interesting conversations with a twenty-year old banker from London, but nothing to say to a shepherd from Denmark? Mentalities, and cultures, are not homogenous entities. This problem is partly caused by Legrand's inversion of a noble tradition of western thought. Traditionally, from Descartes to Locke, Kant to the neo-positivists, it was assumed that the surface structure of language is the main reason of misunderstanding and disagreement, whereas on the cognitive level, the level of ideas and concepts, (cross-cultural) understanding and agreement are possible and desirable.[4]

In particular, we can see in the work of Noam Chomsky how comparative law could profit from "going mental". In taking Legrand's notion of a legal mentality seriously, but reformulating it in the above-mentioned tradition, we do not get a system of legal *apartheid*, but on the contrary a platform for a research into cross-cultural legal universals. Chomsky started with the following three observations.[5] Firstly, we are able as children to learn any arbitrary language. Secondly, we do so despite insufficient empirical input, forming new sentences we have never heard before. Conversely, not every exposure to a grammatically wrong sentence results in acquisition of this ungrammatical feature by the child. Finally, explicit learning of grammar is not necessary to master a language. To account for these findings, Chomsky stipulated that language operates on two levels: a deep structure which contains innate (possibly hardwired) rules of a universal grammar, and a surface structure which is generated by the deep structure but also influenced by "horizontal" historical and cultural particularities. The empirical fact that both English and French speakers will make more mistakes in formulating passive rather than active sentences can then be explained by a universal constraint on languages which says that on the deep level, passive sentences are generated out of active sentences. The cultural character of language

[4] Ian Hacking, *Why Does Language Matter to Philosophy?* (Cambridge, Cambridge University Press, 1975).

[5] Noam Chomsky, *Language and Mind* (New York, Harcourt Brace Jovanovich, 1972).

however is not denied and becomes obvious if we want to explain why for instance the plural of "sheep" is "sheep" and not "sheeps".

Law can learn from an analogy with linguistics. We are able, as students, to learn any arbitrary legal system. This of course is an empirical claim in need of testing, but nothing from our experience in Edinburgh would indicate that the increasing numbers, in particular of Germans, of foreign students doing their first degree in Scotland face any unusual difficulties in doing so. If we master a legal system, then we are able to apply its rules in circumstances different from those we learned them in. Similarly, we do have a notion of a "wrong" court decision, even in common law countries.[6] If law were defined as the set of legal decisions—in the same way traditional empiricism defined language as the set of verbal stimuli received by the child—this would be inexplicable.

We can thus explain the similarities between French and English company law by our shared cognitive ability—that is(on a deep level)—to see collectives as new forms of entities. We "see" forests, not only trees, swarms, not only bees, and companies, not only shareholders. Plural formation has indeed been identified as a likely candidate for a linguistic universal,[7] and this closely related legal application would hence be a good candidate for a "common core" of legal systems, or a universal "legal form". But the fact that French law attributes legal personality also to partnerships would require "horizontal" historical and culture specific explanations.[8]

While this approach emphasises the universal features of law and the possibility of making make cross-cultural comparisons, it is in a number of aspects sympathetic to Legrand and similar sceptical approaches as those of Grossfeld or Samuel.[9] The possibility of cross-cultural legal comparison is explained by a cognitive deep-level. The patterns and activities on this deep level are themselves not legal rules, but generate legal rules on the surface level. A certain disenchantment with a comparative law that focuses on legal rules, propositional knowledge, is fully compatible with the approach outlined here. Clusters of non-propositional, non-verbal knowledge, ways to see, not ways to judge, are indeed crucial for legal systems.

The importance of codification is also put into perspective. Legal codes correspond in this picture to grammar books. But the concept of "noun" or "verb" in English precedes its recognition in formal grammar books by centuries. And just as formal grammar training is not necessary to master a language and to use

[6] Neil MacCormick, "Can Judges Make Mistakes?" in Heike Jung/Ulfried Neumann (eds.) *Rechtsbegründung—Rechtsbegründungen* (Baden Baden, Nomos, 1999), pp. 76–90.

[7] Anna Wierzbicka, *Semantics, Culture, and Cognition: Universal Human Concepts in Culture-specific Configurations* (Oxford, Oxford University Press, 1992).

[8] A further developed version of this point is in B. Shäfer, "Inheritance Principles and the Community of Heirs" in Nicolo Guarino (ed.) *Formal Ontology in Information Systems* (Amsterdam, IOS Press, 1998), pp. 108–121.

[9] Geoffrey Samuel, "Comparative Law and Jurisprudence", *International Comparative Law Quarterly* 47 1998, 817–836; Bernhard Grossfeld, *The Strength and Weakness of Comparative Law* (Oxford, Clarendon, 1990).

its grammatical concepts correctly, neither are BGB-style codified versions of general principles necessary to conceptually structure the legal system. The Nordic legal systems do accept the role of general principles to structure the legal field, without feeling the need to codify them in a BGB-style general part.[10] A good empirical example can be found in information technology. Common lawyers have acquired over the past ten years a huge working knowledge to use effectively the concepts typically associated with the general parts of continental codification—but without knowing it. Whenever they are using a search engine for legal research, particularly ontology based systems as "*Yahoo*" or to a lesser extent "*Lexis*", they navigate along conceptual trees which closely mirror the structure of the *BGB* and the *Code civil.*[11] The "civilising influence" of computer technology is not a conspiracy of continental lawyers, but the automatic side-result of (Anglo-American) computer specialists ordering legal knowledge. To use a European legal code in the way favoured by some proponents of the European Civil Code fraction would mean to mistake the grammar book for the living language itself.[12]

Coming back to the problem of inter-mentality disagreement and intramentality understanding, we can see how this approach avoids the problems of the Legrandian mentalities while preserving his insight into the priority of the cognitive over the propositional. We can do this by elaborating the analogy from cognitive science. Jerry Fodor[13] developed a picture in which the architecture of the mind is described as interacting, but independently functioning special purpose modules or input systems. The modules themselves have their own dedicated processes, their input is strictly domain specific, they are autonomous, fast and quite often insensitive to central cognitive goals. Additionally, they are "normatively closed". Other parts of the mind do not influence the internal working of a module, but have only access to its output.

If we transfer this picture to our discussion, we can understand on one level "legal mentality" as one module between many other task specific input systems. Features of modules "deeper down" the architecture constrain the working of these higher order modules, amongst others the highly specialised legal modules. If we can therefore identify universal features of human cognition in one of these deeper modules, we have equally identified universal features of "the legal mind". On the other hand, we can understand "legal mentality" as made up of several, autonomous sub modules. Sometimes, we work in "defender" mode, sometimes, in "prosecutor-mode", sometimes we think as family lawyers, sometimes as environmental lawyers. A modularised picture of legal mentalities accounts hence both for the possibility of cross-cultural legal

[10] Thomas Wilhelmsson, *Critical Studies in Private Law* (Dordrecht, Kluwer, 1992), pp. 16ff.

[11] Petia Wohed, Paul Johannesson, "Deontic Specification Patterns" in Nicolo Guarino (ed.) *Formal Ontology in Information Systems* (Amsterdam, IOS Press, 1998).

[12] Antti Kivivuori, "Yksityisoikeuden Yleisten Oppien Kriisi?" *Studia Juridica* 1983 at 53–60

[13] Jerry Fodor, *The Modularity of the Mind: An Essay on Faculty Psychology* (Cambridge Mass., M.I.T Press, 1983).

understanding—similarity of modules of human cognition "down the line" and prior to sophisticated legal knowledge modules—and for the possibility of diversion within a legal system—relative autonomy of legal sub-modules.

We do not of course claim, for example, a "hard wired" and innate "Family Law module" to be found in the human brain. The next section aims to take this metaphor and make something more of it; to provide identity criteria for legal modules, and to provide some evidence for the explanatory power of this idea. In particular, we will argue that there is a distinct "private law mentality" which is different from a "public law mentality". Secondly, we will argue that this assumption explains some of the concerns about a European civil code. Both proponents and opponents of such a code employ their "public law module", when thinking about European legal integration, with unsatisfactory results for both of them. We will try to provide an alternative picture, which utilises more a "private law mentality" for integration.

With this we mean more than simply the harmonisation of private law. Rather, we mean to find a new way to conceptualise European integration, which reflects the cognitive particularities of the "private lawyers mind". To explore such a "*privatrechtliche Denkungsweise*",[14] or a "private law mentality", will be the task of the next two sections.

3. PLAYING GAMES

In "*The Player of Games*", the Scottish novelist Ian M. Banks describes a galactic conflict in a far distant future. The culture, a profoundly peaceful and libertarian human/machine symbiotic society takes on the cruel and aggressive Empire of Azad. Azad is unique in its election procedure for its government and administration. It is centred on a game, also called Azad. A game so complex, so like life itself that, that it is the empire's belief that whoever masters the game masters life also. Consequently, the winner becomes emperor. And not only that, the outcome of the game also determines the political tendencies within the ruling class, the economic doctrine to be followed and which creed will be emphasised by the religious apparatus:

> "The idea, you see, is that Azad is so complex, so subtle, so flexible and so demanding that it is as precise and comprehensive a model of life as it is possible to construct. Whoever succeeds in the game succeeds in life".

The final is played between the representative of the culture and the present emperor. The price: the survival of the empire. Both recreate on the board pictures of their respective societies. The empire creates a:

[14] We are hampered to some extent by cultural incommensurabilities especially since the English language has no adjective for "private law", which would be helpful.

> "Centralised hierarchical power structure in which influence is restricted to an economically privileged class retaining its influence through a judicious use of oppression and skilled manipulation of the society's information system. In short, it is all about dominance."

The player of the culture on the other hand, constructs "a grid of forces and relationships, without any obvious hierarchy or entrenched leadership, and initially quite profoundly peaceful". The difference in attitude permeates the whole game:

> "The emperor sent pieces to their destruction with a sort of joyous callousness where Gurgeh would have hung back, attempting to prepare and build up. Where Gurgeh would have accepted surrender and conversion, (the emperor) lay waste. . . . Gurgeh didn't try to mimic (the emperor's) crude but devastating attack-escape, return-invade strategy, but made his position and his pieces in the image of a power that could eventually cope with such bludgeoning."

One can read this novel as a parable concerning the choice between a liberal civic society and a monolithic dictatorship. Arguably, it is this reading that Banks had foremost in his mind. But there is another way of understanding the "Player of Games". Rather than a conflicting normative view of our society, it can be seen as presenting two different *descriptive* accounts of the society we live in. Two different versions which, to some extent, are equally valid, but incommensurable and mutually exclusive. They are two different ways "to see" or to conceptualise society, and to the extent that they are indeed incommensurable, these two cognitive attitudes resemble Legrand's mentalities.

The view of the Empire expresses what we will call the "public law mentality": focused around (an Austinian) notion of the absolute sovereign, it looks for "well defined power structure" and "centralised hierarchies". It defines a society "top-down", focuses on its structural aspects and defines membership as adherence to strict and uniform rules. For the traditional public lawyer, there is always only one state, one sovereign and one law uniformly applied in the territory of the state. The use of force to guarantee adherence to this one set of rules, which is always "down the line" in the hierarchy, is a pre-eminent topic in public law, which could well be summarised as "the doctrine of who is allowed under which circumstances to apply force against whom".

Where the public lawyer sees hierarchies, the private lawyer, the player for the culture, sees a "grid of forces and relationships without entrenched leadership". Where the public lawyer takes society as a given and analyses its *structure*, the private lawyer sees its emergence out of the *action* of individuals. Where the public lawyer concentrates on the (legitimate) use of force, the private lawyer emphasises co-operation between equals.

If we understand "winning the game" as something like "integrating the other side's pieces into one's own", we can extend this picture to the dynamic aspects of state-to-state interrelation. For the emperor, winning the game meant destroying the opposition, to take over its pieces and make them his own. The other player's society truly becomes his, the competing project all but eradicated. The result would have been a bigger version of his initial position, a larger variant of the same hierarchical and static structure he started with. Integration for him is the domination of one model by the other, resulting in a homogenous entity. Outside the game, his only vision of co-existence between empire and culture is the destruction of the latter, to become part of the empire indistinguishable from every other part. His is a hostile take-over that identifies co-existence with subordination under a larger hierarchy, and community with uniformity.

The player for the culture allows for the conversion of his pieces if he cannot save them. His end result is a dynamic system where the empire is absorbed rather than destroyed, his own culture changed in the process. Banks frequently employs the picture of the barbarians invading Rome, only to become assimilated in due course in a process that changes them *and* their host in equal parts. A dynamic equilibrium, an open ended process in which individual pieces on the playing board constantly change and re-affirm their identity is for him an acceptable outcome of the game.

Applying this metaphor to our problem, we can begin to understand some of the problems of the discourse on European legal harmonisation. The question of European integration is traditionally seen as a "top-down" public law problem. Which legislative institutions are required, which general and uniform rules should they enact, and which executive and adjudicative organs need to be in place to implement these rules? This way of thinking is also reflected in the way European law is typically taught at Universities, with the emphasis on the law of European Institutions. And it is also behind proposals for a European Civil Code, if this is understood as a rigid regime of rules imposed from above. This code would display, if at all, only contingent connections to the existing private law systems of the European member states. Integration *of* private law takes precedent over the integration through private law, again, integration is equivocated with uniformity. Both advocates and opponents of a European civil code share the empire's conceptual system. Legrand employs the vocabulary of Darwinism when he describes a European code as threatening "lego-diversity" and eradicating the common law way of life.[15] Zimmerman, with his proposal for a European *Ius Commune*, agrees and thinks that it is a good thing.[16] Both see European law as destroying or replacing existing national legal orders, because this is the only way public law can think about integration.

Our analysis is based on the assumption that this mode of thinking is unable to explain the emergence of a truly European community. Given its conceptual constraint, it cannot but end up with a "fortress Europe", an Empire, not a culture. In respect of legal integration, then, we want to try to develop the converse

[15] Legrand, 1997, p. 49.

[16] Reinhard Zimmermann, "Savigny's Legacy", *Law Quarterly Review* 1996, 112(Oct), 576–605; similarly, with further references, Jochen Zenthöfer, "Brauchen wir ein Europäisches Zivilgesetzbuch?" *Humbold Forum Recht* 4 1999 at www.rewi.hu-berlin.de.

perspective on the question of legal integration, bottom-up rather than top-down, and so we hope, more true to a private law worldview. Such a project should analyse the integrative dynamics of private law on three distinct but interrelated levels. On the first level, private law is seen as a *conceptual* framework to analyse exchange relations between individual human beings. This takes up the topic of the second section, with individual cognitive agents as "community builders" and private law concepts as a descriptive account for their behaviour. On the second level, it will be necessary to abstract from these findings to see private law exchange as a way to understand the *cognitive* impact of the exchange relation between whole legal systems. Individual cognitive agents are here replaced by entire legal systems, understood in a system theoretical perspective. Systems theory has the closest affinities to the notion of cognitive modules as introduced above. If we can understand how individual actors create community through partial understanding, analysed as contractual exchange, then we can use this description to analyse the exchange of "legal transplants" between national legal systems without falling in the trap of presupposing a dominant European power structure. Only on the third level, private law is discussed as the *normative* setting within which the exchanges on the first level take place. Only then does the question of a written European civil code occur. Unlike, for example, Zimmerman's proposal for a *Ius Commune*, this code would not primarily "cause" integration, but reflect and be conceptually determined by the integrative dynamics identified on the lower levels.

4. ON MAKING CONT(R)ACTS

Integration happens if people make connections. Private law is a mode of making those connections between people. Therefore, one can say that people are integrated through private law. European community does not merely happen by establishing a centralised power structure, but in the day to day transactions of its citizens. The conference in of during which this paper was presented, for example, is a contribution to European community not only because of all the relevant and useful political strategies we might come up with, but because we meet in an environment which allows us to exchange ideas and perspectives. We take something from each other back home. On a more mundane level, the taxi driver who extended the normal two minute ride from the station to a half hour sightseeing tour takes with him quite a lot of our travel expenses—but he might send his daughter to Edinburgh for her Masters. From a historical perspective, contractual exchanges (of women, so the anthropologists tell us) were initially less a means of supply and transfer goods, but a way to establish peaceful contacts between normally warring tribes. It is only from understanding the dynamics of this integrative moment that we can analyse the integration *of* law in an arena such as the European Union. Existing positive private law can be seen as a partial description of these empirical exchange relations.

Ernest Weinrib in *The Idea of Private Law* begins his analysis on the basis of such partial explanations, and tries to develop a coherent and complete account of private law relations.[17] If successful, such an endeavour would provide us with a complete description of private law connections between people, a complete conceptual vocabulary for integration through law. As a formalist, he respects the autonomy of private law that gains its coherence and justification internally, without recourse to, for example, politics or economics. This ensures that our approach, as far as we adopt Weinrib, gives us a notion of integration through private law rather than one of integration through economic exchange. His formalism, which emphasises the relative autonomy of law, is also in line with our characterisation of legal mentalities as Fodorian cognitive modules and with the system theoretic approach developed in the second level. Weinrib identifies the notion of bi-polarity as the element which gives private law its coherence and integrity. Private law becomes the theory of the nature of bi-polar exchanges (economic or otherwise). Society is in this picture not presupposed, but emerges out of the totality of individual exchanges.

The notion of "*emergence*" plays a crucial role in cognitive psychology.[18] Higher brain functions are said to emerge from the co-operation of individual cells, creating objects which, on the one hand, are constituted by individuals and their interaction, but are, nonetheless, non-reductive and display properties above and beyond those of their constituting parts. Research in social simulation and artificial societies has recently adopted this view.[19] Societies emerge out of the interaction of individuals, described in game theoretical terms. This approach is particularly close to the view of "private law community" which we want to develop here, and we will make extensive use of findings in this field. It is bottom-up, emphasising individuals and their interaction, contrasting it to a view of society as structure, which we identified with public law thinking. It is non-reductive and therefore compatible with the formalist approach of Weinrib and the idea of normatively closed systems developed above. The notion of emergence is another link between the idea of individual cognitive modules of the first level and the notion of private law community of the second level. But the non-reductive notion of emergence also means that the resulting society is more than the mere sum of its parts. This will allow us eventually to go beyond Weinrib and to argue that some notion of society is indeed admissible even in private law, and the private law view of societies at least compatible with, if not better suited to, Wilhelmsson's Social Contract law than Weinrib's radical liberalism.

[17] Ernest Weinrib, *The Idea of Private Law* (Cambridge Mass., Harvard University Press, 1995).

[18] Wilder Penfield, *The Mystery of the Mind* (Princeton, Princeton University Press, 1975); in this context William Wheeler, "The Ant Colony as an Organism", 22 *Journal of Morphology*, 1903 307–325.

[19] Michael W. Mary, "Social Order in Artificial Worlds", 1 *Journal of Artificial Societies and Social Simulation* 1998 at http://www.soc.surrey.ac.uk/JASSS/1/1/. Nigel Gilbert, "Emergence in Social Simulation" in Gilbert/Conte (eds.) *Artificial Societies* (London, UCL Press, 1995), pp. 144–156.

But in order to have a truly private law view of community, we must first show that legal concepts can indeed help our understanding of emerging societies. Artificial societies research so far does not directly employ legal notions, even if there has been some interest lately in deontic logic and normative constraints.[20] The admissible interactions of individuals in artificial societies have been so far relatively unstructured and heterogeneous. That means that on the one hand, all forms of interactions are taken into account, co-operative exchange relations but also for instance aggressive interactions like killings. For our purpose, we have to restrict these interactions to exchange or contract type interactions. On the other hand, the exchange interactions studied in social simulations have been so far been "bare" interactions. That is, the interaction is successful and completed if the goods are exchanged, the precise nature of the exchange remains underdetermined. To make these exchanges into contractual exchanges, we can add to their "meaning" by adding specific constraints. Not all interactions where goods are exchanged are ultimately successful (contracts can for instance be avoided), nor is the exchange necessarily completed if the exchange is over (for instance product liability rules). Finally, the exchange of one and the same pair of goods can have different structures (for instance lending or buying).

5. MISTAKEN IDENTITIES

A particularly important legal concept, which we will now discuss in more detail, is the contract law notion of mistake. This concept will play a crucial role in differentiating our notion of legal convergence from both Legrand and Zimmerman. But it has also some additional features that make its study particularly interesting. We argued above that private law can be seen as a descriptive, cognitive theory of community making, as a way to make sense of community. Private law describes the actions of individual agents. We analysed these agents as essentially cognitive agents. In the doctrine of mistake, the law makes this notion explicit and analyses the specific cognitive abilities of the individuals it deals with. In this sense, the doctrine of mistake can be seen as providing a reflexive meta-classification of mental states in the same way as the doctrine of offer and acceptance provides a meta-classification of certain speech acts.

Community emerges when people make connections. Private law contracts are one important form of making those connections between two parties. The "meeting of the minds" brings isolated individuals together in a community. But from the doctrine of mistakes, we know that the meeting of the minds is often also a mismatch of the minds. One and the same object will never mean exactly

[20] Nicole Saam, Andreas Harrer, "Simulating Norms, Social Inequality and Functional Change in Artificial Societies", 2 *Journal of Artificial Societies and Social Simulation* 1998 at www.soc.surrey.ac.uk/JASSS.

the same for buyer and seller. If I sell you something I produced, then this object will have for me a radically different significance, it will have a whole world of connotations that I could not and will not communicate to you. Crucially, the law will disregard most of these private connotations and strike down the contract only if the discrepancy in meaning becomes unbearable. For the purpose of the law, partial understandings are more than enough. But if society emerges out of these contractual exchanges, then it is based ultimately on a set of partial and creative misunderstandings. The private lawyer always knew something the public lawyer can never understand; that we are incompletely socialised, that we are living in incomplete communities.[21] If, as we will argue later, legal systems can be understood as cogent entities, then we can transfer this notion of incomplete community to the questions of European legal integration. Individual cognitive agents create community through their partial understandings. In the same way we can say that the legal systems of the European Union can create European legal community through their interaction. The fact that they partially and systematically misunderstand each other is as unconvincing an objection against the creation of a unified legal community as the partial misunderstandings of individual agents an impediment to community *simpliciter*.

Legrand started with a notion of perfect understanding, of strict synonymy. He measured the understanding achieved in comparative law against this standard and found it wanting. From this he concluded that there could not be a cross-cultural legal understanding and therefore not a true conversion of European legal systems which would create a European legal community. But private law mentality teaches us that identity of meaning is not required for understanding, that partial understandings are all that is necessary to create a community and that it is indeed the only form of understanding achievable by us. And for the same reasons, Zimmerman's argumentation for a European civil code fails, because he also as well sees identity of (legal) meaning as prerequisite of a European community and to be enforced, if necessary, from the top. Both play the emperor's game, both presuppose a public law notion of society based on a perfect, not incomplete, community.

6. PLAYING GAMES AND PRIVATE LAW THEORY

We are now in a position to summarise our findings and give an outline of a "private law theory" of European integration. As indicated above, we will distinguish three levels of analysis, community creation by individuals, creation of supra national communities by the interaction of legal systems, and creation of unified law through the internal dynamics of law.

[21] An argument which tries to connect this idea with the above proposal for legal universals can be found in B. Schäfer, "Reinach, Pragmatic Universals and the Methodology of Comparative Law:, in K. Dorn (ed.) *Pragmatics in Contemporary Philosophy* (Beiträge der Ludwig Wittgenstein Gesellschaft, Wien, LWS, 1997), pp. 850–856.

6.1. Playing computer games

What makes the present analysis more than a mere metaphor, are in part results from a very recent development in Artificial Intelligence and sociology, the research into "Artificial Societies". This school uses computer simulation tools to model societies bottom-up, as interactions between individual agents, as described above. Each individual follows a set of strategies, typically maximising its own benefit, without a shared central goal or a hierarchy, which provides a formal framework for their interactions. If these strategies are successful, a stable society emerges, if not, the individuals die) either through aggressive interaction or from starvation. A starting point, set-out for instance where the only available strategy is one of non-co-operation under all circumstances, will soon be "evolutionary eliminated". Nigel Gilbert, in an excellent introduction to this field, started with three observations, which directly link this research to our questions.[22] We rearranged them here for the purpose of our discussion:

1. Simple patterns of repeated individual action can lead to extremely complex social institutions.
2. Members' mis-perception and mis-belief can be functional for groups and societies.
3. Even when there are powerful processes tending to convert a population to a consensus view, minorities may persist.
4. The outcome of some changes is, in principle, unpredictable.

1 is the shared assumption about the priority of individual interaction. What we called the private law view. For Gilbert, this approach goes hand in hand with the rejection of functionalism, and we can compare this to our emphasis on the relative autonomy of law, and the choice of Weinrib as philosophical underpinning. The stability of the computer simulations shows that, in principle, no other ingredients but "repeated patterns of interaction" are necessary to model highly complex social institutions, from the co-ordinated clapping of hands after a concert, to budgetary decision making, to some form of "environmental law". The latter emerged from the model of a computer-based simulation of a Palaeolithic society, which had to "budget" scarce natural resources and had to avoid waste.[23] Gilbert also uses the concept of emergence, where, in his words, "complexity can emerge from social consequences of playing out very simple rules at the level of the individual". He sees emergence explicitly as an alternative to both traditional views in sociology, the idea that social phenomena and institutions as external to individuals (Durkheim), and methodological individualism which argues that there is no such thing as society. This

[22] Nigel Gilbert, "Emergence in Social Simulation", in Gilbert/Conte (eds.) *Artificial Societies* (London, UCL Press, 1995), pp. 144–156.

[23] Doran, Palmer, Gilbert and Mellars, "The EOS Project: Modelling Upper Paleolithic Social Change", in Gilbert/Doran (eds.) *Simulating Societies* (London, UCL Press, 1994).

corresponds to our contention that a "public law mentality" is inappropriate to understanding the dynamics of private law, but that this does not means that we have to adopt a traditional liberal and overtly individualistic version of private law.

2 again played an important role in the computer simulation of Palaeolithic societies. In one version of the simulation, individuals would not attack other individuals they considered as friends, whether or not this view was correct. "Friendship" was furthermore defined locally, that is as expectation of co-operation for the problem at hand. This corresponds to our use of the notion of mistake in contract law. Models with this possibility had a significantly higher success rate. Most importantly, agents could form the mistaken belief of having a "mutual friend". They could, for instance, mistakenly believe in the existence of "pseudo-agents", individuals which do not in fact exist. Because agents exchange beliefs with their friends, such assumptions spread over the friendship network, creating what Doran calls a "cult". We can combine this result with a similar finding from the modelling of budget decisions in families. Here, people's actions were also influenced by imitation of patterns they thought appropriate for their "lifestyle",—"best practice" again spread over the net. Lifestyle distribution and the emergence of cults gives us something much closer to Legrand's "cultural mentalities", sets of collectively held beliefs which are not simply to be explained in functionalist terms, depend on the concrete "history" of the society in question and can be dysfunctional.

3—this particularly interesting result stems from one of the first attempts in what was to become artificial society research. Using "cellular automata", Latané analysed the theory of dynamic social impact.[24] By this he means the change of a person's subjective beliefs as the result of the actions of other agents. Latané considered social impact as proportional to the number of people influencing an agent, and the strength (status, persuasiveness etc.) of the influence. What happens then in a population where all are influence each other, however remotely? The starting parameters in Latané's experiment were that , 60 percent of the agents held the majority view A, 40 percent the minority view B, distributed at random. If the sum of influences on an agent for A outnumbers those for B, she changes affiliation. As a consequence, individuals constantly change their affiliations. Two remarkable results emerged from the simulation. Firstly, distribution of beliefs began to be spatially clustered, holders of the same belief grouped together and kept the members of the group in line. Here again we see how an "ideology" or a mentality emerges, not as a coherent group of beliefs from a hierarchically structured movement, but virtually from nothing.

Secondly, the minority percentage is reduced, but the minority stabilises during the simulation. One of the reasons Legrand' s fears of a European Civil Code is that it would eliminate common law as a way of living, and hence reduce the "genetic pool" of legal ideas and problem solutions.

[24] B. Latané, "The Psychology of Social Impact", 36 *American Psychologist* 1981 at 343–356.

We noted above that he faces in principle the same problem on the level of the nation state. How is it possible to disagree even within a legal culture? Latané's simulation solves the second question, and with that, should reduce the fear connected with the first. Typically, for each proposed legal solution, we will find a minority opinion that disagrees. Sometimes as dissenting opinion within a court, sometimes as conflict between different courts and sometimes as dissent expressed in the academic literature. Each of these will have different dynamic social impact values. A law professor will strongly influence his students, but less so the courts. A court of appeal will influence lower courts (the force will depend on the depending on the actual legal system, but will never be 100%—creative misunderstandings will see to that). Latané's result means that minority opinions will be remarkably resistant to change, at least as long as holders of minority opinions are not eliminated. If we can see the emergence of a European private law as analoguous interaction between different legal systems, as we will argue in the next step, the survival of sufficient disagreement to ensure a healthy pool of legal ideas seems secure.

To recapitulate: what we called above a private law mentality is structurally similar to research carried out on Artificial Societies. The results so far already show that, far from being a mere metaphor, the idea of an emergence of community through interaction is not only plausible, but can be formulated in an absolutely precise and formal way for concrete problems, and empirically tested. With this reassurance at the back of our minds, we can now extend our picture to interaction between entire legal systems.

6.2. Playing the patriot game

On the second level, the players change from individuals to entire nations or legal systems. European legal harmonisation here becomes a process of bargaining and exchange of legal concepts between states. Following our argument from above, we can see how it is possible that while each state is trying to maximise the input from its legal tradition—playing the patriot game—the resulting exchange creates something that transcends the intention of the individual parties and is essentially unpredictable. Our cognitive argument for individuals now becomes a system theoretical argument, of systems theory, dealing with entire legal systems.

We have seen that both the advocates of a European code (Zimmerman) and the opponents (Legrand) have what might be seen as a "statist" view. Any form of the unity of private law (and especially within Europe) has to be seen as monolithic and homogeneous, the former taking a positive, and the latter a negative, view of this. Put in terms of what we called the "traditional public law mentality", this can be seen as claiming that one can have only one sovereignty, bounded by one nation state. In respect of Europe we have what MacCormick[25]

[25] Neil MacCormick, "Beyond the Sovereign State", *Modern Law Review* 1993 1–18.

calls a "monocular" vision. There must be states so there is either a nation state with sovereignty in Brussels (The European option) or many local states related one to another as in international law. The Brunner case illustrates this rather well.[26] In that case the German Constitutional Court denied that the ECJ or any other EU organ could have "competence/competence". The German Court alone had the competence to determine the competence of EU/EC organs in relation to Germany. Thus it followed that if any matters concerning the rights and powers of Germany were involved, then it would determine competence and would not hold itself bound by the decisions of the ECJ or other European organs. In fact, one might say that it claimed a duty to deny the ECJ competence so to interpret EC law that in its application to Germany it would threaten the Constitution. The Constitution was reserved to the ultimate control of the German people. Part of the reason for this was the idea that a polity needed a homogeneous *demos*. Though it could be said that the German state had a *Volk*, the same could not be said of Europe. Implicit in the argument of the court however, was the idea that if Europe were to have a *demos* and it were to be democratic, then the court's decision might be different. Integration can only be theorised on the nation state model—it was not an alleged "top down" hierarchical aspect of Europe that was feared but rather it was not fully that.

But we do not have to see the EU in this way. We can see it rather as a set of interlocking normative orders with no particular one being privileged—the perspective continually changing. Looking at the validity from the point of view of the German system will be different when looked at from a Brussels or even a Westminster viewpoint and what we think of EU law *vis-à-vis* municipal law and *vice versa* will depend upon which perspective we take. What we get in looking at it in this way is a sort of polycentric system with all systems mutually influencing each other, though still having their own protocols—or what we called above a private law point of view. It is the mutual interlocking that creates a unity. A unity that is in the constant cross cutting of these mutually interlocking spheres which do not have to be broken down into homogeneous states—large as in the case of Europe or many small ones relating on an international law model (as in terms of our analogy Legrand would have). In this way we can get a sort of a "view from nowhere"—not necessarily taking any one point of view as fixed. We might here use the idea of "interlegality".

> "Legal pluralism is the key concept in a post-modern view of law. Not the legal pluralism of traditional legal anthropology in which the different legal orders are conceived as separate entities coexisting in the same political space, but rather the conception of different legal spaces superposed [sic], interpenetrated and mixed in our minds as much as in our actions. In occasions of qualitative leaps or sweeping crises

[26] 2BvR 2134/92 and 2159'92 JZ 1993, 1100 cf [1994]CMLR 57. See also Bankowski, Z., Christodoulidis, E., "The European Union as an Essentially Contested Concept", *European Law Journal* (4) 1998 341–354.

in our life trajectories as well as in the dull routine of eventless everyday life. We live in a time of porous legality or of legal porosity of multiple networks of legal orders forcing us to constant transitions and trespassings. Our legal life is constituted by an intersection of different legal orders, that is by interlegality. Interlegality is the phenomenological counterpart of legal pluralism and that is why it is the second key concept of a post-modern conception of law. Interlegality is a highly dynamic process because the different legal spaces are non-synchronic and thus result in uneven and unstable mixings of legal codes."[27]

We are not intending to adopt a "post-modern" perspective here but we can see the "shifting porous world" as indeed the world of the EU. It is the dynamic of the process that is important for us—the system's identity is in its becoming. We can say that Europe is an "essential contested concept" not in the sense that it is vague but rather that its identity is never fixed and each new application, every new penetration and adjustment of the interlocking normative spheres that it makes, might change it.

How does systems theory fit into all this? It appears to talk in terms of radical separateness. Its world consists of systems that grow increasingly more opaque as they become more and more self-referential and self contained. What is important about this "autopoietic turn" in systems theory is that each system is impenetrable (cannot be understood) by any other system. For—for understanding only happens within the system—all understanding and knowledge only takes place within that system's own protocols (or the governing code of the particular system) and all outside knowledge is transformed by the system's codes into its own knowledge form. So, in that sense it can never have knowledge from the outside. But, paradoxically, it is that very separateness that might help us here. For it forces systems theory to develop a range of metaphors for connection—for otherwise regulation and determination would be impossible, which is plainly not the case. And it introduces into systems theory the idea of external input as the determining factor for the identity of systems. Thus the notion of structural coupling binds together systems which then develop, or communicate through "mutual misunderstanding". Though they are normatively closed, they are cognitively open and it is the input from their environment (the other system) which is turned into the other systems way of looking at things) that drives things on. We can now see how this can help us with our understanding of the previous sections. We do not have to buy into the complete implausibility of systems theory to see how this metaphor enables us to get a purchase on how systems mutually help each other to develop in the light of the possibility of mistakes and the never full and complete knowledge that agents have to work with. We can thus analyse the notion of understanding as an incomplete understanding, which results in knowledge that changes with each new application in an infinite series of interactions. But this incompleteness does

[27] Boaventura de Sousa Santos, "Law: A Map of Misreading", *Journal of Law and Society* (14) 1987 279–299.

not mean any longer that we have to accept the in-principle incommensurability of that knowledge.

How is this useful for our problem? The system hears something like "noise" from the outside and it has to respond to it. In so doing it has to translate that "noise" into something intelligible in its own terms. But it is not just a question of translating something from the outside into another language, one's own. For the "outside" is in an important sense "inside". What this means in system theoretical terms is that the system/environment distinction is an internal distinction, that is to say that the distinction between outside and inside is already an inside distinction. Taken absolutely literally, and in autopoiesis's own terms, this has huge problems, both epistemological and ethical[28] but taken more metaphorically it gives us a way of understanding the issues of identity that we raised. For what now becomes important is the fact that, in this way, we can see unity in the mutual interpenetration. We can see, to put it in rather Hegelian terms, unity in becoming and also in diversity.

This can be a way of understanding and seeing "an interlocking system of normative spheres" with no particular sovereignty. But is also useful when applied to national identity within the EU and the possibility of a European identity which is in some sense not statist and homogeneous, but can be seen as something that emerges from the interlocking and mutual interpenetration of various more local identities. If thus we take horizontal interlocking of normative orders, and the systems theoretical distinction made above, we have another way of looking at it: one which does not see all identities as mutually exclusive, by the excision of foreign elements or by the transformation of them into homogeneous units of that identity. It works in the following manner. A system to make sense of itself has to make distinctions. It is in the act of making the distinction between itself and its environment that it knows what it is by indicating what it is not. What it is doing there is conceiving of its whole world as consisting of itself and what it is not, making that indication (making the mark) and "re-entering" the distinction on the side indicated. Thus the distinction between itself and the environment is internal for it, made in order to make sense of itself. This is always, of course, a partial view in that it sees itself in the distinction and with each new distinction it makes its view of itself changes. So its identity is never finished and always in flux.[29]

Let us look at this in more concrete terms. Firstly we may say that European identity is always in flux and in the process of becoming. It is "essentially contested" not because "European" is a vague concept[30]—rather it is something

[28] See Bankowski, Z., "How Does it Feel to be on Your Own? : The Person in the Sight of Autopoiesis" 1994 *Ratio Juris*.

[29] Bankowski, Z., and Christodoulidis, E., "The European Union as an Essentially Contested Project" 1998 *European Law Journal* (4) 341–354 contains much of this argument.

[30] We can also say, that the indeterminacy of the concept of Europe, stems from its application and not its meaning.

that is found in the process of the continual renegotiation of European identity (in the continual making of distinctions in system speak). It is in that process that European identity exists. This conceptualises the Union into a system of interlocking normative spheres whose identities and the larger identity of Europe will not be structured vertically. It will not be a sort of Russian doll model with the smaller identities fitting into, and subsumed by, the larger ones; thus Scottish, British, European. Rather the identities, including the European, one will interlock horizontally. Most important moreover, is that this network of systems will not be seen as static—it will always be in the process of becoming. Thus its identity will be reflexive in the sense that its mode of existence will be the continual creating and recreating of itself anew. The European identity will be formed in the intersection of all of this but will be always in a state of flux—exclusion will thus minimised.

Let us take an example. In defining myself as Scots I do not thereby have to be exclusive even if I can say that I am Scottish because I am not English, because we are both European. This does not have to be a vertical layering of identities on the lines of the Russian doll model. I do not have to exclude the English for I can see it as part of the way that I define myself. For I bring in Englishness into my identity when I try and make sense of myself as European. But the point here is to see myself as *Scottish* European (and not the other way round) so that the identity is a local one at the start. In starting like this, I have to realise that my identity now consists, in part at least, of those whom I excluded in an earlier operation, the English. For to think of myself as Scottish European means also that I have to accept that it means that part of my Scottishness is English for there are English Europeans. So my Scottish identity changes as also does my European one. And the English, the French and Germans and so on do this, as do groups at levels below the nation state. This means that we come to nuanced views of our identities whose crosscutting intersections and inclusions and exclusions means that nobody is fully cut out.[31] Moreover, this is always in flux—I can never be in a permanent state of exclusion for no one can tell where the next encounter might lead. What we have is a form of localised globalism. Here then we have the idea of a polity, which is not vague but is always re-ordering itself. This is because its identity consists in the continual making of distinctions or in the continual re-positioning of its component units. We might call this the process of exchange within its units.

We can also make this point in respect of legal codes. Civil law is a form of life and also a form of national identity, as Collins and Legrand maintain. This poses problems for an integration through private law precisely because it means destroying national identity in an unacceptable manner. But this need not be the case if we look at identity as we did above. It is in this context that we should look at a developing *Ius Commune* in Europe. We can see this coming

[31] Bankowski, Z., and Christodoulidis, E., "The European Union as an Essentially Contested Project" *European Law Journal* (4) 1998 341–354 for some of this argument.

about in two ways. The first is the way that directives and the like are taken and fashioned in Brussels. Starting with solutions from the legal traditions of different countries, these are then recycled back via direct effect where they are adapted to the countries' traditions. This changes these traditions, and so their new input into the legislative effort in Brussels will change as well, a recursive process with no natural determination. Secondly, the ECJ can be seen as a sort of *Grenzstelle* in the sense of Teubner,[32] where it manages the conflict between traditions and also works in different jurisdictions. The European Code might be a sort of *Grenzstelle*, a border post that supplies the grammar and manages the unity in diversity of the various national systems of law.

Finally, we can test our model against some concrete legal proposals. The ill-fated attempt to create a European insolvency law shows all the features, which in our analysis are typical for "public law thinking".[33] The draft proposal contained detailed prescriptions which, if successful, would have resulted in a uniform, that is, strictly identical application of the laws governing insolvency. Unsurprisingly, it failed. The Istanbul convention on the other hand displayed a number of features, which we ascribed to the polycentric, private law view. Rather than prescribing a set of identical material legal rules, it contains primarily "rules of recognition". It allows the German lawyer to recognise the English administrator as "sufficiently similar" to the German *Konkursverwalter*, while keeping their differences. This resembles the situation of "incomplete agreement" which we saw as crucial for contractual relations. The parties retain their identity, are aware of their conflicting frames of reference, but are nonetheless in a "creative misunderstanding" prepared to make temporarily the other's view their own. The transitivity and symmetry of the recognition relation finally results in networks, i.e. incomplete communities.

Throughout this section we have talked a lot about inter-exchanging units and we now go on to consider exchange in more detail. Much of what we have said implies that the way that we develop and progress at all levels, individual and the various group levels, is something to do with exchanging. We develop by being open to the outside. It is this openness characterised in the exchange of gifts that enables both sides to grow to produce diversity and at the same time unity. We might see this as a sort of gloss on communitarianism. It denies the autonomous self-contained self of liberalism and replaces it by the self constituted in community. One might see that as the self that is always in the process of becoming since it gains its identity by exchanging with others. But this way of looking at it gets away from one of the drawbacks of communitarianism. For some strands of communitarianism the community becomes the final context with nothing outside it and thus exchange stops there. The community behaves like the liberal individual that they describe, neatly fitting into a world where people are locked in their forms of life with no real way out.

32 Gunther Teubner, *Law as Autopoietic System* (London, Blackwell, 1992).

33 Ian Fletcher, *The Law of Insolvency* (London, Sweet and Maxwell, 1996), pp. 769 ff.

But in the exchange view put forward here, exchange proceeds at all levels from the individual to the various collectivities that form communities and thus, as we saw, it would be an ideal way of getting the sort of unity and diversity that we want. But we must beware not to lock exchange into the equal commodity exchange of capitalism. That is a way of controlling the exchange and in fact preventing growth, only concerned with getting the equivalent back. Here is no differentiation because everything is the same—the point of the exchange is to make everything the same (note the homogenising effects of capitalism and the market on the European Community). What is important in our focus on exchange is that we do not know the precise outcome of the exchange—unpredictability of social change was, after all, the starting point of the work on social simulation. This openness of the exchange relation makes for growth—that and the unity that it can bring is captured in the metaphors of systems theory.

6.3. Playing power games

So far, we have made the transition of interaction between individual agents to the interaction of nation states. Each system of contract-type interaction leads to the emergence of communities. There is, however, one crucial difference between emergence in its original context, the emergence of consciousness though the interaction of brain cells, and the emergence of human societies. Gilbert notes:

> "The difference is that while we assume that, for instance, wasps have no ability to reason, they just go about their business and in doing so construct a nest, people do have the ability to recognise, reason about and react to human institutions, that is, to emergent features. behaviour which takes into account such emergent features might be called 'second order emergence'."[34]

Above we described legal codes as grammar books. Like grammar books, which reflect and shape the use of language simultaneously, we can now understand laws as "second order emergence". They are feedback mechanism which are primarily determined by agent-interaction, but feed back and inform this interaction as well. Since second order emergence might well be the dividing line between animal and human societies, we must not underestimate their power. But in the picture developed here, they are still secondary to the actual human interaction and in this sense non-arbitrary. Simply to impose a code from above to bring about unity will not do, its largely contingent features could not possibly reinforce base-level interaction. But to enhance unity by reflecting on its mechanism and with that on existing national law will vastly improve the system and contribute to its cohesiveness. If we understand law as an (at least

[34] Nigel Gilbert, "Simulation, an Emergent Perspective", *Journal for Social Simulation* 1998 at 17 at www.soc.surrey.ac.

partly) descriptive account of social interaction, a way of making sense of community, we can re-introduce the idea of a pan-European "general part" of contract law into a picture which superficially seemed to emphasise the heterogeneity of legal systems.

Wilhelmsson has already identified the importance of general principles for European integration, and his use of systems theoretical vocabulary seems to make him an ideal choice for a more concrete legal application of the model presented here.[35] But then, his vision of a social contract law seems to go well beyond what we termed the private law view. Critical contract lawyers seem to rely on the ability of an interventionist state to regulate exchanges to foster predefined social goals while Weinrib on the other hand provides a picture which emphasises the autonomy of legal concepts (similar to that introduced here in the first part). His work could therefore be seen as an ideal theoretical underpinning for the kind of study envisaged here. But this would mean subscribing to a purist version of private law, whose effectiveness as community builder was already called into doubt by results from social simulation. Is there, despite their apparent contradictions, a way to reconcile the two approaches?

As a means of creating understanding, law strives for coherence. This is the main insight Weinrib, writing from a common law background, contributes to our debate.[36] Law itself strives for coherence, in the same way as all our theories do.[37] Coherence is something that comes naturally, something deeply rooted in our cognitive makeup. General principles are the main vehicle for legal coherence, and they are to be found in the common law as much as in civil law, what differs is only the degree of their explicitness. A Pan-European "general part" of private law therefore is not the triumph of one tradition over the other, but can be consistently interpreted as second order emergence that reflects on all European legal traditions. The use of abstract concepts in common law databases as described above proves this point. But, following on both from Weinrib and our analysis of cognitive modules in the first part, this coherence is purely internal and conceptual, a coherence from the point of view of the law. Contradictions with other forms of human endeavour, especially incoherence with social or economic goals, remains possible and indeed likely. The partial autonomy of law and legal concepts is re-affirmed. This explains Teubner's observation that dogmatics trumps statutes[38] (we cannot but be coherent) and Wilhelmsson's observation of the problems of formulating a coherent account of critical contract law which does not conflict with these prior goal specifica-

[35] Thomas Wilhemsson, *Social Contract Law and European Integration* (Aldershot, Dartmouth, 1995).

[36] *Op. cit.* 11 ff.

[37] Burkhard Schäfer, "Form Follows Function Fail—As Epistemological Foundation of Comparative Law, *Social Epistemology* 1999 (forthcoming).

[38] Gunther Teubner, "The Social Responsibility of Contractual Networks" in Thomas Wilhelmsson (ed.) *Perspectives of Critical Contract Law* (Aldershot, Dartmouth, 1993), p. 216.

tions.[39] The strength of the proposal outlined here is that it allows us to transcend. Weinrib's liberal version of private law, accommodates most of the conceptual tools employed for instance by Wilhelmsson and nonetheless remains firmly rooted in *private* law thinking.

For Weinrib the private law exchange is always precisely one of equal commodity exchange. It is therefore based on the exchange relation that Pashukanis saw as definitive of capitalist societies. Distributive goals and any vision of social justice are explicitly ruled out. They, according to Weinrib, would apparently require a source of power that is in a position to enforce these goals, if necessary against the will of the individual actors. In short, this requires public law thinking and public law concepts. But as we have seen, that exchange, seen as the mutuality of obligation between two discrete entities, is not the only form of exchange. We saw instead how, from exchanges, networks can develop where the obligations and mutualities are spread through the network and create, through these interactions, a form of unity.

Weinrib is correct in starting his program with the interaction of individual actors. But nothing forces him to stop there. We have seen above how the interaction of individuals eventually creates a collective unity, which exists above and beyond the individual exchange relations. Here the initial contact spreads beyond the mutual exchange of obligations between two people. Contract as social co-operation, as Wilhelmsson aptly put it,[40] does not require a pre-given social, or state, within which this co-operation takes place. Rather, co-operation creates the social which then feeds back into the primary exchange. The public is not, in this picture, a dangerous supplement, or a conceptual complement, but emergent from the private and private law interaction. Power is distributed over the network of exchanges, not precisely localised, but nonetheless there. Wilhelmsson, rather than Weinrib, turns out to be the "true" private lawyer, for networked exchange models, or models of social co-operation, are simply more efficient in modelling the emergence of "private law communities" than classical private law models.

But entire societies are only one of the emergent features of private law interaction, and we can equally use our model to analyse emergence of sub-national collectives. Again, we can see that despite its individualistic input, the resulting law is not tied to any form of liberal laissez-faire capitalism. Take, for instance, Teubner's analysis of the problem of critical private law dealing with franchising and other hybrid networks. Again we can find a "public law mentality" which searches for clear defined power structures and, in their absence, denies social liability for the loosely connected franchises. Teubner identified the conceptual divide between contract and organisation as a major obstacle for a satisfactory regulation of liability in hybrid arrangements as, for example,

[39] Thomas Wilhelmsson, "Questions for a Critical Contract Law", in: Thomas Wilhelmsson (ed.) *Perspectives of Critical Contract Law* (Aldershot, Dartmouth, 1993), pp. 45 ff.

[40] *Ibid.*, pp. 38 ff.

franchising.[41] In our model the distinction between contract and organisation is gradual; the social networks whose liability Teubner demands are all there is (and is needed) to have organisations of collectives of almost arbitrary complexity and cohesiveness. In this view, even the classical limited company is nothing but, and still something more, than a network of individual contracts. When networks reach a certain "density" law as second order feedback mechanism recognises them as separate entities. But on a conceptual level, there is no natural demarcation line between very loosely and very cohesive networks and both can be dealt with, if so chosen, by the same legal vocabulary.

7. CONCLUSION

Let us briefly summarise the argument that we tried to develop. The question of European legal integration is hampered by a conceptual approach which owes more to public than to private law thinking. This creates a problematic dichotomy, which forces us to choose between a strictly identical application of one private law code throughout Europe, or no integration at all. We tried to develop an alternative, private law picture that took as its starting point nothing but individual cognitive agents and their interactions, rooting it insofar firmly in an individualistic, private law setting. We used as a first step an analogy with Fodor's analysis of the architecture of the mind to understand how different legal mentalities emerge, how different kinds of knowledge and understanding are created internally in individual actors. This gave us a reformulation of the notion of legal mentality, which we argued is more realistic than the idea of homogenous "common law" or "civil law" mentalities and allows for both fragmentation and convergence of mentalities while maintaining their distinct identities. We then looked at the interaction of human actors, and how understanding and co-operation between them results in the emergence of communities. The private law doctrine of mistake was employed to describe crucial features of this interaction, which explained how a form of unity, society, can emerge while respecting the integrity of the individuals who create this community. This view was confirmed by results from social simulation and artificial societies, which could be seen as the operationalisation of the descriptively understood contract law concepts.

From the creation of communities by co-operating individuals, we then moved to the creation of legal communities through the interaction of legal systems. A system theoretical vocabulary which mirrored closely the insights from the discussion on the individual level helped us to argue that a "private law legal community", which precedes the unification of private law statutes, could be perceived which did not threaten the distinctiveness of different modes of legal

[41] Gunther Teubner, "The Social Responsibility of Contractual Networks", in Thomas Wilhelmsson (ed.), *Perspectives of Critical Contract Law* (Aldershot, Dartmouth, 1993).

life. In this way we would not have to see, as in the traditional "public law mentality" legal diversity as primarily a lack of structure and a resulting free for all. We used the notion of second order emergence, and Weinribian insights into the internal coherence of private law, to show the consistency of legal polycentrism and pan-European general principles.

Finally, we dealt, albeit cursorily, with a possible problem of our account. In order to reach a "private law view", we had to eliminate any pre-defined social goals, and had to exclude state-like centralised power structures from our account. Does that mean that the private law we were advocating was a traditional liberal private law, and do we have to rule out *a priori* any attempts to create a European social contract law, as indeed Weinrib does? Using the concept of emergence, we argued that far from excluding social or societal concerns, our view is not only consistent with, but arguably closer to a private law as "Social Co-operation" where the emerging communities are independent enough from the individuals to allow for an "interventionist" feedback mechanism. In this sense, critical contract law was seen to be trapped in a similar dichotomy as that analysed above in the context of private law integration, a view which sees the public and public responsibility, for better or worse, always as a fixed hierarchical power structure. Our approach tried to cut across this divide, not by separating the private from the public, nor by subjugating one under the other, but by focusing on the dynamic of private law interaction as the pre-condition for the emergence of structure.

In the "Player of Games", the Emperor, unable to understand the potential of co-operation, finally destroys himself and his society—neither he nor it are a match for the distributed power networks of the culture. It would be a sad irony if the proponent of European private law harmonisation, and the proponents of a social contract law, destroy their agenda by accepting the conceptual framework of their opponents. We hope that this analysis is a first small step in offering both a conceptual alternative which does nothing but reminds them of what as private lawyers, they always knew.

3

English Private Law in the Context of the Codes

GEOFFREY SAMUEL

1. INTRODUCTION

Whether one is in favour or sceptical about the unification of law within the EU it is of importance that the level of the debate about harmonisation be raised considerably. Weak theorising, simplistic metaphors and the arrogant dismissal of opponents' arguments do Europe no favours. There are some very serious questions that need to be addressed. Happily such a raising of the level of the debate is now more than detectable and it is one purpose of this paper to highlight, if only briefly, two important contributions. This consideration will, however, be in the context of a more general question which needs to be posed to those keen to integrate and to harmonise the private law systems of all the member states of the European Union. Does there actually exist an identifiable and discrete field of "private law" in Western legal systems, which is capable of serving as the base for a harmonisation project? The question is relevant not just because the existence of an identifiable "private law" is rather ambiguous when it comes to the common law. It is relevant because the time has arrived when the kind of thinking that has traditionally underpinned the codes needs to be modified. Harmonisation should be the catalyst for rethinking legal theory since the theories that are presently underpinning legal analysis are, arguably, incapable of handling the epistemological complexities presented by unification.

2. THE PRIVATE AND PUBLIC LAW DIVIDE

Scepticism with regard to harmonisation on the part of some common lawyers (together with some civilians with a sophisticated knowledge of the common law) has of course become manifest.[1] One common law comparatist has even

[1] P. Legrand, "European Legal Systems are Not Converging" (1996) 45 *International and Comparative Law Quarterly* 52; "Sens et Non-sens d'un Code Civil Européen" [4-1996] *Revue Internationale de Droit Comparé* 779; "Against a European Civil Code", (1997) 60 *Modern Law Review* 44.

described the whole harmonisation project as "demented".[2] However other, calmer voices, from the civilian tradition itself are also raising questions that deserve serious consideration by comparative lawyers and legal theorists. Professor Joerges, for example, sees "private law" as a problem in as much as it has actually allowed private lawyers to isolate themselves from European law. He makes the point that most private lawyers assume that their area can be understood from the position of the internal core categories of obligations, property, succession and family law. These internal categories, in turn, appear largely immune from actual European law since "both the Community legislature and the (otherwise activist) ECJ have proved to be extremely cautious in their approach to the traditional realms of private law."[3] However, he goes on to make the point that what European law is in fact doing is to constitutionalise Europe as a private law society. "Private law in this perspective", Joerges observes, "*is* constitutional law".[4]

Professor Teubner has also raised a question about the viability of legal integration. He asserts that some central concepts of civil law—in particular good faith—could prove to be more than just "legal irritants" to the common law. Unthinking transplantation of one concept, fashioned within a set of particular economic and cultural circumstances, from one system to another could result, not in harmonisation, but further legal fragmentation in Europe. From debates in the social sciences:

> "It seems that contemporary trends toward globalisation do not necessarily result in a convergence of social orders and in a uniformisation of law".[5]

Instead new differences can lead to fragmentation:

> "If, under European law, good faith is transferred from the Continent to British law", writes Teubner, "and if it is supposed to play also in the new context its role of linking contracts to a variety of different discourses, then it is bound to produce results at great variance with continental legal orders".[6]

British economic culture is not like German economic culture. This fragmentation would be the result of good faith becoming:

> "A quasi-constitutional constraint on two central elements of the production regime: a constraint on strong hierarchies of private government and a constraint on certain expansionist tendencies of competitive processes".[7]

Contract would move from being a private law device emphasising discretion and commercial freedom to one where it assumed a quasi-public law role setting

[2] T. Weir, *A Casebook on Tort* (London, Sweet & Maxwell, 1996), p. 3.

[3] C. Joerges, "European Challenges to Private Law: On False Dichotomies, True Conflicts and the Need for a Constitutional Perspective", (1998) 18 *Legal Studies* 146, 147.

[4] *Ibid.*, p. 149.

[5] G. Teubner, "Legal Irritants: Good Faith in British Law or How Unifying Law Ends Up in New Divergences", (1998) 61 *Modern Law Review* 11, 13.

[6] *Ibid.*, pp. 23–24.

[7] *Ibid.*, p. 28.

"low-discretionary rules that draw clearly-defined legal limits to quasi-administrative discretion".[8] Like Joerges, Teubner is sensing a destruction of the traditional private and public divide through the operation of European law.

However, before considering in more depth these ideas about constitutionalisation and fragmentation, it might be useful to look first at the background to the notion of "private law" and its general viability as a pan-European category. In the civil law tradition the idea of a "private law" is closely linked linguistically with the Roman law terms of *ius privatum* and *ius civile*.[9] Given the authority with which the Roman sources were treated by the later civilians, these terms must by definition have represented an epistemological (legal knowledge) truth and thus it is not difficult to see why the notion of a private law became so ingrained in the European mentality.[10] *Imperium* and *dominium* were separate power relations binding person with the state (or some more specific *persona* like the *fiscus*) on the one hand[11] and private individuals amongst themselves or with *res* on the other hand. Codification only added to the epistemological authority of the Roman terms. For the great codes took as their object an area of law that was by definition, given the existence of the ancillary codes on commercial law, procedure and criminal law together with the rigid exclusion of the *ius publicum* in France, existing virtually as an empirical reality. This reality was not just a matter of a juristic space resulting from boundaries created by public, commercial, procedural and criminal law;[12] the Romans themselves had defined private law in terms of *utilitates* attaching to the individual in society (*ad singulorum utilitatem*).[13] Private law was about private interests.

3. THE STRUCTURE OF PRIVATE LAW

In addition to this space and interest dimension, private law had, according the teaching manuals of Gaius and Justinian (*Institutiones*), a structure; and it is this structure which was to act as the foundation for all the codes. Private law, whatever the difficulties of definition and delimitation, could not, seemingly, be accused of lacking either form or substance. "All our law", said Gaius, "relates either to persons, to things or to actions".[14] This scheme may or may not have had its logical weaknesses.[15] But it has acted as the basis of all civilian legal

[8] *Ibid.*, p. 29.

[9] Dig.1.1.1.2.

[10] The separation between public and private law seems to have been aided by the distinction between customary and royal (legislative) law see J.-M. Carbasse, *Introduction Historique au Droit* (Paris, PUF, 1998), pp. 187–216.

[11] See generally J.-L. Mestre, *Introduction Historique au Droit Administratif Français* (Paris, PUF, 1985), pp. 106–110.

[12] Cf J.-L. Halpérin, *Histoire du Droit Privé Français depuis 1804* (Paris, PUF, 1996), p. 11.

[13] Dig.1.1.1.2.

[14] G.1.8; J.1.2.12; Dig 1.5.1.

[15] Cf H. F. Jolowicz, *Roman Foundations of Modern Law* (Oxford, Clarendon, 1957), pp. 61–81; R. David, Introduction, *International Encyclopedia of Comparative Law*, Volume II, Chapter 2, Part I, para. 12.

thinking right up to the New Dutch Civil Code (1992) and has given rise to an internal structure of private law which can be described as the "institutional system".[16] This system allows students of the civil law to "study private law as a single whole and progress through the various topics as parts of that whole".[17] In substance there have, of course, been fundamental developments since Roman times. The law of persons has been consolidated into a structured subsystem of personality and status rights—in particular with regard to marriage and the family.[18] And the law of things and the law of actions have been realigned into real rights (property) and personal rights (obligations), actions themselves having been relegated to codes of procedure.[19] Some of the internal developments within the various national systems that make up the civilian tradition have, of course, taken different directions.[20] Yet the extent of such developments and divergences is a point of debate and reflection since it could be argued that many of the modifications fashioned by later civilians nevertheless had their germs in the writings of the Roman jurists themselves. In other words all variation is still referable to a single "source" of private law thinking. For example, the rigid separation between contract and conveyance is as Roman in origin[21] as the inclusion of the law of obligations within the law of things.[22] From the position of harmonisation these differences between the various internal plans of the codes might be problematic. However the most important question is the extent to which each individual legal structure conforms to the "institutional system" and it is evident, given the common "source", that the codified systems present fewer problems in this respect. This is not to imply that harmonisation between codified systems themselves presents no cultural or mentality problem—there are major differences for example between the *Code civil* and BGB legal models and their cultural contexts. But the codes do share a common formal structure inherited from Justinian and the *ius commune* and this structure acts not just as the basis for the classification of rules, but as the foundation for a system of precise rights and legal relationships.[23] It is a formal symmetry, which has been dictated by the legislature and from which the courts and indeed the legislature cannot escape.

It is trite legal history that the common law has grown up in relative (but not complete) isolation from Roman law and its learning and that this isolation has

[16] P. Stein, *Legal Institutions* (London, Butterworths, 1984), pp. 125–129.

[17] P. Stein, *The Character and Influence of the Roman Civil Law* (London, Hambledon, 1988), p. 73.

[18] See generally A. Lefebvre-Teillard, *Introduction Historique au Droit des Personnes et de la Famille* (Paris, PUF, 1996).

[19] See generally Stein, *Legal Institutions*, *op. cit.*, pp. 126–129; *Character and Influence*, *op. cit.*, pp. 73–82.

[20] C. Szladits, The Civil Law System, *International Encyclopedia of Comparative Law*, Volume II, Chapter 2, Part II, para. 77.

[21] See e.g. Dig.41.1.36.

[22] G.2.14.

[23] N. Rouland, *Introduction Historique au Droit* (Paris, PUF, 1998), pp. 251–305.

resulted in a legal system that does not think in terms of codes.[24] Nevertheless the idea of a European private law raises an interesting question about the relationship of the common law with the codified systems of continental Europe. Does the modern common law lend itself to the European plan? The problem, as Stein says, is that:

> "In modern English law, private law is not seen as a system" since its "various branches, such as land law, contract, tort, family law and so on are presented in discrete boxes with little indication of how the boxes, when fitted together, form a coherent pattern".[25]

Now when viewed from the institutions of *persona*, *res* and *actiones*, it is not difficult to conclude that the common law also uses these three institutions as the points of linkage between law and society.[26] Persons and things exist both in the world of fact and the world of law.[27] Indeed status and law of obligations are categories recognised as being separate in English doctrine and case law.[28] However, there are very real differences between common law and civil law at the level of legal structure and categories. For example the codified systems all make a sharp distinction between public and private law and between the law of property and the law of obligations.[29] These conceptual categories have been fashioned by the civilian thinkers into fundamental category structures which underpin not just the detailed rules and principles of each civilian legal system but also legal science itself.[30] Differences between *iura in personam* and *iura in rem* have for example become axioms in turn acting as the basis of a model through which law itself is defined and understood.[31] It is almost impossible for a civil lawyer to conceive of a legal system where public rights or interests are not distinguished from private subjective rights and where owning (property rights) is not sharply differentiated from owing (personal rights).[32] In England, in contrast, because there has never been a foundational textual intervention which has imposed upon legal thinking a formal symmetry, there is seemingly a much weaker internal structure.[33] On the surface, English law remains,

[24] G. Samuel, "Existe-t-il une Procédure de Codification du Droit Anglais" (1997) 82 *Revue Française d'Administration Publique* 209.

[25] *Legal Institutions*, *op. cit.*, p. 126.

[26] G. Samuel, "Roman Law and Modern Capitalism" (1984) 4 *Legal Studies* 185.

[27] G. Samuel, "Classification of Obligations and the Impact of Constructivist Epistemologies" (1997) 17 *Legal Studies* 448.

[28] H. F. Jolowicz, *Lectures on Jurisprudence* (London, Athlone, 1963), pp. 373–380; R. H. Graveson, *Status in the Common Law* (London, Athlone, 1953); G. Samuel & J. Rinkes, *Law of Obligations and Legal Remedies* (London, Cavendish, 1996), pp. 9–14.

[29] Szladits, *op. cit.*, paras 25 ff., 77.

[30] T. S. Holland, *The Elements of Jurisprudence* (Oxford, Clarendon, 13th ed., 1924), pp. 167–168.

[31] P. Ourliac & J. de Malafosse, *Histoire du Droit Privé 2: Les Biens* (Paris, PUF, 2nd ed., 1971), pp. 47–59.

[32] David, *op. cit.*, paras. 12, 18.

[33] T. Weir, The Common Law System, *International Encyclopedia of Comparative Law*, Volume II, Chapter 2, Part III, para 82.

ultimately, an historical phenomenon whose conceptual basis is complex when compared with the simplicity of numbered code articles systematically arranged as between themselves.

4. DEMARCATION BETWEEN CONTRACTS AND PROPERTY LAW

In some areas of law this lack of a formal symmetry might appear irrelevant. Thus harmonisation of contract law in the EU seems to have been achieved at the level of (private) "codification" without, relatively speaking, too much difficulty.[34] Teubner, of course, has his reservations. But, if one leaves these objections aside for the moment, the point needs to be made that contract does occupy a rather special place in the common law in as much as it is a legal structure almost entirely imported from the civil law during the nineteenth century.[35] There are, it must be stressed, important differences between English and civilian contract law.[36] However these differences are not of a kind that prevent the subject from being reduced to a structure of abstract propositions more or less along the lines of a European code. Indeed the treatise writers of the last and the present century have gone far in reducing English contract law to a set of relatively abstract propositions. When one actually examines the case law, the textbook view of contract may look remarkably simplistic of course since cases often tell their own story. But the point to be made is that contract is probably not a subject that will present the harmonisation obstacles. It is other areas of the common law that present serious problems. In particular English property law will offer to contemporary civilians almost exactly the same problems as the customary feudal systems offered to the medieval Roman lawyers. In order to appreciate the task that faced the Glossators and Post-Glossators, it is vital to keep in mind that, unlike contract or even delict and tort, there are two quite separate models of property law.[37]

The first model is the Roman one. This model is based upon a unitary notion of ownership (*dominium*, *proprietas*) which gave expression to an exclusive power (*potestas*) relationship between *persona* and *res*.[38] As Professor Patault has pointed out,

> "*dans la conception romaine du pouvoir de l'homme sur les choses, la propriété confond la chose et la maîtrise de la chose*". And this "*confusion exprime l'idée que la*

[34] *Principles of European Contract Law* (1998). The final revised version can be found on the Internet: <http://www.ufsia.ac.be/~estorme/PECL2en.html>. See generally A. S. Hartkamp *et al.* (eds), *Towards a European Civil Code* (Nijmegen, Ars Aequi, 1994), Part 2A.

[35] A. W. B. Simpson, "Innovation in Nineteenth Century Contract Law" (1975) 91 *Law Quarterly Review* 247.

[36] G. Samuel & J.-C. Montanier, *Le Contrat en Droit Anglais* (Paris, PUF, 1999).

[37] See generally A.-M. Patault, *Introduction Historique au Droit des Biens* (Paris, PUF, 1989), pp. 83–137.

[38] J.2.4.4.

propriété absorbe tous les aspects, toutes les utilités du bien au point qu'on ne peut dissocier la maîtrise et l'objet de la maîtrise".[39]

This structure is unique in two particular ways. First it is a structure that is founded upon the idea of a physical person having a relationship with a physical thing; thus ownership is not a patrimonial right as such. It is *une prérogative*, which attaches to the person and to the thing.[40] This structure grew out of the idea that someone reclaiming his thing in an *actio in rem* was in effect suing the thing itself and this is why the object, or some representative part of it, had to be in court.[41] Secondly, the emphasis of the structure was individualist in its ideological and epistemological pattern. The emphasis was on the individual *persona* and the individual *res* as a social model functioning in a zone, private law (*ius privatum*), quite separate from that of governmental power (*imperium*). It was a form of *potestas* which was equally isolated from correlative proprietary obligations; once an owner had proved his relationship the judge had to order the *res* to be handed back to the owner.[42] There could be no discussion as to whether the particular plaintiff deserved, in some social sense, to be owner. This absolute idea of ownership finds its most perfect expression in article 544 of the *Code civil*: "*La propriété est le droit de jouir et disposer des choses de la manière la plus absolue*". Of course an owner in such a model was, and is, not free to act as he or she wishes in respect of the thing.[43] But many of the restrictions in the Roman model were the result of *imperium* rather than anything attaching to *dominium* itself and thus, for example, Roman magistrates had a range of public law powers and remedies in respect of land and buildings.[44] One might note that the second limb of article 544 goes one to qualify the right of ownership with the *ius publicum* restriction: "*pourvu qu'on n'en fasse pas un usage prohibé par les lois ou par les règlements*".

The second model of property is feudal. One of the main characteristics of feudalism both as a political model and a legal structure was that it made a fundamental distinction between land and other property. The political and legal emphasis was on land since all land was held from the king and thus private ownership of the Roman type was politically inapplicable and socially meaningless.[45] The king devolved land to his lords and barons who in turn granted interests to those lower down the political and social hierarchy. From the legal point of view several persons could at one and the same time have legal relationships in the same piece of land:

[39] Patault, *op. cit.*, p. 17.

[40] F. Zenati & T. Revet, *Les Biens* (Paris, PUF, 2nd ed., 1997), p. 133.

[41] G.4.16–17.

[42] Dig.6.1.9.

[43] J. H. Beekhuis, Civil Law, *International Encyclopedia of Comparative Law*, Volume VI, Chapter 2, Part I, para.15.

[44] See Dig.39.1 and Dig.39.2. In modern civil law there are of course private law restrictions on ownership, in particular the restriction, founded in the law of obligations, of abuse of ownership: Beekhuis, *op. cit.*, paras 16–17.

[45] S. F. C. Milsom, *Historical Foundations of the Common Law* (London, Butterworths, 2nd ed., 1981), pp. 99–101.

> "Ownership belongs to a flat world in which rights in land or other forms of wealth are dependent upon no authority except the state", observes Milsom, but feudal tenure "belongs to a smaller world in which there is no need and no room for abstract ideas like ownership".[46]

In continental Europe this smaller world became enlarged with the reception of Roman law. The feudal land law was transformed, via the Roman law of actions, into a world of *dominium utile* and *domininium directum*. In England, however, there was no reception and as a result English land law remains, relative to the codes, unique.[47]

The central concept in this feudal English model is the notion of an "estate", which is an abstract entity between the holder, or holders, of land and the land itself. It represents the temporal aspect of land—a "fourth dimension"[48]—capable of being divisible between various holders, often during differing time periods, but remaining, metaphysically speaking, as a single whole.[49] There is a Roman element to this term in as much as it is derived from the Latin word *status* and once reflected the idea of a person's status in relation to a piece of land.[50] In a sense, then, the term "estate" is a concept straddling the law of persons and the law of things.[51] However in operation it was far removed from Roman thinking in that several people can enjoy at one and the same time "ownership" rights in the same piece of property and each of these rights is separately alienable. It is not, therefore, the *res corporalis* that is alienated (that was and in theory remains impossible, since all land is owned by the Crown). It is the estate, a *res incorporalis*, that is the thing that is transferred.[52] With the disappearance of feudalism, it may be tempting to apply the Roman model of ownership, but this would be dangerous. Although the full estate may be thought of as the whole quantum of interest in the land, such a whole estate, called the "fee simple", is fragmentable. In civil law, ownership is the coming together of the *ius utendi*, *fruendi* and *abutendi*; but the fee simple of the common law, while in one sense the nearest thing to ownership, is "a fragmentable quantum of interest". And this fee simple "has, more than any other factor, made it both impossible and superfluous to attempt to rivet what a Common Lawyer would consider the oversimplified notion of ownership on the

[46] *Ibid.*, p. 100.

[47] F. H. Lawson, Common Law, *International Encyclopedia of Comparative Law*, Volume VI, Chapter 2, Part II, para. 24.

[48] F. H. Lawson & B. Rudden, *Introduction to the Law of Property* (Oxford, 2nd ed., 1982), p. 88.

[49] "In particular, the beneficial ownership of land may be divided in terms of time as well as space, so that the right to enjoyment of the land for a limited period, such as for life or a term of years, and the right to enjoy land after the expiry of that period, can exist simultaneously as property interests in possession and in remainder or reversion. One such interest may form the subject matter of a gift while the other is retained", Lord Hoffmann in *Ingram v IRC* [1999] 2 WLR 90, 93.

[50] Graveson, *op. cit.*, pp. 7–14; Patault, *op. cit.*, pp. 48–50.

[51] Graveson, *op. cit.*, p. 7. Thus Sir Henry Maine's famous dictum: "we may say that the movement of the progressive societies has hitherto been a movement *from Status to Contract*", *Ancient Law* (1861; Oxford ed., 1939), p. 141.

[52] Patault, *op. cit.*, p. 22.

common law system of real property law".[53] This is why English lawyers talk less in terms of ownership and more in terms of "interests".[54]

The idea of fragmentable interests spreads beyond land law to the law of moveable property and indeed to the law of contract, tort and equity. Certainly something approaching a Roman notion of ownership seems applicable to chattels since the Sale of Goods Act actually talks of the transfer of "property" in goods.[55] However, the law of moveable property is more complex, since ownership is not directly protected by any remedy. What is protected is the immediate right to possession and this is achieved by claims classified, according to the Roman model, in the law of obligations.[56] It is the law of tort that protects direct and indirect interference with possession of property.[57] Thus, where A transfers possession of his chattel to B, this will create a substantive proprietary relationship of bailment, an area of the law of property rather than the law of obligations.[58] However, the actual remedies which will protect the rights of the transferor (bailor) are the torts of trespass and conversion and these torts, according to the logic of the Roman model, are part of the law of obligations.[59] Now, there is nothing necessarily illogical about protecting both title and the *res* itself through actions for damages based upon wrongs. Even Roman law, despite its distinction between property and obligations, treated as law of obligations problems certain invasions of title.[60] But it will appear illogical once one formulates as a premise a distinction between *owning* and *owing* as a matter of subjective right and *scientia iuris*. To allow the law of obligations to protect rights *in rem*, including title itself, appears to be creating a conceptual contradiction. The law of obligations protects only rights *in personam*.

Yet if one abandons the institutional model of "rights" as an operational structure and thinks, instead, of interests defined and protected by a law of actions functioning in more than one dimension, an alternative model presents itself. In one dimension there is the *actio* itself with its own particular relationships and rules, for example the rules of damages or injunctions; in another dimension, there is the law of status.[61] In yet another dimension, there are

[53] Lawson, *op. cit.*, para. 38.

[54] Cf G. Samuel, "La Notion d'intérêt en Droit Anglais", in Ph. Gérard, F. Ost & M. van de Kerchove (eds.), *Droit et Intérêt: Volume 3* (Brussels, Publications des Facultés universitaires Saint-Louis, 1990), pp. 405–436.

[55] *Sale of Goods Act 1979* ss 16–18.

[56] Weir, *Casebook*, *op. cit.*, pp. 491–496.

[57] *Torts (Interference with Goods) Act 1977.*

[58] *Building and Civil Engineering Holidays Scheme Management Ltd* v *Post Office* [1966] 1 QB 247, 261.

[59] For some of the conceptual difficulties arising from the intermixing of property and obligations see *Morris* v *C W Martin & Sons Ltd* [1966] 1 QB 716.

[60] See e.g. Dig.47.2.1.2.

[61] This distinction between remedies (damages, injunction) and rights (contract, bailment) is one of the distinctive features of the common law system: not only are there textbooks on contract, tort, bailment etc, but equally on damages, injunctions and specific performance. See generally F. H. Lawson, *Remedies of English Law* (London, Butterworths, 2nd ed., 1980). See also Samuel & Rinkes, *op. cit.*, pp. 83–151.

causes of action such as conversion, trespass and so on.[62] Such a multi-dimensional model might at first sight appear unnecessarily convoluted. However, it can arguably act as a means for better appreciating the internal workings of the common law. Ownership can in this scheme be a matter both of status and of remedies;[63] equally, restitution can consist of an *actio in personam* based upon a relationship *in rem*.[64] Indeed even the protection of the enjoyment of property can straddle private and public interests.[65] The point to be made, then, is that the common law is not so much a "seamless web"—a metaphor that suggests two dimensions—but more a three dimensional flexible frame structure.[66] The common lawyer uses the institutions of *persona*, *res* and *actiones* to construct and reconstruct frameworks of social structures; and these structures, seemingly descriptive, are in reality quasi-normative. They are "set-ups" whose patterns point towards a normative end result.

This multi-dimensional frame structure is one reason why the common lawyer will have little difficulty in appreciating Professor Joerges' thesis about the constitutionalisation of private law. English tort law has always been constitutionalised. The torts of trespass, malicious prosecution and often defamation are as much causes of action in public law as in private; and even the law of contract can have an administrative law role. The importation or imposition of civilian ideas may cause "irritation" in as much as certain claims are not always easy to translate into common law causes of action or into equitable doctrines. But Professor Teubner's metaphor is, arguably, misleading for the common law. Civilian concepts and categories might well be inappropriate for the English law and might indeed provoke difficulties at the level of social discourse.[67] Yet it is

[62] Causes of action (nuisance, conversion) are in a sense separate from both remedies (debt, damages, injunction) and from rights in the sense of *un droit subjectif* (e.g. ownership, possession). However note the observation of Sir Nicholas Browne-Wilkinson: "In the pragmatic way in which English law has developed, a man's legal rights are in fact those which are protected by a cause of action. It is not in accordance, as I understand it, with the principles of English law to analyse rights as being something separate from the remedy given to the individual . . . [I]n my judgment, in the ordinary case to establish a legal or equitable right you have to show that all the necessary elements of the cause of action are either present or threatened" *Kingdom of Spain* v *Christie, Manson & Woods Ltd* [1986] 1 WLR 1120, 1129. And see G. Samuel, *Sourcebook on Obligations & Legal Remedies* (London, Cavendish, 1995), pp. 65–66, 70–73.

[63] *Stevenson* v *Beverley Bentick Ltd* [1976] 1 WLR 483.

[64] *Lipkin Gorman* v *Karpnale Ltd* [1991] 2 AC 548.

[65] *Miller* v *Jackson* [1977] QB 966.

[66] One might note Kahn-Freund's analogy: "Society handles the institutions of law much in the same way as a child handles his bricks. It uses the same bricks all the time—or for a long time—today to build a manor house, to-morrow to build a factory, and the day after to build a railway station. The number of bricks is limited: the manor house may have to be pulled down to make way for the factory. But—this is Renner's positive axiom—the bricks remain the same. The law provides the bricks. What society makes of them, is none of the lawyer's business", Introduction to K. Renner, *The Institutions of Private Law and their Social Functions* (London, Routledge & Kegan Paul, 1949), p. 6.

[67] Note in particular Walter Jones' warning written over half a century ago: "It is sometimes forgotten that every legal concept has an individuality which is the result of the facts which gave it birth and which leaves its impress upon any new facts to which it is applied. In this way legal technique leaves its mark upon the life of the community, for the law operates through its concepts. But the

much more likely that the internal structure and mentality of the common law will be an irritant for the symmetrical "flat" thinking associated with the codes.[68] A system that thinks in terms of discrete causes of action, treats governmental bodies (on occasions at least) as if they were manufacturers of ginger-beer, functions more at the level of remedies and is prepared openly to use the law of persons to solve a problem of ownership and possession is much more likely to be the irritant. This, of course, is not to question Teubner's central thesis of cleavage and fragmentation amongst the legal systems of Europe. It is simply to make the point that it is the common law that is likely to appear undisciplined and unscientific to a hierarchical mentality of legal dogmatics fashioned within a *mos geometricus* historical tradition.[69] Or, to put it another way, the common law relates to social discourse in a manner that is both seamless and fragmented in a cellular or dimensional way. Thus it is capable of absorbing the impact of potentially irritating imports in ways that ought perhaps never to be underestimated. It is not a brittle structure.[70]

That said, the fundamental differences between the Roman and feudal models of property mean that English real property law cannot be harmonised with this model of thinking without a massive reception of Roman thinking. Such a reception may or may not be socially desirable when compared with the present English property concepts. But it is by no means clear that the civilian (Roman) model of property is that relevant for an economic system that no longer deals primarily in *res corporales*. In a world of futures and time-shares it has to be asked whether the codes are not backward-looking in the way they are based on the Gaian notion of *dominium*, itself dependent on the existence of a physical *res*.[71] Indeed this was an accusation levelled at the *BGB* at the time of its publication.[72] As both Walter Jones and Wolfgang Friedmann pointed out, the relationship between legal concepts and economic theory is delicate and there is always the danger of the two systems getting seriously out of synchronisation. On the one hand,

> "in States where property is constitutionally guaranteed there is always a tendency to extend the concept of property to cover as many interests as possible and the fact that these interests have little in common, except economic value, may be lost sight of".[73]

extension of a concept to cover social and economic facts cannot be prolonged indefinitely without affecting either the concept itself or the facts . . . Thus relations which are essentially flexible or fluid may become rigid and petrified in their legal form, and the law will lose all contact with reality", *Historical Introduction to the Theory of Law* (Oxford, Clarendon, 1940), pp. 266–267.

[68] P. Legrand, "Are Civilians Educable?", (1998) 18 *Legal Studies* 216.

[69] F. Wieacker, *A History of Private Law in Europe* (Oxford, Clarendon, 1995), trans T Weir, pp. 199–204.

[70] Note on this brittleness point the observation of two AI specialsists: W. Bechtel & A. Abrahamsen, *Connectionism and the Mind* (London, Basil Blackwell, 1991), p. 227.

[71] Patault, *op. cit.*, pp. 219–220.

[72] Jones, *op. cit.*, pp. 267–268.

[73] *Ibid.*, pp. 266–267.

On the other hand:

> "Anglo-American conceptions of property are closely in line with the sociological and popular meaning, whereas civilian concepts of property still labour under an artificial analytical division inherited from Roman jurisprudence, and out of step with the reality of modern industrial society".[74]

Harmonisation of property concepts, were it ever to be seriously considered, would need careful research and reflection. Indeed it is worth recalling the view that:

> "The empirical development of the common law, its aversion to theoretical definitions of legal concepts, its preference for thinking in terms of legal relationships, of powers and liabilities, rights and obligations, types of action rather than of abstract concepts, has proved an advantage".[75]

These words were written by a comparatist trained both in German and in American law.

5. LEGAL REASONING AND HARMONISATION: FROM AN AXIOMATIC TO A POST-AXIOMATIC STAGE

This property problem is not confined just to land. How is the model to be harmonised with a legal tradition like the common law which uses the law of tort (the law of obligations) to give expression both to property and to constitutional rights? Indeed, even the notion of a "right" (*droit subjectif*) itself—despite Friedmann's words—has little meaning for the common lawyer.[76] Private law, in as much as it exists at all as a discrete area, is largely expressed in terms of legal reasoning that can take a case from fact to solution without mentioning rules, textbooks or even cases.[77] Litigation is about factual situations where the court's role is to do justice only between the parties; small differences of fact can give rise to quite different conclusions. This is not to say that English cases cannot *ex post facto* be reduced to rules or norms. Professor Van Hoecke indicates how this is more than possible with his analysis of the decision in *White v Jones*.[78] However such an analysis does not in any way undermine the distinction made in Artificial Intelligence between rule defined and rule described knowledge.[79] Rules can indeed be used to *describe* English case law, but this does not mean that solutions in cases are actually arrived at as a result of rules. This alternative epistemological model of legal reasoning has been fully

[74] W. Friedmann, *Law in a Changing Society* (Harmondsworth, Penguin, 2nd ed., 1972), p. 94.

[75] *Ibid*., p. 95.

[76] G. Samuel, "'Le Droit Subjectif' and English Law [1987] *Cambridge Law Journal* 264.

[77] See e.g. *Blackpool & Fylde Aero Club Ltd* v *Blackpool BC* [1990] 1 WLR 1195.

[78] See M. Van Hoecke, "The Harmonisation of Private Law in Europe: Some Misunderstandings", elsewhere in this volume.

[79] Bechtel & Abrahamsen, *op. cit*., p. 227.

discussed elsewhere.[80] Suffice it to say, here, that once it is appreciated that "facts" themselves are reconstructed systems which gradually take on a normative pattern through the juxtaposition of apparently descriptive concepts, then the more it becomes possible to understand Professor Legrand. His point about an epistemological gap between the civilian and the common law mentality is that solutions are not inferred from rules, save perhaps in "easy cases" (and even here the position is by no means clear). All solutions have to be argued for and thus legal method is always a three way debate between the parties' lawyers and the judge.[81] Legal relations and legal concepts are no more than tools for structuring arguments and this has allowed them to be "denatured" in ways that are unacceptable to strict civilian science. Debts and live musical performances can be owned; remedies can trump rights; moveable property is housed in the law of obligations.

No doubt behind the facade of the syllogism legal reasoning in the civil law is not so different.[82] Equally, some English cases are susceptible to translation into civilian structures. But when it comes to attempts to fashion a European code of private law differences of method—the logically disciplined two-dimensional versus the logically flexible three-dimensional—could cause quite serious problems with regard to the kinds of structures applied and arguments deemed acceptable. Do the logically rigid and "flat" systematics of the German *BGB* have a place for the common law multi-dimensional approach to reasoning? Admittedly the systematics of the German Romanists (Pandectists) have been regarded, even in the UK, as the foundation of an international legal science and some modern German writers still see legal science as the main means for achieving harmonisation of private law within the EU. But, equally, other German writers like Joerges and Teubner (and not forgetting Friedmann) with a greater sensitivity to the economic, political and social complexities underpinning European law are beginning, as we have seen, to theorise in terms of a fragmentation. One is moving from an axiomatic to a post-axiomatic stage.[83]

This post-axiomatic stage could have a negative effect upon European legal thought in that it could intensify the cleavages between legal systems not just in terms of norms applicable but, more importantly, in the fragmentation of methodology and theory. Equally one could abandon the structures used in the "axiomatic" stage of legal science and adopt, as suggested, a multi-dimensional model. The idea of a three or even four dimensional model might appear novel, yet such a model has been vital for understanding the role of time with regard to real property rights in English law. Estates, trusts and possession function in

[80] See G. Samuel, *The Foundations of Legal Reasoning* (Antwerp, Maklu, 1994).

[81] See e.g. Bingham LJ in *Blackpool & Fylde, op. cit.*

[82] J.-L. Bergel, *Théorie Générale du Droit* (Paris, Dalloz, 3rd ed., 1999), para. 253. An excellent opportunity for comparison has recently presented itself: see Cass.3e.civ.17.12.1997, D.1998.111 note Aubert and contrast *Fitzpatrick v Sterling Housing Association* [1998] Ch 304; cf. [1999] 3 WLR 1113.

[83] G. Samuel, "The Impact of European Integration on Private Law—A Comment" (1998) 18 *Legal Studies* 167.

more complex structures than the ones to be found in the codes.[84] English private law in the context of the codes is thus not just a matter of re-organising the case law and legislation along institutional lines; nor is it a matter, either, of deconstructing the codes. It is a question of reconstructing the institutions of law within facts and in relation to interests that are now multi-dimensional. Private law has now to function with concepts capable of giving expression at one and the same time to particular and general interests. Legal reasoning is a matter of constructing facts out of institutions (persons, things, actions) and the institutional relationships (ownership, obligations, and so on) which flow between them; and these institutions and relations imply their own solutions. *Ex facto ius oritur* and *ex iure factum oritur* are one and the same process.

Is such a model a recipe for instability in private law or a new stability? It is, evidently, in relation to this question that the contributions of jurists such as Christian Joerges and Gunter Teubner become particularly relevant. They are in their own ways warning that the traditional epistemological models are inadequate for the future. They are models, which have outlived their usefulness. However by way of conclusion, and in order to aid the movement from the "axiomatic" to a "post-axiomatic", it might be useful to draw an analogy with science, in particular with the science of time. The traditional view of time is that of an arrow in which time flies or flows in a linear and uniform way. Such a model is most valuable in the way it identifies with a common sense view of the world in which uniformity of movement seems a natural law. However, difficulties soon emerge when it comes to representing space and time in terms of mathematical models. Einstein thus refused to see time in this uni-dimensional[85] way and, instead, he proposed that time should be appreciated through a multi-dimensional model where past, present and future did not exist in linear form. They existed in an interrelated model where the past and future might well co-exist with the present but in different dimensions. Thus the past might be rediscovered at some point in the future.[86] Of course drawing an analogy between law and time could be most dangerous since the history of science is littered with transformations that proved illegitimate.[87] Nevertheless the analogy is most useful as a symbol, if not as a conceptual device,[88] to provoke a change in the symmetry of knowledge representation. The new symmetry allows the comparative lawyer to rethink the various European models of law within a single structure that is designed not to simplify complexity, but to embrace it. The idea that complex property and commercial relations—together with the legal "facts"—can be reduced to a single "flat" model is far too simplistic for a Europe engaged in re-orientating legal systems at a range of different levels.

[84] See Lawson, *op. cit.*

[85] B. Piettre, *Philosophie et science du temps* (Paris, PUF, 1994), p. 37.

[86] *Ibid.*, pp. 70–72.

[87] A. Virieux-Reymond, *Introduction à l'épistémologie* (Paris, PUF, 2nd ed., 1972), pp. 71–72.

[88] For the difference see A. Leroux & A. Marciano, *La Philosophie Économique* (Paris, PUF, 1998), p. 33.

Indeed it is not just simplistic; it is brittle and will certainly break under the strain of the give and take between the various legal traditions and cultures, as Teubner warns. A complex structure capable of functioning in a range of dimensions at one and the same time will more easily absorb the social, economic and legal structures. But one price for this is that the idea of "private law", as Professor Joerges suggests, will also have to be rethought.

4

*The Debate on a European Civil Code: For an "Open Texture"**

ANTHONY CHAMBOREDON†

1. INTRODUCTION

The fascinating debate on the necessity for, and means of, private law harmonisation has divided scholars, for a long time, between European integration, on the one hand, and the fragmentation of legal systems provoked by legal nationalism, on the other.[1] Among these means of securing uniformity, is the idea of contract law codification, which has its proponents and opponents. However, given the abundant bibliography recently devoted to it,[2] this subject seems, at the present time, to be of great topicality.

Firstly, one may ask why we should have to unify our laws of contract, and why it has to be done under the form of codification. Europe seems "to live" very well without a European contract Code. Why, then, do we have to change? The law of contracts is made by very specific traditions. It is bound by cultural identities strongly linked to each legal system. Is it not hazardous, even dangerous, to create a European law of contracts detached from its local or national roots, which thus risks losing its entire efficacy?[3] What are the compelling reasons, which push us towards the harmonisation of European private law? Two arguments are frequently used:

* This essay has its roots in conversations with Michel Troper, Gérault de Jouffre de la Pradelle, Marie-Jeanne Campana, Jacques Ziller, Geoffrey Samuel, John Bell, Hugh Collins and Igor Stramignoni who commented helpfully on earlier drafts. Thanks to Chris Engert for English corrections. Errors are mine alone.

† Doctoral researcher, Paris X Nanterre, European University Institute of Florence.

[1] Founding of the *Société de législation comparée* in 1869, first Congress on Comparative Law, organised in 1900, by Raymond Saleilles and Édouard Lambert. See, also, Marc Ancel, "Rapprochement, Unification ou Harmonisation des droits?" in *Mélanges en l'honneur du doyen Marty* (Toulouse, 1978).

[2] See, *Vers un Code Civil européen, le débat est ouvert*, (Conference held in The Hague, the 28th of February 1997), European Review of Private Law (ERPL) 1997–5 at 519; see also, La Revue *DROITS*, n. 24–26 and 27, 1997 and 1998; cf., *Faut-il codifier le droit? Expériences comparées*, La Revue française d'administration publique (RFAP) n. 82, April–June 1997; equally, *La codification*, L'actualité juridique de droit administratif (AJDA) 20 September 1997. See, also, *La Codification*, dir. Bernard Beignier, Paris, *Dalloz* 1996.

[3] Christian Joerges, "The Europeanisation of Private Law as a Rationalisation Process and as a Contest of Legal Discipline", *ERPL* 3-1995 at 175.

—An economical argument; the Single Market: The European Community, as an economic entity, has, as its goal, the free movement of goods, persons, services and capital. The opening of the markets entails a considerable growth of trade; these cross border flows are particularly made by means of contracts. The diversity of our laws is considered to be both an obstacle to our trading and to the development of our economic wealth. If we had a uniformed law of contracts, it would be simpler to create and perform contracts.

—A legal argument; "the conflictualistic burden": the international private law of contracts follows the method of the "rule of conflict". Some authors challenge its efficacy. This so-called "artificial mounting" or "highbrow mounting", is a method which would only correspond to,

> "*. . . un besoin de conciliation de la souveraineté des États et la nécessite économique et sociale de ces derniers de ne pas s'enfermer dans une autarcie juridique*".[4]

Even if, according to the principle of autonomy, some contractual clauses determine the applicable law and the competent jurisdiction to the contract, the efficacy of these clauses is always limited because they are susceptible to considerable variations in diverse legislation. According to the nationality of the judge sought, the law applicable to a contract and, accordingly, the determination of the conditions of its formation or the duties of the parties may change. This does not favour legal security. This is the reason why one observes a remarkable development of new private authorities, which are closer to the requirements of business for the settlement of international disputes.[5]

Several means of securing uniformity of private law are thus envisaged:

—A uniform law that is grounded on treaties; however, from a "voluntaristic" origin, treaties decided by States have one major weakness: the absence of agreement leads to legislation *a minima*. The Convention on the International Sales of Goods, for instance, as its name indicates, is restricted to contracts of international sales only.[6]

—A Community private law based on European regulations and directives;[7] but if they provide single rules, their scope of competence remains rather narrow, and they do not "legislate" in fields closely related to them. The harmonisation thus remains very incomplete. They may even have the effect of complicating the already existing national legal rules; this is the case, for example, with the European directive on defective product liability, which has added

[4] (. . . a need of States' sovereignty conciliation, and the economical and social necessity for the States not to close themselves within a legal autarchy). Bruno Oppetit, "Le Droit International Privé, Droit Savant", *Cours de l'Académie de Droit International*, 1992, Vol. 234 at 331 ff. (translation is mine). See, also, Kegel, "The Crisis of Conflict of Laws", *Recueil des Cours de l'Académie de La Haye*, at 260–261.

[5] A. Couret, "La Dimension Internationale de la Production du Droit: l'Exemple du Droit Financier", in *Les Transformations de la Régulation Juridique*, dir. J. Clam et G. Martin, Librairie Générale de Droit et de Jurisprudence (LGDJ) 1998 at 197 ff.

[6] Vincent Heuzé, *La Vente Internationale de Marchandises, Droit Uniforme*, GLN-Joly (eds) 1992. See, also, Antoine Kassis, *Le Droit Européen des Contrats Internationaux* (LGDJ) 1993.

[7] European Parliament Resolution on the harmonisation of certain sectors of the private law of the Member States. OJC 205/1994/07/25/ at 518 (6 May 1994).

a supplementary action into the regime already in force within German law.[8] Instead of contributing to securing uniformity, these forms of legislation may have the opposite effect, that of legal disintegration.

—Eventually, a European common law would allow the implementation of the same private law in every European country. Essentially, two methods are proposed: either a European contract Code or some sort of "restatements" based on the rediscovery of a European *ius commune*. German and Italian scholars (the most faithful depositories of Roman law) are very much in favour of such a return to a *ius commune*.[9] Yet, one has to agree on the notion of *ius commune*. Similar to "taught law" or "scholar law", as a form of thinking or method of reasoning, the *ius commune* was never a framework of rules, but rather, a "higher" law, not issued by any public authority of a State or supra-State. Notwithstanding this, in 1989, the European Parliament chose, as a political objective, the creation of a European Civil Code.[10]

One scholar spontaneously rose up against this project. In "*Against a European Civil Code*",[11] Pierre Legrand argued that the common law[12] and continental civil law belong to such different cultures and traditions that they are constructed with "*mentalités*"[13], which have so little in common that the idea of convergence is simply heresy[14] (Chapter 2). Though this is a very provocative

[8] Peter-Christian Müller-Graff, "Common Private Law in the European Community", in *The Common Law of Europe and the Future of Legal Education*, 1992 at 249, Bruno de Witte/Caroline Forder (eds).

[9] Mauro Cappelletti, *Nouvelles Perspectives d'un Droit Commun de L'Union Européenne* (Leyden, 1977). Reiner Schulze, "Le Droit Privé Commun Européen", *La Revue Internationale de Droit Comparé* (*RIDC*) 1-1995. Claude Witz, "Vers un Droit Privé des Contrats", in les *17e Journées de la Société de Législation Comparée*, at 217, 1995. R. Zimmerman, "Roman Law and European Legal Unity" in *Towards a European Civil Code*, Hartkamp, A., Hesselink, M., Hondius, E., Du Perron, C., and Vranken, J., (eds) (Nijmegen, Ars Aequi Libri, 1994) at 65–81. Helmut Coing, *Europäisches Privatrecht*, München 1985 at 89; also, "Europäisierung der Rechtswissenschaft", *Neue Juristische Wochenschrift*, 1990 at 937–941. Reiner Schulze, "Von Ius Commune bis zum Gemeinschaftsrecht—das Forschungsfeld der Europäischen Rechtsgeschichte" in Reiner Schulze (ed.) *Europäische Rechts- und Verfassungsgeschichte*, 1991. Luigi Mengoni, "*L'Europa dei Codici o un Codice per l'Europa?*" Roma 1993 at 3. Giuseppe Gandolfi, "Pour un Code Européen des Contrats", *Revue Trimestrielle de Droit Civil* (*RTD civ.*), 1992 at 707 and 726.

[10] Resolution on action to bring into line the private law of the Member States 1989 OJC 158/1989 at 400 (26 May 1989); see, also, E. Hondius, "Towards a European Civil Code", General Introduction, *op. cit.* n. 9 at 1–18.

[11] Pierre Legrand, "Against a European Civil Code", *The Modern Law Review* (*MLR*) 60-January 1997. See, also, "European legal systems are not converging," in *International and Comparative Law Quarterly* (*ICLQ*) 1996 at 52–81. Equally, "Comparative Legal Studies and Commitment to Theory", *MLR* 1995 at 262–273. For a general account of his thesis, see his recent book, *Fragments on Law-as-Culture* (Deventer, Tjeenk Willink, 1999). Cf. B. Markesinis, "Why a code is not the best way to advance the cause of European legal unity," *in vers un Code Civil européen, le débat est ouvert*, loc. cit. n. 2 at 519.

[12] About the controversy provoked by the gender of the *common law* in French, see Pierre Legrand, "Pour le *Common Law*", *RIDC* 4-1992 at 941–947. See *contra*, Georges Rouhette, "Le Genre de '*Common law*'" in *Mélanges Maury* at 310–325.

[13] Pierre Legrand defines "*mentalité*" as "l'intériorisation d'une culture juridique dans une culture donnée qui révèle les profondes structures de la rationalité juridique", in "European Legal Systems are not Converging", *loc. cit.* n. 11 at 63.

[14] Pierre Legrand, "Sens et Non-sens d'un Code Civil Européen", 4 *RIDC*, 1996 at 779–812.

and thus stimulating argument, this thesis is too heavily based on stereotypes to be in conformity with the reality of the evolution of legal sources (Chapter 2.1). The pattern of the French Civil Code or of the German *Bürgerliches GesetzBuch* (*BGB*) is, indeed, traditionally defined as a bundle of rules linked by a formal, closed, systemic and rigid structure. But, nowadays, this perception disintegrates in the face of a law that is progressively fragmenting its original sources (Chapter 2.2).

Thus, it would seem that the only acceptable concept to imagine is that of a European Contract Code built with "open textured rules" (Chapter 3). This means that, if one still considers codification as topical, its present methods appear unable to fit the requirements of such an ambitious project of reformation, such as a European Contract Code (Chapter 3.1). Meanwhile, the works of "restatements" of contractual principles achieved by legal doctrine, and the comparative method of the Court of Justice of the European Community (ECJ), seem until now to constitute progressively what could be defined as an "open textured European Contract Code". This project is, thus, a realistic one if it fulfils two primary conditions: first, the legal texture must be understood as a setting whose openness is characterised by a capacity to adapt to the increasingly fast evolution of the law and, also, to the influence of diverse legal sources; secondly, the flexibility and the openness of this texture have limits that must be found in the qualification of the interpretative power of the judges (Chapter 3.2).

2. AN INDICTMENT AGAINST A EUROPEAN CIVIL CODE

The attack against the idea of a European Civil Code, brought by Pierre Legrand, is grounded on a descriptive analysis of the European legal systems that does not really fit the reality of legal practice. Moreover, his quotations of historical literature condemn him to a very hypothetical, retrospective viewpoint. With regard to his normative analysis of "the irreducibility of the differences between traditions and languages of common law and civil law" and "dangers of a European Civil Code construction", the "culturalism" of the Canadian author forces him to ignore the evolution of the sources of positive law, in particular the development of a kind of codification in common law and a *jurisprudentialisation* within the French Civil Code.

2.1. The traps of stereotype and "*rétrodiction*"

2.1.1. *A stereotype of a Civil Code*

To demonstrate the existence of irreducible obstacles between the common law and continental civil law, the description of European legal systems, given by Pierre Legrand, is somewhat grounded on stereotypes, which are "petrified" by a certain school of comparatists for whom nothing should be changed. It has been admitted, for a long time, that French civil law and English common law are two modes of thinking about law, two "*mentalités*", which differ in their understanding of facts, rules and laws. But, the Canadian author illustrates his argument by drawing, at the very least, a caricature of common law lawyers and continental civil law lawyers.

A. *A caricature of a Civil Code*

According to Pierre Legrand, the Civil Code,

> "as a self contained and self-referential system, illustrates the deep conviction held by civilian jurists that experience lived ought to be no longer privileged (. . .) that experience lived can be reduced to proportional knowledge in the form of a panoptic and autarkic body of rules of law, and that it is useful to organise experience lived (and the law) in this way" (. . .). On the other hand, common law, which "has largely fashioned itself through a strategy of resistance to civil law hegemony" (. . .), "offers a *challenge* to the effort to structure the world into a single determined rational order".[15]

And he adds that

> "the English feel definitely uncomfortable with rigid rules" (. . .), while, the Germans "have been programmed since their early childhood to feel comfortable in structured environments", and "look for a structure in their organisations, institutions, and relationships which make events clearly interpretable and predictable" to the point where "even ineffective rules satisfy the people's emotional need for formal structure".

Quoting a French political geographer of the fifties, Pierre Legrand deems that civil law reasoning is based on "suspicion, realism and pessimism, which contrasts with English law, based on custom and trust".[16] These diverse "*mentalités*" are considered as differences of "*moralités*". Civil law lawyers are the

> "oracles of natural law, eternal and universal", and "the guardians of the law"; common law lawyers, on the other hand, are "the high priests of empirical *savoir faire*" (. . .), "the master of the fact". Thus, "civil law is best understood as the law of the *system*" (. . .). "Common law is the law of the *item*", (. . .). Civil law is "centripetal" (. . .). "Common law is centrifugal".[17]

Finally, the contemporary civilian is "ignorantist", he is afraid of the unknown, he is afraid of a "risk of war", which makes him totalitarian,[18] an excommunicator,[19] "arrogant", "retrograde" and "anti-humanist".[20]

15 Pierre Legrand, "Against a European Civil Code" *loc. cit.* n. 11 at 45–46.
16 *Idem* at 47.
17 *Idem* at 48–51.
18 *Idem* at 53.
19 *Idem* at 55.
20 *Idem* at 56–63.

B. A "de-dialectised" Civil Code

Such a repeated use of stereotypes, which define some immutable whole, could be interpreted as a certain mode of "dedialectising" the current reality.[21] The use of stereotypes demonstrates a fear of uncertainty, "this phenomenon of personalisation is a means of keeping contact with the object and of surmounting disorientation",[22] because the more elementary the formulas, the more reassuring they are. Such a mode of thinking could even "lead to an anti-democratic ideological system".[23] We would prefer to believe that the Canadian author uses these commonplaces only with the aim of provocation. However, Legrand not only founds his argument on a list of edifying formulas, he equally illustrates his theses by some bibliographic quotations of authors of some antiquity, who lead him to give a really hypothetical retrospective interpretation.

2.1.2. *Traps of* "rétrodiction"

A. A hypothetical "rétrodiction"

Anxious to give a certain "scientific strength" to his argument, Pierre Legrand constantly refers either to anthropological, sociological, historical or philosophical literature which, at first sight, appears to be very impressive. Unfortunately, he falls into the trap of giving a less than illuminating retrospective interpretation of contemporary facts. This may be similar to the so-called "*rétrodiction*" in history, i.e., an interpretation that is not based on a causal and "scientific" explanation, but only on a completely subjective presumption. The danger of such reasoning is that one can obtain whatever plausible causes one wants.[24] One may, indeed, believe, for example, that there had been for some 600 years animosity between the two great nations of France and England. And the authors quoted—Glanvill in 1187, and Bracton in 1230—had, without doubt, some good reasons to consider, at their time, common law as a tradition of resistance against the brothers from "the other side of the Channel".[25] However, it is quite difficult to conclude from this that we are still at the point of "war", even if this is only an "epistemological war", with England, as Legrand assumes.

B. The taking-up of historical discourse

Finally, these historical quotations are, at the very least, lacking genuine originality. This discourse recalls the ideas already proposed in the last century, by

[21] Cf., J. Gödel, *La Fausse Conscience* (Paris, 1962).

[22] Cf., T. W. Adorno, *The Authoritarian Personality* (New York, 1950).

[23] Cf., "Les Stéréotypes en Sciences Sociales", *Encyclopedia Universalis*.

[24] On the definition of "*rétrodiction*" in history, see Paul Veynes, *Comment on écrit l'histoire* (Seuil, 1971), 97–117 in particular at 101.

[25] Pierre Legrand, "Against a European Civil Code" *loc. cit.* n. 11 at 46.

the historical school of law.[26] From the end of the eighteenth century to the beginning of the nineteenth century, in the context of German Romanticism, a whole trend of thought had condemned the French Revolution for having made, in the name of "Reason", a clean sweep of the past in relation to Nations and States, and the right and the duty of each nation to make its own individuality respected. The historical school of law stressed the "*Volkgeist*", or the particular genius of each people, based on language, morals, habits, customs and law. Thus, Savigny, who was hostile to any codification that was considered to be an artificial and constraining source of law, and thought that the law should arise slowly from the spirit of the people, condemned Thibault's publication, which defended codification in Germany.[27] The revolution accomplished in our understanding of history renewed our ideas about the sources of law in legal interpretation.[28] Despite this, the historical school of law's discourse has been subject to such a nationalistic exacerbation that to take up its argument again, as Legrand seems to do, is quite ambiguous.

The scientific object studied by Pierre Legrand should not be deemed to be immutable, or intangible. Cultures, traditions and legal practices, are not rooted to the spot, but transform themselves with time.[29] Legal traditions, such as a contextual process of resolving conflicts, are constituted by languages, concepts, and legal techniques, progressively elaborated by history and the style of lawyers, according to the political, economical or social circumstances.[30] This idea of law as a tradition, that goes much further than that of law as a system of rules or functions, does not mean that there is a single and unique orthodoxy for

[26] Gustav Hugo, Friedrich Carl von Savigny, *Revue pour une Science Juridique Historique* (founded in 1815 with Eichborn and Goeschen); A. Brimo, *Les Grands Courants de la Philosophie du Droit Et de L'Etat*. A. Pedone (eds). Paris 1978; Helmut Coing, "Savigny et Collingwood, ou Histoire et Interprétation du Droit" in *Archives de Philosophie du Droit* (*APD*) 1959 at 1; J. Droz, Le Romantisme Allemand et l'Etat, *Bibliothèque historique Payot*, 1966; P. Roubier, *Philosophie du Droit*, at 141; A. Dufour, *Droits de l'Homme, Droit Naturel et Histoire*, Puf. Léviathan 1991.

[27] A. E. J. Thibaut, *Uber die Notwendigkeit eines Allgemeinen Bürgerlichen Gesetzbuches für Deutschland*, (1814); F. C. von Savigny, *Vom Beruf unsrer Zeit für Gesetzgebung und Rechtswissenschaft*, (1814); Z. Krystufek, "La Querelle entre Savigny et Thibault et son Influence sur la Pensée Juridique Européenne", *Rev. hist. dr. fr. et étr.* 1966 at 59 ff. Also, A. Dufour, "L'idée de Codification et sa Critique dans la Pensée Juridique Allemande des XVIIIe–XIXe siècles", *Droits* n. 24, Décembre 1996 at 45–60.

[28] See in *APD*, 1974, Vol. 19 "Savigny"; "Une Philosophie Romantique du Droit et de l'Histoire"; "Droit et Langage dans l'École Historique"; see, also, in *APD*, 1978, Vol. 23: "Rationalité et Irrationalité dans l'École du Droit Historique"; and in *APD*, 1982, Vol. 27 "La Théorie des Sources du Droit dans l'École Historique". See, also, "Savigny, Fondateur de l'Ecole du Droit Historique" in *Coll. Genevoise, Les Grands Jurisconsultes* (Bâle, Helbing & Lichtenhahn). P. Stein, "The German Historical School of Law" in *Legal Evolution. The Story of an Idea* (Cambridge University Press 1980); H. Schlosser, *Grungzüge des Neueren Privatrechtsgeschichte* (Heidelberg, 1985) at 98 ff. See, also, R. Zimmerman in "Savigny's Legacy—Legal History, Comparative Law, and the Emergence of a European Legal Science", *Law Quarterly Review* (*LQR*) 1996, at 576–605.

[29] John Bell, "Comparative Law and legal Theory" in *Prescriptive Formality and Normative Rationality* in *Modern Legal Systems* (Duncker & Humblot, Berlin) at 19–31 ff., in particular at 29–30. See, also, Mark Van Hoecke and Mark Warrington, "Legal Cultures and Legal Paradigms: Towards a New Model for Comparative Law", *ICLQ*, July 1998 at 522–523.

[30] Martin Krieger, "Law as Tradition", in *Law and Philosophy* 1986-5 at 237.

all. On the contrary, "if there is a single mainstream "tradition" which provides the correct reading of a text, this tradition is a locus of conflict and debate, competing interpretations and practices".[31] This is why the Canadian author, whose attachment to the preservation of a culture threatened by the hegemonic ambitions of another culture may very well be understood, seems to reach some normative conclusions that really misjudge the evolution of positive law in European legal traditions. These evolutions are characterised by what may be called a double movement of oscillation and fragmentation of the sources of law, illustrated here by the process of a kind of codification in common law and of *jurisprudentialisation* within the French civil law system.

2.2. Codification and *jurisprudentialisation*, or the oscillation and fragmentation of the sources of law

The "culturalist" vision of Pierre Legrand misjudges the evolution of the studied legal systems. His stereotyped presentation of "common law on case law basis", and "civil law on a legislative basis", does not inform us of any reality about the "living law". This snapshot does not reproduce the simultaneous movement of both oscillation and fragmentation of the legal sources in our legal systems.[32] In other words, one may say that our sources of law have moved in a reversed direction in England and in France:

> *"Il y a deux siècles, le droit anglais était exclusivement jurisprudentiel, aujourd'hui il n'est plus que principalement jurisprudentiel et accessoirement légal. Le droit français était exclusivement légal, aujourd'hui, il n'est que principalement légal et accessoirement jurisprudentiel"*.[33]

2.2.1. The development of a kind of codification in the common law

A. *The historical evolution of the sources of law: towards a codification?*

If England has indeed been a country of customary law from its origin,[34] very early on the Royal power asserts itself, not by legislation, but by the creation of jurisdictions, the Royal Courts of *Westminster*.[35] These courts applied a com-

[31] Terry Eagleton, *Literary Theory: An Introduction* (Oxford, Blackwell, 1983) at 72–23 (cited in John Bell, *op. cit.* n. 29 at 29 and 30).

[32] On the terms "system" and "family" of law used in comparative law, see *Dictionnaire Encyclopédique de Théorie et de Sociologie du Droit*, dir. André-Jean Arnaud, 1988. See, also, Joseph Raz in *The Concept of the Legal System* (Oxford Clarendon Press, 1970), 2nd ed. 1980 at 1–2. See, also, René David, *Les Grands Systèmes de Droit Contemporain* (3rd ed., Paris, 1969).

[33] (Two centuries ago, English law was exclusively based on a case law, nowadays, it is mainly on case law and partly based on legislation. The French law was exclusively based on legislation, and nowadays, it is mainly based on legislation and partly on case law)—Philippe Jestaz, Les Sources du Droit: le Déplacement d'un Pôle à un Autre", *RTDC* 1996 at 308 (translation is mine).

[34] About the system of common law, see R. J. Walker in *The English Legal System* (London, Butterworth, 1985). See, also, S. F. C. Milson in *Historical Foundations of the Common Law*.

[35] Cf., J. H. Baker, *An Introduction to English Legal History* (London, Butterworths, 1979) at 290–299. See, also, F. W. Maitland in *English Law and the Renaissance*, (1901).

mon law, not voted by Parliament, but made with a set of common rules opposed to the diversity of customs and jurisdictions of private law.[36] The efficacy of the Royal Courts was such that their scope of competence increased rapidly to become, *de facto*, the jurisdictions of common law. Thus, customary law has been smoothly replaced, not by law made by a legislator, but by law made by courts. Yet, to impose the common law, the Royal Courts could not allow any divergence of interpretation and thus invented the rule of precedent.[37] Broadly speaking, a preceding judgment made by a court imposes itself on the others. This rule is based on a fiction or a utopia, according to which the English judge only reveals the alleged immemorial custom.[38] This "uniformisation" of the law is thus not due to legislation of a statutory nature.[39]

However, the contemporary legal evolution in England has taken another path.[40] It is characterised by a development of State law and seems to be similar to what may be called a kind of "codification" of private law. Private law is understood as the law regulating relations between individuals (which is the core of the law in common law countries) such as family law. But criminal law (*droit pénal*) and other fields that a civil lawyer would be inclined to define as "public law", such as tax law, for instance,[41] are already codified by Statute. The legislator can nowadays modify a precedent and the judge cannot normally disobey a statutory legislation. Obviously, this comparison must be nuanced. Efforts of systematisation and rationalisation under the form of legislation are, without any doubt, not of the same nature as the traditional continental codification, and the case law remains the dominant source of law in England.

Yet, English authors admit that "there is, in many areas of the law, a pressing need for codification".[42] In countries where the authority in private law

[36] F. W. Maitland, *The Forms of Action at Common law*, 2nd ed., 1948 at 52.

[37] Michael Zander, *The Law Making Process* (London, Butterworths, 4th ed., 1994), chs 4–7. J. A. G. Griffith, *The Politics of the Judiciary* (London, Fontana). Smith and Bailey, *The Modern English Legal System* (Sweet and Maxwell), ch. 7; R. J. Walker *op. cit.* n. 34, ch. 3. William Glanvill in *Learning the Law* (Stevens), ch. 6.

[38] About the fiction of continuity in the common law, see Gerald J. Postema, *Bentham and the Common law Tradition* (Oxford, Clarendon, 1986) at 6, citing Sir Matthew Hale, a *History of the Common Law* (1736). See also, Ronald Dworkin, *Law's Empire* (1986) at 238–239, or *Taking Rights Seriously*, 1977 (London, Harper Collins) at 31–32. Also, Joseph Raz, *The Authority of Law* at 181–182. D. N. MacCormick, *Precedent in Law,* in Goldstein (ed). The doctrine thus plays a creative role in the constant construction of the legal system, in drawing a certain type of legal culture as well as in perpetuating a legal tradition.

[39] Cf., H. G. Richardson in *Law and Legislation from Aethelbert to Magna Carta* (1966).

[40] Cf., Guido Calabresi in "A Common law at the Age of Statutes" in *The Oliver Wendell Holmes Lectures* (Cambridge, Harvard University Press 1982).

[41] I use brackets because the distinction between private law and public law is not defined in the same terms in French and English law. On this distinction, see the clear analysis of L. Neville Brown and John S. Bell, *French Administrative Law* (Clarendon Press, Oxford, 1998) at 4–6 and 297–298. See, also, on a possible convergence between various public laws, Jacques Ziller, *Administrations Comparées, Les Systèmes Politico-administratifs de l'Europe des Douze* (Montchrétien, 1993) at 274–280.

[42] R. J. Walker *op. cit.* n. 34 at 91–92. Also, Radcliff and Cross, *The English Legal System* (London, Butterworths, 1977), 6th ed. at 368–378.

normally resides in the case law (*reports of decided cases*), several of its branches have been codified by legislation (*Statutes*):

> "In the nineteenth century, statute was gradually coming to rival decided cases as a source of English law (. . .). The reorganisation of the judicial system and procedure in the nineteenth century was the work of statutes (Judicature Acts 1875), but statutes affected the substance of the law as well".[43]

By the Law Commission's Act of 1965, two bodies of commissioners (one for England and Wales, the other for Scotland) were established

> "to keep the law under review with a view to its systematic development and reform including, in particular, its codification, and generally the simplification and modernisation of the law".[44]

Furthermore, a pilot-study of a code of contract was elaborated and followed by legal doctrine.[45] Moreover, there is a Joint Consolidation Committee at the House of Commons in charge of the preparation of projects for the consolidation of the existing laws:[46]

> "Thus, over the last hundred years, statute has played a considerable part in the development of our private law and is plainly destined to play an increasing part in this field in the future".[47]

English judges, also in favour of a simplification and clarification of legislation in order to facilitate the task, hold arguments that are clearly in favour of some kind of codification. One example is Sir John Donaldson, M.R.[48] who asserts:

> "My plea is that Parliament, when legislating in respect of circumstances which directly affect the "man and woman in the street", should give as high a priority to clarity and simplicity of expression as to refinements of policy. Where possible, statutes (. . .) should not be amended but re-enacted in an amended form so that those concerned can read the rules in a single document".[49]

There are thus no procedural reasons to prevent a codification process in England. Clearly, everything depends on what sort of codification we are talking about.[50] However, we will come back to this later. For example, in texts

[43] Radcliff and Cross, *op. cit.* n. 42: "The need to refer to numbers of cases could perhaps be reduced somewhat by codification".

[44] Radcliff and Cross, *op. cit.* n. 42 at 370.

[45] M. McGregor, *Contract Code: Drawn up on behalf of the English Law Commission* (London and Rome, Giuffrè/Sweet & Maxwell, 1993).

[46] *Consolidation of Enactments (Procedure) Act* of 1949.

[47] Radcliff and Cross, *op. cit.* n. 42 at 370.

[48] Sir John Donaldson, M.R., in *Merkur Island Shipping Corporation v. Laughton*, (1983) 2 AC 570 at 594–595.

[49] This was taken up again by Lord Diplock when the case went before the House of Lords (1983, 2 AC. at 612)

[50] Denis Tallon, "La Codification dans le Système de *Common Law*", *Droits*, 1998 at 39–47.

such as the the two *Sales of Goods Act*,[51] we have two codifications: of existing law (*droit constant*) which lack the will of reform, whereas in the *Law Commission Act* of 1965, everything concerns the development of a systematic reform of law, and, as such, a genuine substantively reforming codification.

B. *With nuances*

To compare this codification process in England, which is often closer to a legislative compilation or consolidation than to codification, with the traditional systems of the continental method, would be going too fast.[52] Some differences of an epistemological nature may subsist; this is Geoffrey Samuel's main argument against the idea of a codification process in England.[53] The author notes that those, who write the laws, only have the goal of solving concrete problems.[54] English laws are only a set of provisions bound by an empirical theme, and interpreted according to an equally descriptive reasoning. Thus, if a procedure of codification in English law really exists, this codification does not lie on the same epistemological continental presupposition"

> "*par lequel la connaissance du droit consiste dans la connaissance des règles dégagée du monde social et organisé en système*".[55]

But, like Pierre Legrand, Geoffrey Samuel bases his analysis on a very strict and classical definition of the French Civil Code:

> "*Un stade axiomatique de la science juridique*" (. . .), "*fruit d'une épistémologie positiviste du droit, fondée sur l'idée de hiérarchie des normes avec comme mission de mettre de l'ordre dans les règles de droit*" (. . .). "*aboutissant au raisonnement judiciaire syllogistique*".[56]

It is clear that such a frozen perception of codification cannot logically be applied to the English system[57] but, as we will see later on in this paper, what is

[51] The original of 1893 is entitled "*An Act for codifying the law relating to the Sales of Goods*", and that of 1979 "*An Act to consolidate the law relating to the sale of Goods*". Cf., M. D. Chalmers, "Codification of Mercantile Law", *LQR* 1993, Vol. 19 at 10–18 (cited in Geoffrey Samuel, "Existe-il une Procédure de Codification du Droit Anglais", *RFAP loc. cit.* n. 2 at 215). See, also, M. Zander, *op. cit.* n. 37, "The Law Commission and Codification", at 429 ff. See, also, The Law Commission, Codification of the Criminal Law: A Report to the Law Commission", Law. com. n. 143, *HMSO* 1985.

[52] Denis Tallon, *loc. cit.* n. 50 at 41: "*Ce qu'on appelle codification n'est autre que la remise en ordre du droit existant à des fins pratiques*" (quoting L. Diamond, "La Codification en Droit Anglais", *Ann. Legisl. fr. et étr.*, 1978, Vol. XXVIII at 1).

[53] Geoffrey Samuel, *loc. cit.* n. 51 at 219 and, "English Private Law in the Context of the Codes" in this volume at 47.

[54] Michael Zander, *op. cit.* n. 37 at 106 ff.

[55] (. . . by which the knowledge of law consists in the knowledge of rules apart from the social world and organised in system). Geoffrey Samuel, *loc. cit.* n. 51 at 219.

[56] (. . . an axiomatic stage of the legal science (. . .) outcome of a legal positivistic epistemology, grounded on the idea of hierarchy of norms, with a mission to put order in the rules of law (. . .) leading to a syllogistic judicial reasoning). Geoffrey Samuel, *idem* at 219.

[57] Geoffrey Samuel calls for the deconstruction of the science, because present presuppositions are outdated and he sees in the Common law a legal science already destructurised, in which we could very well find the epistemological foundations of a post axiomatic stage of the legal science (*idem* at 220).

nowadays, in France, being defined as a "codification" is no longer the nineteenth-century conception of codification.

However, our aim is not to consider the end of the common law system[58] (. . . even if, sometimes, it would indeed be helpful for the "ignorantist" civilian). On the contrary, one may observe the tendency of the common law system to move towards a readjustment between various legal sources: legislation as acts of Parliament and case law; an evolution comparable with what is occurring in France in the opposite direction. Thus, even if the constitution of a "*Code of English Law*"[59] remains only in the imagination,[60] the existence of a trend towards a sort of codification remains, nonetheless undeniable. Thus, Pierre Legrand's and Geoffrey Samuel's perception of the French Civil Code appears to square increasingly less with the topical representation of French positive law. Actually, since its creation, one may find, in the very text of the Civil Code, the conditions for its *jurisprudentialisation*, for a further, and considerable, elaboration of the codified rules by courts.

2.2.2. *The* "jurisprudentialisation" *of the French Civil Code*

Pierre Legrand deems that codification based on the model of the French Civil Code would have the effect of excluding any alternative viewpoint of justice because it would require exegesis.[61] It seems, once again, to privilege the notion of a Civil Code elaborated by some French "legalist" doctrine. Actually, exegesis ceased to be the single method of analysis of French civilians a long time ago[62] (besides, it is the same thing in England, with statutory interpretation).[63] If the rational or syllogistic formalisation still exists, this fiction only serves as a discourse structure and leaves room, in practice, for greater freedom of interpretation by the judge. The functional use of these legal fictions in the argumentation and the decisions of justice in French law have been abundantly

[58] Lord Goff of Chieveley, "The Future of Common law" in *The Wilberforce Lecture* 1997, *ICLQ* 1997 at 745–760.

[59] Scarman, L, *A Code of English Law* (Hull University, 1966).

[60] Franck Lessay, "Blackstone, *Common law* et codification", *Droits*, 1998 at 3–16. Also, "Code et Codification dans la Pensée de J. Bentham", *Revue d'Histoire du Droit*, XXXII, 1964. Thus, the idea of codification is not alien to Common law. After all, The Indian Penal Code was produced in the nineteenth century by common law lawyers such as Sir James Fitzjames Stephens.

[61] Pierre Legrand, *loc. cit.* n. 11 at 55.

[62] François Gény, *Méthodes d'Interprétation et Sources en Droit Privé Positif*, 2d ed. 1919, Vol. 1, nn. 86, 87, 91. Hostile to Napoléon and his regime, the author minimised the range of the civil code and reduced it to a purely technical dimension: "*Le phénomène de la codification, en soi, et en dehors de l'unification qu'il consommait dans la législation de la France, n'apparaît pas comme autre chose qu'une opération de pure forme, de simplification et de classement*". . . (Vol. 1 n. 9); and further on (n. 149) . . . "*la jurisprudence sans constituer en elle-même une source formelle de droit positif, doit du moins compter parmi les autorités les plus puissantes aux yeux des juristes . . .*" See Carré de Malberg, *Contribution à la Théorie Générale de l'Etat*, Vol. 1, (Sirey, 1920), n. 246 at 741 ff.

[63] Michael Zander, *op. cit.* n. 37 ch. 1–3. R. J. Walker, *op. cit.* n. 34 ch. 2; Smith and Bailey, *op. cit.* n. 37 ch. 2. See, also, Lord Browne-Wilkinson, in Pepper v. Hart (1993) 1 All E.R. at 69, 50, 67 respectively.

described.[64] If the part played by the judge, who claims to be the *bouche de la loi,* is a formal fiction, in practice, the authority of case law rivals the authority of law as legislation (Statute or Act of Parliament).

A. *The classical model of the French Civil Code: an "official fiction"*

This model can be analysed from a historical and a theoretical point of view.

From a historical point of view, codification, above all in civil law countries, was deemed to be necessary, because of the extreme distrust towards judges shown by representatives of the French people at the end of the *Ancien Régime*.[65] This distrust, converted into prohibition of interpretation, left its marks on the work of codification, that was being far from accomplished. This conviction soon reached the minds of people and transpired through the "*doléances*" in 1789, indicating the arbitrary interpretation of the laws by judges, and asking for codes that were "not susceptible to the lesser explanation".[66] In this context, it was the vision of a rigid codification that guided most of the subsequent projects:

> "*La fonction des juges n'est que d'appliquer la loi, et leur devoir est de se conformer au sens littéral, sans s'en écarter ni se permettre de l'interpréter*".[67]

But the use of the "*référés législatifs*" quickly appeared to be much more inconvenient in relation to the judge's possible freedom of interpretation. The abuse of this procedure was denounced as ending in a denial of justice ("*déni de justice*"). This is why, as from 1800, the previous suspicion gave way to neutrality.[68] The reintegration of a measure of interpretation did not seem to be unreasonable.[69]

The necessity of a rigid code in civil law countries, which was seen as a machine of war for the legislator against the judge, disappeared. At the very

[64] See Mitchel Lasser, "Judicial (Self-)Portraits: Judicial Discourse in the French Legal System", *The Yale Law Journal*, 1995 at 1325–1420. Even if the jurisprudence is *de facto* equivalent to the law, it cannot do without the fiction of its subordination to the law. Besides, this fiction has never been abandoned since the creation of the Civil Code, which has not impeached a "natural" development of this legal source. One may then ask how the maintenance of this fiction is still justified nowadays? See, in *La Revue Droit*, n. 21, 1995, on *La fiction juridique*, and particularly, Anton Schütz, "L'immaculée Conception de l'Interprète et l'Émergence du Système Juridique: à Propos de 'Fiction' et 'Construction' en Droit", at 113.

[65] Gilles J. Guglielmi, "L'Idée de Codification dans la construction du Droit Administratif Français au XIXe siècle", *Jahrbuch für Europäische Verwaltungsgeschichte* n. 8, 1996 at 109–133. This article can be found in "Codification", on the *Réseau Européen Droit et Société* (REDS) Web site, http://www.msh-paris.fr/red&s/communic/index.htm#codif.

[66] J. van Kan, *Les efforts de codification en France. Étude historique et psychologique* (Paris, Rousseau, 1929) at 383–384.

[67] (The function of judges is only to apply the law and their duty is to conform themselves to the literal sense, without wandering from it or allowing themselves to interpret it). Projet Thouret, sect. IV, Art 12, *AP 1ère série,* Vol. VIII at 331 (translation is mine).

[68] Gilles J. Guglielmi, *loc. cit.* n. 65.

[69] For further developments, see ibid.

most, some attempts might have occasionally subsisted to use the past distrust to justify a supple codification at the very least. Some authors[70] thus advocated a permanent codification. This operation[71] would be undertaken by a national committee that would observe codes and laws, but also decisions of courts, complaints and observations from public prosecutors, who would write projects of modification or abrogation and whose works would be discussed in "a constitutional form".[72] The envisaged codification, even if it does not have the flexibility of permanency, has, however, the flexibility of content?[73]

From a theoretical point of view, according to the "legalistic" and classical vision, the judiciary did not have to do more than applying a rule to facts, on the model of a practical syllogism of the kind:

(1) if Y, then Z ought to be;
(2) Y;
(3) so Z ought to be.

The major premise is the text of the law (1), the minor premise is the fact (2) and the conclusion is the judgment (3). The judge is only an automaton because the major and minor premises are already provided and he merely has to draw conclusions. The validity of this model is questionable.[74] Firstly, one may challenge the validity of the deductive interference: if, in a theoretical syllogism, the conclusion is contained in the major premise, it is not the same with a practical syllogism.[75] One may also show that the validity of a judgment does not depend on the validity of the deductive interference, but simply on the way the judgement has been set down and, in particular, on the authority of the one who set it down. The judgement is valid whatever the premises are, as soon as it is stated in accordance with the required procedure by a tribunal with competent juris-

[70] M. Agresti, *Idées sur le Perfectionnement de la Législation Positive* (Paris, Rondonneau, 1804) at 13 (work dedicated to Cambacérès). This author remains typically suspicious towards magistrates: "*on abuse du mot interpréter, et par le fait, le magistrat crée une loi qui sera nécessairement rétroactive* (. . .) *dans le silence ou l'obscurité des lois* [la jurisprudence de la Cour de cassation] *deviendrait alors une loi de rigueur pour tous les magistrats et cette assemblée se transformerait en quelque sorte en assemblée législative*."

[71] Taking up in the twentieth century, see G. Ardant, "La Codification Permanente des Lois, Règlements et Circulaires", *RDP* 1951 at 35.

[72] M. Agresti, *op. cit.* n. 70 at 15.

[73] With reserve that this content was the positive law. "Le Code ne doit se composer que des dispositions actuellement en vigueur." J. M. Gérando, *Institutes du droit administratif français, ou Éléments du Code administratif réunis et mis en ordre*, Vol. I (Paris, Nève, 1829) at 8.

[74] Michel Troper, review of Théodore Ivainer's thesis: "L'interprétation des Faits en Droit, Essai de Mise en Perspective Cybernétique des 'lumières du magistrat'", Bulletin bibliographique de la *Revue du Droit public et de Science Politique* 1989 at 1193–1195.

[75] Thus, "Socrates is mortal" is already contained in "all men are mortal" because to be able to assert that "all men are mortal", is already to know that Socrates, who is a man, is mortal. On the contrary, "all thieves must be punished" does not contain "Dupont the thief must be punished", the legislator was ignorant of the fact that, one day, there would be a thief named Dupont (see Michel Troper, *idem* at 1194).

diction.[76] One may also challenge the fact that the major premise is given to the judge. It is enough to stress that, according to the doctrine of realism, norms are necessarily expressed by means of a language, which is vague and ambiguous. Thus, above all, interpretations are acts of will, especially those of the judiciary, when interpreting legislative provisions and utterances. Thus, the judge has at his disposal a genuine power, which is considerable in fact.[77] One may finally consider that the minor premise is not a piece of data and that the facts themselves must be interpreted.[78] Various methods may, thus, allow judges to justify their factual conclusions, particularly on the "narrative coherence" model.[79]

B. Case law, an "unofficial" legal source of the French Civil Code

Although "officially" legislative, or even "ultra legalist", French law actually gives substantial room to case law. The separation of powers principle was set up by the Acts of the 16th and 24th of August, 1790, which means that the judge must not "*légiférer*", but must limit himself to the adjudication of the law. However, this principle:

> "*Ne s'est jamais appliqué tel quel, et le juge a toujours, même au temps de la Révolution française, joui d'un pouvoir normateur considérable, lié à de nombreux facteurs: la marge de pouvoir discrétionnaire expressément conféré par le législateur, le pouvoir de subsumer le fait sous plusieurs normes de référence, d'interpréter des textes, de 'dégager' ou de 'découvrir' des principes non écrits applicables à l'espèce, de procéder à la qualification juridique des faits, etc. . . .*".[80]

Even the most renowned draftsman of the Civil Code,[81] Portalis, revealed the openness of the Civil Code to case law interpretation. This vision of the Civil

[76] Laetitia Gianformaggio, *In Difesa del Syllogismo Pratico; Ovvero Alcuni Argomenti Kelseniani alla Prova* (Milano, Giuffré, 1987).

[77] Hans Kelsen, *General Theory of Norms* (Oxford, Clarendon Press, 1991).

[78] Théodore Ivainer, "L'interprétation des faits en droit, Essai de mise en perspective cybernétique des 'lumières du magistrat' ", Paris, *LGDJ* 1988, Bibliothèque de philosophie du droit, Vol. 30, Preface by Jean Carbonnier.

[79] Bernard S. Jackson, *Law, Fact and Narrative Coherence* (Liverpool, Deborah Charles Publications, 1988).

[80] (It was never applied as such, and the judge has always, even during the time of the French Revolution, enjoyed a considerable normative power due to numerous factors: the margin of discretionary power expressly conferred by the legislator, the power to subsume the facts under several norms of reference, to interpret texts, to "clear" or to "find out" unwritten principles applicable to the case, to carry out the legal "*qualification*" of facts, and so on . . .), Michel Troper, "L'Europe et les Principes", *Revue Droit et Société* (*RDS*) 1992 at 165–169 (translation is mine).

[81] The authors of the civil code were the "An III" project's draftmen, the magistrates officially in charge to criticize this project, all legislators, the "*Second Consul*" Cambacérès, as author of three previous projects of codes, Berlier, Treilhard or Jacqueminot, closely associated with the effort of the revolutionary legal unification, but also, Bonaparte himself, the famous Merlin de Douai, called "Merlin-Suspect" whose part in the preparation of the civil code was all the more important since he was, at that time, the president of the "*Tribunal de cassation*". The nineteenth century attributes him with having implemented the first case law from the code. The four official draftmen of the civil code: Bigot-Préameneu and Tronchet, "nordistes" draftmen from countries of customs and Maleville and Portalis. Cf., André-Jean Arnaud, "Origines Doctrinales du Code Civil Français" (Paris, *LGDJ*, 1969). See, also, in "Codification" on the Réseau Européen Droit et Société (R.E.D.S.) website: http://www.msh-paris.fr/red&s/communic/index.htm#codif.

Code in 1804 will be taken up again and developed by the contemporary doctrine. It suffices to read the "*Discours préliminaire*":[82]

> "*L'office de la loi est de fixer par de grandes vues des maximes générales du droit, d'établir des principes féconds en conséquences, et non de descendre dans le détail des questions qui peuvent naître sur chaque matière. C'est aux magistrats et aux juristes pénétrés de l'esprit général des lois, à en diriger l'application. Il y a une science pour les législateurs comme il y en a une pour les magistrats; et l'une ne ressemble pas à l'autre. La science du législateur consiste à trouver dans chaque matière les principes les plus favorables au droit commun; la science du magistrat est de mettre ces principes en action, de les ramifier, de les étendre par une ramification sage et raisonnée aux hypothèses prévues*".[83]

One century later, Planiol echoed the thoughts of Portalis by asserting that the judge was the legislator of the particular case. The judge, from the origin of the Civil Code, clarifies the obscurities of the law, and fills in its gaps:

> "*C'est à l'expérience à combler successivement les vides que nous laissons. Les codes des peuples se font avec le temps. Mais à proprement parler, on ne les fait pas*".[84]

Practice and doctrine have meanwhile demonstrated the modernity of Portalis' vision, and denied Justice Holmes' famous phrase: "General provisions do not decide concrete cases", which has unfortunately inspired a distrust towards codification amongst common law lawyers.[85] From the middle of the twentieth century, French authors have progressively acknowledged the existence of a genuine *jurisprudence* power.[86] This case-law power won fame for

[82] Portalis, *Discours préliminaire*; in Fenet, *Receuil complet des travaux préparatoires du code civil*,Vol. I, 1836 at 463 ff. See, also, Locré in *Législation Civile, Commerciale et Criminelle de la France*, Vol. I, 1927 at 243 ff. See, also, *Motifs et Discours Prononcés lors de la Présentation du Code Civil par les Divers Orateurs du Conseil d'Etat et du Tribunat* (Paris, Firmin Didot, 1886), Vol. I. *Discussions sur le Code civil* (Paris, F. Didot, 1855), Vol. II.

[83] (The office of the law is to fix the great views of general legal maxims and accordingly to set out fruitful principles, and not to go down into details of questions that can spring from each matter. It is to the magistrates and to the lawyers, penetrated by the general spirit of laws, to run their application. There is a science for legislators as there is one for magistrates; and one does not resemble to the other. The science of the legislator consists in finding out in each matter the principles the most in favour of the common law; the science of the magistrate is to put these principles in action, to ramify them, to extend them by a wise and reasoned ramification to the foreseen hypothesis), Portalis *op. cit.* n. 82 (translation is mine). Cf., Otto Kahn-Freund, C. Levy and Bernard Rudden, *A Source Book on French Law* (Oxford, Clarendon, 1973) at 73 ff. about the conceptualism of French law. See, also, F. H. Lawson, *A Common Lawyer Looks at the Civil Law*, (1953) at 62 ff.

[84] (It is to experience of filling in successively the empty spaces that we leave. Codes of the people are made with time. But strictly speaking, we do not make them), *op. cit.* n. 82 (translation is mine).

[85] André Tunc, "La Méthode du Droit Civil: Exposé des Conceptions Françaises", *RIDC*, 1975 at 822. See, also, Sir L. Scarman, *A Code of English Law* (Hull University, 1966) (cited in Geoffrey Samuel, *loc. cit.* n. 51 at 219).

[86] Jacques Maury, "Observations sur la Jurisprudence en Tant que Source de Droit". *Mélanges Ripert*, *LGDJ* 1950, Vol. 1 at 28; Marcel Waline, "Le Pouvoir Normatif de la Jurisprudence", *Mélanges Scelle*, *LGDJ* 1950, Vol. 2 at 613; Esmein, "*C'est trop méconnaître la réalité que d'y refuser d'y voir (dans la jurisprudence) une source du droit*" in La jurisprudence et la loi, *RTD civ.*, 1952 at 19; G. Marty and P. Raynaud: "*L'Observation de la Réalité Juridique Permet de Répondre avec Certitude que la Jurisprudence Crée du Droit . . .*" *Droit civil*, Vol. 1, 2d ed. at 217; H. L. Mazeaud, J. Mazeaud and M. de Juglart, "*La jurisprudence est devenue en France une source de droit d'une importance considérable*" in *Leçons de droit civil*, Vol. 1, 5th ed. at 130).

clarity through the creation of the *Conseil d'État*, the administrative body jurisdiction that gradually emancipated itself from the rules of the Civil Code by inventing an administrative law almost like a legislator.[87] Another example of the creation of legal rules by case law, in the absence of written law, can be found in the theory of general principles of law. The *Conseil d'État* admits that they are applicable in the absence of text, the *Cour de cassation* equally founds its rulings on such principles.[88]

Moreover (taking a textual argument), even in the very bosom of the text of the Civil Code, there is room for rules which develop case law. Article 4 of the Civil Code compels the judge to interpret and decide in the presence of an insufficiency or a gap in the law.[89] This is definitively a text which obliges the judge to create law and to constitute a fully fledged source of law. Equally, Article 1353 of the Civil Code, which leaves the evaluation of presumptions to the discretion of the judge,[90] is among the written provisions in the Civil Code that lead the judge to a factual interpretation. If Article 5 of the Civil Code prohibits judges from "taking decisions by way of general and regulative disposition in cases which are submitted to them",[91] it still leaves the judge a sufficient amount of freedom. Finally, Article 1351 of the Civil Code[92] condemns the system of precedent. It does not, however, ban the use of the hierarchical principle between courts of various levels. The superior courts impart a case law policy, which is generally followed by the inferior courts, which do not want their decisions to be reversed (*cassées*) all the time. If this is not a written rule, it is, however, a common practice in French courts.

[87] "A major characteristic of *droit administratif* (. . .) is that its general principles and framework have developed from case-law. (. . .) There is no code of general principles and so it has been for the courts to integrate the various element into a coherent system." In L. Neville Brown and John S. Bell, *op. cit.* n. 41 at 293–294. The paradox is that Administrative law from case law origin becomes increasingly a written law by the insertion of case law solutions in the legislation. René Chapus, *Droit Administratif Général*, 11th ed. (Montchrétien, 1997) at 73 ff. "Première partie: Les sources du droit administratif"; Gilles J. Guglielmi, *loc. cit.* n. 65.

[88] G. Marty and P. Raynaud, "*La théorie des principes généraux, née de la jurisprudence, est une manifestation de son pouvoir créateur*", *op. cit.* n. 86 at 217.

[89] "*Le juge qui refusera de juger, sous prétexte du silence, de l'obscurité ou de l'insuffisance de la loi, pourra être poursuivi comme coupable de déni de justice*", cf. G. Marty and P. Raynaud, *op. cit.* n. 86 at 218. The English version of the French Civil Code is drawn from the translation by J. H. Grabb, F. B. Rothman & Co, (eds), 1977.

[90] "*Les présomptions qui ne sont pas établies par la loi, sont abandonnées aux lumières et à la prudence du magistrat, . . .*" (presumptions which are not established by law are left to the insight and wisdom of the magistrate) (*op. cit.* n. 89).

[91] "*Prononcer par voie de disposition générale et réglementaire sur les causes qui leur sont soumises*" (*op. cit.* n. 89).

[92] "*L'autorité de la chose jugée n'a lieu qu'à l'égard de ce qui a fait l'objet du jugement. Il faut que la chose demandée soit la même; que la demande soit fondée sur la même cause; que la demande soit entre les mêmes parties, et formées par elles et contre elles en la même qualité*" (The authority of *res judicata* arises only with regard to what was the subject of the judgment. It is necessary that the thing claimed be the same, that the claim be founded on the same grounds, that the claim be between the same parties, and brought by them and against them in the same capacity) (*op. cit.* n. 89).

So, the majority of the disputes are solved in fact (*en fait*), that is to say, following a factual interpretation.[93] Consequently, the counter example, of the *Jand'heur* decision, as quoted by Pierre Legrand, is really not appropriate. The decision of *cassation* in *Jand'heur* should have demonstrated the lack of interest for civil lawyers in the facts of the case when the judge interprets the law. The Canadian author writes: "*In France, as any decision of the Cour de cassation makes apparent, the aim is rapidly to eliminate any trace of the conjuncture and to establish an idea or a concept. Therefore, the facts are immediately inscribed within a pre-existing theoretical order where they soon vanish. It is this order itself—and certainly not the facts—which is regarded as the fount of legal knowledge; the emphasis is on universals. Let us take what is possibly the most famous French judgment in the area of civil liability this century, the Jand'heur decision.[94] Who remembers the facts of Jand'heur?*"[95]

One has to take into account some obvious facts. First of all, the description of a legal system cannot stop just at the analysis of the decisions pronounced by the highest court of justice, but must equally observe those rendered by inferior courts. Thus, facts, both in *Cour d'appel* as in *Tribunaux de première instance*, are really at the heart of the judge's decision in his work of "*qualification*". But even the example of the *Jand'heur* decision about "*la responsabilité du fait des choses*" is, above all, badly chosen because, contrary to what Pierre Legrand sustains, this decision inscribes itself in a purely case law (*praetorian*) construction of Article 1384 of the Civil Code. Compared with "a pyramid built on a pinhead",[96] this case law, the outcome of free evolution, evokes English common law much more than the *jurisprudence* of tribunals applying exegesis of codified texts.[97] Moreover, the contemporary "legislative inflation", often producing "lacunary" or even obscured texts, has increased the interpretative power of the judge. This is why some go even as far as to consider the judge as a political organ logically exercising a normative competence, a third power:[98]

[93] What is a factual interpretation? It is a hermeneutic process which aims at discovering the unknown facts by starting from the known facts of each case, it is this process that leads to the *qualification* of the fact of the cause, the first phase of the interpretation consists in the passage from known facts to unknown facts in order to appropriate them to a normative system, while the second phase focuses on the choice of the normative system. Cf. Théodore Ivainer, *op. cit.* n. 78.

[94] Ch. réunies, 13th of February 1930, *D.* 1930.1.57, note Georges Ripert, rapport le Marc'hadour; *S.* 1930.1.121, note Esmein, *Gaz. Pal.* 1930.1.393 and concl. Matter.

[95] Pierre Legrand, *loc. cit.* n. 11 at 49.

[96] Philippe Jestaz, *loc. cit.* n. 33 at 306.

[97] André Tunc, *loc. cit.* n. 85 at 824.

[98] René Chapus, "Réflexions sur le Pouvoir Normatif de la Jurisprudence", *AJDA* 1962 at 532; Sadock Belaïd, "Essai sur le pouvoir créateur et normatif du juge", Bibliothèque de Philosophie du Droit, Vol. XVII, Paris, *LGDJ* 1974. See, also, Olivier Dupeyroux, "La Doctrine Française et le Problème de la Jurisprudence Source du Droit" *Mélanges Gabriel Marty* (Toulouse, 1978).

"Bref, la montée en puissance de la jurisprudence aura été l'événement français le plus marquant depuis la création du Code Civil".[99]

Thus, it would be too reductive to limit oneself to such an analysis of law as a pure reflection of a culture, a society or a nation, protected by impassable frontiers, and whose "*mentalités*" and traditions are irremovable. On the contrary, within each system, discourse elements about law and the rule of law are subject to endogenous, as well as exogenous, influences. These influences lead us to reconsider the possibility of conceiving a Civil Code that would take new requirements and restraints of the contemporary legal world into account. Our representation of the legal sources evolves, oscillates, balances, varies and changes its meaning periodically. Always in search of an equilibrium, it successively passes through new alternatives. But legal sources also fragment themselves. After an ideal unitary vision, our representation of the law is nowadays in pieces. An adapted vision on a Civil Code must allow us to reconstitute, to recompose, the broken image. It is, indeed, a matter of "resticking", and the texture of the glue used, the concept, has some "magic" properties: while joining up these fragments, it does not change the very nature of these moving and variable sources, these living sources of law.

3. A PLEA FOR THE IDEA OF A EUROPEAN CONTRACT CODE WITH "OPEN TEXTURE"

It seems that the idea of an "open textured rule" could make more plausible the ambitious plan of the harmonisation of contract law by codification. If a "code" is traditionally defined as a set of rules and principles bound by a formal, closed, systematic, coherent and rigid structure, this "nineteenth-century" perception is by now splintered, in face of a law that progressively fragments its very sources. New codifications, in Switzerland, Greece, Italy, Spain, and the Netherlands[100] offer a lot of room for more flexible notions that may fit different legal systems. If we are really keen on the idea of a European contract Code, which would be in a position to solve the weird paradox of unity in legal diversity, we would have to reconsider our perception of the legal rule and adopt a pluralistic vision of a contract Code that abandoned its formal logical structure for a frame of reasoning that is closer to the expectations of the economic sector concerned.[101]

[99] (In brief, the increasing strength of case law will have been the most outstanding French event since the creation of the Civil Code). Philippe Jestaz, *loc. cit.* n. 33 at 308 (translation is mine); see, also, "Remarques en Cascades sur les Sources du Droit", *RTDC* 1993 at 73.

[100] O. Tallon, "Le Nouveau Code Civil des Pays-Bas NBW", in *La Codification*, dir. B. Beignier *op. cit.* n. 2. Cf. Arthur S. Hartkamp, "Judicial discretion under the new Civil Code of the Netherland" *American Journal of Comparative Law*, 1992, at 551–571.

[101] Cf., Hugh Collins, "Formalism and Efficiency, Designing European Commercial Contract Law", followed by my comments, "Form v Substance? An Ideological Venture Beyond the Dichotomy in European law of Contract", Conference at the European University Institute (E.U.I.—October 1998): *Private law Adjudication in Europe's Multi-level*, ERPL I-2000 at 211–235, and at 237–247. See, also, Guido Alpa, "Les Nouvelles Frontières du Droit des Contrats", *RIDC* 4-1998 at 1015–1030.

The outcome of comparative methods, which allow a redefinition of legal notions, such as the works of Unidroit[102] and the Lando Commission,[103] or the case law of the ECJ, all militate in favour of an European contract Code with "open textured rules". But first, one has to explain the reasons why the idea of codification is not outdated and why the existing methods of codification undertaken do not meet plainly the European *uniformisation* requirements.

3.1. Topicality of a codification

Taking into account the fragmentation of legal sources and the development of new forms of adjudication of private law disputes, the idea of codification, as an undertaking of legal rationalisation and democratisation, still appears to be topical. However, the present French method of codification does not seem to satisfy the requirements of such an ambitious project as the European Code of contract.

3.1.1. Why a codification?

A. The perils of a decodification

Alterations to legal sources and modifications in the way of dispute resolutions is a common phenomenon today.[104] A shift of legal sources towards less official pri-

[102] *Principles of International Commercial Contracts* (Rome, Unidroit, 1994), in French, "Les Principes Relatifs aux Contrats du Commerce International", in *JCP* 1995. III. 67399.

[103] Ole Lando, *The Principles of European Contract Law* (Dortrecht, Boston, London 1995). Also, "Principles of European Contract Law", in *Liber Memoralis François Laurent* (1810–1887), Erauw, J. Bouckaert, B. Bocken, H. Gaus, H., and M. Storme (eds) (Brussels, Story-Scientia, 1989), 555–568. See, also, Ole Lando, European Contract Law, 31 *Am. J. Com. Law* 653 (1983).

[104] Mireille Delmas-Marty, "La Mondialisation du Droit: Chances et Risques", *Rec. Dalloz* 1999, 5e cahier Chronique at 43–48, in particular at 45: "*Dans le domaine du commerce international, on observe le dépassement du droit étatique ou inter-étatique au profit de la loi des marchands (lex mercatoria) ayant vocation à être appliquée par les arbitres*" (*qui*) "*. . . deviennent de véritables juges indépendants*". "*Parallèlement, on peut noter l'importance de la normalisation (d'origine privée), ainsi que l'extension de l'éthique d'entreprise et des codes de bonnes conduites*". See, also, A. Couret, "La Dimension Internationale de la Production du Droit: l'Exemple du Droit Financier", in *Les transformations de la régulation juridique*, dir. J. Clam et G. Martin, *LGDJ* 1998 at 197ff. Also, Gunther Teubner, "Global Bukinowa: the Emergence of Transnational Legal Pluralism" (*Working paper. E.U.I.* 1995), *Globale Bukowina: zur Emergenz eines Transnationalen Rechtspluralismus* (Universität Basel, Basel 1996) at 6ff. A. Giddens, *The Consequences of Modernity* (Standford, University Press, 1990) at 70, who shows that some sectors of society such as multinational undertakings, are very inclined towards development away from the sphere of State control or of international public law, or of an internal legal regime. In the same sense, see Gérard Farjat, "Réflexions sur les Codes de Bonnes Conduite Privés", *Le Droit des Relations Économiques Internationales*, Etudes B. Goldmann, at 47. See, also, A. Sayag, who refers to the "phénomènes concomittants de décadence de l'Etat législateur et de développement de sources privées créatrice de droit" and "Quelle prospective juridique?", in *Le Droit des Affaires, Demain, Débat du C.R.E.D.A.*, JCP.E 1986, II, 14637.

vate sources has been observed.[105] In France, institutions are developing such as the *Autorité administrative indépendante*, or the *Commission des opérations de Bourse* (*C.O.B.*), which can simultaneously play the role of arbitrator, adviser, expert, regulating organ and administrative agent, thus combining legislative, executive and even judicial power.[106] This tendency, often considered as "decadence" of the State legislator, would be due to the rejection of classical and formal State rules that no longer match the needs of business. A maximum of security and calculability in order to lower transaction costs is commonly considered to be the expectations of business. Yet one observes an anarchical proliferation of new regulations. This has been labelled a "decodification process" by some academics,[107] who see in this a loss of prestige and adherence to the law. An "inflation of changing statutes" only relating to one category and resulting from fragile compromises, would create both a lack of unity and of continuity in the elaboration of rules of law and an increasing confusion in the texts.[108] This *decodification* would increase the contingency and relativity of solutions, threaten the coherency of the legal order and would shatter the very notion of common law; hence, the development of a legal insecurity in commercial transactions.[109]

B. *The meaning of codification*

In this context, the idea of codification as a rationalising legal process aimed to remedy fragmentation and the dispersal of legal sources,[110] the idea of a code as "a coherent set of legal provisions concerning a more or less extensive domain (. . .) which is dressed in a normative way",[111] seems to remain topical. Besides,

[105] Ph. Gerard, F. Ost, M. van de Kerchove, *Fonction de Juger et Pouvoir Judiciaire* (Bruxelles, Publication des Facultés Universitaires St Louis, 1983). Ph. Fouchard, "L'évolution des Modes de Règlement des Litiges; l'Arbitrage" in *Le Droit des Affaires, Demain, Débat du C.R.E.D.A., loc. cit.* n. 104. J. Viérin, "Le Règlement Extra Judiciaire des Litiges", *Revue de Sciences Criminelles et de droit pénal comparé*, 1982 at 171.

[106] Pierre Lascoumes, "La COB: Entre Magistrature Économique et Gestion du Droit des Affaires", *Déviances et Société*, 9-1985, n. 1 at 1–30.

[107] Bruno Oppetit, "La Décodification du Droit Commercial Français", *Études offertes à René Rodière*, Paris, Dalloz, 1981, (197–207) at 200.

[108] M. Corsale, "La codificazione vista dall' eta della decodificazione," *Materialper una storia della cultura giuridica*, 1993, nr. 2 p. 423–437. N. Irti, "L'eta della Decodificazione", Milano, *Giuffré*, 2nd ed., 1986 at 22 ff. See R. Sacco, "Codificare: Modo Superato di Legiferare?" *Riv. dir. civ.* 1983 at 117 ff. François Terré, "Les Problèmes de la Codification à la Lumière des Expériences et des Situations Actuelles" in *Etudes de Droit Contemporain*, Vol. XXIII, 1962 at 175 ff.

[109] "Rapport du Conseil d'Etat, Rapport Public", 1991, *Doc. fr.*, n. 43, (cited in Bruno Oppetit, "De la Codification", *Receuil Dalloz Sirey*, 1996, 5e cahier—chronique at 35).

[110] On this idea, see J. Vanderlinden, *Le Concept de Code en Europe du XIIIe au XIXe siècle, Essai de Définition* (Edition de l'Institut de sociologie, Université Libre de Bruxelles, 1967) at 74–76 and at 229. This concern was uppermost in the preoccupations of political power in the last century of the Ancien Régime, in particular in commercial matters. See A. Vandenbossche, *Contribution à l'Étude des Sources du Droit Commercial, un Commentaire Manuscrit de l'Ordonnance de 1673*, Cujas (eds), 1976 at 4 text and note 2., and H. Lévy-Bruhl, *Un Projet de Code de Commerce à la Veille de la Révolution: Le Projet Mirosmesnil (1778–1789)* (Imp. nat. Paris, 1932) at 31–32. H. Mariage, *Evolution Historique de la Législation Commerciale* (Pédone, 1951) at 61 ff., with the text of the plan, that changed on numerous points the *ordonnance* of 1673.

[111] (*un ensemble cohérent de dispositions juridiques concernant un domaine plus ou moins étendu (. . .) qui revête un caractère normatif*); Jean Gaudemet, "La Codification, ses Formes et ses

the perception of a Civil Code has always been guided by principles of concision, clarity, and accuracy. Jean-Jacques Rousseau made an outstanding plea on the necessity for the citizen as well as for public authorities, of "*codes clairs, courts et précis*".[112] Such qualities answer the need for legal security, while leaving the judge a margin of assessment in *équité*.

The need to assemble the rules together, publish them and give them both simplicity and coherence inspired the draftsmen of the Civil Code.[113] It thus allows the foundations of "social links" to be fixed. In his *Discours de présentation* Portalis defines a code as "*a corpus of laws which aims to guide and fix the relationships of sociability, family and interests, shared by people who belong to the same community*".[114] Moreover, simplicity, accessibility and communicability also facilitate democratisation. Thus the law must not be restricted to experts and bureaucrats only but must also be accessible to the man in the street and easily comprehensible by him.[115]

Finally, codification may also be considered to be a factor of economic growth.[116] In the world-wide context of deregulation—deregulation, not in the sense of the disappearance of regulation, but, on the contrary, of growing specialisation—codification is necessary in as much as it allows regulatory inflation to be controlled better and its cost in the private sector to be lowered.[117] In assuring greater transparency, it can also enhance competition and international trading.[118] The settlement of cases is facilitated by a co-ordinated, more coherent, more transparent and more adaptable set of rules. The most adaptable method of codification with the objective of securing European uniformity of contract law needs therefore to be determined.

3.1.2. *The limits of the current French co-ordination model of "codification"*

A. *Methods of codification*

There are several methods of codification. Some "codes" are nothing but compilations of gathered texts, which have neither been modified nor put in order.

Fins", *Rev. jur. et pol. indépendance et coopération* 1986 at 244–247 (cited in Oppetit, De la codification, *loc. cit.* n. 110 at 34 ff.) (translation is mine).

[112] (. . . clear, short and accurate codes), J. J. Rousseau, *Considération sur le gouvernement de Pologne et sur sa réformation projetée*, in *Oeuvres Complètes*, La Pléiades, Vol. III at 1001.

[113] J. Gaudemet, "La Codification ses Formes et ses Fins", *Rev. jur. et pol. indépendance et coopération*, 1986 at 250–253.

[114] (*un code est un corpus de lois destiné à diriger et à fixer les relations de sociabilité, de famille et d'intérêt qu'ont entre eux des hommes qui appartiennent à la même cité*), Portalis, *Essai sur l'Utilité de la Codification* (Paris, 1844) at IX (translation is mine).

[115] Habermas, *The Theory of Communicative Actions* (Boston, Beacon, 1984); and *Between Facts and Norms: Contributions to Discourses Theory of Law and Democracy* (Cambridge, Mass., MIT, 1996).

[116] M. Scott Jacobs, "La Codification, Facteur de Croissance Économique", *RFAP loc. cit.* n. 2 at 291–298.

[117] See the statistics given by Scott H. Jacobs, *idem* at 292.

[118] "Il serait impossible d'endiguer le flux sans établir d'abord les moyens de le mesurer": Le Conseil d'Etat in 1992 (cited in M. Scott Jacobs, *idem* at 295).

They are collections of juxtaposed texts.[119] Other "codes" may have a function of consolidation: they are established by the legislator, who takes over solutions to be found in case law and/or puts previously existing texts in a logical or chronological order.[120] The most accomplished form of codification is that which really makes innovative work. This is a unitary set, a corpus of old rules combined with new rules, which express the principles of the new vision on society's organisation; the archetype is the French Civil Code.

However, the most widespread method of recent years has been putting the existing law in order, with a rational division of subject matters amongst different codes, and their methodological structuring.[121] It is a matter of both reordering existing norms, which are gathered and ordered without creating new ones, and enhancing clarity and legal security. These texts are then submitted for parliamentary validation so that the codified provisions replace the previous laws.[122] According to some authors, this exhaustive and permanent "administrative codification" should improve the public services, restore respect for the law, facilitate reforms, simplify public actions and make them more coherent.[123] Thus, thanks to the *Comité supérieur de la codification*, in France, some new codes were born in matters of private law, criminal procedure, and criminal law, for example. But despite the work accomplished by this Committee of Codification, essential criticisms regarding its methods have been raised.

B. *Limits of the method of reordering existing law*

Some authors have argued that "codification", which limits itself to reordering existing law, bears important, and even essential, shortcomings. For example, when codified texts are of bad quality, such a codification does not allow to remedy the incoherence of the existing law,

> "since (this sort of codification) rejects from its domain any efforts of reflection, definition or innovation, as if one considered as accomplished a work that should only be a first draft".[124]

119 Ankum, "La Codification Justinienne était-elle une Véritable Codification?", in *Liber amicorum J. Gilisen*, Anvers, 1984 at 1 ff.

120 Denis Tallon, "Codification of the Law at the Present Time", *Israël L. Rev*. 1979.

121 "*C'est un ensemble unitaire, un corpus de règles anciennes et un apport de règles nouvelles exprimant les principes d'organisation de la nouvelle société; l'archétype en est le Code Civil français*", in 1989, "Le comité supérieur de la codification" in France adopted this new method. See Guy Braibant, "La Problématique de la Codification", *RFAP loc. cit*. n. 2 at 165 à 176. See, also, Cauviere, *L'idée de Codification en France* (Paris, 1910). D. Olivier, *La Codification Administrative* (Thesis, Paris, 1958). J.-L. Sourioux, "Codification et autres Formes de Systématisation du Droit à l'Époque Actuelle", *RIDC* 1988.

122 For a full exposé of the method followed by the French Superior Commission of Codification, see the "5e Rapport d'activité de la Commission", 1994 at 11 ff.

123 G. Ardant, "La Codification Permanente des Lois, Décrets et Circulaires", *R.D. publ*. 1952 at 35–70. V. Adde M. Guibal and L. Rapp, "A Propos de la Codification Administrative", *Cah. dr. entr*. 1995, n. 3 at 1. (cited in Bruno Oppetit, De la codification, *loc. cit*. n. 110 at 35). See, also, M. Suel in "Essai sur la Codification à Droit Constant: Précédents, Débuts, Réalisation", 2nd ed.— Paris *OJ* 1995 (Brochure 4259).

124 ("*. . . puisqu'elle rejette hors de son domaine tout effort de réflexion, de définition ou d'innovation, comme si l'on proposait comme oeuvre accomplie ce qui ne devrait en être que la première*

But, the very idea behind making the "taxonomy" (numeration of articles) coincide with structures such as those of codes of legislation, "is a matter of stamping obsession, and this may create confusing situations".[125] In a more radical way, this "codification" does not solve the real problem of the ceaseless mutation of law. If codification aims to reduce the number of applicable laws, then it implies their adaptation and rectification. The classical codes provided general rules, applicable whatever the quality of the persons concerned is. Nowadays, they have been followed by "codes" that provide specific rules, but as these rules are more and more numerous, the codification is thus led to multiply the number of codes.[126] How, then, can the completeness, coherence and permanency associated with the idea of a Civil Code be obtained with so many codes and such specific texts?

This model of codification, as co-ordination of existing law, is also used by the EU, for Community legislation, but this "codification" has only an informative, not a normative, value.[127] By this, it is in some way close to English methods of codification.[128] However, we do not believe that the French model as such can be used as a means of European private law harmonisation. Only a truly reforming codification could succeed, unless one considers, as Pierre Legrand does, that the difference between codified law and the methods of common law are immeasurable. But if one is really keen to produce a European Code of contract law, it is by adopting a middle course, *"un juste milieu"*, that one has to find a way to allow both common law lawyers and "civilians", to adhere to a project of legal integration in Europe. How then can this paradox of unification, which should respect the different legal traditions be solved?

One starting point might be the use of very common and simple ideas, both very well known and shared by different legal systems. One of these ideas is the "open textured". The concept of "open textured rule" is the result of a dialogue between the various European legal systems. Indeed, a *via media* cannot be reached without a process of dialogue and negotiation.[129] This dialogue already

esquisse"), D. Bureau, "Remarques sur la Codification du Droit de la Consommation", *Dalloz* 1994, Chron. at 291–292. See, also, François Terré and A. Outin-Adam, "Codifier, un Art Difficile" (à propos . . . d'un code de commerce), *Dalloz* 1994, Chron. at 99.

[125] ("*. . . relève de l'obsession de l'étiquetage et peut aboutir à des situations confuses*"), Christian Vigouroux, "Alice au Pays de la Codification à Droit Constant", *RFAP loc. cit.* n. 2 at 187–192. Equally, Stéphane Guy, "Une Utopie: la Codification", *Revue Française de Droit Constitutionnel* 26-1996 at 276.

[126] France could have sixty codes at the end of its codification process.

[127] Gérald Crossland, "La Codification du Droit Européen par les Institutions de l'Union", *loc. cit.* n. 2 at 257–263.

[128] See the equivalent of the codification of constant law in Germany where there is no real code, except the *BurgerlichesGesetzBuch* (BGB) and where legislative techniques consist in making major laws on a particular theme under a consolidated publication form. For German references, see Hans Jurgen Sonnenberger, "Der Ruf unserer Zeit nach einer Europäischen Ordnung des Zivilrechts", *Juristenzeitung* 1998–20.

[129] P. Legrand, "Sens et Non-sens d'une Codification Réformatrice du Droit Européen", *loc. cit.* n.2 at 227–231. See, also, "Sens et Non-sens d'un Code Civil Européen", *loc. cit.* n. 14.

exists within institutions such as Unidroit or the Lando Commission and within the process of adjudication of the ECJ.

3.2. For a European contract Code with "open textured rules"

The present-day French codification model of co-ordinating existing law only encompasses legislative and regulatory provisions. It thus neglects the contribution of case law, which is, as we have seen, a most important source of law. Indeed, for some French authors, case law could be codified when it represents a certain measure of stability.[130] To this classical question in French law,[131] the Superior Committee of Codification replies that inscribing in the law a rule which was previously derived from pure case law, would mean modifying legal authority by changing the borders between what is a matter of choice for Parliament and what belongs to the judge's power of interpretation.[132] However, as we have seen, this is what French legislation in matters of administrative law actually does.[133] Besides, the new Civil Code of Québec, has also integrated case law, as much as legal doctrine and normative professional *usages*.[134]

This would confirm the possibility of a more supple and flexible method for a Civil Code, in other words, the efficiency of a pluralist perception of normativity. The idea of an "open texture" of law partakes of this notion of pluralism. This is a matter of a genuine form of institutional organisation,

[130] Yves Robineau, "A Propos des Limites d'une Codification à Droit Constant", *AJDA* 20 September 1997, (655–659) at 656. See, also, G. Timsit, "La Codification, Transcription ou Transgression de la Loi?" in *Droits*, n. 24, December 1996 at 83–93.

[131] J. L. Aubert, "La Jurisprudence aujourd'hui, Libres propos sur une Institution Controversée" in *Variétés de la RTD civ.* 1992 at 337 ff. For an account of this debate, see G. Timsit, "Les figures du Jugement", *Puf., Les voies du droit*, 1993 at 19 ff. Carbonnier, *Introduction au droit civil* at 164–174 (32). See, in particular, "Politique législative et Pratique judiciaire, distinction entre la *stare decisis* de la *Common law* et la recherche française de 'la dernière jurisprudence'". See, also, L. Silance in *La règle de droit, Etudes publiées par Ch. Perelman* (Bruxelles 1971): "*La jurisprudence n'est pas une véritable source du droit civil, comparable à la loi ou même à la coutume. Mais elle est une autorité, et une autorité considérable en droit civil*" (. . .). "*La loi ne devient règle que lorsqu'elle est consacrée et traduite à l'occasion de son interprétation par les juges*". See, also Grzregorczyk's comments in *APD*, 1972, Vol. XVII, at 437 ff. For a general bibliography, see Sauvel, "Essai sur la Notion de Précédent", *D.* 1955, chron. 93. Dupeyroux, "La Jurisprudence, Source Abusive de Droit", *Mélanges Maury*, II at 349, and "La Doctrine Française et le Problème de la Jurisprudence Source du Droit", *Etudes Marty*, 1978. *Contra*: Esmein, "La Jurisprudence et la Loi", *RT* 1952 at 17 ff. Belaœd, "Essai sur le Pouvoir Créateur et Normatif du juge", 1974. Waline, "Le Pouvoir Normatif de la Jurisprudence", *Mélanges G. Scelle*, II, *LGDJ* 1950 at 613 ff. Maury, "Observation sur la jurisprudence en tant que source du droit", *Etudes Ripert*, I at 28 ff. Cf., Cross and Harris on Precedent in English law.

[132] Yves Robineau, *loc. cit.* n. 131 at 658.

[133] See René Chapus, *Droit Administratif Général*, Montchrétien, 11th ed., 1997 at 73 ff. Première partie: Les sources du droit administratif. Cf. Bibliography, *op. cit.* n. 86, 87 and 88.

[134] Daniel Jutras, "La codification réformatrice—L'exemple du Code Civil québécois", *loc. cit.* n.2. See, also, Jean François Niort, in *Droit* 24-1996 at 135–143, J. E. C. Brierly, "Quebec's Civil Law Codification, Viewed and Reviewed", *Revue de droit de McGill* 14-1968 at 522 ff. J. E. C. Brierly and R. A. Macdonald in, *Quebec Civil Law* (Toronto, Edmond Montgomery, 1993).

which combines the qualities of coherence and solidity of a structure with the use of a flexible language. This "open texture" reveals itself in practice by the phenomenon of "*juridictionalisation*": the content of the law refines itself in the litigation process. The legal rule is no longer pre-established, but reformulated according to the judge's *juris dictio*. This idea and this method, known in common law countries, and seemingly inconceivable for a traditional civil lawyer, is actually not so unfamiliar to civil law reasoning. As explained earlier, the theory of general principles of law has, for quite some time, allowed continental lawyers to create legal rules by case law, in the absence of written rules.[135] Consequently, new projects of contract law harmonisation, stemming from institutions composed of lawyers from civil and common law, make space for such "open textured rules", which are applied in different legal systems.

3.2.1. Doctrinal contributions to a Contract Code with "open textured rules"

If we are really keen on the idea of a European Contract Code, our perception of law must not limit itself to the idea of law as legislation by Parliament. It is a matter of not confusing codification and legislation. The method of European contract law codification should consider case law as a source, which is, at least, equivalent to the law produced by the legislation of Parliament. This is not impossible if one accepts the principle of an "open textured rule of law", a familiar concept in the practice and doctrine of the common law. Contrary to what seems to be the classical representation of the Civil Code, conceptually, this "open texture" of the legal rule does not appear so remote from the Civil Code. In terms of coherence, our perception of the legal system may be comparable to the common law. Indeed, the legislator, the judge, or the legal scholar, also use fictions to fill the gaps, inaccuracies or contradictions inherent to the legal order; each of them rationalises and systematises, in his position, the legal order with the aim of assuring its coherence and its intelligibility.[136] Such legal rules with "open texture" are narrowing gaps in every legal system. They exist both in common law and in continental law. However, we still have to define a general framework of legal reasoning flexible enough to allow judges to do their interpretation work, but rigid enough to assure indispensable legal certainty. How could such a system of European law,[137] that takes these requirements into account, be conceived? The current projects of unification or

[135] G. Marty and P. Raynaud: "*La théorie des principes généraux, née de la jurisprudence, est une manifestation de son pouvoir créateur*", *op. cit.* n. 86. For Vedel, "*Le recours aux principes généraux est un cas particulier de mise en oeuvre du pouvoir normatif de la jurisprudence*", *Droit administratif* (Thémis, 5th ed., 1973) at 283.

[136] "In England this fact is often obscured by forms: for the courts often disclaim any such creative function and insist that the proper task of statutory interpretation and the use of precedent is, respectively, to search for the "intention of the legislature and the law that already exists". H. L. A. Hart, *The Concept of Law* (Clarendon Press, Oxford, 1994) at 135.

[137] On the *uniformisation* by unification or harmonisation, see Mireille Delmas-Marty, *loc. cit.* n. 104 at 46–47.

harmonisation,[138] elaborated by scholars, and the daily work of legal integration of the European judges, such as the ECJ,[139] presuppose the existence of a European legal order in construction, which is only conceivable by means of "open textured norms".

A. *A common concept: "open textured European legal rules"*

The common law judge finds the applicable legal rule in some precedent, or creates a new rule, the scope of which is limited to the facts of the case. Thus, one may find the concept of "open texture" in English legal theory:

> . . . "Nothing can eliminate this duality of a core of certainty and a penumbra of doubt when we are engaged in bringing particular situations under general rules. This imparts to all rules a fringe of vagueness or open texture, and this may affect the rule of recognition specifying the ultimate criteria used in the identification of the law as much as in a particular statute".[140]

In every legal system, courts perform a discretionary power of appreciation,

> "in rendering initial standards determinate, in resolving the uncertainties of statutes, or in developing and qualifying rules only broadly communicated by authoritative precedent".[141]

The open texture of law means,

> "that there are, indeed, areas of conduct where much must be left to be developed by courts or officials striking a balance, in the light of circumstances, between competing interests which vary in weight from case to case".[142]

This perception of the rule of law does not seem to be very remote from Portalis' preoccupations that a code must avoid:

> "*La dangereuse ambition de vouloir tout régler et tout prévoir* (. . .). *Un code n'est pas plutôt achevé que mille questions inattendues viennent s'offrir au magistrat: une foule de choses est donc nécessairement abandonnée à l'empire de l'usage, à la discussion des hommes instruits, à l'arbitrage des juges* (. . .). *L'office de la loi est de fixer par de grande vues, les maximes générales du droit, d'établir des principes féconds en conséquences, et non de descendre dans le détail des questions qui peuvent naître sur chaque matière* (. . .). *C'est au magistrat et au jurisconsulte, pénétrés de l'esprit général des lois, à en diriger l'application*".[143]

138 Cf., Marc Ancel, *loc. cit.* n. 1.

139 B. Oppetit, "Droit commun et droit européen", in *L'internationalisation du droit, Mélanges en l'honneur d'Y. Loussouarn* (Dalloz, 1994) at 311 ff.

140 H. L. A. Hart, *op. cit.* n. 136 at 123.

141 H. L. A. Hart, *idem* at 136.

142 H. L. A. Hart, *idem* at 135. For a more recent reflection on this subject, see Timothy A. O. Endicott, The impossibility of the rule of law, 19 *Oxford Journal of Legal Studies* spring 1999 at 17, "Vagueness in the law is not necessarily a deficit".

143 (. . . dangerous ambition of willing to regulate and foresee, everything (. . .). A code is no sooner achieved than thousand of unexpected questions come to be offered to magistrates: a great deal of things are thus necessarily abandoned to the empire of usage, to the discussion of instructed men, to the arbitrage of judges (. . .). The office of the law is to fix by great views, general maxims

The judge adapts law to the evolution of society and, on the basis of existing texts, he overcomes, as far as he can, the insufficiency of the law when applied to contemporary problems:[144]

> *"De là, chez toutes les nations policées, on voit toujours se former, à coté du sanctuaire des lois, et sous la surveillance du législateur, un dépôt de maximes, de décisions et de doctrine qui s'épure journellement par la pratique et par le choc des débats judiciaires, qui s'accroît sans cesse de toutes les connaissances acquises, et qui a constamment été regardé comme le vrai supplément de la législation"*.[145]

The legislator can try to mention every known form of an activity he wants to regulate, but, by adding a vague and factual formula, he allows the rule to include new forms of this activity, which will be created in social or legal practice.[146]

In the same way, the use of vague notions is common in international public law, as a preliminary condition for reaching an agreement between States with different ideologies. For example, the Universal Declaration of Human Rights,

> *"est un accord sur des notions vagues qui peuvent être interprétés de manière très différentes, chaque membre conservant son droit d'interpréter le texte selon ses vues. Mais le jour où une Cour de justice telle que la Cour européenne des droits de l'homme doit appliquer un tel texte, les intentions individuelles des États membres s'effacent devant l'interprétation autorisée"* (. . .) *"les notions floues permettent la réconciliation dans des accords dont les clauses provoquent des désaccords d'interprétation"*.[147]

According to Mireille Delmas-Marty, one has to use "soft law".[148] Only human intelligence is capable of thinking and reasoning in inaccurate and non-quantitative terms, of deciphering malformed handwriting, of understanding an altered discourse, and of singling out the useful information for a decision.[149]

of law, accordingly, to establish fruitful principles, and not to go into details of questions that can be borne on each matters (. . .). It is a matter for the magistrate and the lawyer, penetrated by the general spirit of laws, to look after their implementation), Portalis, *Essai sur l'Utilité de la Codification* (Paris, 1844) at IX (translation is mine).

[144] André Tunc, *loc. cit.* n. 85 at 821.

[145] (. . . in every civilised nations one has always been able to see, besides the sanctuary of laws, and under the legislator supervision, a deposit of maxims, of decisions and of doctrines that is refined on a day to day basis by the practice and by the shock of judiciary debates that has constantly increased with every acquirement of knowledge, and which has constantly been regarded as the real supplement of legislation), Portalis, *op. cit.* n. 82 (translation is mine).

[146] G. Farjat, "L'importance d'une Analyse Substantielle en Droit Économique", *Rev. int. dr. éco*. 1986 at 9–42.

[147] (. . . is an agreement on vague concepts, that can be interpreted in very different ways, each member keeping his right to interpret the text according to his views. But the day when a court of justice, such as the European Court of Human Rights, has to apply such a text, the individual intentions of Member States will wear away in front of the authorised interpretation (. . .) Vague concepts allow the reconciliation in agreements where clauses lead to disagreement of interpretation), Chaïm Perelman, "L'usage et l'abus des notions confuses", in *Etudes de la Logique Juridique, Dir. Ch. Perelman* (Bruxelles, Bruylant, 1978).

[148] Mireille Delmas-Marty, *Le Flou du Droit* (Puf., 1986).

[149] *"Presque toute la logique du raisonnement humain n'est pas la logique classique à deux ou même à plusieurs valeurs, mais une logique aux vérités floues, aux conjonctions floues, aux règles de*

The use of "soft law" allows the judge to go from one legal order to another, to establish order in a multiple set, and to avoid the dispersal, the inconsistency, and the split of law.[150] The resort to directive and guiding principles is the first means to have been found so far that makes communication between different norms possible. This logical and combinatory "multisystem", arranges the multiple set without destroying it. Taking models of the uniformisation of commercial law in the United States. The current international or European projects for the unification of contract law adopt such a set of principles and rules with "open texture"which are not genuine codes, even if not in the classical sense of a logical and strictly hierarchical structure of univocal norms.

B. *Two institutional consequences: the "Unidroit principles" and the "Lando Commission"*

B.1. Unidroit

In 1994, the International Institute for the Unification of Private Law published the *Principles regarding international commercial contracts.*[151] The aim of this text is to constitute a genuine code of international contract. However, this is not a code. No legislative power has actually voted its texts, as a traditional process of codification would require. Nor is this a "*restatement of contracts*" like the American ones. The "Unidroit principles" are more similar to the rules produced by the International Chamber of Commerce, like the "Incoterms", which are rules of interpretation of commercial terms (such as shipping sales) or the rules of the *London Corn Trade Association*, which become a codification by usage.

Indeed, the obligatory strength of these principles is only deducted from the contractual stipulations of the parties involved. Thus, they are not an

déduction floues". Zadeh, Préface in A. Kaufmann, *Introduction à la Théorie des sous Ensemble Flou à l'Usage des Ingénieurs*, Vol. 1: *Eléments théoriques de base* (Masson, 2nd ed., 1997).—Notion d'appartenance pondérée—(cited by Mireille Delmas-Marty, *op. cit.* n. 148).

150 "*Le désir de rationalité est marqué par la recherche de critères dont la combinaison oriente les choix sans imposer de décision unique*", Mireille Delmas-Marty *op. cit.* n. 148.

151 *Principles of International Commercial Law* (Rome, Unidroit, 1994). See, M. J. Bonell, "Unification of Law by Non-legislative Means: The Unidroit draft Principles for International Commercial Contract", *The American Journal of Comparative Law* 40-1992 at 617–632. Christian Larroumet, "La Valeur des Principes d'Unidroit Applicables aux Contrats du Commerce International", *JCP* 1997.I.4011. F. Ferrari, "Le Champ d'Application des Principes pour les Contrats Commerciaux Internationaux Élaborés par Unidroit", *RIDC* 1995.985. C. Kessedjian, "Un exercice de rénovation des sources du droit des contrats du commerce international: les principes proposés par l'Unidroit", *Rev. crit.* 1995.641 at 646, n. 8. Fr.-M. Bannes, "L'impact de l'adoption des principes Unidroit 1994 sur l'unification du droit commercial international: réalité ou utopie?" *RRJ* 1996.933 at 943. D. Tallon, "L'application des Principes Unidroit par les tribunaux étatiques, Dossiers de l'Institut du droit et des pratiques des affaires internationales de la CCI 1995", *Les principes d'Unidroit, une nouvelle lex Mercatoria?*", pub. n. 490/1 at 243. R. Goode, "International Restatement of Contracts and English Contract Law", *RD* 1997.231 at 238. G. Rouhette, "Les Codifications du Droit des Contrats", *Droits*, 1996, n. 24 at 118. M. Béraudo, "Le Congrès Interaméricain sur les Principes Unidroit", *Bull. de la Cour Internationale d'arbitrage de la CCI* 8-mai 1997 n. 1. J. Huet, "Les contrats commerciaux internationaux et les nouveaux principes d'Unidroit: une nouvelle Lex Mercatoria?", *Les Petites affiches*, 10 nov. 1995. C. Kessedjian, "La codification privée", *Mélanges G. Droz,* Kluwer, 1996 at 135.

autonomous legal source that imposes itself from outside, but *can* be used. As in international private law, one does not admit contract without law; contract must be submitted to rules of objective law that do not depend on the contractual parties, but on the State order. Contractual freedom only exists according to this legal order (Cf. article 1134 French Civil Code). Thus, "independently from the principles, there is an applicable law". The Unidroit principles do not replace the national legal order, but propose stipulations that can be used or not. In this sense, they do not constitute a closed system; they are principles which, though more precise than the *lex mercatoria*, remain open and can be combined with other legal orders.[152]

B.2. The Lando Commission

The Lando Commission's work also aims at unification.[153] This group of professors and practitioners borrowed their method of work from the American Law Institute, whose members compile the laws of each State under the form of restatements. The Lando Commission, however, goes beyond the American restatements or the Unidroit principles, in that their intention is to establish a future European Code of Contract. But, just as with Unidroit, their principles are not compulsory, as they *may* be implemented by contracting parties. Moreover, they do not establish detailed rules, but form a core of general rules conceived with the interest of flexibility to adapt to new circumstances. It is not yet a matter of creating exhaustive codes, but rather a starting point. Thus, the "European principles of contract" seem to establish the basis of what could be a code with "open textured rules", which simultaneously offers guidance for the legislator and the national courts, sufficient autonomy for contracting parties, and a basis for Community law to govern contracts.

3.1.2. Case law's contributions to a European Contract Code with "open textured rules"

These institutional projects for legal harmonisation are still at the first stage. One should go further if one wishes a genuine *uniformisation*. Yet, the question about the possibility of textual flexibility for a normative code remains. One has to go beyond the common place of the observation of a "soft law" or "vague law" development. The solution only seems possible from a reflection on the judge's interpretation. The common and classical analysis in comparative law

[152] Georges Rouhette, *loc. cit.* n. 151. See, also, B. Oppetit, *loc. cit.* n. 140.

[153] Ole Lando, *op. cit.* n. 103: these principles should uniformly be applied in the different Member States, being detached from any national context and being accessible in the common languages (French and English), to become more and more familiar to their users. The strength of such principles lies in the fact that parties to an international contract are put on a same footing. No one has the problem of being confronted with a foreign language, national rules, or even being privileged by the use of his own national rules. These principles could reinforce the development of the single market; by a synthesis of basic principles of contract law (which is the basis of any market), they should eliminate differences which are obstacles to the functioning of the market.

considers the civil law approach as more formal, whereas the common law reasoning would be more substantive. In describing this double movement of oscillation and fragmentation of legal sources, we have tried to demonstrate that this dichotomy does not correspond to the reality of legal practice. On the contrary, one observes a dialectic interaction between the formal and the substantive approaches in the judge's interpretation both in common law and in continental civil law.[154] Through the prism of this interpretation, e.g. by using concepts elaborated by scholars and by adopting a comparative method, European judges are progressively building the "open textured rules" of a new European legal order.

A. *A common case law interpretation between form and substance*

In common law countries, rules with "open texture" are widely used. The most famous examples are the concept of "due care" in cases of negligence, or the concept of "good faith" or "reasonable expectation" in contract law.[155] What means "due care", or "good faith" in a concrete situation without the interpretation of a judge? In other words, the common law system would thus avoid the hermeneutic closure of the legal discourse, that Weber theorised in his paradigm of "formal logical rationality",[156] by this openness, that allows the judge to make the rules fit with the assumed requirements of legal security. For instance, in formal agreements regulating a business relationship before the definitive signature of a contract, the negotiators reluctantly admit the imposition of a rigid, formal and systematic corpus of rules. However, they are ready to adapt to certain formalism if it is alleviated by some sensitivity to the concrete circumstances of the negotiation. This can only be realised by the use of open textured rules.[157]

In continental civil law systems, one finds the same dialectical relationships between formalism and substantive interpretation. Even in the core of private law one may find some

> "illustrations of a sort of do-it-yourself which allows the legal system to master contradictions thanks to the substantive analysis".[158]

An example is offered by the abundance of standards in economic law, such as "*faute*", "*bonnes moeurs*", "*intérêt général*", "*ordre public*".[159] It does not suffice to stick to the official sources of law when measuring the importance of this

[154] For a systematic explanation of the distinction between formalism and substancialism, see Duncan Kennedy in "Legal Formality", *The Journal of Legal Studies*, 1971, (351–398) at 355–366.

[155] H. L. A. Hart, *op. cit*. n. 137 at 132.

[156] See Max Weber, *Wirtshaft und Geselshaft,Mohr* 1980, 5th eds. *Economy and Society*, G. Roth and C. Wittich (eds) (Berkley, University of California Press, 1978), II at 883.

[157] Cf., Hugh Collins, *loc. cit*. n. 101.

[158] Gérard Farjat, *loc. cit*. n. 146 at 41–42.

[159] Cf., André-Jean Arnaud, *Les Juristes Face à la Société du XIXe siècle à nos Jours* (Paris, Puf., 1975).

development.[160] The substantive analysis must go beyond the functionalist, technicist or formal perceptions of law to reveal contradictions and incoherences, and to show possible ways of reconstructing the law.[161] If one observes the interpretative activity of the ECJ, one may find these same dialectical, formal and contextual elements in its comparative approach.

B. The "open texture" conception and the restraints in interpretation

B.1. The creation of "open textured rules" by the European judges

One of the most classical and specific techniques of the ECJ's interpretation is the use of comparative reasoning.[162] Carrying out a genuine "conceptual shopping", the ECJ has chosen high-performance techniques to solve cases.[163] However, it does not only choose amongst the available national concepts, principles and rules, it reformulates them and, in so doing, shows its capacity to create new rules with open texture. An example is given by the ECJ decision of 18 May 1982, in *AM&S Europe limited v. the European Commission* regarding the protection of confidentiality.[164] The European Commission, in the frame of an administrative procedure of verification, according to articles 85 and 86 of the EC Treaty (articles 81 and 82 in the revised Treaty), seized the correspondence of a lawyer with his client. The Community legislation applicable in the matter of competition had not foreseen any particular protection for professional documents with legal character. The court considered that the Community law stemmed from a "legal interpenetrating of Member States", and accordingly, that it should take into account common conceptions of the law in these States.[165] The court thus adopted the confidentiality principle for the correspondence of a lawyer with his client, following Advocate General Sir Gordon Slynn's conclusions:[166]

[160] Cf., S. Rials, "Le juge administratif français et la technique du standard", *LGDJ* 1980 at 57 ff. and at 120.

[161] Gérard Farjat, *loc. cit.* n. 147.

[162] Yves Galmot, "Réflexions sur le Recours au Droit Comparé par la Cour de Justice des Communautés Européennes", *RFDA* 1990-03/04 at 259–262, where the author cites the Johnston case of 15 May 1986 (rec. at 1663).

[163] P. Pescatore, "Le Recours dans la Jurisprudence de la Cour de Justice des Communautés Européennes à des Normes Déduites de la Comparaison des Droits des Etats Membres", *RIDC* 1980, 337.

[164] See Aff. 155/72, *Receuil*. 1982 at 1610.

[165] Regarding the deduction of general principles from a study of the legal situation in the Member States and about the research of the best solution in qualitative term, see P. Reuter, in *Mélanges Rolin*, (1964) at 273. Ipsed, *Europäisches Gemeinshaftsrecht*, (1972) at 114. W. Ganshof van der Meersch, *L'ordre Juridique des Communautés Européennes*, (1975) at 150 and 163. Jean-Victor Louis, *L'ordre Juridique Communautaire*, (1979) at 164. Konrad Zweigert, "*Novelles*" (1969), paragraphe 1203. A similar approach in the Case 14/61, Hoogovens/Haute Autorité, (*Receuil* 1962 at 485–538–539), or again in the Case 5/71, Zuckerfabrick Schöppenstedt/ Conseil, (*Receuil* 1971 at 975–991), and the Cases 63 and 69/72 Werhahn/ Conseil, (*Receuil* 1973 at 1258).

[166] Conclusions of Sir Gordon Slynn, *op. cit.* n. 164, in particular, at 1648–1654.

"It is unanimously admitted that the Court of Justice is not confined, when interpreting comparatively or completing Community law, to found its decision, for example, on the common minimum of the different national solutions, on the arithmetical average or on the solution adopted by the majority of the legal orders. The Court of Justice must weigh, appreciate and find the 'best' solution and the most appropriated to the concrete problem".[167]

Sir Gordon Slynn adds that such a process is applied not to incorporate some national laws, as such, to Community law, but to use this law as a means of discovering a non-written principle in Community law.

"The idea suggested, according to which the plaintiff tried to force, in a non-receptive muddle, a purely local rule of common law, seems to be unfair regarding the plaintiff's argument that has tried to draw from national laws a principle taking an integral part of Community law, but which must be adapted to Community proceedings in its detailed application".[168]

The *Advocate General* concludes:

"The question is not to know if the 'legal professional privilege' (right of the client), is identical to the '*secret professionnel*' (duty, of the lawyer), that is surely not the case, but whether, from diverse sources, a concept of protection of the confidential relations between the lawyer and his client emerge; for example, in England from the 'legal professional privilege' or from any other rules relating to the protection of 'confidentiality', and in France, from the amalgam of '*secret professionnel*', and '*droits de la défense*' and from the rules applicable to the '*secret des lettres confidentielles*'.[169]

The use of national law, which is considered on a comparative basis, with the aim to help to determine the content of Community law, can be found in many other court decisions.[170]

B.2. Open texture and restraints in interpretation

Finally, one has to define the limits in the interpretation of these "open textured rules". The realistic approach considers that the judge not only applies the rule of law, but that he also does a job of interpretation. And, by so doing, he decides on the validity and the efficacy of a legal rule. However, the extensive use of rules with "open texture" could turn out to be dangerous if their use were only founded on the semantic analysis of the rule, on the vague character of the

[167] See, also, "Méthode d'interprétation vues par un juge à la Cour", *Rencontre Judiciaire et Universitaire*, 1976 at 29.

[168] Conclusions of Sir Gordon Slynn, *op. cit.* n. 164 at 1648–1654.

[169] Lord Goff of Chieveley, "The Future of Common law", The Wilberforce Lecture 1997, *ICLQ* 46-October 1997 at 746, ". . . the European Court of Justice is itself open to influence from national laws, including our own *common law*. An example of this is the concept of legal professional privilege, which has been accepted by the European Court as a limit on disclosure which is justifiable in the public interest".

[170] See the cases 3/54, Assider/ Haute Autorité (*Rec.* 1954–55 at 123); 28/76, LTU/Eurocontrol (*Rec.* 1976 at 1541, point 3); 814/79, Pays Bas/Rüffer (*Rec.* 1980 at 3807).

language used. This submission of the legal rule to the assessment of the judge, acting as a legislator, could pose a problem of democratic legitimacy. To acknowledge that the judge is, henceforth, authorised to create general rules, reintroduces the *Arrêts de règlements* and transfers a great part of the creative power to determine the content of rules from the legislator to the judge. How then can this vision be conciliated with the democratic aspirations of the European Union, i.e. a system in which citizens are submitted to the laws made by their representatives?

We conceive the idea of "open texture" within a legal system. The judge, as in the example drawn from the ECJ's case law, applies the law by assessing and weighing principles. He evaluates the facts, makes a value judgement of the objectives proposed by society in general and determines the content of the law according to what seems to be most reasonable for him. The interpretation he makes is not only semantic, linguistic or "meta-linguistic", but also systemic. It must correspond to criteria of coherence and efficiency.[171] The judge is obliged to develop practical argumentation, a rational discourse, in order for his discourse to meet the criteria of coherence with the legal system as a whole. This is why he must justify his interpretation by rational argumentation.[172] This rational and systemic restraint limits the risk of anarchical development of the interpretative power of the judge.[173]

All discretionary power is carried on within a system of restraints. Those of the judge are primarily of an institutional kind and linked both to a hierarchy of jurisdictions and to the necessity of motivation. It is really a matter of necessity and not simply of obligation. Indeed, even in the absence of rules prescribing the judge to justify his decisions, they actually are. The first reason is the impossibility for judges to justify a particular decision without presenting it as the application of a more general pre-existing norm. This will be either a norm expressed

[171] Until the eighteenth century, the legal norms of a society were designated by "Laws" (Bracton, 1265, *Des legibus et consitudinibus Angliae*). From the eighteenth century, Rousseau writes *Les divers systèmes de législation* in 1762, and Bentham describes the *Systems of law* in 1782. Hart suggest that every system of norms is a set of primary rules (rules of conduct) and secondary rules (rules of competence), H. L. A. Hart, *op. cit.* n. 137, VII. On the the concept of coherence see Rawls and Habermas, and the theory of integrity of the rule of law of Dworkin, *op. cit.* n. 38, (the integrity in the legislation and in the judicial deliberation at 182, 195, 238–241, and the coherence at 185, 241–246. See, also, *Postscript to H. L. A. Harts's Concept of law*, Part I, in *Legal Theory* 4-September 1998 n. 3, in particular, Joseph RAZ, "Two Views of the Nature of the Theory of Law: A Partial Comparison", at 249; and Timothy A. O. Endicott, "Herbert Hart and the Semantic Sting", at 283.

[172] Robert Alexy, *A Theory of Legal Argumentation, The Theory of Rational Discourse as Theory of Legal Justification* (Oxford, Clarendon Press, 1989). See at 127, "Whoever utters a judgement of value or obligation implicitly makes a claim to correctness, that is, that the judgement uttered is rationally justifiable". See, also, at 289 ff.

[173] Cf., Duncan Kennedy, *A Critique of Adjudication (fin de siècle)* (Cambridge, Mass., Harvard University Press, 1997) at 3 and 13 ff., "Judges understand themselves to be enjoined to enforce these restraints independently of the views of the executive and the legislature, and of the political parties" (. . .); "judges understand themselves to be bound by a norm of interpretive fidelity to the body of legal materials that are relevant to whatever dispute is before them". Thus, "the rule of law is not absolute value—it is instrumental, its value depends on the context".

in a text that will be subject to interpretation, or an unwritten rule "discovered" in a particular case. Thus, the reasons given in the judgement allow the judge to increase his power, by the production of a general norm. But, at the same time, it contributes to tightening the restraints that weigh on him. This norm is really general and objective only as far as other judges, in their turn, found the justification of their own decisions upon it, and as far as the parties at the trial accept it, in the same way as they accept the law. Thus, this norm cannot be general or objective, just because the judges who have invoked it, submit to it in future cases. Judges are then constrained to their own precedent. They cannot depart from the norm by invoking other objective norms.[174]

Consequently, "the judge is neither a civil servant nor an organ of a State who does not exist as such; he is neither a Lord doted with privileges and untouchable prerogatives, the typical figure of the 'late feudal' institutions, nor is he the simple *bouche de la loi*, applier of the sovereign decision of the people' according to a "republican reading of the adjudication activity of the judge, as Condorcet writes 175 or, as described in the provision of the Constitutions of 1791 and of 1793, a '*pouvoir nul*'. . . . He reproduces, in a concrete context of application, the deliberation that led to the emanation of general measures, of the law in question.[176] In other words, the legitimacy of a decision rendered by a court, that applies standards or rules with open texture, can only be confirmed by justifications of the decision's reasons, which is a sufficiently rational justification. To sum up, the judge must explain it if he wants it to be applied with efficacy, if he wants, for instance, the contracting parties to adhere to this rule with "open texture".

4. CONCLUSION

If we go back to our initial question of whether a European Civil Code is desirable and feasible, the idea of a European codification, even only for contracts, appears to be still only a utopia. It still seems to be excluded that an agreement on new structures and new concepts of substantive uniform law could be reached soon. Indeed, differences of style, of reasoning, of culture and of legal education, of "*mentalités*", cannot be ignored. A uniform code would inevitably meet resistance in its application. Even the very idea of the existence of a single and uniform code already appears to be an illusion *per se*. Either the envisaged text relies on a constitutional modification in each Member State for its adoption, the text adopted being subject to amendments by each national parliament, thus making it different in each Member State, or its adoption will be the

[174] Michel Troper, "Le Bon Usage des Spectres, du Gouvernement des Juges au Gouvernement par les Juges", *Conference*, Paris, 1998.

[175] Condorcet, *Oeuvres*, Vol. 12 at 354–355.

[176] Massimo la Torre, "Le Pouvoir Ambigu, la Figure du Juge à la Croisée de Deux Traditions: la Démocratie Française et le Rechtsstaat Allemand", *Conference, Paris I*, 9 January 1999.

result of modification of international treaties, and here, it will be interpreted by international courts. Thus, there cannot be a unique, single Civil Code; "civil codes", possibly; the ideal "unicity" of a code does not necessarily mean that it has "univocality". Moreover, a judicial and transnational superstructure, a "European Court of Justice", involving a reorganisation of all judicial national systems, should still be worked out. This again appears to be most unlikely.

The alternative, therefore, to the legislative model of codification of a law imposed "from above", would be the constitution of a European *ius commune*, a law imposed "from below".[177] The comparative work undertaken by scholars and practitioners of law, their research on commonalities and differences and the possible mutual understanding and convergence, the thorough study of our concepts, of our reasoning and of our legal cultures, could start to become fruitful.[178] This has already been demonstrated, as we have seen, by the creation of European "restatements". This intense dialogue within institutions, national as well as European, will generate a new legal culture. The daily activity of the ECJ's legal integration, its comparative reflection and its work of reformulating national law, will contribute to the creation of a new legal order.[179] In the same way, the development of a European universitary legal education will create the necessary conditions for the emergence of a much more open new legal "mentality". For some, this emergence of a new common European law will be opposed, in both its object and its method, to a positive law created in its entirety by a national legislator, as a closed system, expressing the ideal of a complete and lasting codification. In fact, everything depends on the objective and the vocation that we ascribe to such a code. Nothing prevents private law "from below" from throwing light on the creation of a private law "from above". The development of the authority of legal doctrine and case law shows what a European Code could look like. In other words, while conserving its classical functions of legal reformulation and simplification, it would not have the purely formal character of a simple ordering of the existing law.

Therefore, we have to go beyond the idea of "soft law". The legal rule with "open texture" is not solely soft law. In fact, it is a normative provision created within a legal system, but it is also the result of a deeper procedure of co-

[177] Cf. F. Hayek, *Law, Legislation and Liberty*, 2 vols (Chicago, Chicago University Press, 1973, 1976).

[178] Christian von Bar, *Gemeineuropäisches Deliktsrecht* (Band I, Verlag C.H. Beck, 1996); see, also, Hein Kotz and Axel Flessner, *European Contract law*, Vol. 1: *Formation, Validity and content of Contracts*; "Contracts and Third Parties" by Hein Kötz, English translation by Tony Weir (Oxford, Clarendon Press, 1997). See also, Walter van Gerven, Jeremy Lever, Pierre Larouche, Christian von Bar, Geneviève Viney, *Cases, Materials and Text on National, Supranational and International Tort Law, Scope of protection (Ius commune casebooks for the common law of Europe)* (Oxford, Hart Publishing, 1998). See, for an account of these three books, Anthony Chamboredon and Christoph Schmid, "Pour la création d'un Institut du Droit Européen: l'Émergence d'une science juridique transnationale en Europe" (to be published).

[179] Walter van Gerven, "Coherence of Community and National Laws. Is there a Legal Basis for European Civil Code?" *ERPL 5* 465–470, 1997. About the part played by the ECJ in the Europeanisation of private law, see Christian Joerges, "Private Law Adjudication in Europe's Multi-level System: a Complex Issue and a Small Example", *loc. cit.* n. 102.

operation between the classical producers of legal rules, the State or supra-State institutions, the judge, the legal doctrine and the society represented for example by the contracting parties. The validity of the "open textured rule" is the outcome of a long and constraining process of negotiation between these different entities.[180] Following the realist inheritance of the American 'Grand Style' and Karl Llewellyn,[181] the European concept of an "open textured rule" could therefore constitute the methodological ground for the creation of a European Code of contract. As we have tried to demonstrate in civil law as well as in common law, it is admitted that a rule in contract law can meet the requirements of business only if it is contextualised, and thus allows the judge to assess the whole of the contractual relationship and the written clauses of the contract simultaneously. If the European Code were not composed of these types of "open textured rules", if it did not allow a contextual reasoning, it would risk freezing into a permanent inefficacy.[182] As a result, it is necessary for the European codification of contract law to avoid some dangers:

> ". . . *l'illusion de perpétuité et d'immuabilité de la loi, la prétention de faire une législation intégrale et massive entraînant la défense d'interprétation des textes, l'identification absolue de l'idée de droit et de l'idée de loi*".[183]

[180] Frier, "Interpreting Codes", 89 *Michigan Law Review*, 1991, (2201) at 2213/4, underlines that a code (such as continental codes or the American Uniform Commercial Code) bring about what he calls "an expanded interpretive community": i.e., the judiciary, the bar and academic legal authors.

[181] For an account of the influence of the American Realism in the American legal uniformisation, see, Françoise Michaut, "Les réalistes américains et la codification", *Droits*, 27, 1998, at 49 ff. Cf., Anthony Chamboredon and Christoph Schmid, "Pour la création d'un Institut du droit européen, Entre unification législative ou non législative, l'émergence d'une science juridique transnationale en Europe" (to be published).

[182] Cf. Hugh Collins, *loc. cit.* n. 102.

[183] (the illusion of perpetuity and immutability of law, the pretension of making an integral and massive legislation, implying the prevention of interpretation of the texts, the absolute identification of the idea of law and the idea of the law as legislation), J. Van Kan *op. cit.* n. 66 at 368.

5

European Private Law: A New Software-Package for an Outdated Operating System?

ALAIN WIJFFELS

1. INTRODUCTION

When I was a little boy, comic strips depicting a mentally disturbed person would invariably revert to the cliché of a man suffering from the delusion that he was Napoleon. Nowadays, I have very little time for comic strips, but it seems to me that the cliché has faded away. Why this is so, I do not know. An historian's optimistic view would be that it is an achievement of the *nouvelle histoire*, which emphasises long-term, structural developments within society, rather than the old school's traditional focus on *histoire événementielle*, politics, military achievements and major historical figures. I suspect (though I have no expertise in this field) that delusions where someone identifies with a cyclical pattern of corn prices tend to be rare, and anyway it would probably defeat the most imaginative of cartoonists. The more pessimistic interpretation of the historian who no longer comes across caricatures of madness in the form of Napoleonic delusions (and an interpretation that I would *prima facie* favour) is simply that over the past quarter of a century, history has largely vanished from our educational system and from our common cultural background, and is therefore no longer anchored in the mind of the general public—whether sound or mad. Even so, something of the old cliché seems to survive, albeit only, apparently, among one of the psychologically most vulnerable groups in our modern society, *viz.* the legal profession. Judging from a trend in contemporary legal publications, at least one Napoleonic-style syndrome is still alive: calls for codifications in all sorts of areas, including areas which are still controversial as academic or professional legal disciplines, have been proliferating during the last decade of our millennium. Many lawyers, whether individually or as members of a specialised group, seem to echo Napoleon's famous remark during his last exile on St Helena's island, that of his many achievements, the *Code civil* would prove the most lasting of all. Similarly, lawyers still seem to believe that, whatever their triumphs may have been in court-room battles or academic disputations, there is nothing such as an adapted version of the *Code Napoléon* in their own field of expertise to ensure an accomplishment that will be remembered by posterity and figure in the annals of legal history.

2. THE CONCEPT OF EUROPEAN PRIVATE LAW

European Private Law may or may not have existed implicitly for a long time, but in any case the phrase has only recently become a more or less recognised and institutionalised legal term of art. Clearly, both its actual scope and its potential are still, at best, undetermined, or, particularly among Eurosceptic lawyers, controversial. Ironically, as the concept of European Private Law made significant progress during the 1990s—precisely at a time when the reinforcement of integrative measures within the European Union (single market, Maastricht Treaty, introduction of the Euro etc.) has led to a strengthening of the politically acceptable contestation of European integration—its much-quoted historical point of reference, *viz.* pre-1800 European *ius commune*, has been increasingly under fire. One might well paraphrase the title of Professor Brauneder's incendiary article "*Europäisches Privatrecht—aber was ist est?*", and ask: "*Ius commune*—all well and good, but what is it?"[1]

Calls for a codification of European Private Law (or more specific areas, such as the law of contracts) may not, so far, have enjoyed a high priority on the agenda of the more prudent pro-European lawyers, and these calls only reflect one particular, perhaps somewhat radical, concept of what European Private Law may be. Nevertheless, even a minimalist concept of European Private Law would seem to suggest a legal discipline which, apart from its transnational nature, follows by and large the wonted patterns and methods of private law as a discipline in the various national legal systems of the European countries involved. Those traditional patterns and methods reached their historical apex at the time of the late eighteenth-century and nineteenth-century codifications and through the positivistic approach to these codes by both practitioners and scholars. At the close of the twentieth century, the whole matrix of values, social and economic interests, and logical principles has changed to such degree as to affect the very foundations of our legal systems. The curriculum of legal education throughout Europe may still reflect the systematisation of the law which imposed itself with the advent of what the Enlightenment's and the Revolution's jurists and law-makers prophetised and, eventually, introduced as the messianic great codes. Indeed legal thinking over the past two hundred years may well have abided by that systematisation even though the boundaries between the conventional legal disciplines became gradually more irrelevant and new disciplines emerged, which did not fit properly in the global systematisation. Nevertheless, there is an increasingly strong, though in general rather diffuse,

[1] W. Brauneder, "Europäisches Privatrecht—aber was ist es?", *ZNR* 15 (1993), 225–235.

feeling that we have reached a stage where the system we have inherited from a combination of "Natural Law" ideas and a "Legal Positivism" disposition is no longer adequate. The common reaction to the often very practical and specific difficulties which reflect that feeling of inadequacy consists in more or less extensive make-shift renovations and adjustments of the existing frame-work. It is probably one of the major challenges to legal theory—and to the other meta-juristic disciplines which may in this context play an ancillary role, e.g. comparative law and legal history—to provide a reflection and a blueprint for a more comprehensive alternative.[2] That reflection will among other questions have to address the dilemma whether the basic tenets of the currently prevailing system should be maintained, or, whether a fundamentally new system can be devised and provide a realistic and workable alternative.

Mentalities among lawyers tend to be, as far as the technical workings of the law are concerned, staunchly conservative. One might compare the attitude with that of most of us when using present-day computer facilities. Unless one is particularly interested and skilled in programming techniques, the vast majority of users simply tend to acquire an adequate command of the soft-ware packages they need (mostly word-processing and data-bases). Innovations of the familiar programmes are tolerated and accepted in so far as they make the programme more user-friendly and provided the changes do not abruptly depart from the previous version of the existing programme. Few of us have the time, know-how or courage to go beyond the ever-improving applications offered by the programme we are wont to use in our day-to-day work, and to fiddle with that part of the software called "operating system" which (as I understand it) is really the software that makes the other software packages (such as whatever commercial word-processing programme we use) work. Therefore, when a major computer manufacturer or software company would decide, for considerations that may be technological or commercial, to change the prevailing operating system, such a change may affect the working and the future of our trusted programme. What happens when the prevailing operating system is no longer adequate to manage the newly developed programmes, or when the development of new, more suitable programmes, requires a different operating system? *Mutatis mutandis*, these are the questions which the current crisis of our legal systems present at the level of legal theory.

3. EUROPEAN *IUS COMMUNE* AND LEGAL HISTORY

What may be the legal historian's contribution in dealing with these questions regarding the future structure of our legal systems?[3] The current debate about a

[2] A. Georgiades, "Zu einem gemeineuropäischen Privatrecht—Illusion oder Realität?", in C. Tomuschat, H. Kötz and B. von Maydell (eds.), *Europäische Integration und Nationale Rechtskulturen* (Köln, 1995), 45–49.

[3] For a critical review of the debate on this question in Germany, see K. Luig, "The History of Roman Private Law and the Unification of European Law", *ZEuP* 1997, 405–27.

common law of Europe[4] (particularly in the area of private law), whether one assumes that the European legal systems are converging or not, tends to refer to the historical concept of a European *ius commune*.[5] In recent years, that very concept has become highly controversial, whereas for most of the post-war period, it had enjoyed by and large a wide-ranging consensus among legal historians.[6] Whatever the state of the controversy, it has always been clear that the term refers to a historically heterogeneous category. In a more technical sense, "*ius commune*" has been used in different ways depending on whether the context was that of a theory on the authority of various legal sources (i.e. a *Rechtsquellenlehre*); or, whether the context was procedural, (e.g.) when a court had to establish which alleged rule of law had to be proved or not. In the context of legal doctrines, the history of *ius commune* has been characterised by fundamentally different approaches throughout the centuries, which, in a specifically legal approach, reflected in each case the major intellectual currents prevailing at the time. These different doctrinal approaches are expressed, *inter alia*, in the systematisation of legal concepts, principles and rules of substantive law, but also in their way of dealing with the relationship between *ius commune* and particular law (*iura propria*). It is one of the legal historian's tasks to show that, far from being an undifferentiated category, "ius commune" refers in fact to very different legal methods and traditions, albeit largely based on a common set of legal materials (*viz.* the texts encompassed in the *Corpus iuris civilis* and, to a lesser degree, in the *Corpus iuris canonici*). The legal historian may not provide an alternative legal theory for the present-day, but he can show that some general categories of our legal thinking, which lawyers have to such degree grown accustomed to, that they tend to view them as evident, universal and absolutely essential, are in fact comparatively specific historical developments, which should not necessarily be seen as the final and definitive stage in the evolution of legal thought.

[4] Apart from the references in the notes of this essay, I have also used the (short) bibliography attached to my article "Aux confins de l'histoire et du droit: la finalité dans le débat sur la formation d'un nouveau *ius commune*", *Revue d'éthique et de théologie morale*, «Le Supplément», No. 205, 33–66, at 55–8. For a general collection of essays, not only on Private Law, see B. de Witte and C. Forder (eds.), *The Common Law of Europe and the Future of Legal Education* (Maastricht, 1992). For a survey of the issues a quarter of a century ago, see M. Cappelletti (ed.), *New Perspectives for a Common Law of Europe* (Firenze, 1978).

[5] A. Padoa-Schioppa, "Il diritto comune in Europa: riflessioni sul declino e sulla rinascita di un modello", *ZEuP* 1997, 706–17; Th. Koopmans, "Towards a new «*ius commune*»", in B. de Witte and C. Forder (eds.), *The Common Law of Europe*, above n. 4, 43–52. More generally, cf. the frequent inclusion of historical essays in *Zeitschrift für Europäisches Privatrecht* (*ZEuP*), or, for a very general (but typical) historical reference, the first editorial (by E. Hondius and M. Storme) of the Dutch-Belgian *European Review of Private Law*.

[6] E.g. Professor Brauneder's article, quoted above; or P. Nève, "Ius commune oftewel «gemeen recht»: traduttore traditore?", in O. E. Tellegen-Couperus et al. (eds.), *Tertium datur. Drie opstellen aangeboden aan Prof.mr.J.A.Ankum* (Tilburg, 1995), 3–58; T. Giaro, "Europäische Privatrechtsgeschichte: Werkzeug der Rechtsvereinheitlichung und Produkt der Kategorienvermengung", *Ius Commune* 21 (1994), 1–43.

From the eleventh or twelfth century onwards, and until the era of national or territorial codifications, scholarship in the "civil law" systems has largely been based, as the phrase "civil law" implies, on the study of Roman law. Throughout these centuries, the texts of the *Corpus iuris civilis* have provided the raw materials for legal scholarship. It would be wrong, however, to assume that this multi-secular tradition of civil law scholarship would imply that legal science was somehow restricted in its capacity to evolve, simply because it would have been bound by the classical jurists' or Justinian's Roman law, whether one would consider its methods and (underlying) theory, its rules of substantive law, or even some of its basic institutions in private law (e.g. in the law of property). In fact, the texts of Roman law provided the bricks and mortar[7] for entirely different legal constructions and systems reflecting each time far more general cultural and scholarly moulds which prevailed at every stage of the development of Western intellectual history. Thus, the history of legal scholarship from the eleventh until the nineteenth century essentially consisted in recasting each time more or less the same texts of Roman law into a new and prevailing, general intellectual mould. This, of course, does not mean that Roman law did not make any difference, or that our contemporary civil law systems might still have reached their essential characteristics if at some stage, materials from a different legal tradition (e.g. customary law) would have prevailed: one only has to consider the contrasting results of uneven degrees of "reception" in the various continental territories to understand that the civil law influence *did* matter. The point is rather that for the first time in the history of the Western continental European legal systems, while a new paradigm for legal science may be needed, and, indeed, may already be in the making, legal scholars will not be able to fall back on the Roman law texts for elaborating a new doctrinal system within the parameters of that paradigm.[8]

4. *IUS COMMUNE*: A LEGAL-HISTORICAL CONTROVERSY

As the ongoing discussion around a "new common law" for Europe often features token references to a pre-codification European *ius commune*, the very concept has become highly controversial in recent legal historiography. The controversy as such is not surprising: legal historians, always anxious to escape the suspicion of irrelevancy in a Law Department, have been quick to jump on

[7] The idiom prevents me from developing a more suggestive metaphor, as in my essay "Aux confins de l'histoire et du droit", *op. cit.*, at 43. In all these Roman law based approaches, "*la pierre a pu servir de matériau premier pour des édifices aussi différents, mais exprimant chaque fois l'esprit de leur époque, que la cathédrale de Chartres, le château de Versailles, la gare d'Orsay . . .*".

[8] A different assessment of the relevance of Roman law for contemporary European Private Law is to be found in R. Knütel, "Rechtseinheit in Europa und Römisches Recht", *ZEuP* 1994, 244–76. For prolegomena to an alternative use of Roman law principles in contemporary legal thinking, see K. W. Nörr, "Das römische Recht zwischen Technik und Substanz: Bemerkungen zu seiner Rolle am Ende des 20. Jahrhunderts", *ZEuP* 1994, 67–76.

the band-wagon as soon as they realised that this was an opportunity to become involved in a sustained (and, by academic standards, potentially lucrative) debate which directly affects current legal issues. Nevertheless, even the legal-historical controversy may indirectly be relevant for identifying some of the key issues raised by legal uniformisation in Europe. Two such (very general) key issues may illustrate the point: (i) the principles and purpose of legal systematisation; and (ii) the relation between the "common law" of a complex legal system, i.e. including distinct sub-systems, and the "particular law" of these sub-systems.

4.1. Systematising the law

Perhaps one of the most underrated features of modern legal methods is its aim at systematising by subject-matter (*ratione materiae*) the law as a whole. Each (national) legal system is divided into areas or branches, and that systematisation is not only the basis for the student's curriculum or the professional lawyer's specialisation (as his particular area of expertise, as the subject-matter of text-books and articles, etc.), it also determines the applicability of (substantive) rules of law. The systematisation is not universal, as some distinctive differences between the civil law systems and the English-based Common Law make clear, but within the traditional Western European civil law systems, the general structure by and large corresponds from one country to another. Certainly, these legal systems all share nowadays a tendency to develop new branches of the law which no longer follow the original arrangement of disciplines; most of the specialisations which have become distinct and established legal disciplines over the past twenty or thirty years are at odds with the "rational" principles on which the general systematisation of the law (and henceforth also the major codifications) was based. Direct or indirect interests of the modern Welfare State in most areas of social life have meant that, particularly during the post-war period, one might have been excused for believing at times that public law had extended its imperium over the entire law, except for a few pockets of resistance. To many Western lawyers, the frantic efforts in Eastern Europe to re-create a private law after the political elites' recanting of the communist ideology came as a shock, as if political reality had forced them to acknowledge that the derided old-fashioned bourgeois Iron Curtain between public law and private law actually still made some sense. But as the 1990s have passed, even that realisation appears to have been but a blip in a general trend where the boundaries between legal disciplines are doomed to wither.

By now, the gradual dissolution of the classical systematisation is generally perceived; bold jurisprudential attempts have been made at devising alternative approaches, though one is far from a consensus yet.[9] This situation echoes the

[9] Compare the approaches of A.-J. Arnaud, *Pour une Pensée Juridique Européenne* (Paris, 1991) and M. Delmas-Marty, *Pour un Droit Commun* (Paris, 1994).

transition in legal methods during the early modern period, which, though on the whole fairly peaceful, caused nevertheless a revolution in Western legal thinking. The main chronology of the change may be summarised as follows.

4.1.1. Mos Italicus

From the late-fourteenth until the late-sixteenth century: the Italian method (*mos italicus*) prevailed, through the standard gloss, a growing number of commentaries, *consilia* and a few other types of legal literature. Traditionally, scholarship tends to emphasise that by the fifteenth century, civil law scholarship was declining; but that assessment depends on one's criteria: if one considers the civil lawyers' originality, or their capacity to stand by the essential issues without being dragged into a web of distinctions, arguments concerning other writers' opinions or other side-issues, the negative judgment on fifteenth- and sixteenth-century *mos italicus* authors may be warranted. However, if the test is not scholarly excellence, those same authors may enjoy more credit, not necessarily because the legal doctrines they developed were more equitable or better adapted to the requirements of their society, but simply because of the influence they wielded on legal thinking among both academics and practitioners. Until the late-sixteenth century, the Italian method represented the mainstream form of legal learning, overwhelmingly in (civil law influenced) legal practice, and to a lesser, but decisive extent, in most law faculties and through the legal book-market.

That method, which pervaded practitioners' arguments in court and much of academic legal teaching and legal learning in print, did not develop its own systematisation of the law. On the whole, it continued to follow the *ordo legalis*, i.e. the sequence of texts (rubrics, leges, paragraphs), as they could be found in the two main collections of Roman law, *viz.* the Digest and Justinian's Code. Although that *ordo legalis* cannot be said to be arbitrary (it partly seems to have been derived from earlier arrangements, which were historically determined, such as the pretorian edict), it has proven difficult to recognise any consistent jurisprudential principles explaining the sequence of texts. Moreover, the selection of both the jurists' opinions in the Digest and the Emperors' constitutions in the Code still often betrays its case-related origins, and as a result, even within the rubrics (which focus around a specific legal institution or topic), the sequence of leges does not provide a systematic outline of the rubric's theme. To some degree, however, the rubrics and their laws brought together the doctrines around a more or less specific topic, and in some cases, a particular *lex* became a *sedes materiae*, i.e. the locus around which a particular legal problem was conventionally developed, a function which was also to some extent fulfilled by *repetitiones*. All this did not amount to a general systematisation of civil law, but it meant that, within the *ordo legalis*, some subject-matters had their specific niche where they found a more extensive doctrinal treatment.

On the other hand, the patterns of legal reasoning ignored to a large degree any partition lines between subject-matters (one can hardly speak of boundaries between different legal areas, as these were practically unknown in any modern sense, though this observation may be qualified by the distinct treatment medieval law often reserved to adjective law—civil and criminal procedure—and to criminal law in general). Therefore, the subsumption of rules, whether general principles (very popular in *mos italicus* reasoning) or specific rules of substantive law, was not strictly bound by a determination *ratione materiae* of the legal issue. To a modern lawyer's perception, legal arguments of that period, whether in scholarly texts or in counsels' opinions, seem to drag into the discussion legal authorities which, because of their proper subject-matter, would not appear to bear any relationship with the question at hand. Far from being inconsistent, the Italian method imposed on the lawyer its own regulation of legal arguments, reasoning and logics. But its "operating system", in the sense of an implied legal theory which dictates how positive rules of law can be put into practice (i.e. incorporated in a legal argument), was essentially different from our present-day approach, where a complex of facts is assigned to a particular area of the law, which then determines the exclusively applicable rules of substantive law.

4.1.2. Usus Modernus

The turning-point can be roughly situated during the latter part of the sixteenth century and the first half of the seventeenth century. The Italian method gradually lost its position as mainstream legal method and gave way to a new approach which took its role as the prevailing approach both in practice and in scholarship, *viz.* the "Modern method" (*usus modernus*). Throughout the 16th century (and beyond), various jurisprudential attempts were made to systematise the law. The premises of these attempts varied considerably: some tried to find a hidden structure in Justinian's compilations; others proposed an adapted version of the classical forms of action; others still were inspired by Ramian configurations. In the end, the most successful "key" became the so-called Institutional System, i.e. the arrangement of Justinian's *Institutes*, borrowed from its classical model. The Institutional System (with its basic structure dividing the law's subject-matters around persons, things and actions) proved particularly apt for introducing a new order in areas of private law, but it was also sufficiently versatile for applications in totally different areas (e.g. the law of nations).

The transition from the Italian method to the Modern method was a gradual one. Some aspects of the new method can already be found under the *mos italicus* rule, but the significant symptoms appear more clearly from about the mid-sixteenth century onwards, at a time when the Italian method still clearly prevailed; after c. 1600, the progress of the Modern method gained momentum and by the mid-seventeenth century it had superseded the old approach. Among these symptoms, legal publications illustrate the change: legal treatises, for instance, not unknown but definitely a secondary source in medieval times, dealing with a (usually fairly specific) topic, grew to a more important genre in legal literature; more comprehensive legal works no longer strictly adhered to the *ordo legalis*, and when they still followed the general arrangement of the Digest or the Code, dealt more systematically with the distinct legal topics of a rubric than in the Bartolistic commentaries. This evolution of early-modern legal literature is only illustrative of a more general and fundamental change: legal questions were progressively regarded within the frame-work of their own specific (and more or less extensive) subject-matter. Simplifying this highly complex transformation in legal thinking, one might say that, of the various attempts at systematising the law, the efforts towards a systematisation *ratione materiae* were in the end decisive—to such an extent that the resulting legal method still governs some basic features of our contemporary legal mind. Because the transition was gradual, some of the main effects of the new method may not always have been apparent at an earlier stage of its development. Thus, a legal author may well have decided to deal with a specific topic, but at that early stage, he might still have adduced rules from well beyond his chosen subject—a *mos italicus* characteristic. Gradually, however, the convention developed that, in principle, the subsumption of the applicable rules (of substantive law) would be exclusively determined by the subject-matter. This form of disciplining legal argumentation and reasoning is probably the most striking change between sixteenth-century and late seventeenth-century civil law scholarship.

As regards legal doctrines, the new method remained much indebted to medieval scholarship. Indeed, the *usus modernus* influence on early-modern legal scholarship, case-law and even legislative techniques, was a major factor in the translation of *mos italicus* doctrines and their incorporation in the eighteenth-century and early nineteenth-century codifications. Legal humanism, which strongly challenged the Italian method during the sixteenth century, before becoming a comparatively marginal current of legal scholarship, not only contributed to early-modern legal science through its philological and historical restoration of Roman law scholarship, it also favoured at least indirectly the systematising efforts of the time. Several major legal writers from the last quarter of the sixteenth century may even give the impression that the *usus modernus* might still have developed more strongly along the lines of legal humanism than by the doctrines of the Italian method. But in the end, legal humanism or, later, the antiquarian studies of Roman law, did not supply an alternative systematisation which could count on the necessary consensus among legal professionals.

4.1.3. Vernunftrecht *and Codification*

The Institutional System may have provided the Modern method with a key for systematising the law in general, but in some ways the new method was too pragmatic and too much involved with positive law to elaborate such a general systematisation and a corresponding new legal theory. During the latter part of the seventeenth century and during the eighteenth century, the rationalistic approach to jurisprudence (the legal offshoot, as it were, of the rationalistic philosophy which prevailed at the time), also known as the *Vernunftrecht* Jurisprudence, or, more commonly (but also more ambiguously), as the "School of Natural Law", worked out such a theory, albeit from a concept of law which was in many ways at odds with that underlying the *usus modernus*. The *Vernunftrecht*'s programme consisted in elaborating a "system" of law in the proper rationalistic sense, i.e. largely as a set of self-defining and by means of deductive reasoning interrelated principles. The principles had to comply to the rationalistic test, *viz.* they had to be universal in time and space (similarly to "natural laws" in the sciences), although in practice, Natural Law treatises appeared to borrow extensively from (classical) Roman law—presumably because the classical jurists' opinions were deemed to have approximated the closest ever in legal history the canons of Rational Law; from a more empirical perspective, the reception of Roman law throughout continental Europe, allegedly "imperio rationis", may also have contributed to attribute the status of "universality" to *ius commune*. As a result, *Vernunftrecht* Jurisprudence was able to incorporate substantive elements of that *ius commune* as it was being applied in *usus modernus* scholarship and practice, but within a truly global systematisation—a feature which ancient Roman law had never attempted, and which had never been a tenet of the Roman lawyers' methods.

The combination of the Modern method (*usus modernus*) and the *Vernunftrecht* Jurisprudence paved the way for the codifications during the last decades of the *Ancien Régime* and during the French Revolution (and its immediate aftermath). The codes may have ruined the Rational Law ideal of a universal legal system, but they pretended to reflect a general systematisation of their national state's legal system. A modern lawyer will be tempted to qualify that pretension by pointing out that the codifications hardly covered the entire legal system: private law, criminal law and procedural law may have been to a large extent encompassed in the new codes, but public law (apart from the written constitutions) remained essentially uncodified territory—a phenomenon which, historically, may be explained by the circumstance that the codified areas represented what was perceived at the time as "real" or "essential" law. The advent of the codifications caused a watershed in legal methods: under the *usus modernus*, the law may have been systematised by subject-matter, but the fragmentation of that systematisation remained a salient feature, in spite of the *Vernunftrecht*'s general theory; now, the code, and henceforth the branch of the law it expressed and represented, became the primary authority through which the law should be accessed. As the law was supposed to be articulated through its main codes, their subject-matters and sub-divisions (i.e. the systematisation within each subject-matter) became the cornerstone of legal learning.

4.2. *Ius commune* and *iura propria*

For several decades, European law in a more technical sense referred to the founding treaties of the European Communities and to the law emanating from the Communities' institutions; European Law was mainly so-called Community Law. By the end of the twentieth century, the term "European Law" appears to pervade most areas of the law, even those which, originally, were generally considered to be beyond the proper prerogatives and jurisdiction of what became known as the European Union.[10] This development has usually been favoured by the Commission, but it is also clear that it has been encouraged by some business interests, and at a more technical level by international law firms and in some cases by academics.[11] Whereas during the first years after the Treaty of Rome, European Law represented a specific body of positive law, the notion of European Law is nowadays much more diffuse. It no longer refers exclusively to an existing set of positive laws, but the term is also used to designate a project *de iure constituendo*, in whatever area of the law. The equivocation has thus offered the possibility of a new orientation to European comparative lawyers: in those areas where the creation or formulation of European Law principles necessitates preliminary comparative research, European Law is sometimes used as being synonymous to a specific form of comparative law. Thus, many of the institutionalised forms of European Private Law as a discipline (e.g. as expressed in the titles of academic journals or chairs) in fact represent a new tendency of comparative law, more specifically aimed at translating its findings into proposals *de lege ferenda*. Moreover, European Law no longer refers exclusively to the legal systems of the European Union's member states.[12]

The idea of a "Common Law of Europe" is, nevertheless, still in many ways controversial. One of the main issues in this controversy is the determination of the relationship between that European Common Law in the making and the national (or in some cases, sub-national) legal systems.[13] That, of course, is a classic issue in any complex legal system, and European legal history provides several examples of political developments which led to a common set of rules within a particular political order along particular laws (see, for instance, the

[10] E. Steindorff, *EG-Vertrag und Privatrecht* (Baden-Baden, Nomos, 1996).

[11] The Italian law curriculum provides a case for connecting the terminology of "European Private Law" with that of European Community Law. See the critical comments by A. Zaccaria, "Die Lehre des Privatrechts der Europäischen Gemeinschaft in Italien", *ZEuP* 1998, 176–8, esp. 181.

[12] Ironically, some critics maintain that legal uniformisation might be easier to achieve outside the EU than among the member states of the EC, cf. M. Zuleeg, "Rechtsangleichung innerhalb und außerhalb der Europäischen Gemeinschaft", *ZEuP* 1998, 506–20, esp. 517.

[13] However, the current debate seems to put less emphasis on the relationship between "positive" rules of law belonging to the supranational and the national systems; conversely, it tends to highlight the importance of the reception of common European rules in different "legal cultures" (e.g. H. Collin, "European Private Law and the Cultural Identity of States", *European Review of Private Law* 1995, 353–65). To a large extent, the debate seems to neglect the variety of "positive rules" which are necessarily interacting in any system encompassing both a *ius commune* and *iura propria*.

English Common Law, the French *droit coutumier commun*, or the *gemeines Recht* in the old German Empire).[14] These historical examples show that a great variety of relations between the "common rules" and the "particular rules" can be envisaged, that the relationship is usually at any time a dynamic one, and that the provisional outcome of the interaction between the political (as well as social and economic) forces represents common and particular interests.[15] In the current discussions about the future of European Law, many different models are proposed, from a politically non-committed "symbiosis" of the legal systems at one end of the scale,[16] to an outright positivistic codification of more or less extensive areas of the law at the other end;[17] in-between, a medley of intermediate formulae abound.[18]

Again, when reference is made in this current debate to a pre-1800 European *ius commune*, such an unqualified reference is far too undifferentiated to offer any meaningful historical contribution to the discussion. Here too, one has to take into account that the various approaches of civil law scholarship evolved and adjusted their doctrines regarding the relationship between *ius commune* and *ius proprium* (the latter referring mainly to customary law and statutory

[14] A. Wijffels, "Aux confins de l'histoire et du droit . . ." (*op. cit.*).

[15] Comp. with H.-W. Micklitz's inaugural lecture at Bamberg (1996), "Perspektiven eines Europäischen Privatrechts. Ius commune praeter legem?", *ZEuP* 1998, 253–76, whose emphasis on *Rationalisierungsdruck*, *Rationalisierungsprozeß*, *Rationalisierungslogik* would appear to see the development of European Private Law (the future of which would depend on a "konstruktiven Nebeneinander von nationalem und sekundärrechtlichem europäischen Privatrecht") as a modern version of the *imperio rationis* model. On civil law influence and "rationality" in a historical perspective see M.-F. Renoux-Zagamé, "Le Droit Commun Européen entre Histoire et Raison", *Droits* 14, 1991, 27–37.

[16] Mackay (Lord—of Clashfern), "Diversity in Unity—European Laws", Churchill Memorial Lecture, Luxembourg, 1992.

[17] For both a general assessment and specific issues related to the idea of a "European Civil Code" see A. S. Hartkamp, M. W. Hesselink, E.-H. Hondius, C. E. du Perron, J. B. M. Vranken (eds.), *Towards a European Civil Code* (Nijmegen, 1994), in which several contributions also refer to the importance of *Unidroit* in particular areas. The controversy around the concept of such a code acquired a new dimension with the European Parliament's call for a European Civil Code (26 May 1989, C 158/400), cf. W. Tilmann, "Towards a European Civil Code", *ZEuP* 1997, 595–8; *idem*, "Zweiter Kodifikationsbeschluß des Europäischen Parlements", *ZEuP* 1995, 534–51; *idem*, "The Case-law of the European Court of Justice and National Courts as a Contribution to the Europeanisation of Private Law", *European Review of Private Law* 1995, 367–78. The issue of a code is still usually raised with a question-mark, e.g.—literally—F. Werro (ed.), *L'européanisation du Droit Privé: vers un Code Civil Européen?* (Fribourg, 1998).

[18] It is impossible to address here the various questions developed in the course of the so-called "Convergence Debate", which has been discussed separately in a 1997–1998 seminar of the European Academy of Legal Theory (cf. the paper by M. Van Hoecke en F. Ost, "Legal Doctrine in Crisis: Towards a European Legal Science", *Legal Studies* 18, 1998, 199–215). Apart from the well-known essays by P. Legrand ("European Legal Systems are not Converging", *ICLQ* 1996, 52–81) and W. van Gerven (e.g. "Bridging the Unbridgeable: Community and National Tort Laws after *Francovich* and *Brasserie*", *ICLQ* 1996, 507–44) et al. (e.g. B. de Witte, "The Convergence Debate", *Maastricht Journal of European and Comparative Law* 1996, 105–7), see also (in a wider context than that of Private Law) B. Markesinis (ed.), *The Gradual Convergence. Foreign Ideas, Foreign Influences, and English Law On the Eve of the 21st Century* (Oxford, OUP, 1994), esp. Markesinis's own introductory contribution ("Learning from Europe and Learning in Europe", 1–32); and P. Häberle, *Europäische Rechtskultur, Versuch einer Annäherung in zwölf Schritten* (Baden-Baden, Nomos, 1994).

law, at different political levels) according to the needs and the opportunities. And here again, one may observe how in that respect, too, the transition from the Italian method to the Modern method expressed a transformation of the underlying "operating system".

Oversimplifying once again a complex set of doctrines, one might contrast the Italian method and the Modern method by differentiating between their respective approach to substantive rules of particular law (for the sake of convenience, the terms "ius commune" and "iura propria" will be used to refer respectively to civil law in a very broad sense—i.e. including the texts of the *corpora iuris*, as well as Roman law and Canon law scholarship—, and municipal law—i.e. mainly statutes and customs).

4.2.1. Ius Commune *and municipal law until the sixteenth century*

The main authorities of the Italian method (commentaries, and in this context, more particularly the *consilia*) were very much involved with *iura propria* but, at the same time, they very rarely incorporated substantive rules of particular law. Perhaps one might characterise its relation to the *iura propria* as that of a "formal" law, i.e. the Italian method, which as a form of civil law scholarship practically enjoyed until the sixteenth century a monopoly for imposing its jurisprudence and legal theory, worked out a theory of legal sources, which determined such questions as the applicability of a *ius proprium* rule, or its construction, or how to resolve conflicts of law, but it did not elaborate doctrines directly based on substantive particular law. In jurisdictions where customary law or statute law prevailed, the gap between the "learned law" taught in the faculties of civil and canon law and the municipal law applied in the day-to-day practice of local jurisdictions was at times very wide. Even then, however, that learned law also fulfilled a bridge-function by determining the relationship between *ius commune* and *iura propria*, and also, increasingly, by imposing elements of its own operating system on municipal law.

4.2.2. Usus Modernus *and national developments*

The Modern method, by contrast, incorporated a growing number of substantive rules of particular law. This was largely due to external pressures: the rise of the early-modern sovereigns' power was reflected in their exercise of increasing legislative prerogatives, and customary law was largely transformed into a written law form, whether through the procedure of an officially sanctioned homologation (as in France), or its incorporation in territorial statute law (as in some German principalities and cities). Civil law learning, partly because it remained the established academic legal discipline, preserved its predominant position in legal science, but by the end of the sixteenth century, its monopoly in legal scholarship was broken; it adapted successfully to the new situation by assimilating the increasingly important body of municipal law, at the price, inevitably, of forsaking to some degree the unity (or relative uniformity) of European *ius commune*. *Usus modernus* became a form of civil law scholarship which developed differently from one (pre-national or territorial) legal system to another. Civil law learning retained on the whole its general European character and provided henceforth the common material for the different territorial variants of the Modern method, while the *iura propria* supplied the distinctive features and materials of each territorial version of the *usus modernus*. It is a matter of speculation whether or to what extent *ius commune* scholarship might have survived the territorial and national codes, and continued to provide these codes with its own legal theory; the political and doctrinal context of the codification from the early nineteenth century onwards precluded such a development. Whatever remained of a "common law" concept in the era of legal positivism, it was now primarily framed within a national context, e.g. that of the *Code civil* as "droit commun" in French (private) law, or the legal profession's articulation of the national *Volksgeist* in Germany.

5. CONCLUSION

Some two centuries after the demise of the European *ius commune* era—an era, it should never be forgotten, where substantive *iura propria* always prevailed—, the idea (or ideal) of a new common law for Europe is once again a major legal issue. The recent development of a concept of "European Private Law" is one of the most striking features of this revival, not least because it deals with the area of the law which was most strongly affected by transnational European civil law scholarship during the *Ancien Régime*, and which thus formed the hard core of pre-1800 *ius commune*. Moreover, it was also the key-target of pre-national and national codifications, because rulers and their law-makers saw the codification of private law as an essential instrument in forging their country's and its population's sense of identity and unity. Nevertheless, the concept of European Private Law remains at this stage relatively undefined, which means that, as for the concept of European law in general, it may stand for several models and types of legal rules.[19] Barring a political débâcle, the question is not so much whether a new European *ius commune* (or, specifically, a European Private Law) will develop, but what type of common law it will be.[20] Legal history shows that several different forms of common law, even within the civil law

[19] J. Taupitz, *Europäische Privatrechtsvereinheitlichung heute und morgen* (Tübingen, Paul Siebeck, 1993).

[20] Cf. H. Dedek's report on the Eighth Conference of Young Civil Lawyers (10–13 September 1997, Mainz), "Europäisierung des Privatrechts—Zwischenbilanz und Perspektiven", in *ZEuP* 1998, 794–7, at 795: "... *Hinter der mottogebenden Wendung 'Europäisierung des Privatrechts' vermisse [Prof. M. Dreher] ein Fragezeichen—der erstrebten Zwischenbilanz habe die Untersuchung vorauszugehen, ob eine (weitere) Europäisierung des Privatrechts überhaupt sinnvoll und wünschenswert sei. Die Beantwortung dieser Sinnfrage blieb indes im folgenden aus. Nicht das 'ob', sondern das 'wie' stand im Mittelpunkt der Debatte* ...".

tradition, have prevailed at different times, and no doubt other forms than those historical examples may still evolve. From an historical, long-term perspective, the various models of European Private Law which are proposed in the current debate can be assessed with reference to the changes which have affected fundamental patterns of legal thinking over the past century. Among other relevant features, the two key issues discussed *supra* may provide indications for such an assessment. Models which tend to hold on to the traditional systematisation *ratione materiae*, or which tend to consider the relation between European law and the municipal laws too rigidly (e.g. too exclusively in terms of positive rules of substantive law), may thus be regarded as regressive, as they fail to offer an adequate response to the tendencies which have increasingly undermined its premises. For example, a few years ago, in the aftermath of the Maastricht Treaty, a seemingly endless debate raged in the British press about the meaning of the notion of "subsidiarity";[21] the debate had the merit of addressing a fundamental question regarding the nature of European law, but at the same time, because it reduced the question excessively to one of a conflict of positive laws, it generally failed to appreciate the variety of legal rules involved and of their potential interactions; at the same time, it considered jurisdictional matters again in far too positive terms, thus emphasising a notion of rigid subject-matters, disregarding the dynamics which have supported the gradual extension of European Law well beyond the original Community Law.

Until now, no clear alternatives have emerged for replacing the systematisation which prevailed two centuries ago, while that systematisation is no longer adequate for supporting modern legal methods. Neither is the finality of European integration plainly defined; whereas the great codes of the nineteenth century represented a multi-secular development which linked political integration and legal uniformisation, one may doubt whether such a link is, at present, perceived as an essential part of European unification. The areas where legal unification at a European level are most strongly advocated (whether among the member states of the European Union or in a wider context) are those with a major economic and commercial relevance. Moreover, a more ideological current advocating human rights and fundamental principles of justice has pervaded most areas of public and private life. These general observations may confirm the conventional expectation that (a) most, if not all, areas of private law, will be closely connected to areas which so far had been categorised as questions of public law; (b) that some specific areas of private law will more readily develop towards a uniform European law than others; and, finally, (c) that the professional demands on lawyers will require a combination of specialisations in very specific fields, but that these specialisations will require a new general theory ensuring the compatibility of the various components of the law.

[21] For a more academic approach to the problem, mainly from a constitutional perspective, see G. P. Wilson, "Nationale Souveränität, Subsidiarität und Rechtskultur. Großbritannien als Sonderfall?", in: C. Tomuschat, H. Kötz and B. von Maydell (eds.), *Europäische Integration und nationale Rechtskulturen* (Köln, 1995), 355–65.

European Private Law, then, only appears to be a generic term for areas which will develop distinctly and very much according to their own agenda. In some ways, the situation will be much more comparable to that of the law under the *usus modernus* than in the era of positivistic codes. Lawyers who aspire at a place in the Pantheon of legal history would indeed be seriously deluded if they would spend their energies on a European Civil Code inspired by the *C.c.*, the *BGB* or any other codification of the past centuries. In the foreseeable future, lawyers who wish to associate their name with statutory law would show more lucidity by looking at the *Code Marchand* or d'Aguesseau's achievements. That, in the long term, may prove in many ways more beneficial to European legal developments. Europe's future is probably better off with a Savary than with a Bonaparte.

6

Studying Judicial Decisions in the Common Law and the Civil Law: A Good Way of Discovering Some of the Most Interesting Similarities and Differences that Exist Between these Legal Families[1]

BASIL MARKESINIS

1. INTRODUCTORY REMARKS

The problems which this essay will look at arise in actions which, in the Common law world, have become known as actions for "wrongful life" and "wrongful birth".[2] Since the way the teacher selects cases for discussion in the classroom can determine the breadth of his sweep, it is important to explain why this subject has been chosen. Five reasons at least can be given for this choice; but, it is submitted, the general tenets of this paper are applicable to other topics besides the one studied here. They are the following.

First, similar relevant decisions can be found in almost all systems. *Secondly*, these decisions reveal clearly the areas where the systems are similar and where they are different. *Thirdly*, the decisions show how the wider legal background affects the style of reasoning as well as the final outcome of the case; and this, incidentally, also points to some of the dangers of legal transplants. *Fourthly*,

[1] This text draws heavily on my contribution to the (posthumous) *Festrschrift* for John Fleming, *The Law of Obligations: Essays in Celebration of John Fleming*, ed. by Peter Cane and Jane Stapleton (Oxford, Clarendon Press, 1998).

[2] Since these terms have not been used consistently, especially in the American literature, it may be desirable to state that in this essay the first—*wrongful life*—is used in a way which refers to actions brought by the handicapped child and can include, among other things, claims for emotional harm and the cost of medical expenses. *Wrongful birth* actions are brought by the parents of the affected child and, likewise, can include claims for moral and pecuniary damages. *Wrongful conception* cases, including claims for the birth of a healthy but unwanted child, are not discussed in this paper though, as we shall see further down, the distinction is not always clear in the French judgments.

the approach in some of these cases does not depend on the inductive versus deductive way of reasoning, which, we have been told time and again, differentiates the two ways of thinking: the English and the Continental. *Finally*, they show how relatively insignificant are the legal concepts used by jurists, at any rate for the purposes of comparing the results reached by the various systems. Let us look at these points in turn, focusing, because of lack of space, on German and American law though, occasionally, also drawing attention to French law.[3]

2. SIMILAR LITIGATION FOUND IN MOST COUNTRIES

At the outset the discussion requires two or three general qualifications. The first is the obvious one namely, that we are talking here of the countries which were once described as belonging to the "Western World" but nowadays are best described as advanced or industrialised countries. For, clearly, the less "developed" countries do not have the same level of litigation for these types of cases, partly for technological reasons and partly because their inhabitants are accustomed (perhaps with greater maturity) to treating many of these incidents as part of the normal vicissitudes of life which are best handled through family co-operation rather than through state help or litigation.

Secondly, even within this group of "industrialised" countries with which we are concerned, indigenous factors may account for a lack of case law. For example, strong religious beliefs on the morality of abortion, coupled with criminal legislation on the subject, which may vary in its breadth in significant details, affect the existence of case law on our subject.[4] Belgium is a good example of a country where no case law of any significance was found for the reasons given above; the Republic of Ireland is another, and that is one of the reasons why they have been totally excluded from the purview of this essay.[5] Overall, however, one must note a degree of similarity in the social, economic, and political backgrounds of the countries, which are looked at in this essay with the consequence that the transplantability of particular legal solutions can be considered with profit.

[3] Italian law also offers interesting analogues—for instance Cass Civ. 22.11.1993, n. 11503, 1994 *La Nuoava Giurisprudenza Civile Commentata* 690, with note by Professor Vincenzo Zeno Zencovich—and so do mixed jurisdictions such as Louisiana. For reasons of space, however, their consideration must be omitted from this paper.

[4] In *Trib. grande inst. Evreux*, 21 déc. 1979, *D.* 1981. 185 the mother's first and unsuccessful abortion took place in France. By the time the mistake was discovered, the time limit (ten weeks from the moment of conception) for having a legal abortion in France had passed; but it was still possible for her to have a legal abortion in England which she did. The (culpable) defendant was held liable for the extra costs of this second operation.

[5] This is also true of French law, though it does not figure in the opaque judgments. (Abortion was first legalised by the "experimental" *loi Veil* of 17 January 1975 and took its definitive form with the *loi Pelletier* of 31 December 1979.) For Professor Le Tourneau, note to Cour d'Appel de Riom of 6 July 1989, *DS* 1990, 284, 286, French law does not recognise a right to abortion but merely "tolerates" it in certain circumstances.

There is a third factor, which may affect the levels of litigation. It is really a variant of the previous one: the Constitution and its interpretation[6] can also have a bearing on these cases. An illustration of this can be found in the recent German case law. Thus, the re-affirmation by the German Constitutional Court that "the child's existence cannot, in law, be classified as damage",[7] effectively continues to bar all direct claims by the child, itself.

In America the "constitutionalisation" of private law can be seen by the effect which *Roe v. Wade*[8] had on this branch of the law.[9] More ominously, one might wish to speculate on the fate of the wrongful life/ birth actions if abortion rights are restricted as a result of the recent and politically orchestrated reactions of the "pro-life" movement. Though one may take heart from the fact that the moods of the American public are often transient, it must be admitted that the current picture, from the claimants' point of view, is bleak if one is to judge from a series of statutes passed by many American States in the eighties limiting or totally eliminating such causes of action[10]. This trend (though not the reasoning) stands in marked contrast to the two most recent decisions of the *Cour de cassation* [11] which may be heralding an expansion of plaintiffs' rights. We shall return to some of these ideas later on.

3. SIMILARITIES BETWEEN THE SYSTEMS

Let us first start with the most elementary observation. Many students (and some courts) have had difficulty in deciding what harm the doctor/defendant has caused in these cases. Both the landmark German and New Jersey cases in this field clarify this point at the outset; and do so using almost identical language. Thus, the German court states that:

> ". . . The defendant did not cause the child's deplorable condition... However, in breach of his obligation towards the mother to treat her, he failed to prevent by means of an abortion the birth of a child, the health of which was severely endangered and in whose person the danger materialised in a severe form."[12]

[6] Which may remain consistent or alter over a period of time. Thus, in the United States, changing attitudes about the constitutionality of abortion, have affected the availability and ambit of the tort actions of "wrongful life" and "wrongful birth".

[7] *BVerfGE* 88, 203, section D.V.6. Article 2 (2), which protects "the right to life", is, of course, the one mainly considered in these cases.

[8] 410 US 113, 93 S. Ct. 705.

[9] See, for instance, the frank admissions which *Procanik v. Cillo,* 97 NJ 339, 478 A. 2d 755 (1984), contain on this matter.

[10] A summary can be found in B. S. Markesinis, *The German Law of Torts: A Comparative Introduction*, 3rd ed. (Oxford, Clarendon, 1994).

[11] *La Semaine Juridique* (JCP) 1996, 156. Contrast, *Conseil d'Etat*, 14 fév. 1997, *La Semaine Juridique*, 22828.

[12] *BGHZ* 86, 240, 250. This elementary point was, apparently, misunderstood by the *Cour administrative d'appel de Lyon* and its decision was thus quashed by the *Conseil d'Etat* of 14 fév. 1997, *Semaine Juridique*, 22828 (with approving note by Professor Moreau).

While in *Procanik* the court said:

> "In the present case, the plaintiffs do not allege that the negligence of the defendant doctors caused the congenital rubella from which the infant plaintiff suffers . . . The essence of the infant's claim is that the defendant doctors wrongfully deprived his mother of information that would have prevented his birth."[13]

Moving next to more important matters, we notice that both systems also reach the same (negative) result concerning the most difficult claim in these actions, namely the child's claim for general damages for being born.[14] The American judgment, reviewing early case law, states simply that ". . . policy considerations have led this court in the past to decline to recognise any cause of action in an infant for his wrongful life".[15] The German court likewise takes the same view and states: ". . . this Division believes that in cases such as the present the limits within which claims can be adjudicated according to law have been reached altogether and even exceeded."[16] A long line of subsequent cases has not budged on this point.[17]

Thirdly, both systems are *at idem* in so far as they make sure that the child's basic needs will be taken care of through damages given to the parents. Could this solution be running counter to the philosophical stance taken by those courts, which have argued that life cannot be damage and cannot justify the award of damages? It is very tempting to give an affirmative answer to this question. But this would produce an overall result, which would be too harsh for most. The decision of 16 November 1993 of the *Bundesgerichtshof*[18] ingeniously wriggles through the (puritanical) obstacles laid before it by the Constitutional court.[19] This section of the judgment of the *Bundesgerichtshof* thus concludes with the following peroration:

> "This Division is rather of the opinion that, especially in cases such as this, granting compensation not only has no detrimental effect on this child [honestly, how could it!] but can rather be beneficial to it, since it improves its financial situation and possibly

[13] *Procanik* v. *Cillo* 478 A. 2d 755, 760 (1984).

[14] The position of French law is, probably, the same despite the recent two important decisions of the *Cour de cassation*, which we discuss further down in the text.

[15] *Ibid.*, at p. 760.

[16] *BGHZ* 86, 240, 254.

[17] In BGH, *NJW* 1994, 788, an attempt to argue this point on appeal was abandoned, obviously because it was hopeless. Likewise, BGH, *NJW*, 1996, 2432, which involved an attempted abortion of twins, which succeeded in the case of one but, left the other fertilised egg alive. The most recent case—BGH 4. 3. 1997, *NJW* 1997. 1639, reached the same conclusion by stating, somewhat blandly, that the child was not included within the protective scope of the contract between mother and doctor. This continuing case law is also giving rise to interesting literature with the result that Germany is no longer following the American debate but, in one sense, leading it. Thus, see Cramer, "Pränatale Diagnostik und Fetaltherapie. Auswirkungen auf die Rechtsprechung des Bundesgerichtshofes zur Zeugung oder Geburt eines genetisch geschädigten Kindes als Schadensfall ("wrongful—birth action")", *MedR* 1992, I, 14; Deutsch "Das Kind oder sein Unterhalt als Schaden—Eine methodische Grundfrage des geltenden Rechts", *VersR* 1995, 609.

[18] *BGHZ* 124, 128, *NJW* 1994, 788; BGH, *NJW* 1997, 1639.

[19] *BVerfGE* 88, 203, section D.V.6. See n. 7, above.

> even its standing within the family. The shifting of the maintenance burden to the attending doctor appears especially satisfactory where, due to his faulty consultation, he is co-responsible for the economic burden which, if a severely handicapped child is in constant need of care, can even threaten the family's existence.[20] As this Division has previously stated . . . even in cases where the doctor is fully liable for all extra expenditure calculated by means of an economic comparison, the parties are still burdened with the total personal care of the child and also with certain a amount of financial losses and sacrifices which they cannot transfer to the person who created the damage. The Court fails to detect any constitutionally objectionable attack on the honour of the child from this partial economic alleviation of the parents burden."[21]

The teacher who uses material such as this in the classroom can, of course, digress here and refer to the cat and mouse jurisdictional game which the Constitutional and Federal Court play from time to time, as the latter shows signs of "irritation" by the generalised fiats which the former sends down from its Olympian heights. Indeed, the discerning teacher/reader obtains a clear glimpse (from judgments such as that of the *Bundesgerichtshof* of 16 November 1993) of how the Federal Court handles these "directives"; and can, thereby at his discretion, add further dimensions to his exposition of foreign law.

4. DIFFERENCES BETWEEN THE SYSTEMS

The appreciation of the two systems comes more into relief when we look at the differences between the approaches of the two courts. They lie in three areas. Firstly, style. As I have discussed this elsewhere[22] little need be added here. Special note, however, must be taken of two features of the cases. The first is how each court uses its respective case law; and let it be noted that, yet again, we are confronted with an area of the law which in almost all countries but England has found its answers through cases and not statutes. The second is the use of the comparative method in the German case (albeit here, unfortunately, displaying a mistaken appreciation of American law.)[23]

Secondly, methodological approach. For reasons which have, again, been explained elsewhere,[24] German law often resorts to contract to perform what we would regard as tort functions. Thus, here, too, the remedies of the various plaintiffs are seen as stemming from the main contract made by the mother of the affected child with the hospital. This part of the German reasoning makes little sense to a common lawyer so little more need be said on this point.[25]

[20] This point, as well, is made by the New Jersey decision at p. 762.

[21] *BGHZ* 124 at 144.

[22] "A Matter of Style" 110, *LQR*, 607 (1994).

[23] *Ibid*. at 251.

[24] See, for instance, *The German Law of Torts: A Comparative Introduction*, 3rd ed. (1994), 46 *et seq*.

[25] The recent double decision of the *Cour de cassation* of 26 March 1996—*Bull Civ*. 1996, 109—also chose to base liability on art. 1147 CC, ie. a contractual rule; but this has puzzled some French commentators. See for instance, Professor Jourdain's observations in *Rev. trim dr. civ*. 1996, 623, 4.

The last area of difference can be found in the substantive answers given; and here we note two major differences. First, in German law the mother is not allowed any damages for pain and suffering except for that which "exceeds the inflictions which accompany a birth without complications". If, for instance, she were forced because of the damage to the foetus, to have an *abortion*, a small sum would be claimable under this heading. More importantly, "no pecuniary damages can be awarded . . . in respect of a violation of the right to plan a family as an emanation of the general right to one's personality."[26] By contrast, the American case allows such claims; indeed, *Roe v. Wade*[27] is the *fons et origo* of the developments in this part of the law.

Secondly, the cases differ in the way they deal with the affected child's claim for special damages. Unlike the New Jersey court in *Procanik*, the German court refuses the child's claims, (for what we would call general *and* special damages), and this irrespective of whether the claim is based on contract (the child being seen, as stated above, a third party beneficiary of the contract made by the mother and the hospital) or in tort. On the other hand, both parents are, as already noted, compensated to the tune of all living and medical expenses incurred for the handicapped child.[28]

Despite this last-mentioned similarity, the American decision remains more generous than the German in that damages for "medical and other expenses" are given to the parents *and* the child. Though the American court is quick to clarify that such damages are not "doubled",[29] in the sense that the damages to the child become payable only when the parental obligation to maintain ceases, the difference is significant since it means that in New Jersey law (but not in German) law the child can go on receiving compensation in the event of surviving its parents. In one sense, however, the extent of this generosity may be exaggerated: statistics suggest that victims with serious injuries rarely live beyond their majority.

5. THE INFLUENCE OF LEGAL BACKGROUND ON THE OUTCOME OF THESE CASES

Professor Fleming[30] has shown how the differences between American and English tort law lie not in the concepts or values adopted by the two systems but on the impact that backdrop factors such as the presence or absence of a written constitution, a Bill of Rights, juries, the welfare state, a differently trained

[26] *BGHZ* 86, 240, 248. Point re-confirmed by BGH, *NJW* 1994, 788.

[27] 410 US 113, 93 S.Ct. 705.

[28] *BGHZ* 86, 240, 247.The Federal Court recently stressed forcefully that the damages must include both normal and extra-ordinary expenses: BGH *NJW* 1993, 788. See, also. BGH, *NJW* 1997, 1639. In France, on the other hand, the lower courts are less generous since they limit damages to extra-ordinary expenses incurred on behalf of the "abnormal" child. See cases cited by Le Tourneau in *DS* 1990, 287.

[29] *Ibid.* at 762.

[30] *The American Tort Process* (Oxford, Clarendon Press, 1988).

and organised legal profession and the like have had on the final outcome of the cases. His pioneering study has not yet been replicated at a Continental European level; but it is submitted that his main ideas hold true also for the comparison of English, American, and German law. This further and significant dimension to the study of the law is well illustrated by the two cases discussed in this paper.

Thus, first, we note how the German court categorically asserts that "Human life . . . is a legally protected interest of the highest order deserving absolute protection. No third party may determine its value".[31] The court goes on to hold that "it is impossible to determine . . . whether a life affected by serious handicaps as an alternative to absence of existence can be regarded at all in law as damage . . ." Significantly the court alludes to its not so distant past and states ". . . generally, having regard to the experience under the National Socialist regime of lawlessness, the practice of the courts in the Federal Republic does not permit, with good reason, any legally relevant judgment about the value of the lives of others."[32] Considerations such as these have led the German courts, as we have already noted, to deny the child/plaintiff any legal redress.

But there is another, more contemporary and pragmatic argument for denying the child special damages; and it is one which, in Professor Fleming's terminology, is dictated by the different national background. A hint of this comes towards the end of the German judgment where the court states that its solution to grant the parents special damages may not be enough "once the duty to maintain [the child] comes to an end, as for instance, when they die".[33] Here, as stated, the American solution appears if not preferable certainly more generous to the child; that is until one notes the way the German court completes the above-mentioned thought. "In all these cases" says the court "a fateful development takes place the interruption of which cannot be demanded by the child and the effects of which must be made good by the community within the bounds of the possible."[34] An admission here, that the social security net (effectively absent in the USA) will thus take over, but also a very important explanation for the fact that American tort law is so often more generous than its European counterparts. That this will provide only a limited relief—"within the bounds of the possible"—and will be less generous than the tort/damages system of

[31] *BGHZ* 86, 240, 252.

[32] *BGHZ* 86, 240, 252.

[33] Note here that in German law the obligation to maintenance continues for life and does not, as in many American jurisdictions, come to an end upon the child attaining majority. This difference in the family law rules may thus explain the lesser generosity of the German tort rules. To put it differently: in the English Common law, tort law often makes up for the defects of the law of contract, family and succession. Yet, in German law at the end of the day a difference still remains at the expense of the child. For what happens to it when the parents die? The solution, as we explain in the text, is found in German social security law.

[34] *BGHZ* 86, 240. In BGH *NJW* 1997, 1639, the Federal Court refused the child's claim on the ground that the child was not included within the scope of the contract made by its mother and the doctor. Why this is so, is not explained, though a few lines further down the court alludes to the dangers of enlarging unnecessarily the extent of medical liability.

compensation, is an undoubted fact. But as Frederick the Great said over two centuries ago: "*Der Mantel des Königs ist Warm aber Kurz*".[35] One could not better this summary of one of the advantages and drawbacks of the social security versus the tort method of compensation!

The way the American court deals with some of the philosophical points of the case is also instructive. With regard to the child's claim for special damages, the court said:

> "We need not become preoccupied . . . with . . . metaphysical considerations. Our decision to allow the recovery of extraordinary medical expenses is not premised on the concept that non-life is preferable to an impaired life, but it is predicated on the needs of the living. We seek only to respond to the call of the living for help in bearing the burden of their affliction".[36]

Without too much distortion one can read into these lines the idea that something must be done about these unfortunate victims of human errors; and, in the absence of any social security provisions in the USA, tort law must perform this function.

If true, this is an important new optic for looking at American tort awards for it suggests that to the extent that they deal with future medical expenses they are rightly more generous than their European counterparts. Additionally, one must bear in mind that a large slice of the damage award will, in America, go to counsel under the contingent fee system which, in one respect at least, is nothing more than a way of financing litigation, alternative to, but just as defective as, our legal aid system.

The judgment in the New Jersey court in *Procanik* becomes even more interesting when it comes to give its reasons for denying the child's claim for general damages. The relevant section deserves to be quoted in full not least because it provides an open admission of how the jury system has affected the operation of tort law in practice. It said:

> " Underlying our conclusion is an evaluation of the capability of the judicial system, often proceeding in these cases through trial by jury, to appraise such a claim. Also at work is an appraisal of the role of tort law in compensating injured parties, involving as that role does, not only reason, but also fairness, predictability, and even deterrence of future wrongful acts. In brief, the ultimate decision is a policy choice summoning the most sensitive and careful judgment. From that perspective it is simply too speculative to permit an infant plaintiff to recover for emotional distress attendant on birth defects which the plaintiff claims that he would be better off if he had not been born. Such a claim would stir the passions of jurors about the nature and value of life, the fear of non-existence, and about abortion. That mix is more than the judicial system can digest."[37]

[35] The cloak of the King is warm but small.
[36] *Procanik v. Cillo* 478 A. 2d 755, 763 (1984).
[37] *Ibid.*, at p. 763.

This is a pragmatic and admirable assessment of conditions in the jury room, especially the context of contemporary American politics. Arguably, it is also a more convincing explanation for denying damages than resorting to philosophical or metaphysical statements, which, even when proclaimed with great conviction, do not enjoy unanimous support.

6. INDUCTIVE AND DEDUCTIVE REASONING

Sixty years ago, in his perceptive but, nowadays, rarely read lecture entitled "Two Ways of Thinking",[38] Lord Macmillan suggested that the Scots and Continental Europeans opt for a deductive way of reasoning while the Anglo-Saxons prefer the inductive approach. "To proceed from principles to instances is the characteristic of the one school [continental European] to proceed from instances to principles—or perhaps not to proceed beyond instances—is the characteristic of the other [common law]." This central theme, however, failed to bring out the fact that the two worlds, though starting from different positions, tend to meet in the middle.[39] For our purposes, therefore, it is interesting to note that one can find abundant German case law, which goes from its starting premise to its conclusion, without really using the one or the other way of reasoning.

The "wrongful birth" and "life" cases we have been comparing offer such an illustration; and to the extent that they do not follow the reasoning pattern one expects of them, but proceed to the finishing point in a very similar fashion, they can help bridge the gap between the two major legal families of the world by showing that even their so-called cardinal difference—their different ways of thinking—is not as omnipresent as one has been led to believe. For one must stress the fact that there are large areas of German law where the same holds true. This tends to happen where the statutory material in the Code is slender; and the pegging of the result on a codal provision tends to be more a formality than a logical necessity.

Here only a few instances of this can be given; but in all of them one can attempt the kind of interpretation/ analysis of the decisional law which we have tried in this piece. From the German law of torts we thus note that the development of contractual ways of circumventing the tort rule of vicarious liability can be included in this group.[40] This tendency to move away from the strict Codal reasoning can also be seen in the judicial development of the general right to one's personality. The deductive reasoning which one finds here derives its force from the hierarchically superior Constitution; and that is as far as deduction

[38] Reproduced in his book *Law and Other Things* (1938) 76 *et seq*.

[39] To be fair to the great jurist he does say that in Scotland "the edges of distinction have been blurred by constant contacts" with England.

[40] This "peculiarity" of German law is extensively discussed in Markesinis, *The German Law of Torts. A Comparative Introduction*, 3rd ed. (Oxford, Clarendon, 1994) pp. 685 ff. and pp. 774 ff.

goes. Yet even here one is left with the impression that the courts are trying to do justice to a problem which has become more acute in our times than it was when the Code was drafted and less concerned to pursue the Code's merciless logic to its end. In that sense, therefore, one could apply to these cases the American dictum that "Law is more than an exercise in logic, and logical analysis, although essential to a system of ordered justice, should not become an instrument of injustice."[41]

The absence in any meaningful way of any deductive or inductive logic is even more obvious in important areas of contract law, which have been transformed over the last century by the courts, the result being dictated by purely practical considerations or iniquities of the codal solutions. This is progressively obvious in the slow enlargement of the codal notion of impossibility of performance, which culminated in the ability of German courts to readjust *(Ausgleichsanspruch)* the contractual obligations of the parties. Here, a mere perusal of the judgments shows how the reference to the Code—§ 242 *BGB*—amounts to little more than paying lip service to the notion that the courts are applying statutory law and hardly disguises their creative powers, often prompted by little more than the desire to do justice during a period of drastic dislocation of the German economy. How creative this power can be, can be seen not only by the courts' ability to move away from the wording of the contract chosen by the parties but also in the extent of their power to re-draw the contract, the entire process finding but the slightest of justifications in the Code. A number of interesting illustrations of this are given in *The German Law of Contract and Restitution*,[42] co-authored by this writer with Professor Werner Lorenz and Dr. Gerhard Dannemann. Two can be mentioned here as illustrations of the point we are trying to make. In these decisions the scant reference to codal provisions, coupled with the insistence, commonly found in cases turning on § 242 *BGB* that they each turn on their facts, demonstrate that neither deductive nor inductive reasoning is dominant here. Instead, the result is dictated by the court's feeling of fairness, at times coupled with an economic analysis of the circumstances of the case before it.

In 1966 the *Bundesgerichtshof*[43] heard a case involving a city dweller who had decided to live in the country and was offered the possibility of a lease of land on which the defendant/builder was to erect for him a pre-fabricated house. When, to the surprise of both contracting parties, the local authority declined to give building permission for the works to proceed, the plaintiff sought to recover his down payment from the builder. In such a case and in accordance with the traditional application of the doctrine of impossibility, the defendant would have been excused his obligation and the plaintiff entitled to recover the pre-paid amount by way of restitution.[44] Yet the court went down a completely

41 *Procanik v. Cillo* 478 A. 2d 755 (1984).

42 (Oxford, OUP, 1997).

43 BGH, *JZ* 1966, 409.

44 Subsequent decisions have shown a greater reluctance to order substitute performance. See OLG Karlsruhe, *JZ* 1972, 120.

different path. For the defendant builder argued that he could build a house on another piece of land, lying near by and having the same characteristics as the first plot (view, clean air etc.). This land belonged to a different land owner who, argued the builder, was willing to grant the plaintiff a similar lease of it as the one the plaintiff had originally obtained of the first piece of land. The *Bundesgerichtshof* was of the view that if these assertions could be proved—as it was left to a lower court to verify them—the substitute performance should be allowed to go ahead. In our view, it is entirely unconvincing that this bold result flowed deductively from any Codal provision even though it was, on the face of things, based on the mundanely-phrased provision about good faith of that enactment.

A more recent decision of the *Bundesgerichtshof*[45] shows the extent of praetorian powers which the German courts have arrogated to themselves when solving a case through the good faith provision of the Code (§ 242 *BGB*). Talk of deductive reasoning once again serves no meaningful purpose in such cases. The litigation arose after the recent re-unification of Germany when the old "West" swallowed up the bankrupt "East". The case involved a buyer (defendant) and a seller (plaintiff) of a machine originally acquired from Austria. Both parties operated within the state-controlled economy of communist (former) East Germany. The two Germany's agreed to unite in 1989; and the currency of East Germany ceased to exist in July 1990. East German marks (for brevity EDM) were converted into West German marks (WDM) at a rate of 2:1. The purchase price of the sold object was 1.7 million EDM; and before the disappearance of the EDM, the plaintiff had paid 400,000 EDM. The *BGH* took the view that the two parties should share the cost of the fiscal disruption to the transaction, which the unexpected political and economic changes had wrought. Pegging this result on § 242 *BGB* was only the first step. The way the court thought the sharing of the costs should be undertaken is even more intriguing; and, again, it bears no connection to deductive or inductive reasoning.[46] Arguably, the result is thus not really based on any kind of "legal principle" but on the court's desire to make some kind of economic sense of a

[45] BGH, *NJW* 1993, 259. Some of the post reunification cases are discussed by EBKE "Legal Implications of Germany's Reunification" (1990) 24 *Int. Lawyer* 1130.

[46] The BGH calculation was as follows. 1.7 EDM (purchase price) minus 400,000 EDM (deposit already paid) left 1.3 EDM unpaid. Exchanged for WDM this meant 650,000 WDM, half of which—i.e. 325,000 WDM should be paid by the defendant (buyer). This may sound as very much less than the originally agreed purchase price of 1.7 EDM but, in fact, it may have been too generous to the plaintiff (seller). For the 1.7 EDM were based on the unrealistically inflated price of EDM and Austrian schilling (from where, it will be remembered, the sold object was originally acquired). If one used the WDM/schilling market exchange rate, the purchase price would have been 380,000 WDM. Now it will be recalled that the plaintiff was allowed to claim 325,000 WDM; and he was allowed to keep the deposit already received (which was 400,000 EDM or, at a 2:1 exchange rate, 200,000 WDM). This means that plaintiff (seller) ended up with a total of 525,000 WDM for a machine which, realistically priced, was worth 380,000 WDM. That covers its cost; and leaves a profit of about 40% That the court would have used its adjusting powers under § 242 *BGB* is understandable and, possibly, even fair; that it should been so generous to the plaintiff is, however, more open to doubt.

transaction which had been completely falsified by the unexpected political developments that shook Germany during the late 1980's.

Cases such as the above are not, of course, the norm. In our afore-mentioned, *The German Law of Contract and Restitution* my German co-authors and I discuss the kind of case which involves the typical German deductive syllogism which will take the judge through a series of paragraph chains before coming up with the result desired by the Code.[47] But not all decisions display these characteristics; and to the extent that one uses as teaching tools decisions which do not depend on deductive or inductive reasoning one can take the comparisons of different systems even further. For in such cases the methodological differences between Common and Civil law are attenuated and thus the mental block, which discourages consultation of each other's, law should also, in theory, be correspondingly weakened.

7. CONCEPTS: VERBAL DEVICES, WHICH FORMULATE JUDGMENTS BUT DO NOT REALLY EXPLAIN THEM

The starting idea is, again, Professor Fleming's. To be sure, it was formulated in the context of the Common law and posited that there was often considerable equivocation between such legal concepts as duty, remoteness, foreseeability, and the like.[48] In later years, another imaginative tort scholar repeated this idea in somewhat more colourful language by maintaining that "it is a question of aesthetics as much as anything else whether one feels that the acceptable solution is better produced by emphasizing causation or duty or damage."[49] But all this can also be applied with profit to the comparative study of foreign law.

If we return to our wrongful life/ birth cases and look at them from a broader comparative perspective than we have done so far, namely by bring in French material[50], we shall see that the results remain broadly similar even though they are justified through the use of very different concepts. The French judgments in particular thus seem to be almost pre-occupied with whether the notion of causation is satisfied in these cases. Whether this is a convincing way of handling their facts is not really the issue. But what these decisions do show, especially when compared with the American or German case law, is that in Professor Fleming's words that the concepts are only "the means of formulating conclu-

[47] Markesinis, Lorenz, and Dannemann, *The German Law of Contract and Restitution"* (Oxford, Clarendon Press, 1997), chap. 1.

[48] "Remoteness and Duty: The Control Devices in Liability for Negligence", 31 *Can Bar Rev*. 471 (1953).

[49] T. Weir in Catala and Weir, "Delict and Torts: A Study in Parallel" 34 *Tulane L. Rev*. 701, 705 (1965). However, this is not always true. Thus, in *Rondel v. Worsley* [1969] 1 AC 191 for instance, the expressed policy aim of the court could not have been achieved through the mediums of causation, carelessness, or damage.

[50] Italian law, not discussed in this essay because of reasons of space, confirms the validity of most of the above general statements.

sions but do not often dictate them."[51] The comparisons of the four systems we have been looking at in this essay confirms this; for though the concepts differ the results are broadly speaking very similar. But let us at this stage of the discussion turn briefly to French law since its study reveals a different set of difficulties when studying foreign law.

The first problem with French law is finding out precisely what the courts allow in such cases. Sir Frederick Pollock is said to have written that "this [i.e. Britain] is the only country in Europe where quite a large portion of important affairs, from the Constitution downwards, are worked by just doing the thing you want and saying as little as possible about it even to yourself".[52] This statement could apply with equal force to the decisions of the highest French courts.

Until March 1996 and February 1997 the French law was basically to be found in two decisions of the *Conseil d'Etat*[53] and one of the *Cour de cassation*.[54] The following dense statement from the latter, denied any *damnum* to the mother "given that the birth of a child conceived by her could not, *in itself*, amount to a juridically recognisable harm to her, even if the birth followed an unsuccessful attempt at abortion." The italicised words supply the only visible clue that the legal position is not as simple as the key statement implies at first glance; and even when the reconstruction of the picture has progressed—with the aid of the *arrêtistes*, the *conclusions du Commissaire du Gouvernement*, and the published versions of the decisions of the lower courts[55]—it is not as complete as the one which we have obtained from the German and American judgments. As instruments of teaching the law, the value of the French judgments is thus very low indeed. So, that observation apart, what is the picture, which emerges from this puzzle?

The first decision of the *Conseil d'Etat* and that of the *Cour de cassation* of 1991 dealt with the mothers' claims. We have no clue whether any claims were advanced on behalf of the children, though given that in both cases the children born were healthy, the probable answer is that none were made.[56] The italicised words of the judgments ("in itself"), alluded to above, have nevertheless allowed the *arrêtistes* to argue that the mother's position might be different if *she* could prove that she had suffered "*une souffrance morale spéciale*", for instance because the child was conceived as a result of rape;[57] or because the child was

[51] *Supra*, note 48 at pp. 497–8.

[52] Cited by Lord Macmillan, "Two Ways of Thinking" in *Law and Other Things* (1938), 82.

[53] Of 2 July 1982, *DS* 1984, 425 and of 27 September 1989 *GP* 1990, 421.

[54] Of 25 June 1991, *DS* 1991, 566.

[55] We are lucky that in the present cases we have all three. In most instances, however, one or more of these "clues" will be missing, making the reconstruction of the case very difficult. This, for instance, is the case of the latest decision of the *Conseil d'Etat*. I have only seen extracts of the revealing *conclusions* of the *Commissaire du Gouvernement* in the *Monde* of 17 February 1997.

[56] In German law the doctor's liability is, in such cases, limited to that of a natural father. It is fixed by means of tariffs and tends to be much less generous than when tort law methods of compensation are used.

[57] Cour d'Appel de Riom, *DS* 1990, 284. It is interesting that the decision of the Court of Appeal stressed that the plaintiff's only complaint seemed to be that the birth of her (healthy) child would

born with grave deformities.[58] However, this last-mentioned decision of the *Conseil d'Etat* was not, really, a case of "wrongful life/ birth" but concerned a claim for damages for injuries inflicted by a negligent doctor to a living foetus. Thus, despite some academic[59] and journalistic *dicta*[60] to the contrary, the better view would appear to be that it cannot be used as a "precedent" in genuine "wrongful life" cases in order to justify any claim by the affected child. This validity of this view was recently confirmed by the *Conseil d'Etat*, which restated its opposition to allowing the child (in contrast to its parents) any damages whatsoever.[61]

Thus far, the reconstruction of the French law has brought it closer to the American and German judgments than its opaque judgments would suggest at first sight. Though we cannot say how substantial this approximation is, since we do not have a comparable, settled list of compensable headings of damage,[62] the overall picture is quite similar, especially since the most recent cases have made it quite clear that the parents' claims for their pain and suffering and the child's cost of maintenance are recoverable.[63] Finally, this picture of similarities is completed by the fact that (until recently) there was nothing in these judgments which could be taken to support the view that any sum could be given to the child for it being born. Indeed, the repeated insistence that life, in itself, cannot be seen as damage made this difficult to accept in any form.[64]

make it impossible for her to lead the ordinary life of a young girl! Incidentally, there no clue as to why she had allowed herself to become pregnant; nor indeed that she had been contributory negligent in failing, despite medical advice, to have timeously an echo test to verify the successful conclusion of the abortion. At First Instance, this claim had led a more sympathetic court to reduce her damages by half.

[58] As is shown by Conseil d'Etat, *GP* 1990. 2. 421. In this case the liability of the hospital, which was held responsible for the doctor's negligence, amounted to just over 1 million FF, 400,000 of which had to go the Social Security for medical expenses etc. and 600,000 to the child for "*des souffrances physiques et du préjudice esthétique*" which he suffered "*ainsi que des troubles dans ses conditions d'existence*".

[59] Le Tourneau, *DS* 1991, 567.

[60] Alluded to by Professor Moreau in his note to *Conseil d'Etat*, 14 février. 1997, *Semaine Juridique* 1991, 195.

[61] *Conseil d'Etat*, 14 février. 1997, *Semaine Juridique*, 1997, 22828.

[62] The cost of a new abortion, to complete the first and unsuccessful attempt has been consistently allowed. See, for instance, *Trib. grande inst. Evreux*, 21 décembre 1979, *D.* 1981, 185. Extraordinary expenses seem allowable; but what amounts to "*circonstances particulièrement inopportunes ou exceptionnelles*" is left to the courts of First Instance and access to their decisions is not always easy.

[63] In *Conseil d'Etat* 14 février. 1997, *Semaine Juridique* 1997, 22828, a proper case of "wrongful birth" claim, the court denied the parents' claim for 2 million FF for pain and suffering and gave them, instead, a paltry 200,000 FF. Additionally, the parents were given 5,000 FF per annum for as long as the child lived to cover the child's annual expenses.

[64] Indeed, pro-life authors such as professor Le Tourneau wax lyrical about this. In his most helpful comment on the decision of the Court of Appeal of Riom he thus states (*DS* 1990, 288): "*La vie même penible, est un don, peut être une grace . . . Toute notre civilisation nous souffle cet axiom et nous pousse à la chanter.*" This view was, again, re-asserted by the *Commissaire du Gouvernement* in the recent decision of the *Conseil d'Etat* of 14 fév. 1997 where Madame Pécresse said: "*Nous ne pensons pas qu'un enfant puisse se plaindre d'être né tel qu' il a été conçu par ses parents, même s'il est atteint d'une maladie incurable ou d'un défaut génétique, dès lors que la science médicale n'offrait aucun traitement pour le guérir in utero. Affirmer l'inverse serait juger qu'il existe des vies*

Yet this picture of trans-border uniformity of the law may have been shattered by two recent (1996) decisions of the *Cour de cassation* which seem incompatible with American, English, and German law and, indeed, irreconcilable with the even more recent (1997) decision of the *Conseil d'Etat* to which we have already referred. The first of these decisions of the *Cour de cassation* was the result of an action brought against a "geneticist" who advised a couple who consulted him to go ahead and procreate assuring them that the symptoms of neurological disorder that concerned them were not likely to be transmitted to any child which the mother conceived.[65] The second case concerned the familiar rubella drama. In both instances, the claims of the impaired *children* succeeded—the argument that life, itself, could not be considered as *dommage réparable* being reformulated to allow a pro-plaintiff result.[66] Once again, however, there is no complete clarity as to who is suing (the judgments only deal with the claims of the children). Opaqueness also exists as to what is being compensated. All that we have here is the almost meaningless generality "*dès lors leur décision* [of *les juges du fond*] *condamant le médecin à réparer les conséquences dommageables définitives des troubles de l'enfant est légalement jusitfiée.*"[67] Notwithstanding these uncertainties, to foreign eyes at least, these decisions can only herald a further liberalisation of the law in the direction of more extensive compensation rights in addition to being in serious conflict with the pronouncements of the *Conseil d'Etat*.

Before we close this brief survey of French law it should be repeated that beyond the general and conclusionary statements alluded to above, the French decisions also display a particular approach to the issue of the existence of a causative link between the doctor's negligence and the harmful event. This, of course, is inevitable for a system that has no device such as own "duty of care" under which it can subsume all the wider policy issues raised by the case. The consequence is that the notion of causation is understood in an overtly normative manner to end up with a result, which we would also adopt relying on a different conceptual methodology. This point is made very clearly in the second decision of the *Conseil d'Etat* where the trier of fact held that the obstetrician's negligence did not take place in the operating room but consisted of failing to check after the operation was over whether the whole of the foetus had been extracted from the mother's womb. The *Commissaire du Gouvernement* thus continued: "*Ainsi, peut-être certains d'entre vous trouveront-ils que le préjudice n'est pas du tout en relation avec la faute reprochée, mais bien plutôt avec la façon dont l'opération a été conduite ou avec la décision d'y recourir, c'est à dire avec des circonstances qui ne peuvent être imputées à faute à l'hôpital*". The

qui ne valent pas la peine d'être vécues et imposer à la mère une sorte d'obligation de recourir, en cas de diagnostic alarmant, à une interruption de grossesse." *Le Monde*, 17 February 1997. It is noteworthy that the judgment itself makes no allusion whatsoever to this important policy reason.

[65] *Bull Civ*. 1996, 109—decision of 26 March 1996.

[66] "*. . . le dommage ne consiste pas à naitre, mais à naitre atteint des séquelles graves et irréversible d'une maladie contractée avant la naissance.*" Jourdain, *Rev. trim. dr. civ*. 623, 4.

[67] *Bull Civ*., 1996, 109.

concluding statement is full of meaning when the *Commissaire* proceeded to say that "*. . . nous hésitons à vous proposer d'adopter un raisonnement où le droit paraît s' écarter de la justice.*"[68]

8. CONCLUDING REMARKS

What is the purpose of this brief essay? To a great extent it must be to impart some information about foreign law. Why should this be desirable? Partly in order to broaden the legal mind by demonstrating to it that similar problems can be approached and solved in different ways; partly in order to convince national lawyers that the study of other people's law may improve their understanding and sometimes the solutions of their own law. Few of those interested in comparative law would doubt the validity of these aims (though, rightly, they would not regard my list of aims as complete). For Comparative lawyers have praised the pursuit of these aims ever since the modern study of foreign systems began to take shape from the turn of this century onwards. The differences that divide the specialists in the subject thus lie mainly in devising a *method* that would best help achieve these aims. Thus, this essay also forms part of my attempt to develop a manageable way of presenting foreign law to my fellow countrymen.

My approach to this task has always been trifurcated. As I have explained elsewhere,[69] being a believer in enhanced European co-operation and integration,[70] I have played my part in stressing the similarities that exist between the systems. Similarities which, though notable, have been obscured by a variety of factors, including nineteenth century nationalism and twentieth century wars with the attendant deep cultural scars that they have left behind them. There is no doubt that those who do not share my ideological belief in Europe will disagree fundamentally with this, the starting point of my approach. But it is important to realise that at this level the opposition is, in essence, political.

A different divergence of views arises when we move to my next objective. The gaze now shifts from ideology to methodology. How does one explain let alone make "attractive" a foreign set of rules, which are often based on a history and a conceptualism that is, for historical reasons different to what one finds in one's own immediate environment—in my case the Common law? Here, being especially conscious of the impact which nineteenth century pandectist theory

[68] *GP* 1990, 422.

[69] *Foreign Law and Comparative Methodology: A Subject and a Thesis* (Oxford, hart, 1997), chapter 1.

[70] Though my enthusiasm for European collaboration and my belief in the growing convergence of the two legal families—the Common law and the Civil law—does not extend to the current fad for a European Civil Code. On this see my "Why a code is not the best way to advance the cause of European legal unity", *European Review of Private Law*, (1997), pp. 519–524. The "convergence" theme has been explored by a number of essays which I edited under the general title *The Gradual Convergence. Foreign Ideas, Foreign Influences, and English Law on the Eve of the 21st Century* (Oxford, Clarendon, 1994).

had on certain parts of German law,[71] I advocated that we must "first deconstruct and then reconstruct" the foreign law—in this instance German law—and "anglicise" it in order to make it more approachable by a Common law audience. The attack to this approach has come from Professor Legrand who sees in it "a manifest expulsion of the values of humility and deference from the relational framework between observer and observed". His conclusion is thus that by adopting such an approach, two German colleagues[72] and I may have "trivialised" German law.[73] The language is so extreme[74] that it makes one wonder whether two German Presidents,[75] a long-serving Foreign Minister,[76]the former President of the *Bundesgerichtshof*,[77]and a number of learned German institutions,[78]who have both praised and honoured this work (and the methodology on which it is based), were totally hood-winked into honouring a man who had trivialised their system rather than made it accessible to thousands of outsiders! But the point needs not to be laboured further, especially in the light of the slowly but steadily growing tendency of high English judges to refer judicially and extra judicially to foreign law *when properly explained to them*.[79] The "deconstruct and reconstruct" method is thus working; and that is a fact and no longer a thesis.

So we move to the third aspect of the methodology: what serves as the best springboard for presenting foreign law: academic writings attempting a codal exegesis or a careful and broad-minded use of decisional law? This essay, along with much of my other work, has laid the emphasis on the latter (without ignoring the former). I have thus, in the present paper, used a fairly narrow set of legal problems to show how their study through decisions can move, depending on the skill of the teacher, from the most narrow and technical point to the wider, philosophical underpinnings of a particular legal system. In my opinion, the great advantage of this approach, coupled where necessary with my "deconstruct and reconstruct" technique, is that it *gently* introduces the foreign and

[71] On which see "The Legacy of History on German Contract Law" in *Making Commercial Law. Essays in Honour of Roy Goode* (ed. by Ross Cranston) (Oxford, Clarendon, 1997), pp. 1–27 (co-authored with Dr. Gerhard Dannemann.). The methodology was applied on a larger scale when writing *The German Law of Obligations*, vol. I, *The German Law of Contract and Restitution* and vol. II, *The German Law of Torts* (Oxford, Clarendon, 1997).

[72] Professor Werner Lorenz of the University of Munich and Dr. Gerhard Dannemann of the University of Freiburg (and now Oxford) who shared this notion with me when writing *The German Law of Contracts* (1997).

[73] "Are civilians educable?" 18 *Legal Studies* (1998) 216 at 227, note 63.

[74] And, one suspects, the logic behind it so dubious.

[75] President Richard von Weisacker and President Walter Odersky.

[76] Dr Klaus Kinkel, former Vice Chancellor of the Federal Republic of Germany.

[77] Dr Walter Odersky in his Foreword to *The German Law of Obligations*, vol. I, *The German Law of Contract and Restitution,* co-authored with Professor Werner Lorenz and Dr Gerhard Dannemann, (Oxford, Clarendon, 1997).

[78] Such as the Ludwigs Maximilians University of Munich which conferred a doctorate *honoris causa* upon me for my work on German and Comparative Law.

[79] See my inaugural lecture at the Royal Netherlands Academy of Arts and Sciences entitled: "Foreign Law and Foreign Ideas in the English Courts. The Contemporary English Contribution to the Use of Foreign Law and Comparative Methodology" *Academiae Analecta* (1998) 50-19.

uninitiated observer into the mysteries of a foreign system. It achieves this result because it remains firmly based on manageable and recognisable factual configurations, which immediately highlight similarities (and differences) in substance, style, and technique in the way that I have tried to show in this paper. Moreover, it does so without having immediate recourse to concepts and notions, which, by virtue of their abstractness and linguistic particularities, can be confusing and even untranslatable. For those who wish to improve understanding and encourage *rapprochement,* the proposed technique thus works. And, as stated repeatedly, it can and will progressively be applied to other parts of the law, eventually proving its universal validity as a method of presenting foreign law.

The above, however, should not be taken to imply that this approach comes without a price. In my view, the highest price it carries with it is that it requires much research time in order to unearth the factual equivalents that will form the basis of the fully blown presentation. Such an acknowledgement will immediately cast a shadow over the mind of any practitioner who may happen to read this text. For practitioners, who experience on a daily basis the pressures that come with legal practice, can understand better than anyone else how precious time is and thus how difficult it is for them (and judges) to do what I am asking them to attempt. But there is also a silver lining to this objection; and it is really quite obvious. For to do properly what I am advocating, requires a closer co-operation between the teaching and practising side of our profession. That carries with it benefits of its own as my mentor and friend Professor Roy Goode has shown in his life's work. On this, I can only concur with him and I have nothing useful to add.

7

Monism and Dualism within the European Jurisdictions

FRANÇOIS RIGAUX

Omnes populi qui legibus et moribus reguntur partim suo proprio, partim communi omnium hominum iure utuntur; nam quod quisque populus ipse sibi ius constituit, id ipsius proprium est uocaturquer ius ciuile, quasi ius proprium ciuitatis; quod uero naturalis ratio inter omnes homines constituit, id apud omnes populos peraeque cutsoditur uocaturque ius gentium, quasi quo iure omnes gentes utuntur. Populus itaque romanus partim suo proprio, partim communi omnium hominum iure utitur. Quae singula qualia sint,suis locis proponemus.[1]

1. INTRODUCTION

The doctrinal debate on the relations between international law and internal law, setting a dualist doctrine against several different monist views, leads to some reflections on a European private law. According to the dogmatic positivist, who created the conflict of systems between international and internal law, these two branches of juridical knowledge are conceived as being separated and fenced-off from each other. The dualist option, common to Triepel and Anzilotti[2] helps to establish the prestige of a doctrine which defines itself as positivist. Each juridical order is posed as a self-sufficient object, using Kelsen's image of a pyramid, whose ramifications with other systems are ignored or reduced to the unreality of one juridical order absorbing the other, with the only other option which may be taken into consideration, being either the absorption of internal law by international law, or the colonisation of international law by internal law, of which, according to the terminology of Hegel, it is only a subdivision, *äusseres Staatsrecht* (*infra* note 44).

[1] Gaius, *Institutes*, I, 1, reproduced in Dig. I, 1, 9.

[2] Hans Triepel, *Völkerrecht und Landesrecht* (Leipzig, Verlag von C. L. Hirschfeld, 1899), p. 131, pp. 258–259, p. 264, pp. 289–323; Dionisio Anzilotti, *Il diritto internazionale nei giudizi interni* (Bologna, Ditta Nicola Zanichelli, 1905), reproduced in *Opere di Dionisio Anzilotti, Il Scritti di diritto internazionale pubblico,* tomo I° (Padova, Cedam, 1956), pp. 281–541, p. 448. The references which follow are from this edition. See also *Corso di diritto internazionale*, Vol. 1, Introduzione-Teorie generali, IVa, in *Opere . . .* t. I (Padova, Cedam, 1955) pp. 49–63, pp. 52–53. The third edition, the last one reviewed by the author, dates from 1927.

Before the positivist drift of the second half of the nineteenth century, international law[3] (also known as European Public Law), was a collection of rules, principles and practices common to European States and their offshoots on the other side of the Atlantic. Before betting on a European private law at the dawn of the third millennium we should remember this European *ius commune,* which belongs to a far distant past. The construction of a European private law[4] for the future rests on a constellation of juridical regulations from which positivist theory, whether monist or dualist, has failed to make a satisfactory synthesis.

The rest of this paper is divided into five parts:

—The *Law of Nations (ius gentium),* earliest formulation of a European Law.
—The conflict between an international treaty and internal law.
—Critique of the monolithic conception of each juridical system.
—The two instruments of European integration.
—The delimitation of a European private area.

2. *THE LAW OF NATIONS* (*IUS GENTIUM*), EARLIEST FORMULATION OF A EUROPEAN LAW

Until the end of the eighteenth century, and doubtless after that, the international custom was seen as

> "a system of rules, deductible by reason, and established by universal consent among the civilised inhabitants of the world."[5]

According to Blackstone, from whom this definition is taken, the law of nations is a branch of Natural Law, containing "principles of natural justice"[6] and inserting itself perfectly into the English constitutional tradition which put an end to the Royal power to introduce new laws or abrogate old ones:

[3] The expression "international law" goes back no further than Jeremy Bentham, who introduced it in 1789 in his *Introduction to the Principles of Morals and Legislation,* ch. XVII, n° 25 (London, The Athlone Press, 1970), p. 296.

[4] The distinction between private and public law is itself debatable. As we shall see later, the protection of human rights has introduced into the public sphere relationships from that of private law.

[5] William Blackstone, *Commentaries on the Laws of England,* 1st ed. 1765–1769, 14th ed. with the last corrections of the author (London, Strahan, 1803), t. IV, chap. V, p. 66.

[6] *Ibid.*, p. 67. David Hume thus attaches the Law of Nations to Natural Law, seeing it as "*a system of morals, calculated for princes, much more free than that which ought to govern private persons" A Treatise of Human Nature* (1st ed., 1739, London, John Noon, reprinted Oxford at the Clarendon Press), Bk III, Part II, Section XI, *Of the Law of Nations*, p. 568, the italics as in the text. In the following section, entitled *Of chastity and modesty*, Hume makes a bizarre comparison with the Law of Nations: "As to the obligations which the male sex lie under, with regard to chastity, we may observe, that according to the general notions of the world, they bear nearly the same proportion to the obligations of women, as the obligations of the law of nations to the law of nature." (p. 573).

"Therefore the law of nature (wherever any question arises which is properly the object of its jurisdiction) is here adopted in its full extent by the common law, and is held to be a part of the law of the land."[7]

It must be said that nothing could be further from a dualist[8] construction, but it is also accompanied by a definition of the object of international law which is much more extensive than that of today, to which Triepel and Anzilotti have so powerfully contributed. For Blackstone, the Law of Nations does not cover only relations between independent States but also those between individuals from different States.[9]

In truth, the *ius communicationis*, which, in the sixteenth century, Francisco de Vitoria placed at the foundation of *ius inter gentes*[10] regulated not only relations between individuals, or between an individual and a State, but also relations between States themselves. Joseph Story, who is a good witness of American juridical science at the beginning of the nineteenth century, not only as a Justice of the U.S. Supreme Court but also as the author of works on constitutional law and private international law, wrote that:

"The truth is that the Law of Nations, strictly so called, was in a great measure unknown to antiquity, and is the slow growth of modern times, under the combined influence of Christianity and Commerce."[11]

The *Law of Nations* includes the *Law Merchant*[12] and the law of the sea; it is not therefore surprising that, in pronouncing in a maritime case in his capacity

[7] Blackstone (note 5), p. 67.

[8] However, after having reaffirmed that "international law is part of our law and as such is the law of all the States of the Union", the Supreme Court of the United States gives to Blackstone's *dictum* an interpretation which would today be qualified as dualist: it applies only to international rights and duties and not to domestic ones: *Skiriotes* v. *Florida*, 313 US 69, 72–73 (1941).

[9] Blackstone (note 5), p. 66: in that intercourse which must frequently occur between two or more independent States, and the individuals belonging to them. See also Louis Henkin, "The Constitution and United States Sovereignty; A Century of *Chinese Exclusion* and its Progeny" 100 *Harvard LR* (1987), 853–884, 853, note 2.

[10] Vitoria, *De Indis*, III, 1–8, revised edition by H. F. Wright, *The Classics of International Law* (Carnegie Institute of Washington, 1917), 257 et seq. It is in the same passage of *De Indis* that Vitoria cites a phrase from the Institutes placed as an epigraph (*quod vero naturalis ratio . . .*) but he substitutes the word *gentes* for the word *homines*; thus the common law of relations between people, (the *ius gentium*) is transformed into a law regulating relations between nations or peoples (*inter gentes*).

[11] Joseph Story, *Commentaries on the Conflict of Laws, foreign and domestic* (Boston, Hilliard, Gray and Cy, 1834), §3, p. 4. For a development of this parallel between Story and Vitoria, see F. Rigaux, "Ius communicationis et droit international privé" in La *Escuela de Salamanca y el derecho internacional en America. Del pasado al futuro* (Universitad de Salamanca, 1993), pp. 67–76.

[12] On the *Law Merchant*, see notably Blackstone (note 5), I, ch. 7, V p. 273; James Lorimer, *The Institutes of the Law of Nations* (Edinburgh-London, W. Blackwood and Sons, 1883), t. I, pp. 379–383; Frederik Pollock, *Essays in the Law* (London, Macmillan, 1922), pp. 55–56, p. 68, p. 209; *The Law of Torts*, 13th ed. (London, Stevens and Sons, 1929), pp. 286–291; Roscoe Pound, "Mechanical Jurisprudence", 8 *Columbia LR* 1908, 605–629, 611; *Jurisprudence* (St Paul Minnesota, 1959), III, chap. 16, p. 398, pp. 429–432. For a detailed historical examination, see William Holdsworth, *A History of English Law* (1st ed. 1924), (3rd ed., London, Methuen and Co. Ltd., Sweet and Maxwell, 1973), vol. V, pp. 3–300.

of Circuit Judge, Story declared himself to be sitting as an organ of the *Law of Nations*.[13] According to an English tradition followed in the United States the customary international law is buttressed by conventional law and can be neither modified nor altered by State law.[14]

Thus understood, the international custom is formed by a convergent practice of the organs of the States, notably their courts, in default of its reception by international jurisdictions.[15] Custom is no more evolved than the law, and the practices of States are developing without it being possible to decide the precise moment at which a new practice becomes convergent enough to replace the solution used up until that point.

Triepel and Anzilotti were too imbued with statist legalism to put international custom in its correct place. The former rejects the Anglo-American tradition as a simple outgrowth of the common law with no relevance for a country of written law,[16] whilst the latter reduces it to an expression of statist voluntarism, not without affirming that the internal judge has the duty to observe it.[17]

3. CONFLICT BETWEEN INTERNAL AND INTERNATIONAL LAW

The belated and partial advent of international justice has meant that jurisprudential practices have been national in their origins and have remained so for a long time. A practice, which was convergent from the superior jurisdictions of the principal States, was qualified as "international".[18] A sample of this practice

[13] *United States* v. *La Jeune Eugénie*, 26 F Cas 832, 841 (C.C.D. Mass. 1822): "Sitting as I do in act of the law of nations . . .". See also the opinion of the Court expressed by Story in *Martin* v. *Hunter's Lessee*, 4 L Ed (1 Wheat 304, 335) 97 (1816) and the concurring opinion of Justice Johnson in *Gibbons* v. *Ogden*, 22 (9 Wheat) US 1, 45 (1824).

[14] In *The Antelope* 10 US 337, 344 (1825), Chief Justice Marshall wrote for the Court: "As no nation can prescribe a rule for others, no one can make a law of nations". See other references in Roscoe Pound, "Common Law and Legislation", 21 *Harvard LR* (1908), 383–407, 394–396 and the references to jurisprudence of note 3, 394: Henkin (note 9) pp. 865–876. Comp. Frederick Pollock, *Essays in Jurisprudence* (1st ed. July 1896) 6th ed., London, Macmillan and Co, 1882, pp. 10–11; *A First Book of Jurisprudence* (1st ed. July 1896) 6th ed., London, Macmillan, 1929, pp. 281–291. In the first of these texts, Pollock criticises the doctrine of Austin, which, to conserve the customary nature of a command emanating from a Sovereign, sees nothing more in it than the affirmation of such a desire by the courts. Pollock retorts to this by saying: "The Courts decide whether an alleged custom is or is not binding not at their pleasure, but according to settled rules." (1882, pp. 10–11). Comp. Austin, *Lectures on Jurisprudence or the philosophy of positive law*, 5th ed. rev. and ed. by Robert Campbell (London, John Murray, 1885), t. I, pp. 101–103.

[15] On the application of custom by international jurisdictions, see notably the case in the International Court of Justice regarding military and paramilitary activities in and against Nicaragua, (*Nicaragua* v. *United States of America*), *ICJ Reports 1986*, 92–98.

[16] Triepel (note 2), pp. 128–155.

[17] Anzilotti, *Il diritto internazionale* . . . (note 2), pp. 510–515. On this point, the Italian author is close to the position of Austin contested by Pollock (*supra*, note 14).

[18] A well-known example is that of immunity from the jurisdiction of foreign States. It is a statist practice, originating from Belgium and Italy, which placed in favour the doctrine of the restricted immunity of foreign States, which later rationalised this practice. See F. Rigaux, *Droit Public et Droit Privé dans les Relations Internationales* (Paris, Pedone, 1977), p. 112. In extending itself to other countries, notably France and the United States, the practice of restrained immunity

before the blossoming doctrinal dispute is provided by the case law of the U.S. Supreme Court. A practice, which would subsequently be qualified as dualist, developed during the last three decades of the nineteenth century, imposing the provisions of a federal law on a conventional earlier obligation, the *last-in-time* doctrine.[19] The solution was first affirmed in relation to a situation which was not, strictly speaking, international. It was judged that the competence explicitly given to Congress by Article I, Section I, Paragraph 3, of the Federal Constitution regulating relations with the Indian tribes, allowed the lawmakers to revoke the terms of a "Treaty" formerly concluded with an Indian Nation.[20]

Some years later, two decisions on immigration adhered to the same solution. The first is about the compatibility with international law, of a tax of 50 cents per head being levied on immigrants under a Federal law, the Immigration Act. The Supreme Court responded by saying that no foreign State had complained, and referred back to *The Cherokee Tobacco* decision.[21] Five years later, a Chinese labourer, living in San Francisco from 1875 to 1887, temporarily returned to China (whilst possessing documentary permission to return to the USA), was refused entry to American soil due to a law of 1 October 1888 highly restrictive of Chinese immigration. A Sino-American treaty was invoked, and, as in the earlier case, the Court upheld two arguments: firstly that the Chinese Government had already derogated from the Treaty, and secondly that the more recent law overruled the earlier one.[22]

Motivated by the equality of status between a treaty and national law, the *last-in-time* doctrine has remained a constant of American jurisprudence.[23] However, it is accompanied by a venerable provision, ceaselessly reaffirmed, to believe that Congress cannot be presumed to have had the intention to transgress an international obligation of the State.

received the status of an international custom. Thus, in addition to their own function as organs of the State, national jurisdictions also help create international law.

[19] See notably Henkin (note 9); Jonathan Turley, "Dualistic Values in the Age of International Legisprudence", 44 *Hastings LJ*, 1993, 185–272, 227–232. The *last-in-time* doctrine, when faced with conflict between two sources of law, gives priority to the most recent one. It implicitly consists of keeping the international treaty "equipollent" to the law (an expression used by the Belgian *Cour de Cassation* in a case of 27 May 1971; *Etat Belge* c. *SA Fromagerie franco-suisse, Pas.*, 1971, I, 886).

[20] *The Cherokee Tobacco Case*, 78 US 616 (1870). On the nature of "Treaties" concluded with the Indians, by the Colonial authorities and, later, by the US Government, see F. Rigaux, "L'autorité du juge constitutionnel: le droit fédéral des Indiens à la Cour suprème des Etats-Unis" in *Le juge: une figure d'autorité* (L'Harmattan, 1996), pp. 409–458, pp. 423–426, p. 433; Mike Townsend, "Congressional Abrogation of Indian Treaties: Reevaluation and Reform", 98 *Yale LJ*, 1989, 793–812, 795–798.

[21] *Head Money Case, Edge* v. *Robertson,* 112 US 580, 597–599 (1884).

[22] *Chinese Exclusion Cases, Chae Chon Ping* v. *United States,* 130 US 581, 9 S Ct 623 (1889), with reference to *Head Money Case*, 9 S Ct 627–628. See also *Alvarez Sanchez* v. *United States,* 216 US 167 (1910). As the matter had not been explicitly decided by the Treaty of Cession (from Spain to the USA) it remained uncertain; in any case, the posterior US law had to prevail (216 US 175–176).

[23] *Whitney v. Robertson* , 124 US 190, 194 (1888); *Lauritzen v. Larsen,* 345 US 576 (1953).

> "An act of Congress ought never be construed to violate the law of nations if any other construction remains possible."[24]

This "canon of interpretation" is not only applied to federal law suspected of transgressing international law, but also in two other sets of circumstances. The first is closest to the subject-matter of this paper; whilst the federal lawmaker had the power to legislate for a situation in another country, his acts only carried weight within US territory. So the law has to be interpreted in the light of territoriality, and, without agreement to the contrary, it cannot be enforced in other countries.[25] This canon of interpretation is accordingly closer to the presumption of conformity of law to international law than international custom, which is sometimes invoked to support the territoriality principle.[26]

The second series of hypotheses aims at verifying the conformity of an ordinary law to a constitutional provision. The same canon of interpretation is in force, the presumption of the constitutionality of the law. Thus, this law receives the interpretation most favourable to its constitutionality, according to the doctrine of "constitutional doubt". This third hypothesis is distinguished from the two preceding ones by their respective effects: if the law is "clearly" unconstitutional the judges must stop applying it, whilst the application of the *last-in-time* doctrine imposes the most recent law over the treaty, and the territoriality principle accepts an impenetrable barrier to the extraterritorial effect of a law if such was the intention of the legislator. On the other hand, the three applications of the canon of interpretation suffer from the same handicap well expressed by the concept of "constitutional doubt". The implementation of the method supposes that we can distinguish a sure interpretation from one which is less so. However, the degrees of incertitude would be of little importance, as any doubt of the unconstitutionality would allow the judge to overturn the objection. But a more detailed examination of a long line of decisions, almost always followed by dissident opinions, reveal the approximations of the terminology.

For law to resist doubt of its constitutionality, it suffices that the interpretation advanced to its support be "fairly possible".[27] The same interpretation can

[24] *Murray* v. *The Charming Betsy*, 6 US (2 Cr) 64, 117–118 (1804). See notably Curtis A. Bradley, "The Charming Betsy Canon and separation of Powers: Rethinking the Interpretation Role of International Law", 86 *The Georgetown LJ* (1997), 479–537; Peter HAY, "Zur extraterritorialen Anwendung US-amerikanischen Rechts", 60 *Rabels Z* (1996), 303–319, 313.

[25] See the opinions of Justice Holmes in *American Banana Co.* v. *United Fruit Co.*, 213 US 347, 357 (1909). More recently, *Foley Bros. Inc.* v. *Filardo* 336 US 281 (1949); *Lauritzen* v. *Larsen*, 345 US 576, 577–578 (1953); *McCullock* v. *Sociedad Nacional de Marineros de Honduras*, 372 US 10 (1963); *Equal Opportunity Commission* v. *Arabian American Oil Cy and Aramco Services Cy.*, 499 US 244 (1991). In this last case, as in *American Banana*, the restrictive interpretation used by the Court has the effect of removing from American companies operating abroad certain protective measures for Third-Parties or workers laid out in American law.

[26] See for example *McCullock* (note 25): "In addition, our attention is called to the well-established rule of international law that the law of the flag state ordinarily governs the internal affairs of a ship. "(372 US 20). The same decision also evokes the preoccupation with avoiding conflict between *lex fori* and a foreign law (20–22).

[27] *United States* v. *Jin Fuey Moy*, 36 S Ct 658, 659, (1916); *Panama R. Co.* v. *Johnson*, 264 US 375 390 (1924); *Crowell* v. *Benson*, 285 US 22, 62 (1932); *Almandarez-Torres* v. *United States*, 118 S Ct 1219 (1998), J. Scalia *dissenting* at 1243.

prevail on "the literal sense".[28] Even if "the language of the law is rather complex", the question must be considered in its context, aimed in one direction.[29] For the Court to be able to overturn the doubt of constitutionality the legislative provision must be able to reasonably receive two interpretations.[30] Of the alternative interpretations, the judge must overturn that which would be "manifestly contrary to the intention of Congress".[31] Finally, the notion of "doubt" itself needs to be qualified: "serious doubt",[32] "grave doubt", or "doubt gravely",[33] "serious constitutional problems";[34] significant constitutional question" and "serious likelihood that the statute will be held unconstitutional".[35]

Not only is the terminology variable, but, as indicated in notes 27 to 37, the judges do not hesitate to multiply the motives of their decision as if none of these sufficiently convinced them. To decisions finding the doubt insufficient to result in unconstitutionality (often accompanied by dissident opinions), must be added decisions declaring a law of Congress unconstitutional whilst according to the dissenting opinions the Court could have avoided such a decision.[36] The presumption of conformity to international law, like the presumption of constitutionality, could be judged a clumsy technique avoiding open conflict,[37] but the first has the advantage of keeping the powers of the lawmaker within the limits fixed by international law, according to the interpretation given by the State judge.

[28] *United States ex rel. Attorney General of the United States* v. *Delaware and Hudson Co.*, 29 S Ct 527, 536 (1906); despite the literal sense of some of the prohibitions, they should all be construed as to accomplish the result intended.

[29] *Almanderez-Torres* (note 27), 118 S Ct 1228.

[30] *Delaware* (note 28) 29 S Ct 535–536, reasonably susceptible of two interpretations.

[31] *Edward J DeBartholo Corp.* v. *Florida Gulf Coast Building and Construction Trades Council*, 485 US 568, 575 (1988): "unless such construction is plainly contrary to the intent of Congress". The intention of Congress, decoded by the Court, is also in the forefront in *Federal Trade Commission* v. *American Tobacco Co.*, 264 US 298, 305–307 (1924).

[32] Opinion of Justice Holmes in *Blodgett* v. *Holden*, 275 US 142 148 (1928); *Crowell* (note 27), 285 US 62.

[33] *Delaware* (note 28), 29 S Ct 536; *Jin* (note 27), 36 S Ct 659; *Almandarez-Torres* (note 27), 118 S Ct 1228.

[34] *Edward* (note 31), 485 US 575.

[35] *Almandarez-Torres* (note 27), 118 S Ct 1228. A traditional solution, already seen in *Ogden* v. *Saunders*, 6 L Ed (12 Wheat. 213), 606, 625, (1827) is "to presume in favour of its validity, until its violation of the constitution is proved beyond all reasonable doubt". The solution had already been extended to the presumption of conformity of a national law to the Federal Constitution in *Fletcher* v. *Peck*, 10 US (6 Cranch) 87, 127 (1810): "such that the judge feels a clear and strong conviction of their incompatibility".

[36] *Kuhn* v. *Fairmont*, 215 US 348, 372 (1909), J. Holmes *dissenting; Erie Railroad Co.* v. *Tompkins*, 304 US 64, 87, 91–92, (1938), J. Butler and J. Reed *dissenting*; *Rust* v. *Sullivan*, 111 S Ct 1759, 1788–1789 (1991), J. O'Connor *dissenting*.

[37] Without, however, "the worry of sparing a difficulty cannot be pushed to the point of transformation in equivocation" *Rust* (note 36) citing *George Moore Ice Cream Co* v. *Rose*, 289 US 373, 379 (1933). In giving the law a restrictive interpretation which avoids the control of constitutionality, the judge arrives at the same result as if he had declared to be unconstitutional an interpretation which would have enlarged the field of application of the law. The restrictive interpretation reduces the problem of constitutionality, but thwarts the desire of the lawmaker to give the measure a wider bearing. See for example *NLRB* v. *Catholic Bishop of Chicago*, 440 US 490 (1979), J. Brennan *dissenting*.

Before asking whether the dualist reputation generally imputed to American jurisprudence (and its English model) is justified, it is advisable to succinctly remind oneself of the key points in the monist/dualist debate. These were clearly laid out by an advocate of the monist theory, Hans Kelsen, in the course he gave in 1926 at the Academy of International Law, entitled "The Relations Between Internal Law and International Law":[38]

> "One can conceive this particular relation in several ways:—either, considering the State order, that is to say internal law and international law, as two different systems of norms, independent of and thus foreign to each other, we could recognise a fundamental *dualism*;—or, admitting on the contrary a certain unity between them, we could comprehend them within a universal system, the *monist* view, which includes two variants, according to which we give preeminence to one or the other of the two elements: the theory of the primacy of internal law, or the theory of the primacy of international law."[39]

The position of Kelsen is decidedly monist and combats the "dualist construction" towards which "most authors lean".[40] The two masters of the so-called dualist school, Triepel and Anzilotti, do not employ this expression, used for the first time in 1914 by an Austrian internationalist, Alfred Verdross.[41]

Of the different criticisms Kelsen levels at the dualist view, the least founded is that which sees in it "a corollary of the dogma of the sovereignty of the State" with, as a consequence, "the complete submersion of international law".[42] Actually, when one rereads the basic texts of Triepel (1899) and Anzilotti (1905), one cannot fail to notice that they strongly affirm the primacy of international law over domestic law,[43] and the duty of State judges to apply and respect the rules of international law[44] as much as they can. It is true that they

[38] *Recueil des cours de l'Academie de Droit International,* vol. 14 (1926-IV), pp. 231–233.

[39] *Op. cit.*, p. 275. The italics are in the text.

[40] *Op. cit.*, p. 275.

[41] Alfred Verdross, "Zur Konstruktion des Völkerrechts", *Zeitschrift für Völkerrecht*, 1914, 329. See Giuseppe Sperduti, "The Principle of Sovereignty and the Problem of Relations between International Law and Internal Law", *Recueil des Cours de l'Académie de Droit International*, vol. 153 (1976-V), 319–410, 333.

[42] *Op. cit.* (note 38), p. 288. Chapter IV of the course (pp. 275–288) criticises the "dualist construction", whilst the two following chapters develop the two branches of the "monist construction" (pp. 289–320).

[43] Triepel (note 2), p. 131, pp. 258–259, p. 264, pp. 289–332; Anzilotti, *Il diritto internazionale* . . . (note 2), p. 448.

[44] Triepel, (note 2), §18, pp. 438–447. Entitled "*Anhang. Die Anwendung des Völkerrechts im Landesgericht*", the last paragraph is very brief on this point which is also the subject of Anzilotti's 1905 work, whose title (note 2) indicates quite clearly that it expands paragraph 18 of the 1899 work. On the duty of internal judges to apply international law, see notably Anzilotti, *Il diritto internazionale* . . . (note 2), pp. 433–436. In truth, the principal adversary of Triepel and Anzilotti is monism, with the preponderance of State law, which in Germany was founded upon Hegel's doctrine of the State, and conceived international law as a subdivision of public national law, *äusseres Staatsrecht*. The expression appeared in Hegel, *Grundlinien der Philosophie des Rechts*, 1. Aufl. 1821 (Hamburg, Felix Meiner, 1955, 1967) in the title of paragraph 330 (p. 284). It was taken up by influential German publicists, notably Jellinek and Bergbohm. According to the first, the limits which international law imposes on the State are freely accepted by it (*Selbstverpflichtung*) and it is significant that it uses a similar expression (*Selbsbeschränkung*) for determining the limits to which

affirm the respective autonomy of the two orders, but they are right not to make the obligatory force of State law depend on a delegation of competence from the international juridical order.[45] The sources and the objects of the two juridical orders do not coincide[46] resulting in one of the principal complaints levelled at dualism, to know the preponderance in each of the juridical orders of the sources of law which emanate from them. This explains that the internal judge cannot make a treaty prevail over a later law, but there is a problem of internal constitutional law, in the forbidding of internal judges to refuse to apply a law due to its unconstitutionality[47]. One finds here the convergence, already noted, between the two hypotheses where law is confronted with a superior commandment, either from international law or from the constitution of the State. Finally, we note that the "dualist" authors adhere to the interpretative canon of American jurisprudence, in that internal law must be interpreted so as to exclude any contradiction with an international obligation of the State.[48]

Has the dualist doctrine, as said in a critical manner elsewhere,[49] influenced the jurisprudence of the Permanent Court of International Justice, several of whose decisions and opinions discuss relations between international and internal law? Whatever the merits of the theory, such influence seems reasonable with regard to the influence of Anzilotti, the only judge to have served throughout the period of activity of the Court, which he presided over from 1928 to 1930.

It is not surprising that the Permanent Court, in its quality as supreme judge of the international juridical order, should have imposed this over the norms of internal law invoked by a State. From its first decision, the Court rejected the argument made by the defendant State, justifying an act of internal law which would have paralysed the execution of an international obligation.[50] Other decisions hardened the position of the Court on this point to an unnecessary degree:

the State submits itself within the internal constitutional order. See Georg Jellinek, *Die rechtliche Natur der Staatenverträge, Ein Beitrag zur juristischen Construction des Völkerrechts* (Wien, Alfred Hodler, 1880); *Die Erklärung der Menschen- und Bürgerrechte. Ein Beitrag zur modernen Verfassunsgeschichte* (Leipzig, Verlag von Duncker und Humblot, 1895). Hegel, Jellinek and Bergbohm are criticised by Triepel (note 2), p. 79, note 1, pp. 131–134. See also Anzilotti, *Il diritto internazionale* . . . (note 2), p. 51; "Il concetto moderno dello Stato e il diritto internazionale" (1915), reprod. in *Scritti di diritto internazionale publico* , II, 1956, pp. 617–630, p. 625.

45 *Il diritto internazionale* . . . (note 2), p. 449, p. 459.

46 Triepel (note 2), p. 27–62; Anzilotti, *Il diritto internazionale* . . . (note 2), pp. 319–322.

47 Anzilotti, *Il diritto internazionale* . . . (note 2), pp. 440–456.

48 Triepel, (note 2), pp. 397–400; Anzilotti, *Ildiritto internazionale* . . . (note 2), pp. 459–462.

49 Krystyna Marek, "Les relations entre le droit international et le droit interne à la lumière de la jurisprudence de la Cour permanente de Justice internationale", *Rev. gén. dr. int. public* , 1962, 260–298, 266; Michel Virally, "Sur un pont ux ânes: les relations entre le droit international et les droits internes", *Mélanges offerts à Henri Rolin* (Paris: Pedone, 1964), pp. 488–505, pp. 500–501.

50 *Case of S.S. "Wimbledon"*, 17 August 1923, *Hague Permanent Court of International Justice Publications*, Series A, no. 1, p. 6, p. 29. But this case also raises a much more interesting question, such as that of alleged conflict between two international obligations. See *infra*, the text preceding note 59.

"With regard to international law and the Court which is its organ, the national laws are simple facts, manifestations of the will and activity of the States, on the same level as judicial rulings or administrative measures. The Court is certainly not called upon to interpret Polish law as such, but nothing stops it from pronouncing on the question of whether, in applying the said law, Poland acted in conformity with the obligations imposed by the Geneva Convention with regard to Germany".[51]

What really constitutes a simple fact is less the Polish law itself, than the application given by the defendant State. Moreover, this fact is justiciable under international law, whatever its legality under internal law.[52] The individual opinion of Judge Anzilotti under the consultative opinion of 4 February 1932 expresses well the reserve which the Court must observe concerning internal law:

"The question submitted to the Court is purely one of Danzig Constitutional Law; international law does not come into the matter. Now, but it is neither arguable, nor is it argued, that the Court was created to be the organ of international law. [. . .] It follows that the Court is deemed to know international law; it is not deemed to know the internal law of different countries."[53]

Anzilotti concludes that the Court does not "occupy itself with national laws", except in two series of hypotheses: when examining them "from the point of view of their conformity to international law", giving as example Decision no. 7, or when such a law "regulates certain facts whose juridical value must be appreciated by the Court",[54] as was the case in the two decisions of 12 July 1929.[55]

The Ihlen Declaration gives an example of the method advocated by Anzilotti and generally followed by the Court. The Norwegian Foreign Ministry had made a verbal declaration which the Danish Government made use of during a disagreement over eastern Greenland. The opposing party submitted that the Foreign Minister, Ihlen, had no authority under constitutional law to bind his country. The dissenting opinion of Judge Anzilotti is very clear on the manner

[51] Decision no. 7, 25 May 1926, Case relative to certain Geman interests in Polish Upper Silesia, Case of the Factory of Chorzòw, *Permanent Court of International Justice*, Series A, no. 7, p. 19.

[52] In another decision on the same topic, the Court reaffirms the principle with regard to a Polish judgment, which, whatever the effect "from the point of view of internal law, [. . .] can neither efface the violation of the Geneva Convention stated by the Court in its Decision no. 7, nor take away from that decision one of the bases on which it is founded", decision no. 13, Case of the Chorzòw Factory, (request for indemnity), 13 September 1928, *Permanent Court of International Justice*, Series A, no. 17, pp. 33–34. This decision thus evokes the obligatory character of an international decision within the internal order.

[53] Advisory Opinion of 4 December 1935, compatibility of certain Danziger decree-laws with the Free City's Constitution, *Permanent Court of International Justice*, Series A/B, no. 65, p. 41, p. 61.

[54] *Ibid.*, p. 63.

[55] Case *re payment of Serbian loans coming from France*, decision no. 14; *Case re payment in gold of Brazilian Federal loans from France*, Decision no. 15, *Permanent Court of International Justice*, Series A, no. 20–21.

in which the international judge must understand the relations between international law and internal law:

> "In my opinion, we must recognise the existence of a constant and common practise of States, which attribute to Foreign Ministers, agents of the Head of State, the power of communicating with foreign diplomatic representatives on current affairs, in particular to declare to them what attitude will be taken on a given question by the Government in whose name they are speaking. Declarations of this nature are binding on the State. As for whether Norwegian Constitutional Law authorised the Foreign Minister to make this declaration, that is a question which in my opinion does not concern the Danish government: it was for Mr Ihlen to withhold his response until he had obtained the consent necessary under Norwegian law."[56]

Unlike the doctrinal theories which pretend to regulate like Sirius the relations between international law and internal law, the international judge contents himself with determining the juridical order to which it belongs and in the name of which is decided the status of internal law. From both sides it is a question of determining the place occupied by a source emanating from another organisation, and the method is close to that of the conflict of laws. Far from being inspired by a dualist construction (in the pejorative sense of the term), the solutions of the Permanent Court impose the rules of international law over the internal laws disdainfully qualified as simple facts. How do these solutions distinguish themselves from monism with preponderance of international law? In the Court's juridical order, international law overrides internal law not by means of its superior obligatory force but because it alone is in force there. Internal law is not, however, without effect in the international juridical order, as a source of subsidiary law (as in the cases of the Serbian and Brazilian loans), or in the form of "institutions of internal law which play an important role and are widespread on the international level". For example, the concept of the anonymous company, "institution created by States in a domain which is essentially in their national competence".[57]

The difficult encountered by doctrinal constructions is caused by the status of international law in the internal juridical order. Here, two principles are opposed. The superiority of international law over internal law conflicts with the duty of every organ of a juridical order to give priority to its own sources of law. This principle has rightly been defended by the dualist school. It also includes the duty of identifying in that juridical order the rules which determine the place to be occupied by other organisations. Two days after the decision of 5 April 1933 on the juridical status of Eastern Greenland, the Norwegian Government revoked the Royal resolution, contrary to the Decision of the

[56] *Juridical Statute of Eastern Greenland*, 5 April 1933, *Permanent Court of International Justice*, Series A/B, no. 53, p. 22, p. 91–92 (dissenting opinion of Judge Anzilotti). While qualifying his opinion as dissident, probably because of profound differences with the method used by the majority, Judge Anzilotti basically agreed with the bulk of the decision.

[57] 5 February 1970, Case of *Barcelona Traction, Light and Power Company Limited* (new request: 1962, *Belgium* v. *Spain*, second phase), *ICJ Reports 1970* , p. 3, p. 33, §38.

Court. One is stunned to read in a commentary of the Permanent Court's jurisprudence that this would be incompatible with the dualist doctrine.[58] If the monist doctrine had prevailed in Norway, the mere pronunciation of the Court's decision would have had the effect of obliterating the act of internal law incompatible with the decision.

The canon of interpretation observed by American jurisprudence (which is of equal bearing in European countries) implies both the presence of international law within the internal order, and the recognition of a hierarchical relation between the two juridical organisations. It makes no sense to believe that the internal lawmaker would have taken into consideration the obligations assumed by the State in the international order, unless he is conscious of such a duty. That the same canon of interpretation be applied to relations between the Constitution and ordinary law cannot but reinforce the recognition of the interpenetration of diverse juridical orders.

4. CRITICISM OF THE MONOLITHIC CONCEPTION OF EACH JURIDICAL ORDER

Whilst a custom can be universal or regional, treaties always institute a particular juridical order. One of the optical illusions of doctrinal theory, whether monist or dualist, is to have treated the international juridical order like an unambiguous system, coherent and fenced-in, forming a homogeneous bloc faced with internal law. Monism is particularly vulnerable in this regard, because it denies any pluralism within the international juridical order. In the fifth section, we will find several examples of conflict between concurrent international obligations, but already the first decision of the Permanent Court of International Justice shows such a conflict. The plaintiff States used Article 380 of the Treaty of Versailles, accusing the German *Reich* of having refused passage through the Kiel Canal for a British steamer bringing arms for Poland in its war against the USSR. Germany invoked its duty of neutrality under its internal law. Whilst the Permanent Court was right to impose the Treaty obligation over the internal law, it made the mistake, stated in two dissenting opinions, of not examining the rules of neutrality according to the international law in force. The dissents of Judges Anzilotti and Huber raise both the question of the interpretation of the Versailles Treaty (did it apply to a situation other than armed conflicts?) and the conflict between Article 380, guaranteeing free use of the Kiel Canal, and the regime of neutrality faced with armed conflict between two other States.[59] Quite curiously, the majority opinion is "more dualist" than the dissident opinion, which clearly evokes the existence of conflict between a conventional obligation and the customary law of neutrality, partially codified by the Hague Conventions of 1907. Such a conflict is elegantly solved if one gives

[58] Marek, op. *cit*. (note 49), p. 282.

[59] *Case of the steamer "Wimbledon"*, *supra*, note 50, dissenting opinion of Judge Anzilotti, pp. 35–40. Compare the dissenting opinion of the German *ad hoc* Judge, Schücking, pp. 45–47.

Article 380 an interpretation which makes it compatible with the rules of the law of neutrality.

In the advisory opinion of 5 September 1931, relative to the Customs regime between Germany and Austria, Judge Anzilotti sets himself apart on several notable points, whilst agreeing for the most part with the majority. Firstly, he believed that Article 88 of the Treaty of Saint-Germain as well as the Geneva Protocol of 4 October 1922 formed an obstacle to the conclusion of a Customs regime between two States so unequal as the German *Reich* and the Federal Republic of Austria. The individual opinion of Anzilotti contains a very fine textual analysis of these two international instruments. But, he interprets them in the light of a particular political context, that of the movements of opinion, in the two countries, favourable to the absorption of Austria by Germany. It also gives the notion of "economic independence" a meaning, which prefigures the developments, unforeseen at the time, of the new international economic order.[60]

A current example of conflict between international norms was revealed during the examination of the demand for the extradition of General Pinochet by the House of Lords. The conflict is between the immunity from jurisdiction of a (former) foreign Head of State and the duty to carry out an extradition treaty, reinforced by his alleged crimes against humanity. This conflict can be resolved, either by the interpretation given to the first rule (it is only in force during the exercise of the functions of a Head of State), or thanks to the supplanting of this rule by the "more pressing" duty to contribute to the suppression of crimes against humanity. Whatever the outcome, the question is not concerned with the relations between international and internal law; rather, it is a matter of international law alone due to the competing claims which it involves.

According to a definition, generally qualified as dualist, the sources of international law have as their object the relations between States, whereas internal law regulates the relations of individuals among themselves, and the extent of the powers exercised by a State over the persons under its control. Inspired by a strict positivism, this aspect of the dualist construction scrapped a proven tradition which included within the field of international law diverse parts of commercial law, private international law, and international criminal law. Without a doubt, the abundant jurisprudence of the Permanent Court of International Justice on the exercise of international judicial action clearly marked out the difference of status between the individual right of a foreigner whom the territorial State was accused of having attacked, and the right which the national State tried to assert in the name of its citizen. In Case no. 13 cited above (*supra*, note 52), given under the presidency of Anzilotti, the Permanent Court laid out very clearly the difference between the two:

[60] Advisory opinion, 5 September 1931, *Customs régime between Germany and Austria* (Protocol of March 19th, 1931), *Permanent Court of International Justice*, Series A/B, no. 41, p. 37. The individual opinion of Anzilotti (p. 55) is followed by the dissenting opinion of seven judges.

> "The rules of law which determine the reparations are the rules of international law in force between the two States in question, and not the law which governs the relations between the State which committed the tort and the individual who suffered the loss. The rights or interests of which the violation causes a loss to an individual are always found on another level from the rights of States to whom the same act could equally cause loss. The harm suffered by the individual is therefore never identical in substance to that which the State would suffer: it can only furnish an adequate measure of the reparation due to a State."[61]

Every blow struck by the organ of a State at the rights of a foreigner, every violation, within the internal order, of a normative provision of an international treaty does not *ipso facto* entail the transgression of an international obligation. In order to constitute that, it would be necessary to have another actor (using the example of diplomatic protection, the State having title to act) declare himself the victim of an event which only his action elevates to the rank of international illicit event, subject to the judicial settlement or negotiated agreement of the dispute. Within the internal order, according to a doctrine which no dualist has ever challenged, the State organ has the duty to apply and interpret its own internal law, and the treaties which are in force there, in such a way as to avoid all risk of calling into question the international responsibility of the State. However, it would be incorrect to think that such an organ itself transgresses an international obligation; it can only commit an illegal act according to internal law. The international illicit act is of a different nature: by putting two States face to face, it supposes that one State has taken over the claim of its citizen, which has to be honoured by the other State. The national judge or civil servant, whose blunder has set off the international action, disappears from the scene, their behaviour being nothing but a simple fact underlying the international illicit event. On this point, the dualist construction remains unwavering.

Most of the norms of international law are meant to be applied within the internal order. Such is the case, notably, for the privileges and immunities of Heads of State and the diplomatic corps. It is only in their internal order that States are able to respect—or violate—their international obligations. Most treaties currently in force relate to matters which in principle come under internal law, whether it be movement of goods and persons, conflict of laws, the recognition and execution of foreign judgments, or the reconciliation of pieces of legislation. The "political treaties", whose object is inter-State relations, treaties of peace or alliance, delimitation of frontiers, certainly have an important place, but one which is statistically marginal.

[61] *Permanent Court of International Justice*, Series A, no. 17, p. 28. It refers to a constant jurisprudence which appears from the second case decided by the Permanent Court: the affair of the Mavrommatis concessions in Palestine (*Greece* v. *United Kingdom*), 30 August 1924, *Permanent Court of International Justice*, Series A, no. 2, p. 12, and repeated in one of its last cases, the affair of the Panevezys-Saldutiskis Railway (*Estonia* v. *Lithuania*), 28 February 1939, *Permanent Court of International Justice*, Series A/B, no. 76, p. 18.

For an international norm to be of "direct" application within an internal order, means that it is a source of rights and obligations for the individual citizens, and that judges and other organs of the State are required to apply it in the same way that they would apply the laws of the State.[62] The rule applies without reserve for international custom, which has no need of a formal act of reception to become part of a country's domestic law, but difficulties may arise as regards treaties.

The direct application of a conventional norm in an internal order of contracting States was affirmed for the first time by the Permanent Court of International Justice in a unanimous advisory opinion pronounced under Anzilotti's Presidency.[63] The passage is too well known to reproduce it here. We will limit ourselves to recalling three elements. The first is the exceptional nature of the solution: in principle, an international agreement "cannot, as such, directly create rights and obligations for individuals".[64] But, and this is the second point, the intention of the contracting parties can have been to derogate from this principle: the direct application depends on an agreement of wishes and not on a unilateral decision from each State. Thirdly, the Court concluded that this had been, in this case, the wish of the States:

> "The text and the general tenor of *Beamtenabkommen* shows that the provisions of these Acts are directly applicable between the officials and the administration."[65]

The elegance and firmness of the language are notable:

> "The adoption by the parties of determined rules, creating rights and obligations for individuals, and capable of being applied by the national tribunals."[66]

and,

> "the provisions of this act are directly applicable".[67]

In its conclusion, the advisory opinion deviates from an article of faith in the dualist *credo*:

> "It follows that article 9 of *Beamtenabkommen* must not be interpreted as making the applicability of the provisions of *Beamtenabkommen* depend on their incorporation in a Polish regulation."[68]

[62] That is to say according to the rules of procedure and judicial/administrative organisation of each State. Such as, for example, the dispositive principle (*Verhandlungsmaxime*) which can limit the power of a civil judge to apply a norm which neither party has taken advantage of.

[63] Advisory opinion no. 15, *Jurisdiction of the courts of Danzig*, 3 March 1928, *Permanent Court of International Justice*, Series B, no. 15. The unanimity is all the more remarkable because the two *ad hoc* judges were present.

[64] *Ibid.*, p. 17.

[65] *Ibid.*, p. 18.

[66] *Ibid.*, pp. 17–18.

[67] *Ibid.*, p. 18.

[68] *Ibid.*, p. 20. Comp. on this point Anzilotti, *Il diritto internazionale* . . . (note 2), p. 366, p. 369 and note 56, pp. 370–381, pp. 421–424.

This is the point by which the advisory opinion of 3 March 1928 seems to deviate the most from certain traditional forms of dualism: in England and the United States the provisions of a treaty could not be invoked before the courts if they had not been incorporated in an Act emanating from the national legislature. The formalities, such as Parliamentary assent, which the constitutions of most Continental States require for the application of certain treaties within the internal order, do not have exactly the same nature in the constitutional order, because it is not required that each of the articles of the treaty (or the Act which reproduces its terms) is the object of a distinct debate or vote. However, the formalities of reception and incorporation of a treaty do not concern the direct effect of certain of its provisions but the immediate application of the whole of the treaty within the juridical order of the States, which have adhered to it.

Under neither of its two variations is the monist vision corroborated by the doctrine of direct effect. The conventional international norm, applicable in the internal order, is no more incorporated therein than the customary norm. Its interpretation obeys its own rules, and its heterogeneity is confirmed by the duty to seek the intentions of the norm's authors, not in the national Act, which, the case arising, introduced the treaty in the internal order, nor purely in the will of the negotiators of the State, but rather in the coming together of wills, and according to the rules of interpretation contained notably in the Vienna Convention on the law of treaties.

As for the provisions of post-war constitutions, which lay down the superiority of international law over internal law, they can be interpreted in two ways: monist, if one wants to see in them a clear affirmation of the subordination of one to the other, but also dualist, because it is the constituent nation which fixes the international law statute in its own internal order.[69]

The difficulty of linking the errors of case law to an exclusively monist or dualist explanation is again shown by the following observations. The ingenuity with which American judges try hard to unknot the conflict between an international norm and internal law, and the *last-in-time doctrine* itself, merit an implicit but certain affirmation of the direct applicability of such a norm in the internal order. The interpretation of international treaties by the domestic judge could have, in other circumstances, justified their removal. Thus, the U.S. Supreme Court decided that an extradition treaty did not form an obstacle to the American authorities taking an accused from the territory of the State, where he was found, rather than requiring extradition.[70] In the same way, the provisions of the Hague Convention on the obtaining of evidence abroad would not be exclusive of other procedures of the internal law.[71] However, the two

[69] Triepel had already made this observation in regard of similar articles of the Weimar Constitution and the Constitution of the first Austrian Republic Carl-Heinrich Triepel, "Les Rapports entre le Droit Interne et le Droit International" *Recueil des cours de l'Académie de droit international*, vol. 1 (1923), 77–121, 90–91.

[70] *United States* v. *Alvarez-Machain*, 119 L Ed 441 (1992).

[71] *Aérospatiale* v. *United States District Court*, 482 US 107 (1987).

decisions have been followed by dissident opinions, which are very critical (6–3 and 5–4). Even the judgments and advisory opinions of the Permanent Court of International Justice where one can recognise the influence of Anzilotti and the dissenting or concurring opinions of the same judge, do not let themselves all gather behind the banner of dualism. The notion of direct effect, which the Court unanimously approved in 1928, provides the most tangible example. Anzilotti's sensibility towards conflicts of international obligations does not correspond to the monolithic perception of international law, which is generally imputed to the dualist school. The numerous decisions and opinions given on the relations between internal and international law are much more differentiated than would appear from the caricatured image of dualist thought which currently holds sway.

5. THE TWO INSTRUMENTS OF EUROPEAN INTEGRATION

Signed in London on 5 May 1949, The Statute of the Council of Europe was the first instrument of European integration. Article 3 of the Statute stipulates that each member of the Council "recognises the principle of the preeminence of law and the principle by virtue of which each person placed under its jurisdiction must enjoy human rights and fundamental liberties". This was only a foundation stone on which would be built, in the following year, the European Convention on Human Rights, signed in Rome on 4 November 1950, which was considerably modified by Protocol no. 11 of 11 May 1994, entering into force on 1 November 1998.

Some years later, European integration took another form, first of all of by the conclusion of the Treaty instituting the European Coal and Steel Community, signed in Paris on 18 April 1951, followed by the Treaty of Rome of 25 March 1957 instituting the European Economic Community.[72] Several other international instruments have reshaped the system of Community integration, notably the Single European Act 1986, the Maastricht Treaty of 7 February 1992 (instituting the European Union), and the Treaty of Amsterdam of 2 October 1997.

Between the two series of instruments there exist certain parallel, but also notable differences. The first and most apparent of these is the diversity of their geographic scope. All of the European Union member states belong to the Council of Europe, but not vice versa. A second difference may seem at first to be an analogy, the institution of a jurisdiction for each of the two organisations. However, the respective functions of the European Court of Human Rights and the Communities' European Court of Justice are very different, as are the procedural mechanisms, which they use. Of the two, it is the former which seems most to conform to the generally accepted image of dualism, or, if one prefers,

[72] Its title was modified by the Maastricht Treaty by removing the adjective "Economic".

to the most traditional forms of international law. Undoubtedly, any person in a contracting State can raise an action against the State (usually the one of which they have citizenship),[73] which must then account for the acts and omissions of its organs before an international judge, who, however, must limit himself to sentencing the State. The European Court of Human Rights does not have the right to abrogate or strike down the judicial or administrative decision, which has engaged the international responsibility of the State. It is for the State itself to implement the consequences of the decision. The Court can neither order the State to take measures demanded by the applicant, nor annul the decisions pronounced internally.[74] Can one imagine a better illustration of the classic dualist definition? The partial international juridical order and the internal law remain autonomous and compartmentalised, each obeying its own rules. The interpretation and application of internal law are the responsibility of the national authorities alone.[75] Article 26 of the Convention, which adopted the traditional exception of the exhaustion of internal remedies, aims at leaving to contracting States to take care of the redressing of their alleged breaches.[76]

The function of the European Court of Justice (and, since its introduction, the Court of First Instance) is of an entirely different nature. While the direct access of the individual to the Court of Human Rights (and, before the coming into force of Protocol no. 11, to the Commission) is the essential element of the protection of fundamental rights, it is exceptional that the persons and companies coming into the scope of Community Law have a right of action before the Community courts. The integration of national tribunals into the system of Community jurisdictions has been pushed very far; it is these national courts which in principle apply Community law, but Article 177 of the EC Treaty has reserved to the ECJ an exclusive competence to pronounce on the incompatibility of derivative law with the Treaties, and, at least in certain cases, to interpret all the provisions of Community Law. This part of Article 177 establishes a schism between the application of law and its interpretation, but the Court has not strived to formulate abstract judgments of interpretation; rather it has

[73] Thus a form of international subjectivity is recognized for the individual, which dualist doctrine seemed to deny him. However, when Anzilotti affirms that in international law, during the period in which he was writing, there were no subjects other than States, he rejects the idea that it must always be thus because such a denial of principle would exceed the limits to which the theorist must confine himself in accordance with juridical positivism *Corso* . . . (note 2), p. 113.

[74] See for example the decision of 18 December 1987, Case of F v. *Switzerland*, *European Court of Human Rights*, Series A, vol. 128, p. 19, §43; 13 July 1995, *Nasri* v. *France*, vol. 320-B, p. 26, §50; 23 October 1995, case *Umlauft* v. *Austria*, vol. 329-B, p. 40, §46–47; 23 October 1995, Case *Palaoro* v. *Austria*, vol. 329-B, p. 41–42, §§50–51; 26 September 1997, Case *Mehemi* v. *France*, *Recueil*, 1997-VI, 1959, 1972, §43.

[75] Decision of 16 December 1992, Case of *Hadjianastassiou* v. *Greece*, *European Court of Human Rights*, Series A, vol. 252, p. 18, §2; 24 February 1994, Case of *Casado Coca* v. *Spain*, vol. 285-A, p. 18 §43.

[76] Decision of 9 December 1994, Case of *Lopez Ostra* v. *Spain*, vol. 303-C, p. 52 §38. The provision of the former Article 26 comes under Article 35, 1st paragraph, in virtue of Protocol no. 11. The two texts contain a reference to "principles of international law which are generally recognised".

intruded to quite a large extent on the domestic courts' exclusive power of application. When the prejudicial question of interpretation of a norm of Community Law arose, regarding the compatibility of a domestic law with this norm, the Court did not hesitate to pronounce, at least implicitly, on such compatibility, the internal judge's own domain.[77]

According to a method, which is much practised by judges, and especially by those who know themselves to be above the appeal process, the ECJ does what it declares not to be allowed to do. The Court underlines the difference between the Article 177 procedure, which does not permit it to "apply Community Law to a determined case, nor to decide on the validity of a national measure in regard of that", on one hand, and the Article 169 procedure, in terms of which the Court can point out the breach of the State,[78] on the other, but, meanwhile, it does do things from which it declares to abstain from.[79]

By the device of the "*acte clair*" doctrine, introduced to the ECJ by Advocate-General Lagrange,[80] the Court has practised a method similar to that of "constitutional doubt". If the question raised can be resolved without a doubt, the national judge need not send it on to the ECJ,[81] but in case of doubt, that is to say, doubt on the doubt, the question must be posed.[82]

In the two European juridical orders the notion of "direct application" of the majority of substantial norms, which they contain, has taken on such a scale as

[77] See notably the jurisprudence cited and commented on in F. Rigaux, *La Loi des Juges* (Paris: Odile Jacob, 1997), pp. 226–230.

[78] Decision of 12 November 1992, Joint Affairs C–134/91, *Kerafina-Keramische- und Finanz Holding AF* and *Greek republic, Recueil (ECJ Reports) I–5699*, 16, §16. See also, 7 March 1990, Case C–69/88, *Krantz GmbH* and *Ontvanger der Directe belastingen, Recueil (ECJ Reports)* I–583; 9 February 1995, Aff. C–412/93, *Soc. Imp. Edouard Lecler- Siplec* v. TF1 *Publicité S.A., Recueil (ECJ Reports)*, I–179. Article 169 Procedure, too, conforms to classic dualism. It is the State which is accused of violating a conventional obligation, and it cannot put forward provisions of its own constitution in its defence *ECJ*, 2 July 1996, Case C–473/96, *Commission* v. *Grand Duchy of Luxembourg, Recueil (ECJ Reports)* I–3207, pp. 3258–3259, §§ 37–38, with references to a constant jurisprudence. The parallel with the first decision of the Permanent Court of International Justice is remarkable (*supra* note 50).

[79] For a recent example which can be added to those noted in Note 77, see the decision of 23 October 1997, Case C–189/95, *Harry Franzén, Recueil (ECJ Reports)* I–5909, point 2 of the operative part affirms that articles 30 and 36 of the EC Treaty "are opposed to the national provisions reserving the import of alcoholic drinks to traders with licenses of fabrication or commerce under the conditions provided for by the Swedish legislation" (I–5979). Clearly, this legislation is incompatible with articles 30 and 36 already cited.

[80] In the conclusions of 13 March 1963 preceding the decision of 27 March 1963, Joint Affairs 28/62, 29/62, 30/62, société *Da Costa and others* v. *Netherlands Tax Administration, Recueil (ECJ Reports)*, 1963, 88–89. See also the conclusions of 25 June 1964 preceding the decision of 15 July 1964, Case 6/64, *Flaminio Costa* v. *Enel, Recueil (ECJ Reports)*, 1964, 1172.

[81] Decision of 6 October 1982, *Srl Cilfit* v. *Ministry of Health, Recueil (ECJ Reports)*, 1982, 3430, para. 16.

[82] As Laferrière, then Vice-President of the French Conseil d'Etat, whose doctrine manifestly influenced Advocate-General Lagrange (although he didn't cite it), wrote: "In doubt we must defer. If one hesitates, one must defer, because when one is embarrassed to say whether a question is doubtful or not, everything points to believing that it really is." (E. Laferrière, *Traité de la Juridiction Administrative et de Recours Contentieux* (Paris-Nancy, Berger-Levrault et Cie, t. Ier, 1896), p. 498. The circularity of the reasoning leaves the reader astounded.

to reverse the terms of the presumption, enunciated by the advisory opinion of 1928 on the competence of tribunals of Danzig: the presumption goes very largely in favour of direct application and is a significant trait common to the two instruments. It is in the internal order of States that the Convention of Human rights and Fundamental Freedoms must be applied, because it is there that rights and liberties are threatened, while the rules of Community Law have supplanted large sections of internal law. This is not to say that these rules are founded in the internal order. Even the provisions of Article 177 of the EC Treaty attest the heterogeneity of Community Law. The double monopoly of interpretation and of control of the validity implies that Community Law remains a specific order, which is distinct from the juridical orders of the member states. When the superiority of Community Law over the law of the member states is affirmed by the ECJ, it is no more than a rhetorical method of conferring on norms in force in a juridical order the exclusive value of a source of law for this particular command. It is from then on, not monist but dualist. On the other hand, when such an order enters into relation with another juridical order, with which it is not integrated, the dispute on the relations of systems reopens.

The maxims, which the ancient jurists applied to the new sovereigns, arising from the collapse of the Holy Roman Empire—*Par in parem non habet auctoritatem,*[83] *Rex superiorem non recognoscens in regno suo est imperator*[84]—can be transposed to the relations between the two institutional systems of European integration. Each constitutes an autonomous organisation with its own organs, whose actions are regulated according to the law, under the control of a supreme jurisdiction within its order. The law of which the ECJ "assures the respect in the interpretation and application of the present treaty" (EC Treaty art. 164) is primarily Community Law and sometimes international law generally.

The relations between Community Law, the legal system instituted by the European Convention on Human Rights, and the internal law of member states, can appear as the three sides of a triangle. The simplifications of monism and dualism cannot give a true picture of this. We will examine successively the relations between internal law and each of the two international systems and, later, the mutual relations of these two.

The judgments, successively pronounced by the ECJ[85] and the European Court of Human Rights[86] in two Irish cases, show that a typical situation can be apprehended by two series of rules emanating from each of the European legal

[83] Cited notably by Rolando Quadri, "Cours Général de Droit International Public", *Recueil des Cours de l'Académie de Droit International*, t. 113 (1964-III), 237–483, 254–256.

[84] Francesco Calasso, *Gli ordinamenti giuridici del rinascimento medievale* (2nd ed. Milano, Guffrè, 1965), pp. 249–252.

[85] ECJ, 4 October 1991, *Society for the Protection of Unborn Children, Ireland, Ltd.* and *Stephen Grogan*, Case C–159/90, *Recueil (ECJ Reports) I* I–4733.

[86] European Court of Human Rights, 29 October 1992, Case of *Open Door and Dublin Well Woman* v. *Ireland*, *European Court of Human Rights*, Series A, vol. 246-A.

orders, both directly applicable within the internal order. An Irish jurisdiction forbade a nonprofit organisation (a student organisation in the first case, a women's group in the second) from spreading information on obtaining abortions in the UK, since the life of the unborn child is protected by the Irish Constitution. Such an injunction could be judged contrary to the free provision of services guaranteed by Articles 59 and 60 of the EC Treaty, and also to the freedom of expression guaranteed by Article 10 of the ECHR. The ECJ had to rule on the matter by a preliminary ruling, before the Irish Supreme Court had to decide the case. The Human Rights Court had to wait until all avenues of internal repeal were exhausted. The ECJ decided that spreading information on freedom of access to a provision of services falls under Community Law, because the service was provided in a member state for a person residing in another member state. The Court considered that it included the freedom to put out information relative to the service offered, on condition that it was exercised by the service provider. In other words, this freedom was connected to the freedom of service itself, protecting commercial publicity, whereas spreading information by a non-profit organisation was outside the scope of Community Law. As for the European Court of Human Rights, it decided that the interference with freedom of expression did not satisfy the conditions laid down in paragraph 2 of Article 10: although it was stipulated in a statute[87] and furthered a legitimate interest, it was unnecessary in a democratic society and so infringed the principle of proportionality.

After the first decision, the Irish jurisdiction, which had asked for the preliminary ruling, decided that the injunction was not contrary to Community Law, while Ireland had been condemned for a similar injunction in the second case. However, there is no contradiction between the two solutions. Not only are they aimed at different kinds of cases, but, above all, they rest on the application of distinct rules. However, if one compares the two, Irish lawyers must conclude that a jurisdictional act could engage the international responsibility of the State for violation of Article 10. The same situation is subject to the different commandments of two international norms, which are directly applicable in the internal order. It involves a conflict of norms analogous to the conflict of laws of private international law, but following the example of this branch of law, for although they are different, the two norms are not irreconcilable. In his internal order, the judge must take into consideration the norm, which restrains the power of the State, i.e. that which supports freedom of expression.[88] This solution is not inconsistent with the declaration of the inapplicability of Community Law.

[87] But this affirmation is contestable. See F. Rigaux, note *Rev. tr. dr. de l'homme,* 1993, 335. Comp. the note under the decision of 4 October 1991, *ibid.*, 1992, 57.

[88] Really, the interpretation which the internal judge is invited to give to the *Open Door* decision can be more nuanced. The use made of the proportionality principle is made case by case and the internal judge can hesitate on the force of precedent of the decision in situations different to those examined by the ECJ.

The situation becomes more complicated if one considers more thoroughly the application of Article 10 ECHR in the Community's juridical order. After some hesitations, the ECJ accepted that the protection of fundamental rights formed part of this order in the name of "general principles of Community Law" applicable whether in virtue of constitutional norms common to member States, or even by reference to the relevant articles of the ECHR.[89] As neither the Communities nor the European Union are party to the Statute of the Council of Europe—nor can they because Article 4 says only States can adhere—the Convention is not as such in force in the Community juridical order.[90]

The application of general principles of law, under the form of a reference to the cited articles of the Convention, gives competence to it in virtue of a rule on conflict of laws. The Convention is applicable in Community Law, following the example of a foreign law in the internal order, and the analogy can be pursued if one adds that the ECJ follows the interpretation given to a specific article by the European Court of Human Rights.[91]

Going back to the cases of *Grogan* and *Open Door,* it must be asked what would have happened if the Court of Justice had followed the conclusions of its Advocate-General proposing to examine as well the validity of the injunction with regard to Article 10 of the Convention, and to admit that the exemption clause of Paragraph 2 could be invoked by Ireland. The Court had the wisdom to move away from these conclusions, limiting itself to say that the general principles of Community Law were only applicable to the extent that Community law as such was, and, as non-commercial publicity did not come into the field of application of Articles 59 and 60 of the EC Treaty, there was no need to extend its deliberations to examine this question.[92]

At present it is enough to suppose that it would have done so, and to ponder next on the order of succession in the timing of the two cases. If the ECJ had decided that Article 10 authorised the interference of the State with the freedom of expression, it is doubtful that the European Court of Human Rights would have declared itself bound by this interpretation the following year. If the order of time had been reversed, it is very likely that, had it pronounced upon the application of article 10, the ECJ would have followed the lead of the European Court of Human Rights.

The relative position of the two legal orders is asymmetrical. While the ECJ regards itself to be bound to respect the fundamental rights guaranteed by the ECHR, the European Court of Human Rights has so far resisted any arguments

[89] On the evolution of the Court's jurisprudence, see notably Joe Verhoeven, *Droit de la Communauté européenne* (Brussels: Larcier, 1996), pp. 118–122.

[90] As the ECJ decided, from the viewpoint of its own juridical order, in Opinion 2/94 given in virtue of Article 228, paragraph 6, of the Treaty of 28 March 1996 (*Recueil (ECJ Reports)* I–1759).

[91] See notably the European Court of Human Rights, 16 December 1992, Case of *Niemietz* v. *Germany*, Series S, vol. 251-B, *Rev. tr. dr. homme*, 1993, 467, and the note F. Rigaux, 480–481. See, moreover, the case cited at note 115.

[92] Decision of 4 October 1991 (note 85), §31.

founded on the application of Community Law.[93] It has, however, recognised the European Union as forming a "specific juridical order", justifying the rejection of a discrimination complaint coming from a citizen of a third-party State against the immigration practices of the Community"

> "As for the preferential treatment given to citizens of the other member states of the Communities, there is an objective and reasonable distinction, in that Belgium, with these other member states forms part of a specific juridical order."[94]

This jurisprudence was confirmed by later decisions, the most recent having stated,

> "that the member-States of the European Union form a specific juridical order having installed an additional citizenship of its own."[95]

Thus, the European Court of Human Rights has recognised the existence of an autonomous juridical order with which it is linked by systemic relations. It is not, however, a coincidence that equal recognition intervened in a domain—immigration regulation—where the Court is tremendously inclined towards the sovereignty of the State.

In principle, there is no doubt that the member states of the Community could not, by the transfer of their competences to the Community, escape from previous obligations, which they had contracted in virtue of their adhesion to the European Convention on Human Rights. A decision of the European Commission of Human Rights confirms this interpretation of the systemic relations between the two legal orders. As the Community organs regard themselves to be bound by the human rights, under the control of the ECJ, the defendant member state cannot be held responsible for a violation of the ECHR.[96] Piquantly, the same argument has been used by the German Constitutional Court in abstaining from verifying whether secondary Community Law transgressed the human rights guaranteed by the Basic Law "as long as" (*solange*) the ECJ controls the conformity of derivative rules of law to the general principles of Community Law, the Federal Constitutional Court will abstain from superimposing its own control.[97] German and Italian[98] constitutional case law have a dualist resonance, unsurprisingly as these are the countries where the doctrine was born and has never lost its influence. Nevertheless, it must be admitted that

[93] See for example the decision of 15 November 1996, Case of *Cantoni* v *France*, *Recueil (ECJ Reports)*, 1996-V, no. 20, 1614, 1628, §30. The occasion, alleged by the French Government, was that Article L 511 of the Public Safety Code was inspired almost word for word by the Community Directive 65/65 did not take away from the application of Article 7 of the Convention.

[94] Decision of 18 February 1991, Case *Moustaquim*, *European Court of Human Rights*, Series A, vol. 193, p. 20, § 49.

[95] Decision of 7 April 1996, Case *C.* v. *Belgium*, *Recueil (ECJ Reports)*, 1996-III, no. 12, 948, § 38.

[96] European Commission for Human Rights, 9 February 1990, *M. & Co.* v. *Federal Republic of Germany*, *Rev.tr.dr.homme*, 1991, 395, note F. Rigaux. This solution is not above criticism.

[97] *BverfGE* 29 May 1974, *Solange I*, *BverfGE* 37, 271; *Rev. trim. dr. eur.* 1975 316; 22 October 1986, *Solange II*, *BVerfGE* 73, 339; *Rev. trim. dr. eur.*, 1987, 537. The expression "solange" appears in the motivation of both decisions *BVerfGE* 37, 271, 285 and *BVerfGE* 73, 339, 387.

[98] Corte constituzionale, 27 December 1973, n. 183, *Giur. cost* 1973, 2401, note Paolo Barile.

a constitutional jurisdiction cannot easily abdicate the responsibility, which it has been given to verify the conformity to the Constitution of sources of law applicable in the internal order. Reiterated by the German Federal Constitutional Court, the *solange* formula effects a diplomatic or political compromise between an ashamed dualism and an unavowed monism.

The decisions pronounced by the German Constitutional Court on the validity of modifications to the Basic Law, made in order to authorise ratification of the Maastricht Treaty[99] and to justify the introduction of the Single Currency,[100] are also wonderful constitutional feats. If the principle of popular sovereignty is one of the intangible values of a State's constitution, the transfer of competences, which are extensive and in practice irreversible, to organs which need not justify their acts before an assembly elected by the sovereign people, is hard to reconcile with this principle.[101] That a particular international jurisdiction only applies the international Treaty, which instituted it, is again shown by a decision of the European Court of Human Rights. A Danish jurisdiction had sentenced a journalist, held responsible for broadcasting racist insults uttered by people he was interviewing, to pay a fine. The Court condemned Denmark for violation of Article 10 of the ECHR.[102] However, this State was also party to the Convention of 21 December 1965 on the elimination of all forms of racial discrimination. It was therefore obliged to prevent and repress all incitation to racial hatred. The European Court did not as such consider the conflict of treaties, which the Danish judge had to face. The ability to repress a form of expression subject to the protection of Article 10, 1st Paragraph, was examined from this angle and not as a duty imposed in virtue of another international treaty, which the legislature had put into effect by inserting a ban on inciting racial hatred into its Penal Code. As a jurisdiction of the legal order instituted by the ECHR, the European Court of Human Rights was not capable of judging an (alleged) conflict between that Convention and another treaty, which was not in force in this legal order. It was in the Danish internal order that the litigants and the judge were put face to face with two different obligations: a triangular relationship, indeed, with the domestic judge being the arbiter of a conflict of treaties in default of an international jurisdiction in respect of which the European Convention of Human Rights would be only a treaty like any other.

It is equally in the internal order that a conflict between Community law and the conventions of the Council of Europe must be unravelled. For example, the Convention of 28 January 1981 for the protection of persons in respect of automated treatment of personal information, which amplified the legal principle in

[99] *BverfGE* 12 October 1993, *BVerfGE* 89, 155; 98 *International Law Reports* (1994), 196.

[100] *BverfGE* 31 March 1998, *NJW* 1998, 1934.

[101] For a critical analysis of the decision of 12 October 1993, and decisions of the French *Conseil Constitutionnel* on the Maastricht Treaty, see F. Rigaux, *op. cit.*, (note 77), pp. 214–220.

[102] European Court of Human Rights, Case of *Jersild* v. *Denmark*, *European Court of Human Rights*, Series A, vol. 298.

respect of guarantee of privacy in Article 8 of the Convention of 4 November 1950. Also, Directive 95/46/CE of the Parliament and the Council, issued on 24 October 1995, on the protection of physical persons with regard to private data and its free circulation.[103] The member states of the two international organisations first put into effect the Convention of 28 January 1981 (which is no more directly applicable than the Directive) and then modified (or started to modify) their legislation in order to comply with the Directive's requirements. The principal problem is not that the protective provisions of the two instruments are not identical and that their respective fields of application do not entirely coincide. It is rather the competition between two parallel legal remedies.

The application of the national law, which is trying hard to satisfy two international obligations, could be the subject of a preliminary ruling of the ECJ, in order to obtain the interpretation of a provision of the Directive and to permit the national judge to decide whether or not the national law conforms to this interpretation. After the exhaustion of internal remedies against this decision, one of the parties is free to allege a transgression of Article 8 of the ECHR, for the interpretation of which the European Court of Human Rights will consult the Convention of 28 January 1981.[104] Whatever the interpretation given by the ECJ to the Community Directive, the Court of Human Rights is competent to verify the conformity of the national judicial decision to a different instrument, the only one which is pertinent for it.

It remains finally to question the effects of a judicial decision on a legal order other than the one from which it emanates. Article 192 of the EC Treaty organises a procedure to become entitled to execution in the internal order of member states. The decision of the European Commission of Human Rights of 9 February 1990 (*supra*, note 96) concerned a case of the application of Article 192. The decisions given by the European Court of Human Rights against the States had long only obligatory force: the condemned State had to "take such measures necessary to carry out the decision of the Court" (EC Treaty, art. 171, 1). The State could now be ordered to pay an indemnity (EC Treaty, art. 171, 2 al. 2 and 3). The European Court of Human Rights could give the injured Party "fair satisfaction" in addition to the verdict given against the State (Conv. art. 50, replaced by article 41 in virtue of Protocol no. 11). On the other hand, as has already been indicated, the decisions of the Court could not annul the judgments and rulings of the internal order, which had engaged the international responsibility of the member state. Therefore, if the internal law had not organised a procedure of retraction, these acts would keep their internal validity, depending on the administrative measures of the government. The "fair satisfaction" of Article 41, and the indemnities which the State could be forced to pay within the

[103] JOCE No. L 281/31 of 23 November 1995.

[104] For a precedent, see the decision of 25 March 1993, Case of *Costello-Roberts* v. *United Kingdom*, vol. 247-C, p. 60, § 35, being founded upon the UN Convention of 20 November 1989 on the Rights of Children.

internal order compensate for the prejudice which cannot be made up for in kind. A comparison with classic international case law is imperative.

The courts and tribunals, having posed the preliminary question of validity or interpretation, must conform to the decision of the ECJ, but if they do not, or if they fail to pose a question which they should have, the only remedy is action in breach of conduct against the State in conformity with articles 169 and 170 of the EC Treaty. Here too the old dualist model gives a better impression of the state of the law than the aspirations of monism.

As for interpretative decisions, notably those of the European Court of Human Rights, they are incorporated in the interpreted provision and are also obligatory in the internal order. Their force is that of a precedent; As the Permanent Court of International Justice has stated, the law of a State must be interpreted in light of the court decisions of that State (see the cases cited in note 55). This vision has not aged and can be applied by analogy to the force of precedent of a ruling of the European Court in the internal order.

6. THE DELIMITATION OF A PRIVATE EUROPEAN SPACE

The competition of two European instruments having approximately the same purpose renders at first sight sceptic on the notion of a European private law. In admitting that the protection of private life relates to private law—although in many ways it belongs to the field of constitutional law—the jurist finds himself in the presence of two channels of normativity. It matters little that the formulations of the two instruments are similar, while they both use vague concepts and give way to the jurisdictional application of the method of balancing of interests,[105] which confers a decisive weight on the controls exercised respectively by the ECJ and the European Court of Human Rights.

The direct applicability of an international norm in the internal order, with its power to supplant any contrary rule of national law, would seem to be a decisive victory for monism, with preponderance of international law. So seem to reason, each in his own domain, the specialised jurists of Community Law or Human Rights. The dualism of the institutions of European integration confuse this simplified image: according to which method can we choose between two directly applicable norms emanating from different legal orders?

The procedural mechanisms instituted in each of the two systems do not provide an adequate response to such a problem. The supreme jurisdiction would, indeed, have a necessarily unilateral perspective, limiting itself to assert the sole superiority of the originating norm of its system over not only the internal law but also over the other international order(s).

[105] For a more detailed analysis, see F. Rigaux, "Libre Circulation des Données et Protection de la Vie Privée dans l'Espace Européen", *Festschrift für Ulrich Drobnig* (Mohr, Siebeck, 1998), pp. 425–441.

Several articles of the ECHR use concepts of internal law or refer implicitly to institutions governed by state law. The most significant, in this regard, is Article 8, which guarantees respect of private and family life. The notion of "morality" which appears in Paragraph 2 of Articles 8, 9, 10, and 11, once called "public morality" (art. 9), and the freedom of religion guaranteed by the same article take on different meanings according to the member-States. Except in two cases, which we will return to, the Court did not force the development of the State accused of violating the Convention, whilst it occupied a minority position among the member-States. One can, henceforth, advance the idea that in these domains the jurisprudence of the ECHR has contributed little to the formation of a European private law.[106]

Thus, despite the central place occupied in the scope of the Convention by the protection of freedom of expression, the Court excluded that "one could extract a uniform European notion of "morality" from the internal law of the contracting States".[107] The same moral relativism allowed the Court to decide that restrictions imposed by Irish law on dissemination of information about abortions in the UK was "a legitimate aim of protecting morality", in that "the protection guaranteed by Irish law for the right to life of unborn children rests, on the evidence, on profound moral values concerning the nature of life".[108]

To moral relativism is added the particularism of dominant religions which the Court tends towards, concerning the persecution of Jehovah's Witnesses in Greece,[109] and the repression of blasphemy in the Austrian Tyrol where "the Catholic religion is that of the majority of the population".[110] Now, contrary to the affirmations of the Court, it is not an attack on religious freedom, guaranteed by Article 9 of the Convention, for other currents of opinion or thought to use Article 10 to support spreading a minority belief, or to combat or contradict even majority opinions. In the Austrian case, as in the Greek cases, the Court gave to a dominant religion a support, which the principle of pluralism reinforced by that of freedom of expression should have commanded it to abstain from. Also, as the Court has said in earlier cases, it is these minority or unpopular opinions, which are most in need of the protective mechanisms of the ECHR.[111]

106 See F. Rigaux, "Interprétation Conventionnelle et Interprétation Évolutive" in *L'interprétation de la Convention Européenne des Droits de l'Homme*, Fréderic Sudre (ed.) (Brussels: Nemesis and Bruylant, 1998), pp. 41–62.

107 Decision of 7 December 1976, Case of *Handyside* v. *United Kingdom*, *European Court of Human Rights*, Series A, vol. 24 §48. In the same sense 24 May 1988, Case of *Müller and others* v. *Switzerland*, vol. 133 § 36.

108 Decision of 29 October 1992 (*supra*, note 86), 27, 563.

109 Decision of 25 May 1996, *Kokkinakis* v. *Greece*, vol. 260, and of 26 September 1996, *Manoussakis* v. *Greece*, *Recueil (ECJ Reports)* 1996-IV, no. 17, 1346.

110 Decision of 20 September 1994, Case *Otto Preminger Institut* v. *Austria*, vol. 295-A

111 Decisions of 7 December 1976, Case of *Handyside* v. *United Kingdom*, vol. 24, 23, § 49, of 26 September 1979, Case of *Sunday Times* v. *United Kingdom*, vol. 30, p. 40, § 65, 8 July 1986, Case *Lingens* v. *Austria*, vol. 103, 11, §41. American jurisprudence is in the same vein since *West Virginia State Board of Education* v. *Barnette*, 319 US 624, 642 (1943).

The justification of a decision of 25 November 1996, relating to the refusal of authorisation to distribute a video because of the UK criminal blasphemy laws, is more ambiguous than that of *Otto Preminger*. The Court maintained the idea already advanced in the latter case:

> "There is not yet, in the juridical and social orders of the member states of the Council of Europe, an agreement of views sufficient to conclude that a system permitting a State to impose restrictions on the dissemination of writings reputed to be blasphemous is not in itself necessary in a democratic society, and to find it consequently incompatible with the Convention."[112]

However, certain arguments of the Government, to which the Court seemed to adhere, evoke the erotic and even pornographic character of the film, which would constitute an entirely different juridical foundation for the banning of the film. Moreover, it referred to a case of precensorship, which, as Judge De Meyer pointed out in his dissent, would constitute a much more important blow to freedom of expression.

In the area of family relations and the regulation of sexual relations, the Court has not extracted from the comparison of systems of internal law a consensual interpretation of the notions of private life and family life, with two exceptions. It refused "an evolutionary interpretation", which would have allowed to deduce from Article 12, guaranteeing the right to marriage, the right to remarriage after the dissolution of a former marriage by divorce.[113] In the case of delay of remarriage, imposed by the Swiss Civil Code on those divorced for adultery, it was by a weak majority (9–8) that the Court condemned the defendant State for violating the principle of proportionality.

The case is interesting for its justification:

> "The fact that a country criticises, after a gradual evolution, an isolated situation regarding an aspect of its legislation, does not necessarily imply that this aspect infringes the Convention, especially in a domain—marriage—quite strongly linked to cultural and historical traditions of each society and to profound conceptions of the family unit."[114]

The conservatism of the ECHR is also shown in its jurisprudence regarding transsexuals, which shows not only a total misunderstanding of the phenomenon of transsexuality and an obsolete attachment to a morphological definition of sexual identity, but also an ignorance of the road taken by numerous European countries.[115]

[112] Decision of 25 November 1996, Case of *Wingrove* v. *United Kingdom*, *Recueil (ECJ Reports)* 1996-V, no. 23, 1937, 1971, §57.

[113] Decision of 18 December 1986, Case of *Johnstone* v. *Ireland*, vol. 112, 25, §53.

[114] Decision of 18 December 1987, Case of *F.* v. *Switzerland*, vol. 128, 16–17, §26.

[115] See notably the decision of 27 April 1997, Case of *X, Y, Z* v. *United Kingdom*, *Recueil (ECJ Reports)*, 1997-II no. 35, 619, *Rev. trim. dr. h.*, 1998, p. 121, note F. Rigaux, pp. 130–144. Also the decision of 30 July 1998, *Sheffield and Harsham* v. *United Kingdom*. One compares the more liberal solution of the ECJ in a decision of 30 April 1996, Case C–13/94, p. S., *Recueil (ECJ Reports)* I–2143. It is true that the attribution to a transsexual of a right guaranteed by a Community Directive does

In only two areas has the European Court of Human Rights truly adhered to a consensual and evolutionary definition of family life and private life. That is, in cases on the incompatibility with the former of discrimination against illegitimate children,[116] and the incompatibility with the latter of the criminalisation of homosexuality between consenting adults.[117] Two States in the first case, three in the second, were condemned for having kept in force legislation which had certainly not been deemed contrary to the Convention at the moment of their accession. A more recent decision set aside the application of Article 8 ECHR to the criminalisation of sado-masochistic practices between consenting adults.[118] The argument which they had used, that they were homosexuals and that therefore the disputed practices came under "private morality"[119] was overturned by the Court. Although it explained its decision by the right of a State to protect health, it didn't exclude "the right of a State to seek to discourage such acts in the name of morality".[120] Does this refer to a European conception of sexual morality, which would set aside the moral relativism of the *Handyside* and *Müller* decisions?

Another recent decision, this time for the ECJ, refused a same-sex couple the same social advantages available to cohabitees under company regulations.[121] As has already been said (note 115), when comparing decisions of the two Courts one must exercise caution. It is one thing to prohibit same-sex relations between consenting adults, with the threat to private life which that implies; it is another thing to deny same-sex cohabitants the benefit of measures designed for cohabitants full-stop. However, the ECJ expresses itself very explicitly on the jurisprudence of the Commission and Court of Human Rights denying transsexuals the right to marry. The reference to homosexuality is of little relevance, for two reasons: homosexuality and transsexuality are very different phenomena; also, extending the same rights to same-sex couples as other cohabitants poses no risk to marriage because it concerns an extra-conjugal relationship coming under Article 12. One could say that heterosexual cohabitation poses more of a risk to marriage than homosexual cohabitation.

The essential difference between the two Courts is their function. In interpreting Community law the ECJ has a freedom of interpretation as extensive as

not have the same weight as the condemnation of an accused State of having broken the law in respect of respect for private life, for not having adapted its legislation to take account of transsexuals. The very different functions of the two jurisdictions must always be borne in mind when considering their respective decisions.

116 Decisions of 13 June 1979, Case of *Marckx* v. *Belgium*, vol. 31, 28 October 1987, Case of *Inze* v. *Austria*, vol. 126, and of 29 November 1991, Case of *Vermeire* v. *Belgium*, vol. 214.

117 Decisions of 22 October 1981, Case of *Dudgeon* v. *United Kingdom*, vol. 45, of 26 October 1988, Case of *Norris* v. *Ireland*, vol. 142 and 29 April 1993, Case of *Modinos* v. *Cyprus*, vol. 249.

118 Decision of 19 February 1997, Case of *Laskey, Jaggard and Brown* v. *the United Kingdom*, *Recueil (ECJ Reports)*, 1997-I, no. 29, 120, *Rev. trim. dr. h.*, 1997, 733, note Michael Levinet

119 See note 118, § 45.

120 See note 118, § 51.

121 Decision of 17 February 1998, Case C–249/96, *Grant* and *South-West Trains Ltd.*, *Recueil (ECJ Reports)* I–636.

that of a constitutional jurisdiction or a national Supreme Court. The European Court of Human Rights, on the other hand, can only condemn or absolve a defendant State. It must not research the most plausible interpretation of the Convention, only an interpretation which the State could not oppose without infringing its international responsibilities. This explains the minimalist interpretations of many of the Court's decisions.

The European Court of Human Rights recently recognised that "a greater margin of appreciation" is left to contracting States when they regulate freedom of expression on questions capable of offending intimate convictions in the field of morality or, especially, religion".[122] Thus, the Court perseveres in an unhappy confusion of morality and religion, which occupy entirely different positions under the Convention: the first, but not the second, is mentioned among the aims, which States may legitimately pursue in interfering with freedom of expression. Freedom of religion is certainly guaranteed, but does not mean that religious beliefs (especially those of the majority) deserve protection against freedom of expression.[123] Even more, it must be considered discriminatory to other beliefs and opinions to maintain a selective protection of dominant religions against blasphemy.[124]

Another consequence of the "margin of appreciation" left to States is that in its application of the Derogation Clause of paragraph 2 of Articles 8, 9, 10, 11, the Court usually bases its condemnations on transgressions of the proportionality principle. It reasons as follows: the measure by which the State restricts liberty is provided for by law, it pursues a legitimate end, but, when it is unnecessary in a democratic State, it lacks of proportion between the harm and the counter-measures put in force. Thus, the first group among the cases commented on above expressed an insufficiently critical deference for the State's margin of appreciation (*Handyside, Müller, Otto Preminger, Wingrove*), whilst the second group condemned the State for violating the proportionality principle (*F. v. Switzerland, Open Door, Kokkinakis, Manoussakis*). All this does not give a clear message to the States: similar interferences with free expression can be made, on condition of being more circumspect and calculated.

In none of these fields has the Court of Human Rights contributed to the formation of a "European privacy law". It is doubtful that it will do so in the future, with the considerable geographical enlargement of the Council of Europe making consensual interpretation of the Convention's concepts of internal law even more complicated. Another consequence of the different configuration of the two European fields is that the distance between their respective jurisdictions may grow wider, with the ECJ giving the Convention, conceived as

122 Decision of 25 November 1996 (note 112), 1958, § 58.

123 See notably F. Rigaux, "L'Incrimination du Prosélytisme Face à la Liberté d'Expression" note under the decision *Kokkinakis, Rev. trim. dr. h.*, 1994, 144–150; "La Liberté d'Expression et ses Limites", *ibid.*, 1995, 401–415.

124 Guy Haarscher, "Le Blasphémateur et le Raciste", *Rev. trim. dr. h.*, 1995, 417–422; Jean-Manuel Lavalde, "La Liberté d'Expression et le Blasphème", note under the decision in *Wingrove*, *ibid.*, 1997, 725–732.

a set of general principles of Community law, an interpretation more respectful of fundamental liberties than the Court of Human Rights. The extension of the competences of the European Community, and the institution of the European Union means that the protection of fundamental freedoms will gradually become much more than just a complement to the original economic freedoms.

The doctrinal theories obscure rather than enlighten the reality of the multiplication of international legal orders, and the complexity of relations between them and the various legal orders of the States. The principle of the subordination of internal law to international law cannot give an answer faced with the competition of international juridical orders. Conflicts between internal and international law are often unravelled with the interpretation of norms. State tribunals strive to give internal law an interpretation imputing to the lawmaker a willingness not to infringe the international obligations of the State. This is undoubtedly, in the internal order, the best test of the interpenetration of the systems and of adhesion to the principle of hierarchy which necessarily controls relations between internal and international law. However, the international juridical order is itself plural. It imposes on the State conflicting obligations, and it would be exceptional that a judge with no links to one of the conflicting legal orders could arbitrate such a conflict. Neither the European Court of Human Rights nor the ECJ can be impartial judges of a conflict of a norm emanating from their own juridical order against another international norm. The internal judge is no worse placed to pronounce on the scope of the obligations contracted by a State, because he too, no less than the lawmaker, must try to make international law prevail over internal law, to be guided by an ingenious method of interpretation and by a correct evaluation of the interests at stake.

Outside the particular fields covered by the two instruments of European integration, do there exist other domains in which one can perceive the formation of a European private law? Is it possible to reconnect with the tradition of *Merchant Law*, of maritime law (and transport law in general) banking documents and credit instruments, which, flowering at the end of the Middle Ages were the spontaneous manifestations of a European private law, which later has been laid down in international treaties.

In the nineteenth century intellectual rights were the object of a similar convergence ending in the various Treaties of Union. Even if the field of application of these quickly became universal, their European origin was not in doubt. With the shift in world commercial centres, it is to be expected that Europe has lost the initiative in this field. The example of the Euro is significant: the establishment of a single currency is an attempt to adapt to the globalisation of banking power, and to cut a better figure in the financial exchanges, which Europe has ceased to dominate. The same is true for so many successive revolutions in the means of communication, the growing economic fields of entertainment, of sport, of celebrity, inspired the American *right of publicity*. The personalised notion of private life has been supplanted by the economic exploitation of individual characteristics, physical image and existential image (*Lebensbild*).

Also derisory are the current terms of the controversy about a European *ius commune*. Contrasts between Civil Law and Common Law have some significance in the fields of procedure, administrative law, and criminal prosecutions, but they are artificial in private law, more exactly, under different names the substantial rules largely converge. However, the new contractual figures, just as banking practices and telecommunications law are imported from the dominant economic and military power, leaving no room for a European private law. The example, mentioned earlier, of the link between protection of personal data, and its free circulation, confirms that the two European domains in which this matter is regulated are too strict. If we want to avoid "information paradises" being established outside the frontiers of one Europe or the other it is imperative to enlarge the spatial domain of the protection. There too it is a question of domains in which a universal law—or one with pretensions to such—tends to be installed, but it cannot be qualified as "European".

8

The Adjudication of Law and the Doctrine of Private Law

FRITZ JOST

1. THE LAW, RULES AND THE INDIVIDUAL CASE

When we are asked, what the law is, we might answer from the point of view of a system, which uses codified rules: "The law is what the codes say it is". We all know that this is an unsatisfactory answer, especially for common law systems, but also, to some extent, to the civil law tradition as well. We feel uneasy with this concept as law might be determined by non positive principles as well as by statutes.[1] Moreover, the reason for feeling uneasy with this statement is caused by the fact that the rules within the codes (mostly) are in force for a long time and are, thus, applied to an infinite number of individual cases. Therefore statutes must be abstract. As a result of this, the rules in the statutes, and the terms used within them, need interpretation, when they are applied to individual cases. Even the sentence "*interpretatio cessat in claris*"[2] cannot make us feel any easier. "Is there such a thing as clarity within a legal rule ?" is an interesting question which may be asked on closer scrutiny of the litigation and problems posed with the introduction of new statutes into the law.

If we take the above proposition as granted, one answer to the question of "What the law is" could be "The statutes which we find within the codes, being applied in a proper way, and following the rules of interpretation". Whether those tools or methods themselves are rules of law[3] is not a question at issue here. However, what we have to point out is the fact that in referring merely to the codified rules and the rules of adjudication and interpretation, we cannot give a reasonable answer to our initial question.

Taking into account particular facts or individual cases will not be sufficient either. Studying the law and the methodology of legal reasoning, we find out

[1] For a summary of the discussion on principles and policies see Langenbucher, K., *Die Entwicklung und Auslegung von Richterrecht* (München, Beck, 1996), p. 4.

[2] See Esser, J., *Grundsatz und Norm in der richterlichen Fortbildung des Privatrechts*, 3. Aufl. (Tübingen: Mohr, 1974), p. 177; Van Hoecke, M., *Norm, Kontext und Entscheidung* (Leuven, Acco, 1988), p. 71.

[3] We find those rules fixed in the older codes, for instance, §§ 6 pp. Austrian ABGB, § 46 Prussian ALR (Einleitung).

that we need much more rules and sentences than we find in statutes and rules of adjudication.

Let us take article 1382 Cc. "*Tout fait quelconque de l'homme, qui cause à autrui un dommage, oblige celui par la faute duquel il est arrivé, à le réparer*". As we know, the German Civil Code BGB has not adopted this wide frame application of that fundamental French statute of torts. According to § 823 sec. 1 German BGB the duty of compensation depends on the violation of special goods and rights.

In the common law we find various types of torts. Let us have a look at negligence. The name of this tort might give reasons to believe that everybody who causes damage, by negligent behaviour, to another person is obliged to compensate for that. However, the frame of application is not as wide as it may seem, neither in common law nor under French law. In France compensation is confined to special cases of "*faute*",[4] and, in the common law compensation is dependant on the breach of a duty to take care. As well as this, the German rule contained within § 823 sec. 1 German BGB is rather narrow, and can only be applied or understood if special types of cases and their valuation are familiar to the lawyer.

The English court decision of *Donoghue v. Stevenson*[5] is very important in the context of negligence, especially as regards the way in which one deals with the whole matter. This decision was concerned with product liability. Everyone who has a basic knowledge of the German law of torts knows that it was very difficult, and took considerable theoretical efforts to include cases of product liability within the scope of § 823 sec. 1 German BGB.[6]

Consequently, we can conclude that a (codified) rule has to be abstract, to a certain degree, to enable legal control. Therefore—irrespective of the wording of the rule—the contents of law can only be grasped by knowing how to cope with the rule, the methods of interpretation, and also, a more or less extensive theoretical context of application, that we call dogmatics or legal doctrine.

2. LEGAL DOCTRINE—DOGMATICS

Speaking within such a theoretical context, in order to establish the features of such a system,[7] it is necessary to discuss the nature of such a system, as well as its possible aims or uses.[8] The term dogmatics in German ("*Dogmatik*") is asso-

[4] See Ferid, M. & Sonnenberger, H. J., *Das französiche Zivilrecht*, Bd. 2, 2. Aufl. (Heidelberg, Verlag Recht und Wirtschaft, 1986), Rdnr. 2 O p. 113.

[5] (1932) A.C. 562. The successful plaintiff was a person who drank ginger beer out of a tumbler. When some more beer, manufactured by the defendant, was poured into the glass, a rotten snail appeared that had been in the bottle. The plaintiff suffered from shock and severe gastro-enteritis.

[6] For instance, BGHZ 51, 91.

[7] From an analytical point of view, Doctrine as a system of sentences, see Gusy, Chr., "'Wirklichkeit' in der Rechtsdogmatik", *Juristenzeitung* 1991, 213, 215.

[8] There are different opinions, if we are more or less on a pragmatic or theoretical level, so doctrine nearly is absorbed in the description of adjudication on the one hand or it is taken for a

ciated with theology. The Greek word *dogma*, which dogmatics is derived from, originally meant opinion.[9] This is a particularly apt meaning, especially as certain problems of adjudication would fit very well within such a definition. However, dogma stands for a special issue of belief, or at least thinking. This theorem is not merely one amongst many others, but is a fixed doctrine, which is to be taken as read, and therefore needs no explanation.

Even if there are some doubts as to what extent dogmatics fits, as a concept, within the idea of law and adjudication, it is still in use and shall be taken here as a synonym to the word "doctrine" in any future use. In my opinion, the English term doctrine is closer to my definition, or opinion, as the result of learned but pragmatic thinking.

Dogmatics, or doctrine, are a reaction to the use of particular sections, or words, within statutes, to help in the interpretation and application to so many different cases, in a plausible, and indeed, reasonable way. On the other hand, those cases and the needs of everyday and commercial life, call for legal provisions that could not be foreseen by the legislator. For this reason, dogmatics, or doctrine, are necessary to make abstract statutes practicable.[10] They prevent that in the eventuality of a hard case, corresponding to particular statutes, we are forced to start again "from the beginning" with our attempts at interpretation. Rather, we are provided with means that make our adjudication even and equal, in order to fulfil one premise of justice. This is necessary for the justification of the decisions made within a judicial system.[11] In any case, dogmatics is not bound to adjudication in special and individual cases, even if it often provides an inductive way of reasoning, from individual cases to axiomatic items. It can, and indeed has to embed new aspects and invented rules within the given framework of the law, in order to prevent contradictions. On the other hand, it can mark where there are gaps in the legal system, which may give rise to a need for legal protection.

It is sometimes likened to a separate layer between case and statutes. However, this is not the totality of the idea. Besides the existing rules, dogmatics forms new legal institutions which cannot be found in the law books, however much you try to find them there. In German law, I use examples such as *culpa in contrahendo*, breach of contract and the protection of third parties in contracts, but there are many more examples to be given.[12]

separate part of legal thinking on the other (surveys: Bydlinski, F., *Juristische Methodenlehre und Rechtsbegriff*, 2. Aufl. (Wien, Springer, 1991), p. 8; Meyer-Cording, U., *Kann der Jurist heute noch Dogmatiker sein?* (Tübingen, Mohr, 1973), p. 14.

[9] Meyer-Cording, U., *op. cit. supra*, n. 8, p. 7.

[10] For the following see Esser, J., Möglichkeiten und Grenzen des dogmatischen Denkens im modernen Zivilrecht, *Archiv für die civilistische Praxis* 172 (1972), 97, and *Vorverständnis und Methodenwahl in der Rechtsfindung* (Frankfurt: Athenäum-Fischer, 1972), p. 90.

[11] Gusy, Chr., *op. cit.*, n. 7, p. 217.

[12] See, for instance Larenz, K., & Canaris, C. W., *Methodenlehre der Rechtswissenschaft*, 3. Aufl. (Berlin: Springer, 1995), pp. 49, 56.

What we have heard up to now could make us think that the features of a code-based legal system evoke doctrinal work. However, this story has already begun, especially if we take a look at the origins and constructions of a code. Resystematisation of Roman law, canon law, customary law and existing statutory law was necessary as preparatory work to draft the French Napoleonic Code, as well as the German *Bürgerliches Gesetzbuch*, to mention these examples as great and influential codifications of the last century.[13] So, as we can see, doctrinal work is not only the consequence of any given legal system, and the rules it is composed of, rather that it is the fundamental framework, upon which such a system can be built. The draftsmen of these codes are often conscious of this, with the results that statutes are not any longer than they essentially need to be. Of course this is the reason why, as we have said before, dogmatics or doctrine are able to make abstract statutes practicable. Therefore, doctrine is indispensable for creating law in a systematic way, and for shaping a code of wide application, as well as being required to make it operate.

3. THE INGREDIENTS

3.1. The elements of legal doctrine

Van Hoecke and Ost have specified what items legal doctrine contains: theories of legal sources and of interpretation of the law, an argumentation theory, a theory concerning the task of legal doctrine itself and "a common basic ideology amongst lawyers and/or legal writers".[14] This is a description on rather a high level, and in rather a broad sense. If we try to find doctrinal reasoning in academic writing, or within judicial decisions, we should be able to differentiate terms that we have cited before (the case, the wording of the statutes and the adjudication tools) from those that could be termed as doctrinal. Attempts to specify what is the content of legal reasoning, have been tried several times before.[15] A simple enumeration could be: there are sentences and utterances about statutes, definitions of terms, records on case, hypotheses on social or economical facts, argumentation and conclusions about relevant statutes/rules and cases.

There is no doubt that the features outlined by Van Hoecke and Ost above belong to the doctrinal kind, which encompasses also the reference to interpretation theory.[16] Hereby, the theoretical framework of doctrine is described.

[13] Van Hoecke, M., & Ost, F., "Legal Doctrine in Crisis: Towards a European Legal Science", *Legal Studies*, 18 (1998), pp. 197, 200.

[14] *Op. cit. supra* n. 13, p. 197.

[15] For instance Rottleuthner, H., "Plädoyer für eine empirische Argumentationstheorie", *ARSP* (Beiheft 14), 1980, 87–118; Jost, F., "Tatsachenbehauptungen als Elemente Juristischer Argumentation", *Zeitgenössische Rechtskonzeptionen*, Verhandlungen des 9. IVR-Weltkongresses, 1979, Part III, p. 163.

[16] Although I mentioned "interpretation tools" as a category of utterances that are outside of doctrine and belong to "mere" application. For different opinions see n. 8.

However, the systematic point of view in doctrinal work[17] as well as the material that is dealt within, should be emphasised now. Therefore, statements on the meaning of categorical terms are to be cited, as well as the attempts at systematisation of different phenomena. Reference must also be made to given institutions, the comparison of those institutions in different fields and the shaping of new ones.

3.2. A case study

Let us take the adjudication concerning § 1365 German BGB as an example. The statute says that a married person is not allowed to transfer the whole of his assets to a third party without the agreement of his spouse. The way the *Bundesgerichtshof* handles this prescription shows a broad development of this idea, and a fundamental alteration as to the way in which this statement is applied. The first step can be found in BGHZ 35, 135, 143. The wording of the statute deals with the transfer of assets as a whole ("*Vermögen im ganzen*"). That suggests that the parties really refer to that ensemble of all goods the transferring party actually owns ("*Sachgesamtheit*", "*en bloc*").[18] However, the judges apply the statute to transactions of single goods as well, if they economically represent the whole assets of a spouse.

As a result of this, another question arises. The statute does not mention if, or how, precisely, the third party should know that he gains the totality of the spouse's property. If the parties intend that, or even state it in their contract, it is a clear matter. However, there is a problem if the contract is about single goods, perhaps even individual ones. Therefore, should the third party not know in this case, that he is going to acquire (economically) everything, if § 1365 BGB is applicable? Otherwise he would be surprised to find out later on, that the transaction is void. The BGH states that only on the precondition that the contracting party of the spouse knows what it is all about, may a transfer like that need the agreement of the other spouse to be valid.[19]

If the first step (BGHZ 35, 135) is meant to adopt the "*Einzeltheorie*" (applying the statute to the transfer of single goods), then the second step added the doctrine of taking into account what the third party knew about the economical consequences for the transferring spouse ("*subjektive Theorie*"). However, this is not the end of the story. The time the third party finds out about the goods he has received from the spouse, may also be relevant (third step). First the parties, for instance, make a contract on a piece of land, by which the seller is obliged to transfer it to the buyer, and then according to German law, further acts have to be accomplished to make the buyer the proprietor of the real estate.

[17] See Van Hoecke, M. & Ost, F., *op. cit. supra* n. 13, p. 199.

[18] It is remarkable, that the BGH uses a foreign (French) term, to make that clear (BGHZ 43, 174).

[19] BGHZ 43, 174.

But what about § 1365 BGB, when the buyer is ignorant as to the true nature of the sale, but recognises that the plot was all the spouse owned before the whole transaction took place?[20] There is, therefore, a doctrine needed, concerning the time a contract is made.

What we find, is that doctrines arise when we attempt to apply the statute to cases, and that there might be consequences of producing further interpretation, to round off[21] the way the statute or the rule can be handled, in different cases, or causes of application. When we have to explain, and to figure out, the meaning of § 1365 BGB, we have to say much more than to quote the wording and define the particular terminology terms within. The doctrinal item is only partly derived using interpretation methods (step one). Indeed, the precondition of the buyers knowledge is not found by mere interpretation of the paragraph in question (step two). The need for protecting the buyer acting in good faith, who would be surprised by the inefficiency of the transaction afterwards, and who might sustain losses, is a thought much closer to a general principal than to a single section in a statute. As well as this, step three has to do with the buyers' certainty and safety. If the transaction is accomplished to a certain extent, it is upheld, although it has not been completely performed before the acquiring party gets to know that the contracting spouse has sold all his assets.

Thus, in the description of the scope of application of a statute, doctrinal items ("*Theorien*") play an important role, and we willingly name them, and refer to them, in our daily work as lawyers. Once recognised and accepted, they are treated as more or less independent features, thrusting aside questions of immediate interpretation.

4. PRODUCING LEGAL DOGMATICS

Now let us see who it is that produces doctrine or dogmatics. It is easy to mention professors of law in the first place, because the task of legal doctrine is not only to make adjudication possible, but also to support it. Describing and systematising the law[22] is a precondition of teaching it. On the other hand, in different legal cultures, the academic doctrine is of differing importance,[23] even if there is an assimilation of both the continental and English legal system in this, as well as in many other respects.[24] Of course, solicitors, barristers and other

[20] See BGHZ 106, 253 and Jost, F., Anmerkung zum Beschluß des Bundesgerichtshofes vom 12.1.1989 (V ZB 1/88) zu § 1365 I BGB, *Juristische Rundschau* 1989, 506.

[21] Going on with our example see, for instance, BGHZ 77, 293 or (as a summary, too) Wolf, C. H. R., "Übertriebener Verkehrsschutz", *Juristenzeitung* 1997, 1087.

[22] Van Hoecke, M. & Warrington, M., "Legal Cultures, Legal Paradigms and Legal Doctrine: Towards a New Model for Comparative Law", *I.C.L.Q.* 1998, 495, 523.

[23] See Van Hoecke, M. & Warrington, M., idem, 525 (67) citing Kekewich J. (Union Bank v. Münster (1887) 37 *L.R.Ch.* 51, 54: "It is to my mind much to be regretted, and it is a regret which I believe that every judge on the bench shares, that text books are more and more quoted in court".

[24] Van Hoecke, M. & Ost, F., *op. cit. supra* n. 13, 210. Oehler, W., "Working with a Code: Is there a Difference between civil-law and common-law People ?" *University of Illinois Law Review*,

legal advisors must be mentioned. They have to develop inventive powers to do their job. In addition, with new kinds and forms of contracts, they are challenging the system of law.

Let us now turn our minds to the question of the courts. They have to adjudicate individual cases. Their task is to resolve social conflicts in a reasonable way. If this cannot be done in the simple statement of facts, and in logical conclusions they also have to argue more generally and more "dogmatically". This is because in order to determine the ratio of the case, one needs more reasons of justification, especially in cases where the outcome is doubtful. Those reasons must find support within the system of law.

One difference between various actors in the field of law should be mentioned here. Advocates have to prepare a case, when the client commissions them to do so, and judges must decide on a case, when an action is brought to the court,[25] whereas scholars can pick up problems of interpretation, when they get interested in them. They can save their conclusions until many others have uttered their opinion. Judges and advocates have to dare, when the question is asked.

So what is doctrine made of? We repeat this question again after our glance at the creators of doctrine. It consists in systematisation, in conserving the results of decided cases in a normative sense, referring to the principles and body of rules, in the shape in which they have been interpreted up to now.[26] The doctrine is something like the "experience" of law. Thus, the results of interpretation and systematisation can be employed again in adjudicating further cases. However, the process of legal reasoning has to be elastic enough, in order that social change can be perceived and be met with regard. Therefore, doctrine has to provide variety in its concepts to face variety in the social world.

Thus, we can say doctrine is necessary for codified law, but also, for a case law system,[27] although the process of law and legal reasoning here might not be as axiomatic as that of a codified system.[28] Doctrine has both a conserving function, and a bridge function, to the non-normative world and its development. A common law system, or case law system, needs a medium like this too, even if Lord Justice Cooper, late Lord President of the Court of Sessions of Scotland, is right. He assumes that in a code based system judges silently ask themselves: "What should we do this time?", whereas in common law their question is: "What did we do last time?"[29]

1997, 711, 716. On the other hand Oehler points out the different styles of legislation (714), how the techniques of interpretation are preferred in different ways (715) and the distinct ways of legal education in civil law and common law systems (716).

[25] Larenz, K. & Canaris, C. W., *op. cit. supra* n. 12, p. 55.

[26] See Van Hoecke, M. & Warrington, M., *op. cit. supra* n. 22.

[27] Esser, J., *op. cit. supra* n. 2, p. 183

[28] Emphazising differences Langenbucher, K., *op. cit. supra* n. 1, p. 83. See also Oehler, W., *op. cit. supra* n. 24.

[29] Quotation by Oehler, W., *op. cit. supra* n. 24, p. 711, 715.

5. THE STATUS OF LEGAL DOCTRINE, GENESIS AND PROBLEMS OF APPLICATION

5.1. Legal Doctrine: not a source of law

If legal reasoning of the doctrinal kind is so important, as is claimed here, its results should be as obligatory and valid as the statutes (indeed, the law) itself. We would have to agree to this, especially if doctrine could be developed and derived from the statutes directly by accepted means of interpretation. However, it is more than this. Its task is to make statutes determine cases for a long period of time, and under changing circumstances. This can only be achieved if the law is versatile enough. Therefore, doctrine, or dogmatics, is not binding law itself, or indeed, a source of law, but only means by which one to judge according to the law.[30] In adopting results of doctrinal considerations in adjudication, the lawyer has to control such considerations, if he is in conformity with the authority of the law.

5.2. Legal doctrine as an intermediate level

This has to do with the origins of doctrines. It is not the legislator, empowered by the constitution, that gives rise to the doctrine. It is of a more general method than adjudication, but with its outcome on a lower level than that of statutes. The workers in the field of doctrine are those who are busy with adjudication or systematic endeavours, as explained before. However, even if just a single case is to be decided, they have to deal with legal propositions of a more general degree, because it requires so much to fill the gap between statute and case law. Finally, we have to be aware of the fact, that in elaborate legal systems, it is often the ubiquitous doctrine, or the meaning it gives to statutes, that is ruling the process of interpretation, or even substituting it.[31]

5.3. Doctrinal rules and interpretation

The last question concerns the mentioned patterns or independent institutions, originating in doctrinal reasoning.[32] They can turn to customary or common law. Whatever it may be, if doctrine forms such immediately determinate patterns, they are expressed and shaped like specific rules. They are as abstract as

[30] Müller, F., *Juristische Methodik*, 7. Aufl. (Berlin: Duncker & Humblot, 1997), p. 270 : "Rechtserkenntnisquellen".

[31] See *supra* 3.2. (at the end).

[32] Above 2 (at the end).

statutes.[33] Now we are faced with the same problems in application or adjudication, as we are in applying statutes.[34]

Let us take, for example, a contract that gives protection to a third party, in the way it has been developed within German law. It has even been mentioned by the House of Lords.[35] Doctrine states very clearly what the rule is, adopting genuine terms, as the legislator does when issuing statutes. In accordance with this, we have to judge whether or not a third party will earn benefits of protection in special cases, in order that the third party may recover damages from one of the contracting parties (transferred losses).

If we fall back upon the methods of interpretation, considering particular wording, the systematic aspect, the genesis of the rule, its history and, last but not least, the purpose of a rule, we shall get into the well known problems of a methodological nature. In every case, we would start with the wording of the doctrinal rule; in order to begin, there is no other way to put the case in touch with the rule.[36] Nevertheless, we must consider that it is hard to compare the process of shaping the rule in legislation, as well as in doctrinal work. If the rule of doctrine arises out of precedents, it depends on individual cases that had to be adjudicated. If it stems from legal reasoning, on the opinion of various authors, anyone of them might use completely different terms, or indeed similar terms, but with a different meaning.

The systematic point of view in interpretation cannot be missed out. However, it has another reference. At first sight, the systematics of statutes cannot be taken as a basis because our rule is not a statutory one. On the other hand, our doctrinal rule may often have the task of mending a gap in the body of the law. Thus, there are relations between where the edges of these gaps are.

The genesis of the doctrinal rule is also different from that of statutes. There may only have been one suit or case that induced the initial doctrinal reasoning, from which the "new" rule arose.[37] That is its "history". As well as this, the case in question and the "facts"[38] now have to be compared with the precedents,[39] in order to determine to what extent the features are equal; we get very near to the techniques the judges use within the common law. Anyway, we are not dealing with a sequence of former statutes, or with material that came out of the legislative process.

[33] Müller, F., *op. cit. supra* n. 30, p. 271. Müller states that for doctrinal reasoning in principle, because a theoretical context is concerned, that cannot predict and take into account all particularities of individual cases. I would like to differenciate as I did under 5.2.

[34] Bydlinski, F., *op. cit. supra* n. 8, p. 502. Often authors only deal with the question, how to handle precedents (to get to "stare decisis" or to "distinguishing"). But we have to realize that there are similiar problems with the output of legal reasoning, if it is rather far and independent from single judgements.

[35] White v. Jones (1995) 1 *All ER* HL 691.

[36] Langenbucher, K., *op. cit. supra* n. 1, p. 77.

[37] Or at least a series of similar cases.

[38] Langenbucher, K., *op. cit. supra* n. 1, p. 78.

[39] Bydlinski, F., *op. cit. supra* n. 8; Zweigert, K. & Kötz, H., *Einführung in die Rechtsvergleichung*, I, 2. Aufl. (Tübingen: Mohr, 1984), p. 300.

I think all that underlines this, is that the purpose of the doctrinal rule is to determine a point of view, with regard to its interpretation. The reason for the establishment of the rule, and the end which it must achieve, seems to have a strong significance.[40] If the aim cannot be achieved, indeed, if the special need for legal protection vanishes, the doctrinal rule has no effect, without any act of the legislator.

6. LEGAL DOCTRINE IN EUROPE

There are many efforts to unify the law in Europe and this is, and can, be done by unified statutes to some extent. If it is true, as I have argued, that doctrine is (inevitably) like a layer between statute and case, and that it saves the experience of a system of law, this could suggest that the different national doctrines might be obstacles to the way of unification. However, the experiences of legal systems in industrialised countries are often similar, even if the legal institutions differ from each other. As well as this, when we remember what has been said about doctrinal task as preparatory work[41] before enacting statutes, we look to the Roman law as a source for different codes in different countries. Maybe old-fashioned subjects become (or are already) very modern-day and important for the process of unification.

As far as more recent developments are concerned, it is important to know what the framework of the various legal systems in Europe is made of. This is a challenge for legal education. Offering tools of unification, there should not be a total *melange* of all differences on the one hand, and, on the other hand, there cannot exist fifteen economic regions distinct from each other by very different legal rules. So where economic and social exchange takes place, legal arrangements across the borders are necessary. How they ought to be shaped and embedded in the set of existing legal institutions, must be considered on the doctrinal level as this includes systematic aspects. This task has to be carried out further in relation to adjudication. The way of interpreting such statutes, and rules, must take into account the experiences in different countries in which they hold true. If general directions had to be transformed into national statutes, their interpretation would be ruled by the terms of these directions. Thus, a common doctrine will arise in this field too. Therefore, there are two branches of scholarly legal reasoning: the common sources of different legal systems and the needs and the outcomes of handling the same, or similar, statutes and rules. However, it is necessary to consider the differences between particular traditions. There is no doubt that it is hard to perform duties like this, especially during a time, when acceleration and specialisation are common features of the

[40] Here it again becomes apparent that there are strong links between the "historical" and the "teleological" approach in interpretation.

[41] *Supra* 2.

development of law in a national context.[42] Therefore, if doctrinal work within the national sphere cannot be done on easy terms, it is even more difficult in a European context. However, without it, there is nothing that can be regarded as a working legal system.

7. CONCLUSIONS

I would like to sum up as follows:

1. There is no law (developed like private law in industrialised countries) without doctrine.
2. Doctrine does not have the authority of a legal source but, in fact, reduces the significance of "pure" interpretation of statutes and precedents.
3. If doctrine shapes an applicable rule, the same problems of interpretation arise as those which arise in the application of statutes. However, the handling of the methodological items is different.
4. Doctrine is not an obstacle in the process of unification. In contrast, we should be busy investigating its foundations and role in adjudication.

[42] Van Hoecke, M. & Ost, F., *op. cit. supra* n. 13, p. 200.

9

Unfair Terms in Consumer Contracts: An Anglo-Italian Comparison

PAOLISA NEBBIA

1. INTRODUCTION[1]

This paper aims at highlighting some of the difficulties which may be encountered in the interpretation and application of the measures implementing Directive 93/13 on Unfair Terms in Consumer Contracts in the United Kingdom and in Italy. A quick survey of the pre-existing legal frameworks in the two countries will reveal that the impact of the Directive may be different from what can be *prima facie* imagined and that values, legal thinking and tradition are elements which must be taken into account at least as much as words and concepts when assessing such an impact.

2. MEANS OF IMPLEMENTATION

Implementation of Directive 93/13 in the United Kingdom has taken place, in accordance with the European Communities Act 1972, by Statutory Instrument, the Unfair Terms in Consumer Contracts Regulations 1994.[2] The Regulations, which follow quite closely the wording of the Directive, do not repeal or amend the pre-existing law, but rather supplement it and often overlap with it. As a consequence, contractual terms may be subject to scrutiny under more than one legal framework, which provide a range of remedies historically stratified and derived from the common law, statutory law and European law.

In Italy, after long discussion,[3] the Directive was implemented by an Act

[1] This paper reflects the ideas put forward not only in the Conference "European Private Law in Context" held in Brussels on 5–6 February 1999, but also in the Symposium "European Legal Harmonisation and National Private Law Systems" held in Bad Homburg on 18–20 February 1999 and in the Acts of this Symposium to be published by Nomos later this year under the title *Rechtsangleichung und Nationale Privatrechte*.

[2] SI 1994, No.3159. At the time of writing this paper the 1994 Regulations had not been repealed by the 1999 Regulations (S.I. 1999, No. 2083) yet. Such change, however, does not affect the substance of this paper.

[3] See F. Contri, *Presentazione della proposta ministeriale di attuazione della direttiva comuniaria*; L. Barbiera, *Il recepimento della direttiva del 5 Aprile 1993 del Consiglio CEE sulle clausole*

(*Legge* of February 6th 1996 n. 52), which inserted articles 1469bis to 1469sexies in the Civil Code. Amending the Code via *Leggi*, however, is not a common route to implementation of Directives, which usually takes place via *Decreti Legge*. Those are items of delegated legislation, which are free standing, in the sense that they are apart and separate from the legislation contained in the codes, and are used in order to deal with matters requiring efficient and quick legislative response. The more radical choice to amend the Code instead of resorting to the usual means proves the will to reaffirm the primacy of the Code as the fundamental body of private law over the ever increasing amount of separate legislation and at the same time to stress the importance of the Directive within the Italian law of contract.

As with England, the addition of the new provisions did not entail a repeal of the framework already provided by the Code. Rather, the newly inserted articles create a number of exceptions to the Code provisions on penalty clauses, assignment, limitation of liability[4] and, above all, they introduce principles which are incompatible with the spirit and the nature of the Code thus seriously endangering its self-consistency and coherence.

3. PRE-EXISTING LEGISLATION

In the UK, control over unfair terms is performed through the common law doctrines of incorporation and interpretation (which are applicable to all types of unfair terms, but that are less used after UCTA came into force) and the statutory provisions of the Unfair Contract Terms Act 1977 (UCTA), which deals specifically with exclusion clauses.

The doctrines of incorporation and interpretation impose duties of disclosure of the terms of the contract in the interest of those against whom such terms may be enforced. In the first place, the party who sets terms which are particularly harsh must take reasonable steps to bring them to the attention of the other party: "If one condition in a set of printed conditions is particularly onerous or unusual, the party seeking to enforce it must show that the particular condition was fairly brought to the attention of the other party".[5] Second, failure to disclose the terms clearly may result in the proposed terms being enforced with a meaning contrary to the intention of the *proferens*: thus, for example, a provision that the seller gives "no warranty, express or implied" does not exempt him from liability for breach of a condition.[6]

abusive nei contratti stipulati con i consumatori nell'alternativa tra inserzione nel codice e redazione di una legge speciale; L. Bigliazzi Geri, *A proposito della proposta di attuazione della direttiva comunitaria sulle clausole abusive nei contratti stipulati con i consumatori*; A. Di Maio, *Proposte e scelte dei progetti di recepimento;* G. D'Ippolito, "Il recepimento e la tutela dei consumatori" in: *Le clausole abusive nei contratti stipulati con i consumatori*, 1st ed., 1996.

[4] Compare art. 1382, 1406, 1228, 1229 and art. 1469bis nn. 6, 17, 1 and 2.

[5] *Interfoto Picture Library Ltd.* v. *Stiletto Visual Programmes Ltd.* [1988] *1 All ER* 348.

[6] *Wallis, Son & Wells* v. *Pratt & Haynes* [1911] AC, 394.

In addition, UCTA imposes a total ban on clauses which exclude or restrict liability for death or personal injury resulting from negligence and subjects the other exclusion or limitation clauses to a judicially administered requirement of reasonableness. The test is applied "having regard to the circumstances which were, or ought reasonably to have been, known to or in contemplation of the parties when the contract was made" (section 11(1)); in the case of clauses limiting a person's liability to a specific amount of money, regard has to be had to the resources which that person could expect to be available for the purpose of meeting liability, and how far it was open to him to cover himself by insurance (section 11(4)). In a number of specific cases, further guidelines are available focusing mainly on the bargaining position of the parties and the customer's knowledge of the terms.[7] As a matter of social policy, courts seem to be willing to take into account, in their decision making, factors like the bargaining power of the parties, the value of the subject matter, the availability of insurance, the difficulty of the task undertaken, the existence of a duty of care between the parties and possible market failures (e.g. competition or information deficit). In *Smith v. Eric S Bush*, however, the House of Lords recognised that it is "impossible to draw up an exhaustive list of factors to be taken into account when a judge is faced with this very difficult question".[8]

On the other hand, the English law of contract does not recognise at any stage of the contractual relationship a duty of good faith. The refusal to accept such a principle is based on the idea that individuals should be allowed to act in their own best interests without any concern for the others. As a matter of market efficiency, ability to enter negotiations and to perform contracts without any extra commitment to the other party would allow traders to discover the most advantageous bargain and to perform it in the most advantageous way, thus promoting the goal of wealth maximisation. If the utility of contract as an instrument of self-government is not to be seriously weakened, parties must be free from any extra duties due to the others. This is especially true for pre-contractual duties, where the absence of a duty of good faith entails as its most remarkable consequence the freedom for the parties to break off preliminary negotiations without being hold to an accounting, as recently confirmed by the House of Lords in the case of *Walford v. Miles*.[9]

In Italy, unfair terms are addressed by art. 1341 and art. 1342 of the Civil Code.[10] Those articles apply to terms which are found in "*contratti d'adesione*" i.e. those contracts where one party adheres to a contractual text, which is pre-formulated by the other party in order to regulate in a uniform way certain

[7] See Schedule 2 of the Act. Even though the guidelines contained in the Schedule refer to specific cases, it must be said that in practice they are followed in all decisions involving a question of reasonableness.

[8] [1990] 1 *AC* 831 at 858.

[9] [1992] 2 *AC* 128.

[10] In addition, art. 1228 and 1229 of the Civil Code address specific cases of exemption and limitation clauses. In particular, para. 1 of art. 1229 prohibits clauses, which exempt or limit liability in cases of fraud (*dolo*) or serious negligence (*colpa grave*).

contractual relationships.[11] Art. 1341 of the Code provides that standard terms of contract set by one party ("*condizioni generali di contratto*") are effective only if the other party is aware of them, or he could have been aware of them by ordinary diligence. In addition, some types of clauses (commonly known as "*clausole vessatorie*") are not effective unless specifically approved in writing. Such clauses are, for example, those which limit one party's liability or allow suspension or termination of the contract according to that party's wish, or which impose on the other party tacit renewal of the contract or restrictions to the freedom to negotiate with thirds.[12] Art. 1342 adds that forms and standard form contracts clauses, subsequently added to the form, prevail over the pre-written ones in case of incompatibility.[13] The formalism and inadequacy of the control provided by these articles are clear: terms will be effective against one party to a contract if he is aware of them or has the opportunity to be aware of them and if specifically approved, but this does not ensure the clarity and comprehensibility—not to mention the fairness—of clauses which may be approved by the subscriber without any understanding of their meaning and of their importance in the contract. This can be easily explained if one analyses the *ratio* of the 1942 Civil Code.

The attitude of the Civil Code, which dates back to 1942, but is still deeply rooted in the ideology of Enlightenment, is that of neutrality towards the socio-economical position of the parties. Private law, as *jus privatorum*, is the law of private individuals and as such shall encourage them to pursue their interests by allowing them a high degree of autonomy and self-determination and by ensuring in the first place formal equality before the law. Accordingly, the Code does not consider any special category of economic agent, or any form of direct and substantive control on fairness of contract bargains, and judges have no power to interfere and modify parties' obligations, save few exceptional cases (art. 1447, *rescissione di contratto concluso in stato di pericolo* and art. 1448, *rescissione per lesione*).[14]

[11] The 1942 Civil Code was, actually, the first code in Europe including provisions specifically addressed at the "*contratto d'adesione*".

[12] 1341 (Condizioni generali di contratto) "Le condizioni generali di contratto predisposte da uno dei contraenti sono efficaci nei confronti dell'altro, se al momento della conclusione del contratto questi le ha conosciute o avrebbe dovuto conoscerle usando l'ordinaria diligenza. In ogni caso non hanno effetto, se non sono specificatamente approvate per iscritto, le condizioni che stabiliscono, a favore di colui che le ha predisposte, limitazioni di responsabilità, facoltà di recedere dal contratto o di sospenderne l'esecuzione, ovvero sanciscono a carico dell'altro contraente decadenze, limitazioni alla facoltà di opporre eccezioni, restrizioni alla libertà contrattuale nei rapporti coi terzi, tacita proroga o rinnovazione del contratto, clausole compromissorie o deroghe alla competenza dell'autorità giudiziaria".

[13] 1342 (Contratto concluso mediante moduli o formulari). "Nei contratti conclusi mediante moduli o formulari, predisposti per disciplinare in maniera uniforme determinati rapporti contrattuali, le clausole aggiunte al modulo o formulario prevalgono su quelle del modulo o formulario qualora siano incompatibili con esse, anche se queste ultime non sono state cancellate. (. . .)".

[14] Those are the cases where one party agrees to an extremely disadvantageous contract for the reason that he finds himself in a situation of danger or need, and the other party takes the opportunity to derive an unfair profit for himself.

In the preparatory works to the Civil Code the *Relazione al progetto preliminare del libro delle obbligazioni* (the report to the preliminary draft of the part relating to the law of obligations) explains that the importance acquired by *contratti d'adesione* in regulating in a uniform way transactions of the same type, justifies the insertion of specific provisions addressed to them. According to the *Relazione*, a "*contratto d'adesione*" can be identified wherever those two features are present: unilateral formulation and use for an indefinite number of transactions. Reference to these features is reiterated by art. 1341 and art. 1342 which refer to "standard" terms of contract ("*condizioni generali di contratto*") and "forms and standard term contracts which are pre-formulated by one party in order to regulate in a uniform way certain contractual transactions" ("*moduli o formulari predisposti per regolare in maniera uniforme determinati rapporti contrattuali*").

Formulation in advance and uniform regulation are, therefore, the reasons justifying intervention in the eyes of the Italian legislator. However, the causal link with inequality of bargaining power of the parties does not appear to be taken in due account, as neither the text of the articles above mentioned nor the Relazione suggest that the lack of negotiation underlying "contratti d'adesione" is the most common and clear sign of a structural failure of the market due to the inequality of parties' bargaining position. On the other hand, the fact that one party to the contract is unable to negotiate its content is in itself irrelevant if the contract is drawn for individual use.[15] Lack of negotiation, combined with consideration of the position and quality of the parties, is not a sufficient reason to trigger the application of art. 1341 and 1342.

4. JUDICIAL DEVELOPMENTS

Having previously mentioned the refusal of the English courts to resort to good faith as a guideline for decision making, it is now necessary to point out that this does not mean that judges have not tried to find from time to time different solutions to problems of unfair contractual behaviour, as proudly declared by Lord Bingham in *Interfoto Picture Library Ltd. v. Stiletto Visual Programmes Ltd.*:

> "In many civil law systems, the law of obligations recognises and enforces an overriding principle that in making and carrying out contracts parties should act in good faith. This does not simply mean that they should not deceive the other party, a principle which any legal system must recognise; its effect is perhaps most aptly conveyed by such metaphorical colloquialism as 'playing fair', 'coming clean', or 'putting one's cards face upwards on the table'. It is in essence a principle of fair and open dealing. English law has, characteristically, committed itself to no such overriding principle

[15] See A. Tullio, *Il contratto per Adesione,* 1st ed., (1997), pp. 11–17; S. Troiano, "L'ambito Oggettivo di Applicazione della Direttiva CEE del 5 Aprile 1993: la Nozione di Clausola 'non Oggetto di Negoziato Individuale'" in *Clausole vessatorie e contratti dei consumatori, op. cit.*, p. 599.

> but has developed piecemeal solutions in response to demonstrated problems of unfairness."[16]

Accordingly, some regulation of the negotiation process is considered justifiable and desirable by English courts. A few examples can show that, even in the pre-contractual stage, a duty to take into account the other party's interest exists and comes close to giving in practice the same results which would be attained if the criterion of good faith was used. A quick survey of those examples, even in the absence of specific reference to unfair terms, can be useful in order to proceed to the analysis of the impact of the Directive.

In the first place, a duty of care and to take the other party's interest into account is imposed on the party who makes certain statements during the negotiation of the contract if this party has specialised knowledge and expertise. In the case *Esso Petroleum Co. Ltd v. Mardon*[17] a representative of Esso gave a prospective tenant of a petrol station an estimate of the potential throughput of the station, which was exceedingly high. The tenant was dubious about the accuracy of the statement, but the employee's greater expertise quelled his doubts and he entered into a tenancy agreement. The throughput turned out to be below expectation and the tenant sought compensation for the damages in respect of the representation made by the representative (he had lost all the capital he had and incurred a substantial overdraft). The Court of Appeal considered that, even if the estimate was an expression of opinion rather than a statement of fact and therefore could not amount to a misrepresentation, it contained the implied promise that it was made with reasonable care and skill:

> "Where, during the course of pre-contractual negotiations, one party, who had special knowledge and expertise concerning the subject-matter of the negotiation, made a forecast based on that knowledge and expertise with the intention of inducing the other party to enter into the contract, and in reliance of the forecast the other party did enter into the contract, it was open to the court to construe the forecast as being not merely an expression of opinion but as constituting a warranty that the forecast was reliable, i.e. that it had been made with reasonable care and skill. (. . .). Accordingly, since the estimate was negligent and was therefore unsound, Esso were liable to the defendant for the breach of that warranty".[18]

Another instance of pre-contractual duty is provided by the case Barclays *Bank* v. *O'Brien.*[19] Mr. O'Brien persuaded his wife to sign a guarantee for an overdraft facility on the matrimonial house, and lied about the extent of liability. The bank failed to explain the transaction and recommend that the wife takes independent legal advice. The House of Lords considered that the bank should have realised from the nature of the relationship between the parties and the content of the transaction that there was a risk of fraudulent behaviour from the

[16] [1988] 1 *All ER* 348.
[17] [1976] 2 *All ER* 5.
[18] *Ibid.* at p. 6.
[19] [1993] 4 *All ER* 417.

husband, and therefore should have taken reasonable steps to ensure that consent to the contract was properly obtained by informing the weaker party of the extent and nature of the transaction. Accordingly, the transaction was set aside.

With regard to unfair terms, as already mentioned, the doctrines of incorporation and interpretation impose duties of disclosure, which increase in the cases where the offeree is a consumer or is not likely to be familiar with the normal terms of trade and lacks the experience, skills and knowledge necessary to evaluate the meaning of the terms of the contract.[20]

In all the above-mentioned cases, the law recognises a "duty to negotiate with care".[21] The rationale of such a duty is not an abstract standard of correctness and honesty: it is a practical and flexible consideration of the market context, which Collins explains as follows:

> ". . . the full extent of the duties during negotiations for a contract has been explained by reference to the concept of relations of dependence. In these situations the relative skills and knowledge of one party have led to the imposition of a duty to take into account the interests of the other party. (. . .). Similarly, when discussing the terms of a contract, one party who is in better position to understand the legal consequences of the contract will be under a duty to explain the full import of the terms, or else risk liability for misrepresentation. These, and many other instances of relations of dependence, imply that a purely self-interested exercise of freedom during the negotiation process is impermissible where one party stands in relation of dependence to the other".[22]

The same idea is reflected in the guidelines used in the application of the reasonableness test under UCTA to the extent that factors such as the bargaining position of the parties and the customer's knowledge of the terms are taken into consideration. Accordingly, the view that English law does not impose any duties of taking into account the other party's interest is not correct to the extent that it fails to explain such a duty to negotiate with care.

On the other hand, little judicial development has occurred in Italy with regard to unfair terms. The *Corte di Cassazione* has not gone any further than the legislator in determining the scope of application of art. 1341 and 1342, and has on many occasions confirmed that ". . . *contratti d'adesione* . . . are those aimed at regulating an indefinite number of transactions . . . accordingly, the mere fact that a contract has been formulated in advance by one party, so that the other has no option other than taking it or leaving it, without participating in its formation, is not enough to trigger the application of art. 1341 so far as the form and the terms are not meant to regulate an indefinite number of contracts".[23]

[20] See, for example, *Thornton* v. *Shoe Lane Parking Ltd.* [1971] 1 *All England Law Reports* 686; *Interfoto Picture Library* v. *Stiletto*, *op. cit*.

[21] As defined by H. Collins, *The Law of Contract* (London, Butterworths, 1997), pp. 168–205.

[22] H. Collins, *The Law of Contract*, *op. cit*., p. 204.

[23] Corte di Cassazione, 14.5.1977, n. 1952 in *Giustizia Civile, Repertorio*, 1997, item Obbligazioni e contratti, n. 86; see also Cassazione, 21.4.1988, n. 3091 in *Giustizia Civile, Massimario*, issue 4.

The *Corte di Cassazione* has also confirmed the neutral attitude of the law to the contract and disregarded socio-economical considerations in many other decisions concerning "*contratti d'adesione*", the most remarkable example being that of "*clausole bilaterali*". "*Clausole bilaterali*" are those clauses, which give a specific right or deprive of a specific right both parties to the contract, i.e. which apply in favour or to the detriment of any of the parties, so as to maintain formal equality between them. In substantial terms, the same clause can have remarkably different effects, depending on the party, which relies on it. The *Corte di Cassazione*, after some uncertainty, has held that a clause, which can operate in favour or to the detriment of any of the parties, cannot be "*vessatoria*" and is not covered by art. 1341.[24]

Yet, the Civil Code would not be completely deprived of potential for more creative and innovative judgments. The law of obligations, and more specifically the law of contract, is dominated by the principle of good faith. A duty to behave "in good faith" is imposed at several stages of the contractual relationship, from pre-contractual dealing to performance, to interpretation; in addition, a duty of good faith is specifically mentioned by the *Relazione al Codice Civile* with regard to *contratti d'adesione*. However, judges have not made sufficient use of such a potential and have refused any form of innovative and creative routes to controlling unfair terms.[25] The case law shows no attempts at applying the principle of good faith in order to mitigate the consequences of the use of harsh contract terms.

5. THE IMPACT OF THE DIRECTIVE

The introduction of the principle of good faith[26] in the United Kingdom is expected to bring a shock to the common law legal culture, as it would entail a whole range of new duties and standards of behaviour. However, it is argued in this paper that the above mentioned examples of pre-contractual duty of care show that the fact that the common law does not impose on parties a duty of good faith does not mean that judges have not been concerned with matters of contractual fairness. Rather, what is explained in terms of good faith in continental systems is viewed in terms of "duty of care" in the English system. The extent of the duties during negotiations for a contract is explained by reference to the concept of dependence and to the market context and not to an abstract duty of behaviour. It is therefore likely that English judges, instead of being

[24] See, for example, Cassazione, 28.4.1981, n. 2594 in *Giurisprudenza Italiana* 1982 I, 1, 1449, where it was held that a clause limiting responsibility of both parties in a contract of carriage cannot be considered as a "*clausola vessatoria*" and therefore needs not specific written approval.

[25] See V. Rizzo, *Condizioni generali di contratto e predisposizione normativa*, (1983), pp. 11 ff., 64 ff., 74 ff.

[26] Described as "mysterious and exciting to an English lawyer" by H. Collins, "Good faith in European Contract Law", (1994) *Oxford Journal of Legal Studies* 249.

"irritated"[27] by the new concept, will simply interpret and apply it according to their tradition as a flexible standard, which captures the way in which legal duties increase in relation to the market context.

In Italy, the Directive seems to have a twofold importance within the system of private law. Firstly, it introduces the category of consumers in the corpus of the Code, traditionally and steadily based, as described, on formal equality of individuals before general and abstract rules. For a long time, the consumer had merely economical-sociological relevance, but had no right of citizenship in the Italian legal system until the obligation to implement EC consumer legislation has made its introduction compulsory. In the name of the substantial inequality and of the different bargaining power of the parties, consumer law supports the consumer as the weak party of the contractual relationship. Its insertion in the Code brings the unavoidable consequence that, within that fundamental *corpus* of law, the focus shifts away from the contract itself to the parties and their subjective qualities, while "the" contract loses its unity and its central position.[28] In addition, the new legislation takes into account the motives for which parties act as a means to determine its scope of application, while any reference to motives is irrelevant in the system envisaged by the Code.

Second, the new legislation entails, by introducing the combined criteria of good faith and significant imbalance, a substantive assessment of the balance of the contractual bargain. It is not clear yet how this assessment will be carried out in practice[29] and the first litigation is more likely to revolve around the list of potentially unfair terms. What is clear is that judges will not any longer be able to restrict their role to a mere control of the form of transactions. The new criteria impose an assessment of the balance of the transaction inspired by considerations of social policy, which have nothing to share with the principles inspiring the Code and its judicial application. Accordingly, in the example of *clausole bilaterali*, the new test will require that in practice, beyond the *prima facie* symmetry of legal effects, parties' duties and obligations are reviewed so as to make sure that a clause of that type does not act to the detriment of the consumer and to the unfair advantage of the other party.

In addition, the new provisions have not repealed the ones already existing in the Code, so the two regulations, different for *ratio* and type of control, will coexist in the Code.[30] The type of contract envisaged by the new framework,

[27] The word is used by G. Teubner, "Legal irritants: Good Faith in British Law or How Unifying Law Ends Up in New Divergencies" (1998) 61 *Modern Law Review* 11.

[28] Before the 1942 Civil Code, the Italian system was based on a dualist approach to private law: the civil code regulated relationships between private individuals and the commercial code was applied when at least one of the parties was a trader. The current system, on the other hand, is based on a single code and has eliminated every distinction between civil and commercial contracts, mainly by extending the application of the rules of the commercial code.

[29] The inaccurate translation of the provision on good faith, for example, suggests that a subjective notion of good faith should be adopted. However, comparison with other languages and compliance with the word and spirit of the directive would suggest the requirement has to be interpreted objectively.

[30] On the problems of co-ordination between the two frameworks, see A. Tullio, *op. cit.*, p. 99.

however, does not overlap with the previous concept of "*contratto d'adesione*": the clauses subject to art. 1469bis ff. are simply those, which have not been individually negotiated, no matter whether the contract is for individual or general use. To increase confusion, clauses, which may be caught by art. 1469bis ff., are called "*vessatorie*" (while the more appropriate and Directive-compliant term "abusive" could have been used), thus adopting the same word commonly used for clauses subject to art. 1341.

6. CONCLUDING REMARKS

The cases of Italy and United Kingdom are paradigmatic in showing what different ranges of issues and problems the implementation of Directive 93/13 can create in the Member States. Law is a matter of values, tradition and legal thinking, as well as a matter of written words. The example of Italy shows that the potential of words can remain unexploited and underdeveloped if the necessary policy considerations and "*mentalité*" are lacking. Thus, implementing the Directive will be a matter of changing values, tradition and legal thinking, rather than words. On the other hand, as a matter of words and legal techniques, the introduction of a duty of good faith will simply provide to English judges an easier route for justifying certain decisions. It can be argued[31] that the interpretation envisaged by this paper for the English judges confines good faith to procedural issues and does not capture another possible meaning of the Directive that the terms themselves can be contrary to good faith. The Directive does not state that the significant imbalance of the obligations must be caused by actions contrary to the requirement of good faith and it may be wrong to confine the requirement of good faith to defects in the negotiating procedures. The fact that the requirement of good faith can have several possible meanings and that courts can apply it according to their own understanding and tradition, however, can be considered as a strength rather than a weakness of the Directive. All depends on whether one believes that "*textures ouvertes*"[32] can be one of the key routes to harmonisation.

[31] See the remarks made by H. Collins in *Good faith in European Contract Law*, *op. cit.*, p. 250.

[32] See A. Chamboredon, "The Debate on a European Civil Code: For an 'Open Texture'", discussed elsewhere in this volume.

10

*Current Problems of Legal Dogmatics in European Regulation: The Principle of Equality and the Policies of Affirmative Action**

JOSÉ GARCIA AÑON

The purpose of this work is to point out the classical problems of legal doctrine, or *legal dogmatics*, which are reproduced in the application of European Law. I will use, as an example of this, an analysis of recent cases solved by the Court of Justice of the European Communities, in relation to the principle of equality and the policies of affirmative action, more specifically, the decisions in the Kalanke (1995) and Marschall (1997) cases.[1]

1. INTRODUCTION: THE LIMITS OF LEGAL DOGMATICS

The characteristic functions of Legal Dogmatics, both in academic work and in legal practice, are those of carrying out the interpretation, application and systematisation of the law, as well as providing the roads for its transformation.[2]

* I would like giving thanks to professor Mark Van Hoecke, to Ruth Mestre, James Varney and Karen Nimmo for the language revision of the English version of this paper.

[1] The purpose of this paper is to examine problems of European legal dogmatics in the context of harmonisation of law in Europe. The German dogmatics approach, as analysed in the paper by María Elósegui elsewhere in this book ("The Kalanke case and the Marschall case in the Court of Justice of the European Communities"), seems interesting. However, Elósegui's approach as a moral philosopher prevents her from really seeing the legal perspective. Moreover, the influence of German legal dogmatics on European legal doctrine should be comparable to the influence of others, such as Spanish, Italian, English, French or Belgian legal doctrine, in order to construct a truly *European Law*.

[2] Alexy, R., *Theorie der Juristischen Argumentation* (Frankfurt, Suhrkamp, 1978) [*Teoría de la Argumentación Jurídica*, spanish translation M. Atienza and I. Espejo (Madrid, CEC, 1989)]; Van de Kerchove, M. and Ost, F., *Le Système Juridique entre Ordre et Désordre* (Paris, Presses Universitaires de France, 1988), p. 117 ff. [Spanish translation I. Hoyo, Universidad Complutense de Madrid, 1997]; Van Hoecke, M., "La Systématisation dans la Dogmatique Juridique", *Rechtstheorie*, Beiheft 10, 1986, 217 and ff., and, in the same volume, see: Aarnio, A., "On Changes in the Systematics of Law", 161–170; and Bulygin, E., "Legal Dogmatics and the Systematization of Law", 193–210.

However, the limits to the development of this activity do not appear to be defined, and this causes some problems in establishing the characteristic functions of legal operators.

Without aiming at an exhaustive delimitation of doctrinal activity, it is necessary, for the purpose of this exposition, to keep in mind, among others, the following aspects: Firstly, the transforming function of law has to be linked to existent social reality. The structure, context and history of the society which the transforming proposals of legal institutions seeks to modify should be kept in mind. This limitation, or indeed, delimitation, is necessary in order to maintain the pretences of the law. This aspect has been termed the "external systematisation of the law", and implies the task "to integrate to the maximum the legal system in the society, continually in evolution, as well as in the system of values and norms that dominates within society."[3]

Secondly, the limit or ideological conditioning. Despite the chimera of the neutrality of legal scholars, the interpretation, systematisation and transformation of works of law are not presented as value-free instruments. The use of a concept, a classification or an objective as inspiration for law, reflects and finds an unavoidable ideological load that transcends mere doctrinal discussion. In this work delimitation is illustrated by the policies of affirmative action in relation to European norms.

This unavoidable ideological conditioning and the lack of entailing to reality, that is to say, the transgression of these limits, is manifested in diverse ways within the doctrine:

1. Firstly, by trying to search for the essences and legal nature within the concepts of delimitation. It is not necessary to give particular meaning to certain words or, once meanings are well-known, to give a description of the phenomena denoted by these expressions. It is better to take a more implicit approach, where the intention is to obtain an explanation that allows them to infer a series of relevant principles. The problem is that behind the appearance of descriptive neutrality, a certain ideological and methodological conception has slipped into the law.[4]
2. Secondly, by means of the construction of elaborations that transcend the interpretation of a legal system.[5]

[3] Van Hoecke, M., "La Systématisation dans la Dogmatique Juridique", *op. cit.*, 224.

[4] Nino, C. S., *Consideraciones Sobre la Dogmática Jurídica. (Con Referencia Particular a la Dogmática Penal)* (México, Universidad Nacional Autónoma de México, 1989), p. 41 and p. 77; Carrió, G. R., *Notas Sobre Derecho y Lenguaje* (Buenos Aires, Abeledo-Perrot, 1976), p. 74; Calsamiglia, A., *Introducción a la Ciencia Jurídica* (Ariel, Barcelona, 1990), 1st ed. 1988, p. 21. In short, the use of these type of positions by the European Court of Justice, also in questions related to equality, may be seen in the decisions of the Defrenne case: when using a systematic interpretation approach, the Court also make reference to the approach of the "nature of the principle of same paying." (Defrenne II, C–43-75; Defrenne III, C–149/77). About this, see Bengoetxea, J., *The Legal Reasoning of the European Court of Justice. Towards a European Jurisprudence* (Oxford, Clarendon Press, 1993), esp. pp. 267 ff.

[5] As an example, here, we could frame the elaboration of theories as "legal goods protected" in penal law. See Nino, C.S., *Consideraciones Sobre la Dogmática Jurídica*, *op. cit.*, p. 55 and ff. In

3. Thirdly, and as a consequence of the latter , the "reformulation" of a legal system.[6] The problem of "reformulation" consists of using terminology that is not within the realms of law and that implies different consequences to those that could be extracted from the legal system.
4. Finally, the use of fictions linked to the concept of rationalism.[7]

I will attempt to describe the tension which exists between the delimitation of legal dogmatics and the problems that cause its transgression, focusing mainly on the second and third problems.

2. SOME PROBLEMS OF LEGAL DOGMATICS IN THE CONFIGURATION OF EUROPEAN LAW REGARDING EQUALITY: THE POLICIES OF AFFIRMATIVE ACTION

The legitimation of the principle of equality and the adoption of policies of affirmative action may be a good example to study the position of European legal dogmatics, especially in relation to the formulation and application of European Law. As it is known already in this area, one can verify the influence or inspiration from North American Anti-discrimination Law. This starting point allows us to frame other problems that are to be exposed. We could stress the following discussion points:

1. The lack of *precise* conceptual elaborations. An example of this is the use of foreign concepts such as "rigid quotas" and "flexible quotas."
2. The creation of *new concepts* and a terminology existing both by doctrine and case law, without connection to national or European norms, nor with national or European judicial decisions, such as the criterion of "automatic or absolute preference", or the alternative concept of "opening clauses."
3. Using conceptual elaborations with a lack of foundation, as well as the use of reductive foundations, such as the reduction of the foundations of law to one single model, the liberal State.

Before analysing these questions, we will first contemplate the legal-political context of the problem, using as an example the reception of North American Anti-discrimination Law and, in short, the policies of affirmative action.

European environment law, the approach of the "public interest" criterion, starting from the interpretation of the article 10 of the European Covenant on human rights by the European Court on Human Rights, can also be pointed out. I am not developing this aspect in my paper, but see Bonet, J., "El Criterio del «interés público» en la Práctica Jurisdiccional Relativa al Artículo 10 del Convenio Europeo para la Salvaguardia de los Derechos Humanos y las Libertades Fundamentales", *Derechos y Libertades*, 2, 1993, 541–596.

[6] See Nino, C. S., *Consideraciones sobre la dogmática jurídica*, *op. cit.*, p. 49 and ff.

[7] Nino, C. S., *Consideraciones Sobre la Dogmática Jurídica*, *op. cit.*, p. 103 and ff.; Ost, F., and van de Kerchove, M., *Jalons pour une Théorie Critique du Droit* (Brussels, Publications des Facultés Universitaires Saint-Louis, 1987), p. 100 and ff.

3. THE INFLUENCE OF NORTH AMERICAN ANTI-DISCRIMINATION LAW ON EUROPEAN LAW

Domestic laws of European legal systems first conceived the idea of Anti-discrimination Law in the seventies. This idea was also aided by interpretation through constitutional jurisprudence. At this time, European Labour Law also took a limited stand, in relation to gender-based discrimination.

3.1. Regulation within the European Union

In the constituent Treaty of the European Union, there is no reference to formal equality, except in a generic way, nor to the type of measures that can be used to make it effective. For instance, Art. 117 of the *Treaty of Rome* (1957) says:

> "Member States agree upon the need to promote improved working conditions and an improved standard of living for workers, so as to make possible their harmonisation while the improvement is being maintained."

And relating to equal payment, it is specified in art. 119 that:

> "Each Member State shall during the first stage ensure and subsequently maintain the application of the principle that men and women should receive equal pay for equal work."

It was not until the seventies, when a series of Directives developing some aspects relating to equal treatment of men and women in specific fields of Labour Law were introduced, that this principle was given leverage. Headway was made in relation to access to employment, equality of payment and social security. More precisely, it is interesting to read Directive 76/207, about the application of the principle of equal treatment of men and women, in the light of access to employment, formation and promotion, as well as standards of working conditions.

In contrast, one must consider the decisions of the European Court of Justice, which had previously approached some questions relating to non discrimination policy,[8] but had not, as yet, decided any case in which measures of affirmative action were questioned, at least until the *Kalanke case* (1995). In this case, measures of affirmative action are forbidden if an acknowledgement of absolute priority is made in respect of women (the aforementioned *rigid quotas)*, although the lack of clarity within this judgement could also be interpreted as allowing no types of quota at all.

In light of the need to clarify such a controversial decision, the judgement was an object of intense interpretation by the Commission.[9] Proposals were even

[8] The elimination of discrimination for sex reasons, considered as a fundamental human right, guaranteed by European law, was held in the *Defrenne III* case (1978).

[9] "Communication of the Commission of the European Union to the European Parliament and the Council relative to the interpretation of the Judgement of the Court of Justice in the *case Kalanke*"; Brussels, March 1996, 27 COM (96) 88 end.

being made to modify Directive 76/207 (COM (96) 93). In its *Communication* to the European Parliament, the Commission argued that the Court had excluded the automatic system of quotas and gave no importance to the idea of substitution of equality of opportunities by its effect, such as appeared in paragraph 23 of the Kalanke judgement. The Commission also considered modifying section 4 of art. 2 of the Directive, which expressly allowed measures of affirmative action, except in the case of rigid quotas. The later case of Marschall (1997) seems to follow the interpretation of the Commission.

The Amsterdam Treaty, signed in October 1997, and having immediate effect once ratified by the fifteen member States according to their constitutional norms, modifies some provisions of the European Union Treaty and, also, of the constituent Treaties of the European Communities. In short, regarding equality, the Treaty of Amsterdam gives a new legal basis to integrate the jurisprudence of the Court of Justice with the Kalanke and Marschall cases.

Amongst other measures, the Council, following consultation with the Economic and Social Committee, may adopt measures of affirmative action to ensure the application of the principle of equal opportunities and equal treatment in matters of employment and occupation. As well as this, the new Art. 119.4 allows Member States to adopt or maintain positive-action measures for the underrepresented sex regarding professional careers, with limitation placed on the adoption of "rigid quotas".

3.2. From Kalanke to Marschall

The position of the European Court on the concept of equality is found in the Kalanke and Marschall cases. We shall now examine these two cases in more detail. They are similar, although they do have certain peculiarities that I will attempt to point out: in the *Kalanke* case, Mr. Kalanke disagreed with the law of the Land that prevented him from being Head of Section of the Gardens of Bremen, in contrast to Mrs. Glissman, who had the same merits.

The controversial article in this case was Art. 4 of the Act of 20 November 1990 of the *Land of Bremen*. The question is whether or not this norm, and the decision taken, contravened art. 2.4° of European Union Directive 76/207 which states that:

> "The present Directive won't prevent the measures guided to promote equality of opportunities between men and women in particular to correct the inequalities in fact that they affect to the opportunities of the women in the matters contemplated in section 1 of article 1."

In this case, the Court, in its judgement of October 1995, established that a national Act is discriminatory on the basis of sex, if it states that, in a job promotion, women having the same training as their male competitors, automatically enjoy a preference in sectors where they are underrepresented.

Although we will look at this in more detail, the reasoning of this interpretation is that the Directive prohibits measures tending to equality of results, as those foreseen in the law of Bremen. The "automatic preference", according to the Court, is a case of equality of results.

I will also refer to the Marschall case, brought before the Court by *Hellmut Marschall* against the *Land Rheinland-Westfalen,* for which a preliminary decision was asked for on the interpretation of the same sections of Directive 76/207/EEC, because it was in contravention of section 5 of Art. 25 of the *Law of the Public Function of the Land of Rheinland-Westfalen,* which states:

> "When, in the sector of the competent organism in which the promotion should take place, there are less women than men on the level of the corresponding position of the career, preference will be granted in the promotion to women, if there is equal aptitude, competence and professional capabilities, unless reasons converge in the person of a candidate that incline the decision to his favour, (. . .)"

In application of this norm, Hellmut Marschall was not promoted to a higher rank in his career as a teacher at the school in the city of Schwerte, where he lived. The promotion was given to a female candidate who had the same level of competence. The reasons adduced by the school were that both had the same training, and the number of women promoted to this position was inferior to that of men. Hellmut Marschall appealed to the competent national Court, and outlining the preliminary question, attempted to explain that the law of the *Land* should be in line with the Directive.

The Court, in this case, decreed on the 11th November 1997, that contrary to the decision in the previous case of Kalanke, the controversial disposition contains a clause, according to which, women do not enjoy automatic preference in promotion, if the male candidate has good reasons to incline judgement in his favour (the idea again of "opening clause").

In both cases, the controversial arguments could be summarised in three main points:

a) The existence, or not, of "tolerated" discrimination, regulated by the exception in art. 2.4º of Directive 76/207/EEC. This determines, primarily, what instrument we have (affirmative action, reverse discrimination, a subjective fundamental right . . .) and whether or not these cases are tolerated by such a disposition.
b) The sufficiency or not of the approach of *under-representation* to configure the exceptions foreseen within the context of the Directive. This implies the determination of necessary approaches to determine the scope of the exceptions in the Directive.
c) If the foreseen measure supposes an *equality in the result* and this is found as an exception to the Directive, which would appear to allow only measures whose purpose is that of *equality of opportunities*.

4. PROBLEMS OF AFFIRMATIVE ACTION POLICIES IN EUROPEAN LAW

A definitive decision does not exist, either in legal doctrine or socio-legal opinion, as to the exact meaning of the concept of affirmative action or, indeed, which policies are in place to carry out the protection of this fundamental principle of equality. This has led to a weakening of the concept, as well as doubt as to whether or not such policies can be legitimately carried out.

Normally, one would adopt the terminology and foundations of the evolution within North American anti-discrimination Law. However, it is true that one must take into account the lack of similarity in their relative socio-political and historical backgrounds. We will now look at the problems surrounding such a reception of terminology and foundation.

4.1. Lack of precise concepts

The lack of precise concepts produces confusion, and causes negative effects in relation to the extension of such ideas. For example, there is no distinction between the concepts of affirmative action and reverse discrimination, as well as no resolution of the relationship between gender and species. Indeed, no clarification exists within normative European Jurisprudence, or indeed doctrine. There is not even a definition of what affirmative action really is. In this sense, one could say that although no *normative definition* exists, or even an agreement on what the measures or policies of affirmative action are, it could be understood that these measures suppose the creation of mechanisms, or the use of policies, to favour individuals or groups that have been discriminated against, or who are in a disadvantaged situation.

The measures of affirmative action are a type of characteristic norm of the Welfare State, the function of which is promotional, that is, it uses stimulus measures to favour the realisation of actions or to use means for reaching a result, which is considered as advantageous.[10] The measures of affirmative action are of an indirect character, and we can distinguish them according to their functions, as follows: diffusion measures, measures of facilitation and retribution measures. The *diffusion* measures are generally formation measures, or of an advertising nature, that seek to create a statement of opinion or a sensible approach to the problem. For example, the campaigns of publicity for sexual equality, or the development of specialisation courses.

[10] Bobbio, N., "Sulla funzione promozionale del diritto", *Rivista Trimestrale di Diritto e Procedura Civile*, XII, 4, 1969, 1313–1320; and "Sulle Sanzioni Positive", *Scritti Dedicati ad Antonio Raselli*, vol. I, Milano, Giuffrè, 1971, 229–249. Both compiled in *Contribución a la Teoría del Derecho*, Spanish translation A. Ruiz Miguel, Valencia, Fernando Torres ed., 1980, especially pp. 375 ff. (Reed. Debate, Madrid, 1990).

The measures of *facilitation*, impulse, or promotion, are measures primarily tending to the attainment of some means, which are necessary to reach an end, notably the elimination of a disadvantage. By this, equality is promoted for the future. We can make a distinction between: a) *incentive* measures, used to increase the means or decrease the impact of the disadvantage, as is the case with the awarding of grants, scholarships, and the so-called *recruitment measures*; b) measures of *reverse* or *positive discrimination*: they are characterised as such, because in the case of two unequal positions, they carry out a methodology of inequality in order to benefit the weaker position. Examples of measures of reverse discrimination can be the establishment of different scales for men and women in relation to salary, the quotas or reserve of places for these disadvantaged groups in jobs, education, and the like; and c) measures of *preferential treatment*: the establishment of a priority or advantage. That is to say a preferential or unequal treatment, in the supposition that a similar situation exists, but there still remains a contextual disadvantage in one case. And finally, the *retribution* measures, or *positive sanction*: measures that are adopted after the realisation of the desired action. For example: the assignment of a prize or a fiscal exemption.

A second type of problem in this section is the lack of distinction between types of affirmative action as quotas (reverse discrimination) and preferential treatment. In another way, the enlargement of the interpretation of the idea of "quota" includes within it the measures of preferential treatment. The consequence of this is that one has to make continuous adaptations, in order to explain, for example, the difference between quotas for decision / quotas for result; flexible and rigid quotas.[11]

This confusion may outline some problems: the preferential treatment supposes a similar situation, whilst favouring one of the two. The quota system does not suppose a preferable treatment, but a "privileged" treatment, using this terminology. This means that the persons in the weaker position would not be successful in their application for employment, if such quotas were not in place. In the previous case, preferential treatment could have been produced towards any of the two persons concerned, depending on which "breaking the tie" approach is used. On the other hand, the system of quotas (in a strict sense) is different as to those "extra points", or to preferential treatment: this approach always benefits the weaker party, who would not be able to accede to the position if it were not by a criterion concerning "discrimination". However, this is too wide a notion of "quota" and implies a continuous redefinition about what precisely the term denotes in each use of it. For example, use is made of diverging expressions, such as "quotas for decision" and "quotas for results". "Quotas for decision" is what we understand as preferential treatment, whilst "quotas

[11] See "Communication from Commission to Parliament and Council", *op. cit.* The same terminology and confusion can be found in Elósegui's paper, where she tries to elaborate the concept of affirmative action and classification (section 2).

for results" would be what we describe as quotas in the strictest sense of the word.

The question gets more complicated when we use terminology such as *flexible quotas* and *rigid quotas*. This, precisely, is the interpretive solution adopted by the European Commission to clarify the judgements in Kalanke and Marschall. In this way, flexible quotas are allowed and rigid quotas prohibited. The terminology is used to denote something which has already been defined in another way, but to something else. These permitted flexible quotas are those of preferential treatment, provided the preference is on the part of the individual who is part of the disadvantaged group, and the system does not operate automatically; that is to say the possibility exists of using other elements, other than those that are kept in mind in the circumstances of the individual. As we will see, the resultant conclusion is confusing. The forbidden quotas, the rigid ones, would be those characteristic of the measures of reverse discrimination and those of preferential treatment, being those that grant the preference in an automatic way.

As it has already been said, this is due to an ambiguous use of the terminology. There exists an a-critical import of the terminology on the part of the legal culture and, indeed, of European Law; which implies, as a consequence, that instruments characteristic of positive action are not looked for within the European context. Besides producing terminological confusion, it also favours the stigmatisation of measures that are not strictly reverse discrimination, but are considered to be similar, such as those of preferential treatment. As well as this, it is intended to carry out a classification exercise and to make a distinction between different types of measures of affirmative action. In this sense, and within the measures of facilitation, we can distinguish quotas from measures of reverse discrimination, on the one hand, and from measures of preferential treatment, on the other.

4.2. The lack of connection between concepts and terminology of doctrine in relation to national or European norms and judicial decisions

The second aspect, as has already been pointed out, is that of the creation of concepts and terminology on the part of doctrine and jurisprudence, without connection to either national or European norms, or, with national or European judicial decisions.

4.2.1. The problem from the point of view of a European interpretation of law

The interpretation of Directive 76/207 on the part of the European Court of Justice, requires the definition of the *discrimination* cases *tolerated* in the exception of the section fourth of its article second. These are the permitted measures, which are,

> "guided to promote the equality of opportunities between men and women, in particular to correct the inequalities in the fact that they affect the opportunities of women."

In the first place, this supposes to determine which type of measures of affirmative action are allowed. Secondly, this implies defining the requirements of "tolerated discrimination": the under-representation of parties, the principle of equitable merit and the lack of automatic preference. The last point will take us to the problem of the "opening clause" which arises in the case of Marschall.

Before examining that, it is necessary to specify that terminology used in the interpretation by the Court comes neither from Directive one, nor the Acts in question (that of Bremen in the *Kalanke case,* and that of Nordrhein-Westfalen in the *Marschall case*). The categories discussed next, which are at the core of polemic decisions, are built by European doctrine, influenced by North American Anti-discrimination law, with abstraction of our legal context and history.[12]

4.2.2. *The requirements of "tolerated" discrimination*

A. *Rights and guarantees*

In both cases a number of enumerative approaches are carried out in a negative way. In Art. 2.1° of the Directive, the principles of equality and non-discrimination are consecrated, and the drawing of allowed actions appears as an exception to this principle. As the Court recognises "it constitutes an exception to an individual right", that should be interpreted restrictively.[13] Perhaps this is the fundamental problem of the first section, which regulates *formal equality* and of the fourth section, which supposes a nexus between formal and *substantive* equality.

The way in which the resolutions focus on this matter is not contrary to the form in which it is necessary to understand these measures. This means, the measures are not configured as rights, but as exceptions or limitations of a right, in order, from a teleological point of view, to make that right effective. This way, as regards the right to equality, they cannot be opposed to what is termed as "women's rights." These "rights" are guarantees of equality.

A further point to note is that the Directive is understood in a restrictive way, as regards the concept of equality, and is limited to formal equality, allowing only conducive measures in relation to equality of opportunities, not to the equality of results. The exception to the right of equal treatment does not imply that measures are reduced to equality of opportunities. This reduction is that of the conception maintained by the Court, and not of the concept of equality. The correct formulation, from my point of view, is that measures of affirmative

[12] See Barrère Unzueta, M., *Discriminación, Derecho Antidiscriminatorio y Acción Positiva en Favor de las Mujeres* (Madrid, Civitas, 1997), p. 115; Ruano, L., "Acciones Positivas y Discriminación Positiva", *Actualidad Jurídica Aranzadi*, n. 227, 1995, 3; Charpentier, L., "L'Arrêt Kalanke. Expression du Discours Dualiste de l'Égalité", *Revue Trimestrielle du Droit Européen,* n. 2, 1996, 287.

[13] Case Marschall section n. 32., and section n. 21 in the case Kalanke.

action may be adopted in some cases to make the principle of equality effective in its substantive dimension. The problem is that these measures may harm other dimensions of the principle-right of equality, its formal dimension. However, for this reason affirmative action measures have some limits, not only in their setting up, but in their application too.

In order to do this, one can distinguish between "tolerated discrimination" and "justified discrimination." The measures that can be adopted in the standard of the interpretation of the Court would be understood in a *negative* sense, as *exceptions* to equal treatment. In the same way, "tolerated measures" are limited to *formal equality*. On the other hand, the "justified discrimination" or "just" discrimination, is the only way of making *equality in rights or in law* effective.[14] That is to say, it is "just" discrimination because it allows us to adopt measures that, though in principle seem to contravene the idea of equality, they are necessary to make it effective in two dimensions, formal and substantive, since they cannot be understood separately.

From another point of view, once the unnecessary conflict between the right to equality and the measures taken to make it effective, is shown, it is possible to underline the possible conflict, with reference to both European and National laws. An example of this is the Spanish. The question should not be viewed merely from the idea of content, but also from the point of view of the structure of the norms.[15]

Article 2. 4 of the Directive would be a *permissive guideline* and, if we compare it with article 9.2 of the Spanish Constitution, we note, not a permissive guideline, but a *command guideline*. From this point of view, the possibility of conflicting solutions to the problem takes place for the Judge of the Spanish Courts, and, indeed, in the same way for a judge of the European court when

[14] Bobbio, N., "Equaglianza", *Enciclopedia del Novecento*, vol. II, pp. 355–364, Spanish translation in *Igualdad y Libertad* (Barcelona, Paidós, 1993), pp. 75–76. In the same sense Ferrajoli, L., "La Differenza Sessuale e le Garanzie dell'Uguaglianza", *Democrazia e Diritto*, 1993/2, 49–73, and *Diritto e Ragione. Teoria del Garantismo Penale* (Laterza, 1989) (Spanish translation by P. Andrés Ibáñez, A. Ruiz Miguel, J. C. Bayón, J. Terradillos, R. Cantarero, *Derecho y Razón. Teoría del Garantismo Penal* (Madrid, Trotta, 1995), esp. p. 905 ff.). See de Lucas, J., *El Concepto de Solidaridad* (México, Fontamara, 1993); "La Polémica Sobre los Deberes de Solidaridad", *Revista del Centro de Estudios Constitucionales*, 19, 1994, 9–88; *Puertas que se Cierran. Europa como Fortaleza* (Barcelona, Icaria, 1996).

[15] The distinction between principles and rules, and especially Alexys's theory of principles, is an interesting perspective from which to examine affirmative actions problems. But it might, perhaps, be better not just to gloss over it, as in Elósegui's paper, but to clarify Alexy's theory in the light of the later critical assessments. However, Elósegui's reading of Alexys's theory is mistaken. She distinguishes, as Alexy does, the ponderation theory, which is applied to principles, as opposed to the proportion theory, which is applied to rules. However, the principle of ponderation is used to determine normative premises, whereas, in her paper, she uses it to clarify premises of facts. For example, when she says "According to what the Theory of Principle states when this type of collision comes up, the granting of a right to one of the parties (in this case, to the woman) cannot be automatic. It is necessary to ponder the case with more reasons." (section 7). Next I analyse the concept of automatic preference and uselessness of the "opening clause". These are elements of the premises of facts, and it is not possible to use ponderation for determining them. Other mistakes may be found in her interpretation of constitutional principles in the Spanish Constitution.

deciding on Spanish law. For the Spanish Judge, in the case that has to use a norm that includes measures of affirmative action, supported by article 9.2 of the Constitution, and forbidden according to the interpretation of the European Court of Justice, he could request a pronouncement of the Court of Justice with "preliminary character", based on article 177 of the Treaty of Rome, before applying, or not, the interpretation of the Spanish Constitutional Court in light of the contrary interpretation of the European Court.

In that perspective, if a Judge has to decide, and in doing so contradicts a norm (the Directive), then this *authorises* in a restrictive way an action, whilst in application of the other (art. 9.2 of the Spanish Constitution) it *obliges* in a more extensive way the same action (that is to say, it facilitates a wider performance). The decision would not be simple, as it would be a contradiction between two guidelines. The solution to this conflict would only take place at the level of an axiological or evaluative contradiction, in relation to indetermination of the legal consequence, in which it would even be necessary to consider the concurrence of alternative solutions, and available means for the realisation of the objectives marked in the guideline. Therefore, the balance,

> "does not necessarily finish with the preferable and excluding application of one or both programmatic norms, but with the harmonisation intent between means and available ends".[16]

On the other hand, if we accept that there are two possible decisions, the result of the decision of the European Court, in relation to that of the national Constitutional Court, they must follow formal rules, and the conflict should be solved on the basis of a prevalence criterion. If we assume that no conflict of rules exists, there would be a conflict of jurisdictions.

From the perspective of the communitarian Judge, in light of recent interpretations, it would not be possible to have measures of affirmative action either on the basis of preferential treatment or of reverse discrimination, if this supposes an "automatic preference" for the member of a disadvantaged group. Obviously, this interpretation of the European Court does not keep in mind, or understand the contextual, relational, and temporary character of the concept of affirmative action, etc.[17] However, it supposes a re-interpretation, and possibly an annullation, of the interpretation of article 9.2 by the Spanish constitutional court, regarding the connection between substantive equality and formal equality. There also appears to be an emptying of the prevailing doctrine starting from judgement 128/1987, of July 16 1987, on affirmative action.

[16] Ruiz Sanz, M., *La Coherencia en el Derecho. Antinomias, Conflictos y Argumentación* (Madrid, 2000), in print.

[17] See de Lucas, J., "La igualdad ante la Ley", *El Derecho y la Justicia*, eds. E. Garzón and F. J. Laporta (Madrid, Trotta, 1996), p. 495.

B. "Tolerated discrimination"

Use of this terminology is also pejorative as a consequence of the previous conception that considers these measures as exceptions to rights. Normative configuration and doctrinal interpretation should have purified these concepts, technically, in the sense of defining clearly some exigible suppositions with the purpose of making effective the principle of equality. However, they may take another road. In this way, one can deduce that there is discrimination, and the measures foreseen in national norms cannot be tolerated if:[18]

a) a man and a woman have the *same merits* when competing in a process of promotion within employment;
b) there is an under-representation of women in that particular employment sector;
c) the norm establishes that women *automatically* enjoy a *preference* in the acquisition of a particular position of employment.[19] In other words, the woman has a "absolute and unconditional"[20] priority to employment.

The first two requirements are necessary in relation to the term *equal policies*. The first requirement is necessary for the distinction of measures of reverse discrimination within measures, as a whole, of positive action. This means, equal measures should be carried out between people that should be treated equally, and who are not in the same competitive situation, as any contrary treatment to this is discriminatory. Otherwise, if individuals are in the same situation, the applicable measures could be the rest of those measures which we have named as measures of *facilitation*.

The second requirement is absolutely necessary to characterise an affirmative action, and refers to the disadvantaged situation of the group. The third is the not tolerated approach to discrimination; that is the established doctrinal limit of these policies: automatism. Alternatively, a presumption of "*tolerated discrimination*" would exist in two circumstances:

1. If the measures "are dedicated indeed to eliminate or to reduce the inequalities in fact that could exist in the reality of social life"[21] and, alongside this, one can improve the capacity to compete and, also, to develop women's careers on an equal footing, in terms of equality.[22] Although such measures tend to produce an equality of results, one can deduce from the following sections that the decision which is reached, is based on the equality of

[18] Case Marschall , par. n. 23 and 32, and in paragraphs number 16, 22, 24 in the Kalanke decision.

[19] Paragraphs n. 16 and 22 in the Case Kalanke.

[20] This supposes a "reformulation" of the legal system, in Nino's terminology, by the doctrine of the Court, with terms not used in the law. See Nino, C.S., *Consideraciones Sobre la Dogmática Jurídica*, *op. cit.*, p. 41 ff.

[21] Case Kalanke, par. n. 18.

[22] Case Marschall, par. n. 27 and 28.

opportunities. As a result, the judgement allows measures of positive action in a generic way.

2. If the measures of reverse discrimination do not bear an automatic preference approach for the woman, but incorporate, for example, an "opening clause",[23] then we are also facing a supposition of tolerated discrimination. I suggest that this "opening clause" becomes configured by the norm as an exception to a legal consequence, and in this way, as is understood by the Court in the case of Marschall, it is in fact adapting one of the requirements of the supposition: that of equal competition. Therefore, as I point out next, it does not seem that there is much sense in setting a norm configured like an exception, nor to follow the interpretation made by the Court.

C. *The automatic preference*

The automatic configuration, or the existence of an automatic approach, that always attributes a preference towards women, is characteristic of understanding the rights as absolute. However, this is not the required characteristic of the measures of affirmative action or of reverse discrimination. These characteristics are: temporality, relational comparison, proportionality, context, extra-justification, etc. Therefore, it should not be understood in terms of limitation criteria, but as a characteristic of its definition.

This way, in both cases, one could deduce that the Court could accept "a system that grants priority to women, but whenever it is not in an automatic way." The Court understands that the "opening clause" settled down by the norm of the *Land Nordrhein-Westfalen*:

> ". . . unless they converge in the person of a candidate reasons that incline the scale to their favour, (. . .)"

can avoid the concept of automatism. However, I suggest that the interpretation of the Court is erroneous, as I will point out next. More sense can be made of the measures which Atienza proposes:

> ". . . another series of elements, of properties that the Court does not specify, but that should be of such a nature that it allows them to make some «balance», etc. (because it seems that these are, exactly the ideas that are opposed to the «automatic»)."[24]

In this sense, either the norm provides more precise criteria, so that the judge cannot use the approach of preference on the basis of sex in an automatic way, or, on the contrary, should keep in mind that the preference approach cannot be absolute and unconditional, but that it has to have a contextual, and temporary, justification. As a result, from the interpretation that can be made (from a teleological, grammatical and systematic point of view), it seems that the Court

[23] Case Marschall par. n. 24 and 33. This clause would be an "equitative exception" to priority rule as it is called by M. V. Ballestrero, "A Proposito di Azioni Positive II: L'Eguaglianza del Signor Marschall", *Ragion pratica*, 1997/8, 99–100.

[24] Atienza, M., "Un Comentario al caso Kalanke", *Doxa*, 19, 1996, 121 and 122.

admits reverse discrimination, and not only measures of affirmative action, provided that this idea of automatic preference does not exist.

However, within the norm of the *Land Nordrhein-Westfalen* it seems to be deduced that inequality which *still exists*, is "always" (in an automatic way) opted for by the *less favoured party* (that is to say, in this case, the woman). However, I think that this is not an absolute limitation, but rather it is the own character of the measure: a context measure that demands a public performance, both giving reasons and justifying this "tolerated discrimination." This means strengthening legal argumentation and justifying equalisation measures. In the Marschall case, this seems to be avoided with the term "opening clause"

> "according to which women do not enjoy preference in promotion if they converge in the person of a masculine candidate reasons that incline the balance to their favour."[25]

D. The uselessness of the opening clause

In the controversial Act of the *Land Nordrhein-Westfalen* we can distinguish with clarity the description of fact from the normative consequences in the structure of the norm. The requirements of the description of facts are:

a) women are underrepresented, in relation to men, in the organisation where the promotion is carried out;
b) there is equal merit (aptitude, ability, competence . . .) among the applicants.

The *legal consequence is* that: "preference in promotion will be granted to women."

The *exception clause or the opening clause is:* "*unless reasons converge in the person of a candidate, that incline the balance to his favour.*" Once the structure of the norm is certain, it seems clear that the *clause* is not an exception to the legal consequence, rather is it a delimitation to the second requirement of fact. That is, another norm. In addition, if this exception is about the description of facts, we are not in a case of equality of conditions, in cases where discrimination will take place. The outlined exception does not seem to make sense, if it is a description of facts in which a stronger aptitude or male competition exists. This is because "reasons" converge that incline the scale to their favour. That is to say, that an individual has more merits or capacity. Consequently, one does not understand what the "opening clause" contributes to the norm, or the justification that a court makes of it. In fact, the description in the reasoning and argumentation of the clause is characteristic of the reasoning and argumentation that the judge should make when he applies the norm, which could refer as much to a case of affirmative action as to reverse discrimination.

From the point of view of the application of the norm, the supposition is evaluated in the phase of determination of facts, as a requirement for the possibility

[25] Case Marschall par. 23 and 24.

of applying measures of equalisation. If there is inequality, objectively, that is to say, when women have more merits than men, then there is not any reason to apply equalisation measures. If women have less merits than men, one could think about a supposition of reverse discrimination that seems to be forbidden by the normative definition within the European Union, except in cases not decided in an automatic way.[26] Since automatism should be understood as an application and evaluation criterion of the circumstances, and the context of the case, the "opening clause" does not solve this problem.

On the other hand, the existence of the "opening clause" as a criterion for justification of the quotas, the aptly termed *flexible quotas,* is insufficient to explain the way in which appropriated measures are explained in terms of *rigid quotas,* which are not legitimated for the attainment of the principle of equality. This is so, because the use of the "opening clause" and the justification of the *flexible quotas, are not* formulated in relation to the principle of equality, but to other approaches like "automatic preference", which is a procedural criterion, with an indirect relationship to equality.

4.3. Conceptual elaborations with lack of foundation, or with reductive foundations: the problem of concept and conception in European Law

Policies of affirmative action make reference to State decisions carried out by a model of Welfare State, opposed in this sense to the classic liberal State.[27] Summarising, the differing opinions in the decisions of the Court would reveal conflicting conceptions of justice, and, in this case, of equality. In this section, we will investigate whether the concept of equality has been adopted as a concrete conception within a European normative context.

It seems that European norms and the decisions of the Courts maintain a liberal-individualistic conception of equality: equality is reduced to formal equality and to the equality of opportunities. This conception collides, somehow, with the conception of equality within some national States, as is the case in Spain. In our Constitution, a complementary reading should be carried out amongst articles 9.2 and 14 in relation to art. 1.1. This is, the vision of the Spanish Constitution on the State as a *Welfare State*, in which we include not only aspects of equalisation, or of non-discrimination, but also of *compensation.*

As we have argued, the import of American anti-discrimination law has been restricted with an excluding intention. That is, it seems that some of the North American criteria have been adopted in a reductive way, and without contextualisation. However, this restriction enters into conflict, not only with national

[26] Legal dogmatics may not explain why gender reverse discrimination measures are forbidden in this sense, but in all domestic laws handicapped reverse discrimination measures are allowed.

[27] Alexy, R., *Theorie der Grundrechte* (Frankfurt, Suhrkamp, 1986) (Spanish translation, *Teoría de los Derechos Fundamentales*, trans. E. Garzón (Madrid, CEC, 1993), especially p. 419.)

normatives, but rather with a generous interpretation of art. 117 of the Treaty of Rome. In fact, some of the modifications of the Treaty of Amsterdam clarify the position in relation to the attainment of equal treatment and equality of opportunities in employment, allowing the adoption of measures of affirmative action. However, as it has been shown, the Directive 76/207 is restrictive in the way it refers to the concept of equality.

In my opinion, the problem appears in the wording of the fourth section and, indeed, the previous one, according to which the equality of *treatment* and the *equality of opportunities* are comparable on the same basis, or, at least in light of an exclusive interpretation of other dimensions of equality. However, equal treatment does not eliminate the substantive aspects and equality in results, which are not opposed to equality of opportunities. This means, that equal treatment is reduced to equality of formal treatment, and the equality of opportunities, which excludes the equality of results. In a less fortunate formulation of the Directive, alongside a less favourable aspect of social policies in Europe, a restrictive interpretation takes place, on the part of the Court. Although the normative does not impede it, the European Court carries out a reductive interpretation of the concept of equality, located in a liberal-individualist conception that seems to be in contradiction with the concept of equality within domestic legal systems.

5. CONCLUSIONS

1. Policies allowed by European decisions limit the possibility of measures of reverse discrimination because it seems that they are not recognised beyond the confines of equality, from a formal perspective.
2. The permitted measures of reverse discrimination are not defined in a concrete way in the case of Kalanke, and their enunciation in the case of Marschall is erroneous, as it determines the lack of automatism in an incorrect way. Many argumentative elements in these decisions use a foreign terminology, not clarified in our context, and whose construction on the part of legal dogmatics has left little of European regulations, of domestic statutory law and of the decisions of the domestic Courts.
3. A reduction of the measures of affirmative action, to those that are compatible with the equality of opportunities, is a reduction of the concept maintained by the Court, but not of the concept of equality, which should continue to be based on our distinction of substantive and formal equality.
4. The criterion of automatism is not a good basis to differentiate the measures of reverse discrimination from the rest of the measures of affirmative action. It serves to exclude policies, that are not policies of equalisation, but rather policies which seek configuration as rights. This is not possible for the type of measures used (contextual, temporal, etc..)
5. One may doubt the legitimacy of measures proposed by the European normative. In the first place, because a certain deficit of legitimacy follows from

the relationships among the European institutions, as the separation of powers principle is not respected. Secondly, the measures are insufficient to make the value of equality effective.

6. The legitimacy of measures of affirmative action, according to the interpretation that has been carried out here, is coherent with superior values enunciated in domestic legal systems, such as the Spanish, that go beyond the strict interpretation of average lawyers and of judgements of the European Court of Justice, and beyond the convenience of political interpretations of the Commission.
7. European domestic constitutions, as well as the European normative, offer possibilities that should not be reduced by the restrictive interpretations of the liberal-individualistic conception of the European Court of Justice. This normative mark allows an extension of ideas in relation to individuals, object, environment and content of measures, to apply and make effective the principle of equality. In this sense, and keeping in mind the social, political and economic contexts, measures of affirmative action should be assured, and even in some cases be extended to other disadvantaged collectives, not only women, for example, foreigners, ethnic minorities, linguistic minorities, the handicapped, etc. In fact, it is necessary to remember that the reason for the existence of these measures is the effectiveness of the equality in both dimensions (formal and substantive). The *equality in the law* demands that fundamental rights are guaranteed, and this guarantee supposes a connection among the normative levels of concept, validity and effectiveness of rights.

11

*The Kalanke Case and the Marschall Case in the Court of Justice of the European Communities. The Women's Quota and Alexy's Principles Theory**

MARIA ELOSEGUI

1. INTRODUCTION

In this paper, I shall try to clarify some concepts that are usually somewhat confusing, such as affirmative action, preferential treatment, inverse discrimination and the controversial issue of quota.[†] At the same time, I shall comment on the discussions around whether or not affirmative action plans are needed to achieve male-female equality within Europe. We currently have the Third Spanish Plan for Equal Opportunities Between Women and Men[1] and the Fourth Community Action Programme for Equal Opportunities For Men and Women (1996–2000) approved by decision of the Labour and Social Affairs Council of the European Commission on December 22, 1995.[2]

I shall attempt a comparative analysis of the situation within one of our neighbouring countries, specifically, Germany. Our main concern, here, will be the problem that has arisen in this country before the Court of Justice of the European Communities regarding the laws that most of the German *Länder* have about quota for women to accede to and be promoted within public administration.

* Text revised as to the English language by James Varney and Mark Van Hoecke.

† I have to thank, especially, Robert Alexy, with whom I discussed the content of this paper. Of course, the interpretation is mine. I thank also the Humboldt Foundation, which enabled me to be a Humboldt Fellow during the years 1997 and 1998 in the Faculty of Law of the *Christian-Albrechts Universität* in Kiel (Germany), working with professor Alexy.

1 *III Plan para la Igualdad de Oportunidades entre Mujeres y Hombres. 1997–2000* (Madrid: Ministerio de Trabajo y Asuntos Sociales, Instituto de la Mujer, 1997).

2 *IV Programa de Acción Comunitaria a Medio Plazo para la Igualdad de oportunidades entre Hombres y Mujeres (1996–2000),* Decisión del 21.12.1995, Comunicación de la Comisión sobre integrar la igualdad de oportunidades entre hombres y mujeres en el conjunto de las políticas y acciones comunitarias, 21.2.1996.

The problem has transcended the borders of Germany due to the fact that several issues of prejudice have come before the Court of Justice of the European Communities, which is the organ that must interpret European directives regarding equality. Therefore, the interpretation handed down by this Court must be complied with by all the EU countries.

Three years ago, the German Federal Labour Court consulted the Court of Justice of the European Communities on whether or not a certain Bremen Act was compatible with the European Directive on Equal Opportunities. This particular statute required, in contests for posts and staff promotion in the case of a tie between a man and a woman and in professional categories in which women were under represented, that the post be given to the woman. It is the famous case of *Eckhard Kalanke*. The Court contended that Art. 4 of the Bremen Act was not compatible with the European directive on Equal Opportunities because it discriminated against men.[3]

This was considered a step backwards with regards to European policies concerning Equal Opportunities. Later, a court in the *Land* of Rheinland-Westfalen (*Verwaltungs-gericht* Gelsenkirchen)[4] submitted a new preliminary question regarding a new case, that of *Hellmut Marschall*.[5] This time it had to do with the compatibility of the Equal Opportunities Act in the Public Administration of Rheinland-Westfalen with paragraphs 1 and 4 of Article 2 of the Council's directive 76/207/CEE of February 9, 1976, regarding the application of the principle of equal treatment between men and women with reference to access to professional employment, training and promotion and working conditions. In this case the Court determined that this law of quota was compatible with the European directive. The Advocate General, Jacobs, considered that the same resolution had to be applied as in the Kalanke case.[6] However, in the Court's judgment, the law of Rheinland-Westfalen about quota and that of Bremen were not equivalent.

Both judgments have been the object of numerous comments, especially among the defenders or detractors of quota in the German Scholars. The issue is not trivial, since almost all German *Länder* have statutes about quota with

[3] Gesetz zur Gleichstellung von Frau und Mann im öffentlichen Dienst des Landes Bremen, (Landesgleichstellunggesetz), *Gestzblatt der Freien Hansestadt Bremen*, 29 November 1990, Brem GBl. S 433; *Aus Millimeterarbeit. 5 Jahre Bremisches Landesgleichstellungsgesetz*, Freie hansestadt Bremen, Bremische Zentralstelle für die Verwirklichung der Gleichberechtigung der Frau; *Gesetz über die Errichtung der Bremischen Zentralstelle für die Verwirklichung der Gleichberechtigung der Frau*. 16.12.1980 (in force as from January 1st, 1991); *Frauenförderplan nach dem Landesgleichstellungsgesetz (LGG) für die senatorische Dienstelle des Senators für Arbeit und Frauen*, Bremen, 15 November 1993, Senator für Arbeit und Frauen, 1993; Arbeitsgericht Bremen, 8 Ca 8034/91.5 December 1991 (Kalanke); Bundesarbeitgericht, 1 AZR 590/92 (2 Sa 322/91 Bremen). 22 June 1993; Bundesarbeitgericht, I AZR 590/92 (A) (2 Sa 322/91 Bremen). 5 March, *Der Personalrat* 1996,12, 508–512; Landesarbeitgericht Bremen. 8 July 1992. 2 Sa 322/91; BAG, 22.6.93—1 AZR 590/93. *SAE*, 242.

[4] Beschluß OVG Nordhrein-Westfalen, 21.12.1995.

[5] ECJ 11 November 1997, case C–409/95, *Hellmut Marschall* vs. *Land Nordhein-Westfalen*.

[6] ECJ 17 October 1995, case C–450/93 (*Eckhard Kalanke vs Freie Hansestadt Bremen*). Directive 76/207/EEC Art. 2; BremLGG & 4. *JZ* 1996, 4: 196–197.

different judicial configurations. Although they existed before, the German Constitution introduced, in 1994, a modification in Art. 3.2. on equality between the sexes, creating a constitutional mandate addressed to the powers of the State with obligation to remove the obstacles that could impede factual equality, not only legal.

All of this has triggered, in recent years, an immense and fruitful doctrinal discussion on the legal justification of affirmative actions to achieve *de facto* equality in a "Social State". It has led to delimiting terms like affirmative action, affirmative discrimination, and reverse discrimination.

The thesis maintained in this article is, firstly, that the legal arguments presented before the Court of Justice of the European Communities in both preliminary questions are coherent; secondly, that there has been no change or rupture in the Court's line of jurisprudence; thirdly, it is asserted that the key for this interpretation lies in the problem of weighing constitutionally protected legal goods. To this aim, we shall use Robert Alexy's[7] theory of "Principles and Fundamental Rights".

The difference that the German doctrine establishes between subjective rights and the objective mandate directed to the State to achieve *de facto* equality helps to solve this problem. That is, the distinction between a subjective right to have a job and an objective mandate directed to the State to achieve real equality as contemplated in Art. 3.2. of the German Constitution.

On the one hand, we are facing legal issues with correct or incorrect interpretation of current statutes, but, on an ethical political plane, we must go beyond this and discuss what are the most desirable equality policies. In short, law is an instrument to serve justice, or indeed it should be. Laws are not something immutable, but rather debatable and changing, and this is where each one must forge an opinion, but with a fundamental basis and structure and not at the mercy of clichés and customary standards.

This is why we are going to proceed along the following steps.

1. Define some concepts to focus the discussion, with particular regard to what affirmative action means, and including reverse discrimination, also termed affirmative discrimination.
2. We shall analyse whether or not the quota system is justified from the point of view of Robert Alexy's "Theory of Principles". The key question is what kind of quota harm subjective rights and what kind of affirmative actions are legal according to constitutional and European Community law.

[7] Alexy, R., *Theorie der Grundrechte* (Baden-Baden, Nomos), 2nd ed. (Frankfurt am Main, Suhrkamp, 1985); Alexy, R., *Theorie der Juristischen Argumentation* (Frankfurt am Main, Suhrkamp, 1991); Alexy, R., *Begriff und Geltung des Rechts* (Freiburg, 1992); Alexy, R., *Recht, Vernunft, Diskurs* (Frankfurt am Main, Suhrkamp, 1995). English trans. "Individual Rights and collective Goods", in NINO, *Human Rights*. Published as "Individuelle Rechte und kollektive Güter", *Internationales Jahrbuch für Rechtsphilosophie und Gsetzgebung* 1989, 49–70; Alexy, R., "Discourse Theory and Human Rights", *Ratio Iuris* 1996, 9, 209–35.

The answer to these problems lies within the framework of the philosophy of law; that is, what kind of State do we want to conceive? A liberal State is not the same as a social State.[8] It embraces social rights in general and not just women's issues. At the same time, it requires an anthropological framework from which to respond to the issue of what kind of male-female relationships we want in our society and which distribution, if any, of roles is the fairest.

In this sense, this issue, contrary to how it is approached in many debates, affects men just as much as women, because it affects society as a whole. It is not a female caprice just to rid herself of domestic chores and achieve self-fulfillment through insertion in the labour market. This vision arises from a fairly short-sighted perspective. The achievement of real equality between men and women contributes to making society fairer and richer for everyone: we all end up winning. Measures to achieve true equality is not a feminist claim; it is a question of justice that must concern all citizens. If we are not capable of tackling this challenge, the result will be social imbalance, the consequences of which will be suffered by all. A society with second class citizens is a sick society.

2. THE CONCEPT OF AFFIRMATIVE ACTION

The aim of affirmative action philosophy was to achieve justice and equality by helping both people in need and the least fortunate. This policy started in the United States in the 1970's, triggered by the discrimination against Afro-Americans and other minorities. Later, it was applied for achieving equality between women and men. Initially, it attempted to repair or compensate for the racial discrimination that the coloured, black, population had suffered in the past.[9] However, the underlying philosophy today is not so much to repair something from the past but rather to reach *de facto* equality in the future, especially in the case of the female population.[10]

This policy has been applied more recently to the integration of disabled persons in our society, both physically and psychologically. This has meant a great change in mentality and is successful in that it has brought about a radical change in attitude towards these people. By way of example, the change in Germany, which is not so far away, is from the Nazi philosophy, which sought to eliminate these people, to the current German law that truly protects the disabled. This German law requires 6% of all company's jobs to be reserved for the disabled, while in Spain it is only 2%. Moreover, it grants real economic

[8] Denninger, E., "La Reforma Constitucional en Alemania: entre Ética y Seguridad Jurídica", *Revista Estudios Políticos* 1994, 84, 69.

[9] Grafrath, B., *Wie gerecht ist die Frauenquote?. Eine praktisch-philosophische Untersuchung* (Würzburg, Königshausen & Neuman, 1992), p. 14.

[10] Rössler, B., "Quotierung und Gerechtigkeit: Ein Überblick über die Debatte", in *Quotierung und Gerechtigkeit: eine Moralphilosophische Kontroverse* (Frankfurt/Main, New York, Campus Verlag, 1993), pp. 7–28.

support. This would require a special analysis, but, our interest here is to focus on affirmative actions relating to women.

Moving to consider the subject of affirmative actions, as Bernard Gräfrath[11] points out, we should say that no stereotypical affirmative action program exists, but rather that there are many programmes and different measures existing, depending on the individual country's legislative and philosophical approach. Many different plans are framed within this concept. Besides, it is necessary to differentiate between affirmative actions, preferential treatments, affirmative discrimination and the quota policy. It is also necessary to distinguish between measures that attempt to promote *de facto* equality between women and men and the attainment of equal opportunities in society.[12]

For the following distinctions, we follow Fernando Rey, Professor of Constitutional Law at the University of Valladolid.[13] According to this author:

> "Affirmative actions are all those measures to impulse and promote, the objective of which is to establish equality between men and women, especially, through the elimination of *de facto* inequalities".[14]

Some of the affirmative actions for achieving equality for women would be:

> "The measures that tend to integrate or remedy any discriminatory aspect that characterises female presence (or absence) in the labour market (specific occupational training, training for jobs traditionally considered only for men, recycling courses, encouraging private hiring of women, etc.)".

For example, for some professional training measures or for retraining older women, who want to reinsert themselves into the labour market, etc., there can be a sufficient offer of places available through the state employment offices. Measures for integration and against discrimination in the job market include occupational training, education against stereotypes in schools, educational policies on the role played by the new distribution of functions for men and women, for example, in Spanish legislation on education (LOGSE). It is foreseen that the topic of equality will be taught through the *syllabi* of all subjects. In addition there might be flexible schedules to make family and professional responsibilities compatible and joint responsibility, that is, co-responsibility and mutual co-operation, in the distribution of domestic obligations and of educating and caring for children. There could also be fiscal incentives for companies to hire women or young people, as well as women that decide to reinsert themselves into the labour market after a period of child bearing, and policies of providing incentives for companies that establish measures to facilitate the integration of work and the family, i.e. installing nurseries in the workplace, for

[11] Gräfrath, B., *op. cit.*, 15.

[12] Barrere Unzueta, Mª A., *Discriminación, derecho antidiscriminatorio y acción positiva en favor de las mujeres*, Madrid: Cuadernos Cívitas, 1997.

[13] Rey, F., *El Derecho Fundamental a no ser Discriminado por Razón del Sexo* (Madrid: McGraw-Hill/Interamericana de España, 1995).

[14] Rey, F., *op. cit.*, 91.

example, *el Corte Inglés* in Madrid, the University of the Basque Country, Nestlé etc.:

> "Favour, within work conditions and hours, balance between family and professional responsibilities and a better distribution of them between the two sexes. That is, an organisation of work tailored to women".[15]

Some laws have been adopted in Spain along this line. Act 64/1997 of 26 December 1997, on measures to encourage permanent contracts for women consists in the creation of a contract for encouraging permanent posts, another for training and another for on-the-job practice. The aim is to create stable employment and convert temporary contracts into permanent contracts. Act 64/1997 consists in urgent measures to improve the labour market and encourage permanent contracts. Annex III of the Directive of 6 August 1992 established the list of professions or trades in which women are underrepresented. These statutes substitute Act 22/1992 of 30 July 1992, that established urgent measures to encourage employment and protect unemployed workers over 45 years of age and the disabled. A subsidy of 500,000 pesetas was established for an employer who hired an unemployed woman over 25 years of age in a profession or trade in which women are underrepresented, or a woman that wanted to reinsert herself into professional activity after an interruption of at least 5 years. Act 42/1994 of 30 December 1994, now repealed, established, in art. 44.1, the collectives that benefited from encouraging temporary employment. The Royal Decree 11/1998 of 4 September 1998 regulated the discounts on social security contributions for temporary contracts with unemployed people to substitute women employees on leave for maternity, adoption or temporary care of an orphan.

Opposed to the foregoing general measures of affirmative action, preferential treatment and affirmative discrimination and, within the latter, the quota system, are different measures of affirmative action with stricter and more concrete provisions:

> "Reverse discrimination is a specific, more incisive and effective, version of affirmative actions that adopts the form of quota and preferential treatment. Through reverse discrimination measures, a rigid reservation of a minimum guaranteed number of posts (jobs, places on electoral tickets, etc.) are established by assigning a number or percentage or attributing special points or qualifications to the groups that are to be favoured. Quota are the genuine measure for inverse discrimination".[16]

In a general sense, we could say that both systems produce an inequality in treatment, in this case, favourable to a group that was previously discriminated against or that is triggered by a situation of *de facto* inequality, but there is no move afoot to remedy such a situation. This is why it is called affirmative dis-

[15] Ballestrero, M. V., "Le Azioni Positive fra Eguaglianza e Diritto Desiguale", *Le Nuove Leggi Civile Commentate* 1994, 1, 11.20; REY, F., *op. cit.*, 91.

[16] Rey, F., *op. cit.*, 85.

crimination; it discriminates against some in order to favour those that were previously being discriminated against, for example, blacks, Indian minorities,[17] women, the disabled, etc. who were discriminated against for racial or cultural reasons.

In spite of all this, there is a great legal and philosophical difference between the affirmative actions of preferential treatment and the quota system. The affirmative actions that we have mentioned above in the European context do not place two people, who are demanding a right, into direct confrontation with each other; they only produce indirect discrimination.

The quota system for people that apply for a job, however, produces direct discrimination.[18] In order not to break with the fundamental principles of justice and constitutional demands, law requires differential treatments to be strictly justified. In principle, there should be an attempt to apply the general Aristotelian rule of treating what is equal the same and what is unequal differently, in order to favour formal equality. The idea is to justify why we accept that we reserve a quota of jobs, and even a parking place, for persons who start with an initial disadvantage, that they are never going to overcome, like a disabled person. On which basis, and under what conditions, do we justify that a train car is reserved for women with children, or a seat on a bus for war invalids or senior citizens?

Before making a judgment about quota, we should take into account other distinctions within the quota system, which vary according to the country and the legislation. There is an essential difference between the USA and Europe in the case of affirmative action regarding women. In Europe, quota are only applied when two candidates, man and woman, compete for a post in public administration and present equal merits; that is, in the case of a tie (*Pattsituation*). Therefore, the case of a woman with less merits displacing a man never arises.

Having clarified this point, we move on, briefly, to mention some types of quota:

(a) *Fixed quota*. The idea is to cover a set percentage, independently of merits:

In political parties. In Italy, for example, there existed a statute that made it obligatory for the lists of candidates to alternate, in rigorous order, between a woman and a man. This law has been declared unconstitutional by the Italian Constitutional Court.[19] In Germany, there exist quota in lists of candidates in the statutes of some *Länder* like Schleswig-Holstein. In Spain, some parties like the PSOE have percentage quota, but they are not so rigorous. The same is valid for almost all German political parties: the first were the Greens; it then

[17] Kymlicka, W., *Multicultural Citizenship* (Oxford, Oxford University Press, 1995).

[18] Young, I. M., *Justice and the Politics of Difference* (Princeton, New Jersey, Princeton University Press, 1990). Goldman, A. H., *Justice and Reverse Discrimination* (Princeton, New Jersey, Princeton University Press, 1997).

[19] Ballestrero, Mª V., "Acciones Positivas. Punto y Aparte", *Doxa* 1996, 19, 91–109.

extended to the Socialist Party (SPD); then to the Party of the Christian Democratic Union (CDU) and to the Federal Party, etc.[20] These rules are drawn up in the statutes of each political party through democratic decision of its members; they are not imposed by the State.

With equal qualifications. For example, the law for the disabled in Spain requires companies with more than 50 employees to hire 2% of physically or psychologically disabled. But these persons must previously present equal qualifications to those of the rest of their peers. In public administrations, they must pass the same exercises or tests to accede to that post.[21] In Germany, the law is more generous, because it requires 6%.[22] In both cases, there is a threat of economic sanction if this requirement is not complied with.

Without equal qualifications. For example, there are minimum numbers for certain races for university posts in the United States or Canada for Afro-Americans, Indians, Chicanos and Eskimos. The reason is the philosophy of compensating for past injustices and there being in a situation of underrepresentation.

(b) *Quota as a target* or an objective: they aim at reaching parity between men and women, up to 50%, but are applied only when the woman has the same qualifications as the man. That is, in the case of a tie, and only if, in that sector or professional category, women are underrepresented.[23]

The mechanism for implementing this policy is also different. The difference is not just a nuance, but rather determines the limits within which the quota system can be legal or illegal. *Automatic quota in case of a tie.* They would automatically grant priority to the woman without taking into account the personal circumstances of the male candidate. This is the type of quota that seemed to be present in the Bremen Act on equal opportunities in Public Administration. It does not contemplate the possibility of exceptions. The Court of Justice of the European Communities determined that this type of quota harms the other candidate's individual rights because it does not admit weighing the subjective rights that are in play. As Gräfath states, the quota problem becomes clear when one asks under what conditions women's quota can be admitted.[24]

(c) *The quota are not automatically applied,* or the regulation contains a social clause or reservation, or clause of exception (*Härtefall, Härteklausel*), whereby, in spite of the policy of promoting women, the other candidate's social conditions are taken into account in such a way that the woman will be given priority with equal merits when women are underrepresented, unless the other candidate's social circumstances, in an exceptional case, require otherwise. In principle, preference should be granted to the woman in the case of promotion.

[20] Ebsen, I., "Verbindliche Quotenregelungen für Frauen und Männer", in *Parteistatuten* (Heidelberg, R. v. Decker & C. F. Müller, 1988).

[21] Royal Decree (*Real Decreto*) 1.451/ 1983, Constitutional Court Sentence 269/94.

[22] Pfarr, H. M., & Bertelsmann, K., *op. cit.*,108, 91–94.

[23] Sacksofsky, U., *op. cit.*, 406.

[24] Gräfath, B., *op. cit.*, 25.

But, if circumstances would require so, equity imposes an exception to this privilege.

This is exactly the type of legislation of Rheinland-Westfalen,[25] that the Court of Justice of the European Communities considered compatible with Directive 76/207. Point 9 in the Kalanke sentence says:

> "The referring court considers that the quota regime is compatible with the aforementioned German constitutional and legal provisions in paragraph 6. They specify that article 4 of the *Grundgesetz* must be interpreted in agreement with the German Constitution in the sense that, although, in principle, preference should be granted to the woman in the case of promotion, equity imposes an exception to that privilege, if circumstances so require."

(d) In the case of quota that tend towards a 50% parity, but depending on the circumstances, we talk about *flexible quota*, or quota that depend on the candidates' conditions. There is no fixed reservation of posts.[26]

Let us now apply Robert Alexy's theory of principles to the affirmative actions in favour of equal opportunities for women, to the subject of quota in general as well as to rigid quota.

3. ALEXY'S THEORY OF PRINCIPLES. ITS APPLICATION TO THE PROBLEM OF QUOTA LAWS FOR WOMEN. RULES AND PRINCIPLES

Robert Alexy's theory of principles is enlightening for analysing the constitutionality of affirmative actions and quota for women. For this purpose, three questions must be examined:

1. Individual rights and collective goods.
2. Fundamental rights as subjective goods and objective norms.
3. Justification of unequal treatment to achieve equal opportunities and promotion of women, according to the "treat unequal equally" principle. In this sense it is necessary to distinguish between:
   —*Affirmative actions.*
   —*Preferential treatment.*
   —*Reverse discrimination.* The regulation of quota. Quota for women. Within this, we must differentiate between *indirect reverse discrimination* (legal), and therefore, constitutionally allowed, and *direct reverse discrimination* (illegal), which goes beyond the limits of what is constitutionally allowed, and which also transgresses European community directives.

[25] Gesetz zur Förderung der beruflichen Chancen für Frauen im öffentlichen Dienst (Frauenförderungsgesetz) v. 31.10.1989, GVNW, S, 567. Nordhrein-Westfalen, 1989.

[26] Classen, C.D., "Wie viele Wege führen zur Gleichberechtigung von Männern und Frauen?", *JZ* 19: 927; Hermann, E., *op. cit.*, 230.

To this purpose, we shall use Alexy's well-known distinction between rules and principles:

> "The decisive point for the distinction between rules and principles is that principles are norms that order something to be done to the maximum degree possible within existing legal and real possibilities. Therefore, principles are mandates of optimisation, which are characterised by the fact that they can be fulfilled to a degree which is different from the measure due to their fulfillment, not only depending on the real possibilities, but also on the legal ones".[27]

By way of contrast:

> "On the other hand, rules are norms that can only be fulfilled or not. If a rule is valid, then exactly what it says must be done. Therefore, rules contain determinations of what is possible in reality and in law. This means that the difference between rules and principles is qualitative and not a matter of degree. All norms are either a rule or a principle".[28]

4. INDIVIDUAL RIGHTS AND COLLECTIVE RIGHTS

Individual rights are *prima facie* rights. They can be limited when they collide with a collective good or with another individual right.[29] When we refer to a collective good, we are talking about an object, a good, which belongs jointly to several subjects. When speaking about collective rights, we refer to a group of people that are entitled to a right. This distinction is important in the theory of principles, because, while it admits the legitimate existence of collective goods, it rejects the concept of collective rights.[30]

A collective good is that which cannot be distributed, nor divided into parts. A collective good for our society would be to achieve the greatest possible equality among its citizens or to act so that there would be less poor people. This would improve the welfare of all, not just that of the people directly affected: it would reduce the delinquency rate, it would increase the citizens' safety (collective good). The reduction in unemployment, through policies that encourage

[27] Alexy, R., *Theorie der Grundrechte*, 75–77; "Der für die Unterscheidung von Regeln und Prinzipien entscheidende Punkt ist, dass *Prinzipien* Normen sind, die gebieten, dass etwas in einem relativ auf die rechtlichen und tatsächlichen Möglichkeiten möglichst hohen Masse realisiert wird. Prinzipien sind demnach *Optimisierungsgebote*, die dadurch charakterisiert sind, dass sie in unterschiedlichen Graden erfüllt werden können und *dass das gebotene* Mass ihrer Erfüllung nicht nur von den tatsächlichen, sondern auch von den rechtlichen Möglichkeiten abhängt".

[28] Alexy, R., ibid., "Demgegenüber sind *Regeln* Normen, die stets nur entweder erfüllt oder nicht erfüllt werden können. Wen eine Regel gilt, dann ist es geboten, genau das zu tun, was sie verlangt, nicht mehr und nicht weniger. Regeln enthalten damit *Festsetzungen* im Raum des tatsächlich und rechtlich Möglichen. Dies bedeutet, dass die Unterscheidung zwischen Regeln und Prinzipien eine qualitative Unterscheidung und keine Unterscheidung dem grade nach ist. Jede Norm ist entweder einer Regel oder eine Prinzip".

[29] Alexy, R., *Recht, Vernunft, Diskurs*, *op. cit.*, 238; Alexy, R., *Theorie der Grundrechte*, *op. cit.*, 164.

[30] Alexy, R., *Recht, Vernunft, Diskurs*, *op. cit.*, 239–240.

employment, could be a collective good. Nevertheless, the right to work is an individual *prima facie* right, that each individual, as an individual, bears, but it is not a definitive right. An unemployed person does not have a special collective right inasmuch as he belongs to the collective of the unemployed. Likewise, each job is not a collective good, since it can be distributed and is not occupied by all of us, but rather by concrete individuals. The right to work, and not be discriminated against in terms of sex (for women as well as men) is an individual right or subjective right.

The State's affirmative actions to encourage *de facto* equality of women would be a collective good or objective right (although, as we shall see later, the State's affirmative actions are sometimes aimed at achieving individual rights). The promotion of women's equality is a collective good.

The Theory of principles jointly sustains:

—the non reductibility of individual rights to collective goods and
—*vice versa*, the non reductibility of collective goods to individual rights.

The graphic representation would be two circles that overlap a little.

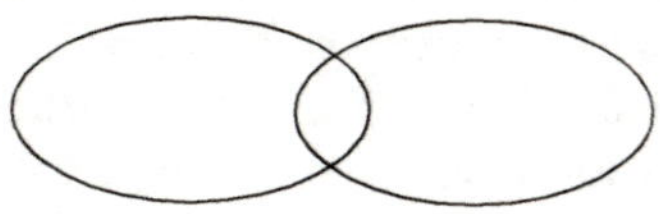

There can occasionally be good reason to attribute (grant) rights to the individual, so that he can choose collective goods for himself or for the community. However, this situation cannot be generalised. As a rule, there exist more persuasive reasons in favour of establishing collective modes of imposing collective goods, as occur in the democratic process.

The State's affirmative actions for achieving a collective good must be established, in democratic societies, through democratic decisions, but this is not sufficient for its legitimation, because they have limitations. For example, the Bremen Act, establishing quota for acceding to posts and for promotion in public administration, was decided at the time by majority agreement, that is, democratically. Nevertheless, the Court of Justice of the European Communities considered that the Bremen legislator overstepped his competence and violated an individual right, which cannot be infringed in the name of encouraging equality. The directive promotes equal opportunities, but does not permit direct reverse discrimination against the other party's individual right. The end of achieving *de facto* equality does not justify the automatic violation of the parties' subjective rights, but rather, in any case, requires balancing (*Abwägung*).

5. COLLISION BETWEEN INDIVIDUAL RIGHTS AND COLLECTIVE RIGHTS

According to the "Theory of Principles", as well as to the German Constitutional Court's jurisprudence, individual rights as well as collective goods are principles. Art. 3.2. of the *Grundgesetz*, in its second part, formulates a principle, which implies a *prima facie* mandate directed to the State for achieving *de facto* equality. Only in a second instance, when the legislator makes specific decisions, does this mandate become a rule. In our case, the State's concrete regulations of affirmative actions, statutes on equality, have the rank of rules. Equal opportunities should not be achieved through direct reverse discriminations.

Objective rights are born in the "Social State". The State has the obligation to encourage or make the achievement of individual rights possible, as well as to take care of collective goods.[31]

The Spanish, as well as the German States, are social States. Art. 1 of the Spanish Constitution reads: "España se constituye como un Estado democrático de derecho" (Spain constitutes itself as a democratic State under the rule of law). And Art. 9: "Corresponde a los poderes públicos promover las condiciones para que la libertad y la igualdad del individuo y de los grupos en que se integra sean reales y efectivas: remover los obstáculos que impidan o dificulten su plenitud y facilitar la participación de todos los ciudadanos en la vida politica, económica, cultural y social" (It is in the competence of the public powers to promote the conditions for freedom and equality for the individual, and for the groups of which he is a member, to be real and effective: remove the obstacles that impede or hamper its fulfillment and facilitate the participation of all citizens in political, economic, cultural and social life). But the problem lies in what the limitations on the State's intervention to achieve real equality are. Which State actions are just and which are not?.[32]

In the case of a conflict between an individual good and a collective good or a conflict between two collective goods, the "Theory of Principles" requires that the case be pondered by using the principle of equity. *A priori* solutions cannot be given.[33]

6. SUBJECTIVE RIGHTS AS FUNDAMENTAL RIGHTS AND OBJECTIVE NORMS

Subjective rights are actionable fundamental rights, that is, claimable in court, as opposed to the States' objective rights. These objective norms, directed

[31] Alexy, R., *Recht, Vernunft, Diskurs*, op. cit., 262–264; Alexy, R., *Theorie der Grundrechte*, *op. cit.*, Chapters 8 and 9.

[32] Rodríguez-Piñero, M., and Fernández, Mª.F., *Igualdad y Discriminación* (Madrid, Tecnos, 1986). Ruiz Miguel, A., "La Igualdad en la Jurisprudencia del Tribunal Constitucional", *Doxa* 1996, 19: 39–88.

[33] Alexy, R., *Recht, Vernunft, Diskurs, op. cit.*, 258.

towards the State, do not grant a subjective right, which is claimable in court, e.g. the right to a job. Both are principles. Only when they are made specific in the form of rules will they be definitive.[34]

binding				not binding			
subjective		objective		subjective		objective	
definitive	prima facie	definitive	prima facie	definitive	prima facie	definitive	prima facie
1	2	3	4	5	6	7	8

The Spanish Constitution, as well as the German Constitution, in its art. 3.3, contains a fundamental right in the defence of individuals (subjective side), which is spelled out in the rules that prohibit all direct and indirect discrimination. However, at the same time, art. 3.II expresses an objective value decision (rooted in the principle of the social State, but particularly, in the special extra protection granted by the anti-discriminatory principle), according to which, the legislator must lead the public powers and society to equal opportunities for men and women (objective side).

"The objective side is not legally a rule, but rather a principle (that is, a mandate to optimise according to the existing *de facto* and legal conditions): the principle of affirmative actions for encouraging women's equality".[35]

Affirmative action could be of two types, some more programmed, others more concrete rules. However, the ones which are not concrete are something more than rules.

—Art. 3. I. GG. is a type 4 principle. A binding, *prima facie* objective norm.
—Art. 3.II. GG. is a type 4 principle, directed to the State. Binding, objective, prima facie: for example, objective norms that contain *prima facie* obligations and which, in turn, possess the nature of principles. A parallel could be established with the Spanish Constitution's art. 14, on equality. The first sentence, which prohibits discrimination, is an obligatory principle, subjective, *prima facie*, since it admits recourse to the courts in case of violation. Nevertheless, the last part of article 14 is an obligatory principle, objective, *p. f.*, but not claimable in court.
—Art. 3.III. A type 2 principle. Subjective right. Obligatory, subjective, *prima facie*.

Affirmative actions can give rise to different judicial norms:

[34] Alexy, R., *Recht, Vernunft, Diskurs, op. cit.*, 265–266 and 274–275.
[35] Rey, F., *op. cit.*, 83; Alexy, R., *Theorie der Grundrechte, op. cit.*

—Some are only advice, merely promotional norms; for example, tax deduction measures, i.e. if women fulfilling certain age conditions are hired. These dispositions are type 7 rules, non-obligatory, objective, definitive.
—The typical political goals of the affirmative action plans, which are mostly vague, pertain to type 4 principles, obligatory, objective, *prima facie:* for example, the general equal opportunities plans.
—Rigid quota for the disabled could be considered in the following way;

For the company, it is a type 3 rule, obligatory, objective, definitive, since it is obligatory.

For the disabled person, it is a type 1 rule; obligatory, subjective and a definitive right.

—Women's quota laws are, for the State, type 3 rules: obligatory, objective and grant definitive rights, because they are objective obligatory norms which cause definitive obligations and are rules by nature.
—Women's quota for jobs and promotions in the German public administration are type 1 rules: obligatory, subjective and grant a definitive right.[36] This same outline can be applied to the European Directive on equal opportunities. In the text of this norm, we can distinguish between (a) an individual right, which is a type 2 principle, obligatory, subjective, *prima facie*, and (b) art. 4.2. of the Directive, which is directed to the public powers, and is a type 4 principle, obligatory, objective, *prima facie*.
—Within European Directive 76/207 itself, there are two levels:
  (a) an individual right consecrated by the Directive and
  (b) point 4.2, which is directed to public powers.

[36] Cf., the German Länder equal opportunities Acts concerning access to State jobs: Berlin: Landesgleichstellungsgesetz (LGG) of 31.12.1990 (GVBl. 1991, S. 8) changed by Gesetz of 26.6.1994 (GVBL. S. 182) and Gesetz of 26.1.1995, GVBl. S. 26; Bund: Gesetz zur Durchsetzung der Gleichberechtigung von Frauen und Männern (zweites Gleichberechtigungsgesetz-22.GleiBG) of 24.6.1994 (BGBl. IS. 1406); Brandenburg: Gesetz zur Gleichstellung von Frauen und Männern im öffentlichen Dienst im Land Brandenburg (Landesgleichstellungsgesetz-LGG) of 4.7.1994 (GVBl. I S. 254); Bremen. Gesetz zur Gleichstellung von Frau und Mann im öffentlichen Dienst des Landes Bremen (Landesgleichstellungsgesetz) of 20.11.1990 (Brem. GBl. S. 433); Hamburg: Gesetz zur Gleichstellung von Frauen und Männern im hamburgischen öffentlichen Dienst (Gleichstellungsgesetz) of 19.3.1991 (GVBl. I S. 75); Hessen: Hessisches Gesetz über die Gleichberechtigung von Frauen und Männern und zum Abbau von Diskriminierungen von Frauen in der öffentlichen Verwaltung (Hessisches Gleichberechtigungsgesetz-HGlG) of 21.12.1993 (GVBl. I S. 729); Mecklenburg-Vorpommern: Gesetz zur Gleichstellung von Frau und Mann im öffentlichen Dienst des Landes Mecklenburg-Vorpommern (GleichstellungsG M-V) of 18.12.1994, GVBl. S. 343; Niedersachsen: Niedersächsisches Gleichberechtigungsgesetz (NGG) of 15.6.1994 (Nds. GVBl.S. 246); Nordhrein-Westfalen. Gesetz zur Förderung der beruflichen Chancen für Frauen im öffentlichen Dienst (Frauenförderungsgesetz-FGG) of 31.10.1989 (GV.NW.S 567); Rheiland-Pfalz:Landesgleichstellungsgesetz of 11.7.1995, GVBl. S. 209; Saarland: Gesetz zur Förderung von Frauen und zur Änderung sonstiger dienstrechtlicher Vorschriften of 10.5.1989 (Amtsbl. S. 977); Freistaat Sachsen: Gesetz zur Förderung von Frauen und der Vereinbarkeit von Familie und Beruf im Öffentlichen Dienst des Freistaates Sachsen (Sächsisches Frauenförderungsgesetz—SächsFFG) of 31.3.1994 (SächsGVBl. S. 684); Sachsen-Anhalt: Gesetz zur beruflichen Förderung von Frauen im öffentlichen Dienst des Landes Sachsen-Anhalt (Frauenfördergesetz) of 7.2.1993 (GVBl.LSA S. 734), changed by Gesetz of 27.6.1994, GVBl.S. 762; Schleswig-Holstein: Gesetz zur Gleichstellung der Frauen im öffentlichen Dienst of 13.12.1994. GVBl. S. 562.

7. CONFLICT BETWEEN A SUBJECTIVE RIGHT AND AN OBJECTIVE NORM

Next, we shall attempt to analyse what happens when a conflict between subjective rights and an objective norm directed to public powers arises. In the case of conflict, the "Theory of Principles" leans towards the individual's subjective rights as opposed to the State. This does not exclude the possibility of there being justified State interventions; for example, the limited number of places for students at university, tax scales, etc. Individual subjective rights are also limited by third party rights or collective goods. But, here, we are referring to the case of collision between a clearly constitutionalised right and an objective right (objective norm directed to the State). Any legitimate limitation of individual rights must be justified. There must be reasonable arguments.

In the issue of affirmative actions for achieving *de facto* equality for men and women, affirmative actions, in general, as promotional measures are justified. It is only in the case of direct conflict with a constitutionally protected individual right, that the affirmative actions must be limited in favour of the individual right. And, in the case of two individual rights in conflict, the principle of proportion must be applied by weighing and balancing the concrete case, in order to establish a hierarchy of the rights in conflict.

There are quota, which directly harm individual rights, but are considered promotional measures; for example, the reservation of a minimum number of posts for the disabled. A direct reverse discrimination is also produced here, but we generally find it justified, because we consider that the principle of proportion justifies it.

Political parties' candidate list quota would also be constitutional. The lists of candidates are democratically drawn up within the political parties and these organisations are flexible. They are private organisations. The State is not the employer in this case.

Nevertheless, the case of the automatic quota for acceding to a job through public contest, with objective criteria, violates article 33.2. of the German constitution, which speaks about equal opportunities, and not discrimination based on sex, in the case of acceding to a civil service job by the merit system: "Jeder Deutsche hat nach seiner Eignung, Befähigung und fachlichen Leistung gleichen Zugang zu jedem öffentlichen Amte".

The question is whether there would be sufficient reasons, from a social point of view, to justify that automatic quota and the direct reverse discrimination that derives from it. By way of justification, it could be alleged that quota for women are part of the affirmative action system that the State determines in favour of *de facto* equality for men and women. The State would, thereby, be attempting to facilitate the fulfillment of a subjective right, the subjective right of women to equal opportunities in obtaining a job: more precisely, an individual right specified in article 3, paragraphs I, II, and III of the German Constitution.

It is the State's obligation to help putting individual rights into practice;[37] each woman's equality is an individual right (legally there are no collective rights). But if, with an aim to achieving this objective, the State were to give rise to a direct reverse discrimination, it would be granting a woman an individual right, but at the same time violating a third person's individual right, who could be a man.[38]

According to what the "Theory of Principle" states when this type of collision comes up, the granting of a right to one of the parties (in this case, to the woman) cannot be automatic. It is necessary to ponder the case with more reasons. The final result may be favourable to the woman, but it would require a concrete weighing and balancing, and not an automatic decision based on the consideration of sex.

We insist that it is necessary to ponder each case, because justice demands that no automatic preferences are given. The social State's capacity to intervene to correct inequalities has a limit, especially when it comes to restricting each individual's freedom, as happened in the cases relating to employment. The difference between rules and principles turns out to be useful here:

> "Principles order something to be carried out to the greatest possible degree taking into account the legal and *de facto* possibilities. Therefore, they do not contain *definitive* mandates but rather only *prima facie* ones. From the fact that a principle is valid for one case, it cannot be inferred that what the principle demands for this case is valid as a definitive result (*definitives Recht*). Principles present reasons that can be displaced by opposite reasons. The principle does not determine how the relationship between one reason and its opposite is to be solved."[39]

Applied to the Kalanke case or to automatic priority, this means that the awarding of that job must take into account the woman's promotion and the other candidate's particular conditions. To go from a *prima facie* right, to a *definitive* right, demands reasonable justification and pondering. (When the contest was later repeated, Frau Glissmann won the post again. This time it was alleged that her background was more adequate for the job). In the Marschall case, this condition of weighing and balancing is respected. Thus, the law of Rheinland-Westfalen abides by the established jurisprudence, while the law in Bremen did not.

[37] Alexy, R., *Recht, Vernunft, Diskurs*, *op. cit.*, 10

[38] Alexy, R., *Recht, Vernunft, Diskurs*, *op. cit.*, 282

[39] Alexy, R., *Theorie der Grundrechte*, *op. cit.*, 87–88: "Prinzipien gebieten, dass etwas relativ auf die rechtlichen und tatsächlichen Möglichkeiten in möglichst hohem Masse realisiert wird. Damit enthalten sie keine *definitiven*, sondern nur *prima facie-Gebote*. Daraus, dass ein Prinzip in einem Fall einschlägig ist, folgt nicht, dass das, was das Prinzip in diesem Fall verlangt, im Ergebnis gilt. Prinzipien stellen Gründe dar, die durch gegenläufige Gründe ausgeräumt werden können".

8. CONCLUSION

According to the "Theory of Principles", equality at law is a value in itself, but so is *de facto* equality.[40] When a conflict between the two arises, the concrete case must be weighed and balanced. Both are *prima facie* rights. In case of collision, we must ponder each case, in order to determine the *definitive* right.[41] But, a direct reverse discrimination is not possible. The Theory of Principles permits considering affirmative actions for achieving *de facto* equality with *de facto* affirmative actions. From the point of view of subjective rights, it also includes the right to regulated benefits, e.g., in labour legislation: regulation of maternity leave, leave for caring for a child, etc.

This is compatible with the fact that affirmative action measures, in the European Community and in German law, are not only permitted, but even rather encouraged, promoted and regulated,[42] as has been acknowledged by the Court of Justice of the European Communities in the Marschall case. The promotion of *de facto* equality in the case of women abides by established jurisprudence in two senses. On one hand, it is constitutional according to the German Constitution and Community law. On the other hand, it is fair according to the theory of equality, upheld in Robert Alexy's "Theory of Fundamental Rights".

The "Theory of Principles" would permit, advise and demand measures to promote equality; that is, affirmative action measures. The achievement of *de facto* equality is an essential content of the Constitution; it is part of fundamental rights. Taking all this into account, one may conclude that the legal arguments used by the Court of Justice of the European Communities in the Kalanke case, and in the Marschall case, fitted with jurisprudence and, moreover, observed continuity in their line of argument.[43]

[40] Huster, S., *Rechte und Ziele: Zur Dogmatik des Allgemeinen Gleichheitsatzes* (Berlin, Duncker and Humblot, 1993). Huster, S., "Gleichheit und Verhältnismäßigkeit.Der allgemeine Gleichheitsatz als Eingriffsrecht", *JZ* 1994, 11, 541–549.

[41] Borowski, M., *Grundrechte als Prinzipien. Die Unterscheidung von prima facie Position und definitiver Position als fundamentaler Konstruktionsgrundsatz der Grundrechte,* diss., Kiel. For the difference between Stefan Huster and Robert Alexy, see pp. 389–393. Now published.

[42] BVerfGE 74, 163 (180); 85, 191 (207), BVerfGE 92, 91. I. 109

[43] I have to say that I have read, in detail, the paper of José García Añón. I disagree with so many things, that I would need to write a new article in order to develop my response. In short, firstly, although German doctrine is central to his discussion, he does not quote any German writings; García Añón does not place the two cases within a German legal context. For me, this is essential in order to understand what is going on here. The European Court of Justice knows very well that Germany and its laws are to be seen in the context of a social State. Article 3.2 of the German Constitution is much stronger than the Spanish art. 9.2. In fact, in Spain we do not have any obligatory quota, except for handicapped, whereas there are many obligatory German Acts about quota, as can be seen from my footnotes. However, I think that the opening clause is very useful. It clarifies the difference between an unjust and just intervention of the state searching material equality. It marks perfectly the way of justification of a different treatment in German legal dogmatics, that is the principle of proportionality (*Verhälnismässigkeit*) and the principle of weighing and balancing (*Abwägung*) of such measures when two individual's rights are in conflict. I think that the European Court of Justice has clearly shown the necessity of a Social State, and also the necessity of equality

of results, not only of opportunities, and of material equality, not only formal equality on this point José García Añón confuses the argumentation of Advocates General (Jacobs and Tesauro) with real sentences. In fact, The Court does not follow the argumentation of the Advocates General on these points. In fact, the Court distinguishes between affirmative action and reverse discrimination, and accepts also the latter, within the limits of making a balance between both candidates. Actually, the Court follows rather the excellent report made by the German professor Juliane Kokott, who represented the Land of Nordhrein-Westfalen for the preliminary question.

Further, Professor García Añón does not discuss a key matter, namely; can we speak about collective rights from a constitutional point of view? I agree with him on the necessity of a social state in searching for real equality; equality of results. But it is at this point the problem starts, what does "legal" mean in a state under the rule of law, without going to the other extreme of a tyrannical State? Germany has a sad experience of forced equality, on the right with National Socialism, and on the left with communism.

12

*The Right to Personal Identity in Italian Private Law: Constitutional Interpretation and Judge-Made Rights**

GIORGIO PINO

1. THE RIGHT TO PERSONAL IDENTITY: A DEFINITION

According to relatively wide-spread opinion in Italian legal culture, the right to personal identity can be described as the right everybody has to appear and to be represented in social life (especially by the mass media) in a way that fits with, or at least does not falsify or distort, his or her personal history. In the Italian debate, the right to personal identity is often considered a "new" personal right. This means that:

(a) It is a right that belongs to the person, in the sense that it is an entitlement or claim of human beings as constitutional subjects, in contradistinction to, for instance, juristic persons (however, the question will be discussed in due course if and in what cases, a similar right can be recognised also to juristic persons).
(b) It is a somewhat "new" right, in the sense that it has only recently been recognised by judges, legal theorists, and (finally) by the legislator, in a period that can be restricted to the last two decades.

Nevertheless, the concept itself of "personal identity" was not unknown to Italian legal culture even in less recent times. In a rather obsolete conception, personal identity was understood as the whole of the official personal data resulting in public records, and important mainly for the public purpose of making the citizen identifiable by the public administration: name, pseudonym, date of birth, address, status, and so on.[1] Later, a civil law relevance of personal identity arose, in relation to the right one has to be identified and to be distinguishable from other subjects. To this purpose, the protection of this right

* Text revised, as to the English language, by James Varney and Mark Van Hoecke.

[1] See for instance Falco, "Identità Personale", *Nuovo Digesto Italiano*, vol. IV (UTET, Torino), 1938.

was necessarily implied in the protection of the main distinctive features of the person, such as name and likeness.[2]

The new concept of "personal identity" adds to the traditional concept a sort of "abstract", "moral" or "ideal" feature that can be expressed as the interest everybody has to be represented with his/her real identity, i.e., with the identity that appears in concrete and unequivocal circumstances of social life. In other words, it is the claim that one's (ascertainable) cultural, professional, religious, political, social experiences should not be distorted, misrepresented, falsified, confused, contested, or the like, by means of the ascription of false (even if not necessarily defamatory) statements or acts.[3]

The shift towards this "ideal" conception of personal identity is related to two important cultural and social factors: firstly, the growing interest in the legal protection of the various aspects of human personality, which characterises the evolution of almost every European legal system in the second half of this century (on this point, see sec. 2.1 below); secondly, the striking diffusion of the mass media, whose intrusive power and technological development can cause serious (and sometimes irremovable) damage to the moral integrity of the person. These two factors can be considered as the origin of many "new" personal rights (new to the Italian legal system at least), such as the right to personal identity and the right to privacy.[4]

Before proceeding with a more precise definition of the right to personal identity, it is important to clarify that in Italian private law this right has little in common with such fashionable topics such as the "right to group identity" or "community rights". These rights, indeed, are usually defined as political rather than legal claims advanced by a minority group against the government, in order to obtain the protection or the recognition of cultural or religious demands.[5]

Rather differently, the right to personal identity means the protection of individual personality against false representations elaborated by the mass media, or displayed in data bases, and the like (more examples will be shown in sec. 3.2 below).

[2] This view is expressed by A. de Cupis, *Il Diritto all'Identità Personale* (Milano, Giuffrè, 1949), and by G. Bavetta, "Identità (diritto alla)" *Enciclopedia del diritto*, XIX, 1970.

[3] This is the commonest definition of the right to personal identity, which can be read the decision of the *Corte di Cassazione*, I, 22.6.1985, n. 3769, in *Nuova Giurisprudenza Civile Commentata*, I, 1985, pp. 647–654.

[4] In this sense, see V. Zeno-Zencovich, "Identità Oersonale", *Digesto delle Discipline Privatistiche*, vol. IX (UTET, Torino 1993).

[5] The debate on the relations between personal identity and community is vast; the interested reader will find many useful remarks on this point in W. Kymlicka, *Liberalism, Community and Culture* (Clarendon, Oxford, 1989); W. Kymlicka, *Multicultural Citizenship. A Liberal Theory of Minority Rights* (Oxford U.P., Oxford, 1995); C. Taylor, *Multiculturalism and "the Politics of Recognition"* (Princeton U.P., Princeton, 1992); M. Toraldo di Francia, "Valori Costituzionali e Diritto all'Identità Personale", in F. Cerutti (ed.), *Identità e Politica* (Laterza, Roma-Bari, 1996), pp. 113–129.

2. PERSONAL RIGHTS IN GENERAL

The general category of "personal rights" (*diritti della personalità, droits de la personnalité, Persönlichkeitsrechte*) is quite a new field of analysis for European continental legal doctrine: the lack of interest that legal science showed in this topic, until two decades ago, was justified by the scarce provisions concerning the protection of "moral personality" in positive law. In the Italian Civil Code (1942), for instance, the only explicitly recognised personality rights were (and still are): the right to one's own name and pseudonym (art. 6–9), the right to one's own likeness (art. 10), and the so-called "moral" copyright (art. 2577).

The reason for this somewhat limited consideration of the moral profiles of the human personality in the Civil Code, is to be found in an ideological stance common to European continental legal culture; according to this position, which dates from the last century, the legal system has to protect two basic values: liberty and property.

The value of "liberty" concerns the relations between citizen and State, in the sense that liberty is the result of the delimitation of the political sphere, and at the same time the right to participate in political power: "liberty rights" are essentially a matter of constitutional law. "Property", on the other hand, is the fundamental model of legal interaction between private subjects. In this sense, it has been repeatedly noted that in the primary and traditional structure of Italian private law, every model of legal right (*diritto soggettivo*) is based on the "property" scheme.

It is easy to conclude, then, that according to this traditional position, the Civil Code regulates only patrimonial-economic relations, while the moral development of the human being is committed to constitutional law, and protected only by penal law.[6] This situation has radically changed in the second half of the 2twentieth century. Among other factors, the need for a different way of conceiving of, and giving protection to, personal rights in the Italian legal system was clear in the context of the new Italian Constitution (1948), and also after the ratification in 1955 of the European Convention on Human Rights (1950). Many authors have pointed to this deep change in legal culture, which has replaced the traditional "liberty and property" formula with that of "liberty and personality". This "paradigm shift" brings, on the one hand, a weakening of economic liberties, which are not recognised as fundamental rights; and, on the other, a strengthening of personal rights and freedoms.[7]

[6] This distinction is common to nearly all the civil codes drawn up between the last century and the first half of this century. About the French *Code Napoléon*, for instance, it has been said that the Code *"se présentait plutot comme le droit du patrimoine que comme le droit des personnes"* (Nerson, "De la Protection de la Personnalité en Droit Privé Français", in *Travaux de l'Association Henri Capitant*, XII, I (1963), pp. 60, 63.

[7] In this sense, see F. Modugno, *I "nuovi diritti" nella Giurisprudenza Costituzionale* (Giappichelli, Torino, 1995), p. 11.

2.1. The "Personalistic Principle" in the Italian Constitution

The Italian Constitution, like the constitutions of the large majority of contemporary Western legal systems, is based on the concept of the intrinsic value of the human being. In this regard, it has been said that the most important substantive principle in the Italian Constitution is the "personalistic principle". The key-norm to this concern is considered to be art. 2, according to which Italy:

> "Acknowledges and protects the fundamental rights of the human being, both as an individual and as a member of social groups".[8]

Compared to other contemporary constitutions, the Italian constitution is probably less explicit in recognising a right to the development of the person (which could represent a direct constitutional foundation for personal rights).[9] Nevertheless, an overall view reveals that the autonomous development of the person, and the related concept of "human dignity", are implied in the structure of the first two parts of the constitution ("*Principi Fondamentali*" and "*Diritti e Doveri dei Cittadini*").

Indeed, several Constitutional provisions concern the development and the protection of the human personality. These provisions are not only concerned with strengthening the "liberty" sphere in the traditional sense, but also regard the defence and promotion of human dignity in different social contexts. For instance, art. 3(1) recognises "equal social dignity" ("*pari dignità sociale*") for every citizen; art. 29(2) recognises "legal and moral equality" ("*eguaglianza giuridica e morale*") for husband and wife; art. 32(2) states that compulsory health treatment shall not infringe human dignity; art. 36(1) regards wages as a means to assure the worker and his family a decent existence ("*esistenza libera e dignitosa*"); human dignity is also a limit to economic enterprise (art. 41(2)).[10]

In legal dogmatics there has been (and still is) a radical opposition regarding the interpretation of art. 2. The question is whether it is to be regarded as an "open clause" or, on the contrary, a "recapitulatory provision". According to the first approach, art. 2 is considered a necessary technical tool by which the legal system recognises general moral or social needs.[11] The opposite conception regards this constitutional norm only as a strengthening of the fundamen-

[8] The complete formulation of art. 2 is: "La Repubblica riconosce e garantisce i diritti inviolabili dell'uomo, sia come singolo sia nelle formazioni sociali ove si svolge la sua personalità, e richiede l'adempimento dei doveri inderogabili di solidarietà politica, economica e sociale".

[9] An explicit right to the development of human personality can be read in the German *Grundgesetz*, art. 2(1); in the Spanish Constitution, art. 10(1); in the Greek Constitution, art. 5(1); and in the Swedish Constitution, art. 1(2).

[10] For more examples, and an analysis of the use of the concept of human dignity by the *Corte Costituzionale*, see A. Ruggeri, A. Spadaro, "Dignità dell'Uomo e Giurisprudenza Costituzionale (Prime Notazioni)", *Politica del Diritto*, 3, 1991, 343–377.

[11] In this sense, A. Barbera, "Commento all'art. 2", in G. Branca (a cura di), *Commentario alla Costituzione. Principi Fondamentali* (Zanichelli, Bologna-Roma, 1975.

tal rights and liberties specifically stated in other constitutional provisions (particularly at art.13-54).[12]

Both conceptions are based on policy arguments (and on ideological presuppositions) rather than on logical or conceptual reasons. The "open clause" approach, for instance, aims to keep the Constitution in a dynamic and vivid correspondence with society, by way of the possible introduction of "unenumerated rights", and seems to be inspired by a "jusnaturalistic" attitude. The "recapitulatory" conception, on the other hand, is more "positivistic" in character, and is intended to prevent the concentration of an excessive discretionary power in the hands of the lawyers (judges in the first place), also considering that the introduction of new rights in favour of certain categories of citizens requires the imposition of correlative duties and costs upon other subjects.[13]

The *Corte costituzionale*, in a first period (more or less until the first half of the 1980s), embraced the restrictive, "recapitulatory" interpretation of art. 2.[14] Then, in a series of important decisions concerning fundamental rights, it explicitly accepted the "open clause" conception, thus granting constitutional foundations to many "unenumerated" rights.[15]

Indeed, it has been noted that the adoption of the "open clause" approach by the *Corte costituzionale* is not clearly defined. Rather, the Court holds a more moderate, middle-way approach, according to which the open catalogue of art. 2 can be filled only with values and principles that are already *inside* the system of the Constitution. Moreover, the introduction of a "new" right should never cause the erasing of an explicit constitutional right (even if a comparison between the two is possible). In this sense, the function of art. 2 is not merely that of a summary of the other specifically declared constitutional rights, but on the other hand the introduction of new rights cannot be radically discretionary, or merely dependent on "social morality".

In these cases, for instance, the expanded protection of human dignity and of the development of human personality can be obtained by considering art. 2 in conjunction with art. 3(2):[16] new rights, then, are considered to be constitutional

[12] See for instance P. Grossi, *Introduzione ad uno Studio sui Diritti Inviolabili nella Costituzione Italiana* (CEDAM, Padova, 1972), p. 159 ff.; A. PACE, *Problematica delle libertà costituzionali. Parte generale* (CEDAM, Padova, 1990), p. 4 ff.

[13] For an evaluation of the use of jusnaturalistic and positivistic arguments in constitutional interpretation, see G. PINO, "The Place of Legal Positivism in Contemporary Constitutional States", in *Law and Philosophy*, European Special Issue 1999, ed. by N. MacCormick.

[14] See for instance Corte cost. 11/1956 (in *Foro italiano* 1956, I, 1038; and *Giurisprudenza costituzionale*, 1956, 612); 53/1957; 30/1958; 81/1958; 29/1962 (in *Foro italiano*, 1962, I, 603; and *Giustizia penale*, 1962, I, 164); 98/1968; 1/1969; 84/1969; 101/1971; 42/1972; 77/1972; 14/1973; 147/1973; 159/1973; 33/1974; 102/1975; 106/1975; 238/1975; 57/1976 (in *Giurisprudenza costituzionale*, 1976, I, 396); 181/1976; 98/1979; 125/1979; 188/1980; and so on.

[15] In this sense, see Corte cost. 54/1986, on the inviolable right to life, health, and physical integrity; 561/1987, on the right respect for sexuality; 139/1990, on the right to privacy; 278/1992, on the right to leave one's own country; 13/1994, on the right to keep one's own name as an aspect of personal identity.

[16] Art. 3(2): "E' compito della Repubblica rimuovere gli ostacoli di ordine economico e sociale, che, limitando di fatto la libertà e l'eguaglianza dei cittadini, impediscono di fatto il pieno sviluppo

fundamental rights insofar as their content is intended to ensure a full development of the human personality, by removing economic, social (or even physical, as we will see) obstacles. The result is that even if the Court apparently says that art. 2 makes possible the entrance of "new rights" into the system, as a matter of fact such new rights are often new means of protection of traditional rights against new assaults, or the extension of the entitlement of traditional rights to new subjects.[17]

The most evident example of this technique of "moderate self-integration" of the constitutional text is represented precisely by the introduction of new personal rights into the Italian system (such as the right to privacy, or the right to personal identity), or by the consideration under private law of aspects of human personality formerly protected only by penal law (such as honour and reputation).

The tendency towards an expansive protection of personal rights is echoed by a similar attitude of the organs of the European Convention on Human Rights, i.e., the Commission and the Court, as to the protection of private life under art. 8 of the Convention. The Commission has held that the right to respect for private life "comprises also, to a certain degree, the right to establish and develop relationships with other human beings especially in the emotional field, for the development and fulfilment of one's own personality".[18] Commentators have suggested that this norm of the Convention has to be interpreted so as to protect the individual against attacks on physical or mental integrity or moral or intellectual freedom, attacks on honour and reputation and similar torts, the use of a person's name, identity, and the disclosure of information protected by the duty of professional secrecy.[19]

2.2. Personal Rights, or the General Right to Personality?

The debate on the interpretation of art. 2 is paralleled, in the specific field of the civilian consideration of personal rights, by a similar debate on the conceptual alternative between a "pluralistic" and a "monistic" approach. According to the

della persona umana e l'effettiva partecipazione di tutti i lavoratori all'organizzazione politica, economica e sociale del paese".

[17] On this matter, see M. C. Ponthoreau, *La Reconnaissance des Droits Non-écrits par les Cours Constitutionnelles Italienne et Française. Essai sur le Pouvoir Créateur du Juge Constitutionnel* (Economica, Paris, 1994), pp. 87–115; A. Beyere, A. Cerri, *Il Diritto di Informazione e i Diritti della Persona* (Giuffrè, Milano, 1995), pp. 43–49.

[18] App. 6825/74, X v. *Ireland*, 18 May 1976, *Decisions and Report of the Commission*, 5, 1976, p. 86 ff.

[19] See F. Jacobs, R. White, *The European Convention on Human Rights*, 2nd ed. (Clarendon, Oxford, 1996), p. 172 ff.; Doswald-Beck, "The Meaning of the 'Right to Respect for Private Life' under the European Convention on Human Rights", *Human Rights Law Journal*, 4, 1983, 283 ff.; Loucaides, "Personality and Privacy under the European Convention on Human Rights", *British Yearbook of International Law*, 61, 1990, 175 ff.

"pluralistic" conception, there are different and distinct personal rights, such as the right to one's own name, the right to one's own likeness, the right to personal identity, the right to privacy, and so on. According to the "monistic" conception there is just one single right of personality, or rather *to* personality, i.e., to the autonomous development of one's own personality, which is articulated in several "faculties" or aspects.

Apart from the above-mentioned "constitutional" argument, this debate is influenced by other technical factors and, again, by relevant policy arguments. The pluralistic approach seems to be based on a more traditional attitude that recognises personal rights only as far as they are structured as precise rights (*diritti soggettivi*), and explicitly worded in a positive provision (of course, the use of analogy is possible, in order to extend legal protection to cases similar to those regulated). This approach has fitted quite well with a more general tendency in the field of civil liability, which used to apply this remedy only in cases of violation of explicitly recognised rights (*diritti soggettivi perfetti*). As regards the constitutional foundation, moreover, this view is linked to a restrictive interpretation of art. 2 as a "recapitulatory provision".[20]

The monistic conception, on the other hand, is related to a more flexible consideration of civil liability that covers any damage to legally protected interests. This evolution popularised the monistic conception, which is considered also more in line with the "personalistic" stance of the Constitution and with the concept itself of human personality. In this sense, the main argument is that human personality is unitary in character, and therefore legal protection concerning only some pre-determined and fixed aspects (name, likeness . . .) would be incomplete and distorted. Human personality, in this view, is not the object of *diritti soggettivi*; it is rather a value, whose primary legal relevance is testified by art. 2 of the Constitution, and which deserves protection in all its relevant aspects.[21] The monistic approach seems to be based on an "open", "liberal" interpretation of art. 2 that makes possible the constitutional legitimacy and protection of new personal rights.[22] Moreover, it has been suggested that the adoption of a monistic approach to personal rights encourages the recourse to a common-law attitude in the courts, because it attributes to the judges the task

[20] The pluralistic conception was shared by the first theorists to deal with personal rights, such as A. de Cupis, *I Diritti della Personalità* (Giuffrè, Milano, 1959); for a more recent restatement of this theory, see P. Rescigno, "I Diritti della Personalità e la Loro Rilevanza Costituzionale (a proposito di un recente libro)", *Il Diritto dell'Informazione e dell'Informatica* (1986), pp. 333–341; P. Rescigno, "Personalità (diritti della)", *Enciclopedia Giuridica*, XXIV, 1991.

[21] The monistic approach is consolidated in the courts, and shared by the majority of writers. See for instance D. Messinetti "Personalità (diritti della)", *Enciclopedia del Diritto*, XXXIII, 1983.

[22] This point is not always sufficiently clear, especially in judges' legal reasoning; indeed, the *Corte di Cassazione*, in a very important decision for our present concern (n. 3769, 22.6.1985, quoted *supra*, ftn. 3), explicitly held a pluralistic approach, but claimed on the other hand that the rights of the personality must be based on an "open clause" interpretation of art. 2. To my mind, this view is radically contradictory.

of protecting (and, indeed, creating) rights that lack a precise and specific legislative foundation: "remedies precede rights".[23]

For simplicity's sake, the differences between the two approaches can be expressed as follows: according to the pluralistic approach, every sort of intrusion in the personal sphere is allowed, except for those that are explicitly prohibited; according to the monistic approach, every sort of intrusion in the personal sphere is prohibited, except for those that are explicitly allowed.[24]

3. A RIGHT IN THE MAKING

The right to personal identity is essentially a judge-created right. Indeed, it is possible to regard the introduction of the right to personal identity as an interesting example of a common-law technique in a civil-law system, such as that in Italy.

The "landmark case" is usually considered *Pretura Roma* 6-5-1974 (*Pangrazi and Silvetti* v. *Comitato Referendum*).[25] The facts of the case are quite interesting. In the days of the referendum about the abrogation of divorce in Italy, the anti-divorce committee, for the purpose of its campaign, used the picture of a man and a woman working in the country. The picture was meant to evoke a "traditionalist" context (an old-style family) and was of course associated with an anti-divorce message. The problem was that, first of all, the picture was taken without the consent of the people portrayed. In the second place, they were not married. Last, but not least, they were in favour of the existing divorce legislation.

The *Pretore* accepted the complaint of the two plaintiffs, on the assumption that the use of the picture was first of all a violation of their right to their own likeness, as explicitly protected by art. 10 of the Civil Code. However, the judge added that the picture damaged another relevant interest of the plaintiffs, i.e., their right to personal identity. On this point, the judge stated that the law protects one's right to the acknowledgement of one's own acts, and conversely the right to repudiate acts that one has never done: in other words, the right to personal identity.

The way was open for the judicial recognition of the new right. Many other decisions in the following years have used the "personal identity" paradigm in order to offer a new protection of the person from the misrepresentations of the mass media. In this sense, it is possible to say that the right to personal identity

[23] Curiously enough, English judges seem to show an extreme self-restraint in the field of personal rights; see V. Zeno-Zencovich, "Personalità (diritti della)", *Digesto Discipline Privatistiche*, XIII, 1995, 433.

For a comparative analysis of the English and German experiences, see B. Markesinis, "The Right to be Let Alone Versus Freedom of Speech", *Public Law*, 1986, 67.

[24] In this sense, see M. Dogliotti, "Le Persone Fisiche", in P. Rescigno (ed.), *Trattato di Diritto Privato*, vol. 2, t. I, pp. 5–188 (UTET, Torino, 1982).

[25] In *Giurisprudenza Italiana*, 1975, I, 2, pp. 514 ff.

shows a considerable "elasticity", because it covers a wide, and not *a priori,* determinable range of assaults on the integrity of one's personal history, perpetrated by the mass media.

3.1. The Object of the Right to Personal Identity

Since the earliest judgements on the matter, personal identity has been perceived as an autonomous right, and not merely as a kind of extension of the protection of more traditional and consolidated *biens de la personnalité*, such as name and personal likeness. Of course, name and likeness are fundamental attributes of the personality, and attacks on personal identity can easily involve their misuse (indeed, we have seen *supra* that the very first case about the right to personal identity dealt also with a violation of the right to likeness). Whatever the case, the conceptual differences between those aspects of the personality are clear. To put it crudely, both name and likeness identify the subject only with reference to his/her material existence and corporeal appearance. The right to personal identity, on the other hand, expresses the global and concrete individual personality of the subject, in the sense that we have seen above.[26]

The positive discipline of name and likeness, then, could be used only by means of analogy (as far as relevant resemblances with personal identity are envisaged), but it could not work as a proper normative foundation for the new right. To this purpose, instead, the courts have repeatedly referred to the legislative provisions on the so-called "right of reply", i.e., the right to obtain the rectification of a false statement concerning personal facts that have appeared in a newspaper[27] or a TV broadcast.[28]

The higher courts, more than ten years after the first judgement, have developed a different way of reasoning, in the direction of the recognition of the right to personal identity as an autonomous right. The *Corte di Cassazione*, in 1985 (n. 3769), explicitly recognised the autonomy of this right, and rooted its normative foundation directly in art. 2 of the Constitution, in conjunction with art. 3(2). The *Corte Costituzionale* in 1994 (n. 13) followed the same line of argument.[29]

Also, in the field of legal doctrine, the first comments showed a reductionistic attitude: some commentators assumed that the "new" right to personal identity was empty and useless, because its scope was almost the same as that of honour and reputation. In other words, there is no need to talk about a new right,

[26] A more detailed distinction between name, likeness, and personal identity is in V. Zeno-Zencovich, "Identità personale", quoted above.

[27] See art. 8, l. 47/1948 ("*Legge sulla stampa*").

[28] See art. 10, l. 223/90: "Chiunque si ritenga leso, nei suoi interessi morali o materiali da trasmissioni contrarie a verità, ha il diritto di chiedere che sia trasmessa apposita rettifica".

[29] In *Giurisprudenza costituzionale*, 1994, 95. See also *Corte di Cassazione*, I, 7.2.1996, n. 978 (in *Foro italiano*, 1996, I, 1253–1262.

because the relevant interest falls entirely within an already protected field.[30] According to other writers, there is no such right to personal identity; personal identity is not an autonomous right but rather an intrinsic limit on the freedom of the press that reflects the need for exact and accurate information.[31]

In favour of the autonomous relevance of the right to personal identity, on the other hand, it can be noted that the right to personal identity has some important distinctive features, in consideration of which it is necessary to distinguish it from other personal rights. The first feature of the right to personal identity is that its protection can be invoked only if a false representation of the personality has been offered to the public eye. This feature makes it possible to distinguish the right to personal identity from both reputation and privacy. In the first case, indeed, it can be noted that the false statements must not be necessarily defaming: personal identity can be violated also by the attribution of (false) merits. In the case of privacy, instead, legal protection does not concern the correct exposure of the personality to the public eye, but rather the interest of the subject not to be exposed. The conceptual distinction between privacy and personal identity, anyway, is not always clear. In American jurisprudence, for instance, the tort of "false light in the public eye" is often considered a specific aspect of general privacy torts.[32]

A second feature of the right to personal identity is that the concept of personal history it refers to must be interpreted only in a factually-objective way. This means that this right does not cover all those personal ideas and thoughts that have never been publicly exposed or actually revealed in concrete acts. The object of the right is the social projection of the personality, as can be ascertained using an ordinary duty of (professional) care.[33] The third feature is that this right is "relational" in character: it protects the interest to preserve the social image one has concretely revealed.

[30] This view has been expressed, for instance, by G. Visintini Tarello, "Il c.d. diritto alla identità personale e le reazioni della dottrina di fronte alla attività creatrice di un diritto della giurisprudenza", in G. Alpa, M. Bessone, L. Boneschi (eds.), *Il Diritto all'Identità Personale* (Cedam, Padova, 1981), pp. 70–77; and F. Macioce, *Tutela Civile della Persona e Identità Personale* (Cedam, Padova, 1984).

[31] In this sense, A. Pace, "Il c.d. Diritto all'Identità Personale e gli artt. 2 e 21 della Costituzione", in Alpa, M. Bessone, L. Boneschi (eds.), *Il Diritto all'Identità Personale*, quoted above, pp. 36–41.

[32] According to W .L. Ptosser, "Privacy", *California Law Review*, 48, 1960, 383–422, the "right to privacy" refers, individually and collectively, to four distinguishable rights, that apply in the following situations: 1) intrusion into seclusion; 2) publication of private or embarrassing facts; 3) publicity placing another in a false light; 4) commercial use of another's name, likeness, or identity. This view has been recently contested by R. Gavison, "Privacy and the Limits of Law", *Yale Law Journal*, 1980, 421 ff.

[33] This point has been clearly expressed by *Tribunale Roma*, 27.3.1984 (in *Giurisprudenza Italiana*, 1985, I, 2, p. 13 ff.), and *Corte di Cassazione* n. 3769, quoted above. On this point, see A. Beyere, A. Cerri, *Il Diritto di Informazione e i Diritti della Persona*, quoted above, p. 164.

3.2. Cases and Legislation

The "relational" or "social" dimension of the right to personal identity is the reason why this remedy has been invoked in many different contexts. Indeed, personal identity is a complex entity that can be displayed in a variety of social circumstances, depending on the personal concerns or the professional activity of the person involved.

The analysis of the different cases in which the protection of personal identity is recognised suggests an articulated conception of the concept of personal identity, the core of which can be configured in some recurrent groups of hypotheses. We will see also that some specific articulations of personal identity have found an *a posteriori* recognition in legislation.[34]

Political identity: this can be defined as the sum total of publicly adopted positions, statements, traditions, and attitudes that have been shown by the subject in respect of political and social matters.[35] For instance, a politician was reported to have assumed a certain position in the parliamentary debate, which was disproved by the Parliamentary Reports.[36] In this field there is the more recurrent and complex conflict between personal identity and freedom of the press (some remarks on this point will be developed in the conclusion of the paper). An (implicit) legislative recognition of political identity can be found in the already mentioned provisions on the right to reply.

Intellectual patrimony: this refers to the results of an individual's intellectual and professional activities. For instance, some propositions made in an interview by a famous surgeon (who devoted all his research to combating cancer) were used in a cigarette advertisement, thus suggesting his (false) medical approval for a particular kind of cigarettes.[37]

Ethical and moral attitudes: these are the ideas and beliefs, that everybody has in the moral field. As seen *supra*, the very first case on personal identity concerned a misrepresentation of the plaintiffs' moral attitudes. A specific recognition of this aspect of personal identity against public administration can be found in the new law on conscientious objection to military service (L. n. 230/1998).

Sexual identity: sexual identity can be regarded as a specific aspect of personal identity. The main problem involved, is the possibility for those wishing to do so, to change sex by surgical means, and to obtain the consequent rectification of sexual data in the Public Registry. The *Corte Costituzionale*,[38] at first, denied

[34] For a more detailed case study, see B. Iannolo, G. Verga, "Il Diritto all'Identità Personale", *Nuova giurisprudenza civile commentata*, II, 1987, pp. 453–470.

[35] In this sense, see *Tribunale Roma*, 15.9.1984 (in *Foro italiano*, 1984, I, 2592 ff.).

[36] *Pretura Roma*, 2.6.1980 (in *Foro italiano*, 1980, I, 2046)

[37] *Corte di Cassazione*, I, 22.6.1985, n. 3769 (quoted *supra*, ftn. 3).

[38] *Corte costituzionale* 1.8.1979, n. 98 (in *Giurisprudenza costituzionale*, 1979, I, 719); on this point, see the comment by S. Bartole, "Transsessualismo e Diritti Inviolabili dell'Uomo", in *Giurisprudenza costituzionale*, 1979, I, 1178–1197.

the existence of a fundamental right to sexual identity, with rather weak arguments (the European Court of Justice shared a similar undecided attitude in a number of cases between 1986 and 1992).[39] Later, when the Italian law on sex changes was passed (L. 14.4.1982, n. 164), the *Corte* explicitly attributed constitutional relevance to the right to sexual identity, as an essential feature of the principle of the full development of human personality, under art. 2 and 3 of the Constitution.[40] From a conceptual point of view, this specific articulation and the preceding one of the right to personal identity, are probably the only cases in which a "subjective" concept of personality is accepted for legal purposes.

Publicity: the so-called "right of publicity", i.e., the right one has to profit by one's fame, finds its first formulations in the U.S. courts. The *ratio* can be expressed as follows: if somebody gains a certain degree of fame (as an actor, an artist, a sportsman, or the like), then it is not fair that somebody else should take economic advantage of this publicity without consent. In Italian law, there is no autonomous relevance to the right of publicity. Rather, the unauthorised use of one's celebrity is prohibited insofar as it causes a distortion to personal identity.[41]

Right to oblivion: this is, in a certain sense, the opposite of the right to publicity. This figure was first formulated in French jurisprudence, under the name of *droit à l'oubli*.[42] It is the right to silence on past events in life that are no longer relevant/current. For instance, after a conviction for murder, a man was granted a pardon and made a completely new social and family life. Then, after thirty years, his vicissitude was used in a prize-game in a newspaper. The court ruled that the disclosure of this information was not justified by any current public interest, and "shed false light in the public eye" about the present personality of the subject.[43]

Right over personal data: explicit reference to personal identity is made in the new Italian law on personal data.[44] Under the new law, any sort of systematic collection and treatment of personal data must be guided by such criteria as exactness, pertinence, and completeness (art. 9). Moreover, under art. 13, the

[39] See the references in F. Jacobs, R. White, *The European Convention on Human Rights*, quoted above, pp. 192–194.

[40] *Corte costituzionale* 6.5.1985, n. 161 (in *Giurisprudenza Italiana*, 1987, I, 235).

[41] *Pretura Roma*, 15.11.1986 (in *Foro Italiano*, 1987, I, 973). On this point, see C. Scognamiglio, "Il Diritto all'Utilizzazione Economica del Nome e dell'Immagine delle Persone Celebri" in *Il Diritto dell'Informazione e dell'Informatica* (1988), pp. 1–40.

[42] See for instance R. Lindon, *Les Droits de la Personnalité* (Paris, 1983), p. 90 ff.

[43] *Tribunale Roma* 15.5.1995 (in *Il Diritto dell'Informazione e dell'Informatica*, 1996, p. 422 ff., with a comment by G. Napolitano, "Il Diritto all'Oblio Esiste (ma non si dice)", *ibid*). A more explicit recognition of the right to oblivion is in *Corte di Cassazione*, III, 9.4.1998, n. 3679 (in *Foro italiano*, I, 1998, 1834–1840, with a comment by P. Laghezza, "Il diritto all'oblio esiste (e si vede)", *ibid*).

[44] L. 675/1996, art. 1: "La presente legge garantisce che il trattamento dei dati personali si svolga nel rispetto dei diritti, delle libertà fondamentali, nonché della dignità delle persone fisiche, con particolare riferimento alla riservatezza e alla identità personale; garantisce altresì i diritti delle persone giuridiche e di ogni altro ente o associazione."

interested person has a right to amendment of inexact data, similar to the right of reply seen above.[45]

4. CONCLUDING REMARKS

The preceding analysis of the right to personal identity, as a new personal right, leads to some concluding considerations.

1. The first consideration is that the right to personal identity is a multiform, adaptable right: the consolidated definition of personal identity is flexible enough to grant legal protection to different situations.
2. This makes it possible to take into consideration a plurality of possible legislative constructions in which this right finds a normative rooting. Moreover, this makes it quite hard to apply to the right of personal identity, the traditional distinction between a monistic and a pluralistic approach to personal rights.
3. However, the normative foundation of the right to personal identity finds a unitary aspect in art. 2 of the Constitution, interpreted as an open clause, in conjunction with art. 3(2) and art. 21 (freedom of expression clause). In fact, if the violation of personal identity is made, for instance, by attributing false statements or political attitudes (which is the more recurrent case), then the subject is harmed in his/her freedom of professing openly and explicitly his/her own ideas.[46]
4. The need for a constitutional foundation of the right to personal identity depends on the source of the most recurrent attacks it receives, i.e., the mass media. Given that the activities related to the mass media are in most cases covered by the constitutional clause of free expression (explicitly), it is necessary to find a constitutional foundation for personal rights (especially unwritten ones), in order to reach a suitable compromise between the two.[47]
5. Insofar as personal identity conflicts with freedom of expression, it can be protected only in its objective features. To put it crudely, respect for personal identity can be required in news reporting, but it does not apply to evaluative or critical exercises.
6. The right to personal identity is also recognised for juristic persons, but it is preferable to limit it only to private ones. Indeed, if this kind of protection were also granted to public juristic persons (States or the like), it could easily be used as an instrument for the repression of dissent.[48]

[45] See V. Zeno-Zencovich, "I Diritti della Personalità dopo la Legge sulla Tutela dei Dati Personali", *Studium Iuris*, 5, 1997, 466–469.

[46] Of course, art. 21 Cost. cannot be invoked in the case of sexual identity.

[47] As pointed out by Esposito, only a situation endowed with constitutional relevance can limit the exercise of a constitutional right, see Esposito, *La Libertà di Manifestazione del Pensiero nell'Ordinamento Italiano* (Giuffrè, Milano, 1958).

[48] In this sense, see A. Cerri, "Identità Personale", *Enciclopedia Giuridica*, XV, 1995.

13

The Power of Aspiration. The Impact of European Law on a Non-EU Country

IRENEUSZ C. KAMIŃSKI

1. HISTORICAL BACKGROUND

Poland is a nation of 40 million people which, as a consequence of the unhappy course of post-war history, had to become a member of the Communist bloc. The Polish shared their fate with other nations of this region. Some of them—Hungarians, Czechs—have their tradition strongly rooted in Western European civilization, others—such as Bulgarians and to some extent Romanians—have been influenced by Eastern European culture. Notwithstanding historical and cultural differences, all the countries of the region were governed by communist regimes, installed and subsequently remaining in power against the will of the vast majority of the populations. In Poland, however, ruling communists had to accept, to a much greater extent than in other countries, some particularities resulting from the fact that—as it is alleged Joseph Stalin once said—communism fits Poland in the same way as a saddle suits the cow. The strong position of the Catholic Church, a dominant private agriculture sector and the existence of a growing opposition which culminated in the Solidarity movement are only a few examples which made Poland the, so called, funniest barrack in the camp. Nevertheless, Poland was a totalitarian state—or at least an authoritarian one—precluding private property in almost all areas outside agriculture, enforcing strong laws against opposition, introducing preventive censorship, as well as prohibition of independent manifestations, free trade unions, associations and other forms of activity. No person could have his/her passport at home and each visit abroad was preceded by a screening of the applicant by the Secret Service. Although the majority of Poles considered that the communist rulers were not their own, they had to live with these rulers and the laws these rulers enacted.

In June 1989, only after the "Round Table" talks between ruling communists and the opposition, were Poles allowed to express their real political views for the first time. These elections were not, in fact, entirely democratic. The communists agreed that only election to the upper chamber of the Parliament was free, whereas in the lower chamber 65% of the places were reserved for them and the remaining 35% chosen on a democratic basis. There was also the requirement that the candidate had to obtain 50% of the given votes to be an MP; otherwise he had to stand in the second round. The election's results left no doubts about the political preferences of the population. In 100 members, Senate Solidarity won 99 places almost entirely in the first round (the remaining one senator was independent). In the *Sejm*, the lower chamber, all Solidarity candidates but one were also elected in the first round, whereas no communist candidate entered the Parliament. Even within the ambit of the reserved amount of places, the communist candidates were crossed off the ballot card and not surprisingly humiliated, as they had to take part in the second round of voting. The results simply meant the end of communist rule, and with the accompanying changes in other countries of the collapsing Soviet bloc, there was already no way back.

At the turn of the 1980 and into the 1990s Poland was at last allowed to start changing its political and economic system towards a viable market oriented economy and a democratic form of government. All these changes needed patterns to be followed in order not to get lost in ineffective experimenting. Few normative solutions could be offered by the prewar Polish law, which had been enacted during the short period (1918–1939), when Poland existed as an independent state, since it had been erased from the map of Europe in consequence of three partitions at the end of the eighteenth century. Regarding itself part of (Western) Europe, Poland has applied for membership of the main European institutions. In 1991 Poland joined the Council of Europe, two years later it ratified the European Convention on Human Rights and Fundamental Freedoms. It also was accepted as a member of NATO and its full accession was formally finalized in April 1999. The next target is the European Union. Already in 1990 Poland, together with Hungary and then Czechoslovakia, started negotiations on an association agreement with the European Community. It was signed after a year of talks on 16 December 1991 and came into force on 1 February 1994. Although the status of an associate member does not guarantee Poland full membership of the EU, the Association Agreement "recognizes that the final objective of Poland is to become a member of the Community and that this association, in the view of the Parties, will help achieve this objective".[1] This day is fast approaching, as last year Poland was mentioned among a few countries which would be considered as the first new members of the European Union in years to come. The vast majority of Poles support and have always supported membership of the Union as well as other European institutions. There is, however, a substantial change in the reasoning and politics behind this. During the first period following the collapse of the communist empire the membership of NATO and the European Community was perceived first of all as offering guarantees of national security, especially at the time of the botched *coup d'état* in

[1] Preamble of the Association Agreement.

Russia, increasing tensions around the new Baltic republics and volatile fighting on the outskirts of the former Soviet Union. It would seem that the Polish are now accustomed to the somewhat "predictable instability" of its Eastern European neighbours and think about membership of the European Union in more proper terms: those of economic well-being, a broadening of the common market, and a development of a community with strong political values.

2. DESPERATELY LOOKING FOR GOOD PATTERNS . . .

The process of changes requires the new Poland to reshape its political and economic system as well as its law. "The return to Europe" is an attractive slogan but it must be followed by more practical steps in order to actually be in Europe. In the context of law, these steps consist of the substitution of domestic law for the norms of European law or, at least, European legal standards. Such a process always—to a greater or lesser extent—puts into question the concept of national legal heritage. It is fortunate, therefore, that the Poles did not accept the rules by which they lived at the time of communism. The ruled citizen did not take legal rules seriously, but, strangely enough, neither did the ruling party. In consequence, communist laws have not generated a deeper level of accepted legal tradition or legal culture. Legal culture is a configuration of values, concepts, practices and institutions through which individuals interpret and apply legal norms.[2] All these elements are rooted in general culture. In a stable state, under democratic rule, there exist mechanisms, which enable connections between law, legal tradition and culture. Legal rules are efficient because they answer social expectations and value judgements. Accordingly, legal solutions enter culture and become part of it. In such a situation, changing law by the adaptation of foreign pattern may create difficulties since the change requires a revision of schemes which have been molded during a long period and which a given population perceives as own. In Poland, however, it was not the case. Rejecting legal rules of communist origin did not amount to the rejection of a culturally shared practice or model.

All I have written above should not be understood as suggesting that Poles began to live in a legal vacuum at the beginning of the 1990s. Old communist laws were still in force and new acts could not be prepared overnight. There were some novelties introduced into the Constitution of 1952, but the majority of ordinary statutes were unaffected by the changes. A profound adaptation to new circumstances was, however, necessary and unavoidable. When the Institute for the Administration of Justice, the research institution of the Ministry of Justice, organized a series of conferences in the early 1990s for judges, their subjects were on topics such as law and values or law and justice.

[2] J. Bell, "English law and French law—not so different?" (1995), *Current Legal Problems* 63, at 65–66.

Despite their topics, these conferences were not intended to be purely theoretical or academic, but were very practically oriented with the major aim to propose some applicable modes of adjusting the old law to the requirements of the new state. Presentations delivered there advocated such legal techniques as dynamic interpretation of the law, availing of legal argumentation and taking advantage of systemic, functional and purposeful approaches to law. Good examples were given, from above, by the Constitutional Tribunal which in its decisions has laid down fundamental principles of the new legal order. Interpreting Art. 1 of the amended Constitution (now Art. 2 of the new Constitution), which provides that Poland is a democratic state of law enforcing principles of social justice, the Tribunal referred to such principles as the requirement of *vacatio legis*, prohibition of retroactivity, the protection of acquired rights, legal security and prediction of the legal decision, a right to court and the duty to fulfill legal obligations. These principles form a substantial element of modern Western legal tradition.

Encouragement also came from other sides. The Chief Justice (the First President of the Supreme Court as he is called in Polish), Professor Adam Strzembosz, who took his office in 1990, proposed that Parliament would enact a bill of rights which could serve as the yardstick to measure the old statutes.[3] The task of screening was to be given to the Constitutional Tribunal and the Supreme Court. Eventually his idea was not accepted but nevertheless it encouraged courts to take a more active course in relation to communist law. It is also worth mentioning that despite its critics, even adversaries of the proposal of the Chief Justice themselves pointed out some legal possibilities as to how to cope with communist law. Their suggestions were not, however, very far reaching. They referred to general clauses which exist in different parts of the law and whose primary role was to allow different value judgments and non-legal normative criteria to enter into the law.[4]

General clauses are mostly known in private law. In the Polish civil code of 1964, still in force, the main general clause is that of the principles of communal life. It had been introduced into private law already in the late 1940s and was patterned after the solution existing in the Soviet law. The new clause replaced the traditional general clauses of equity, good manners and public order. The change was to adjust the prewar "bourgeois" private law to the requirements of the new "progressive" communist state. Now the clause of principles of communal life has been used to justify changes that might have terrified the authors of the clause. In a democratic Poland—as many outstanding Polish lawyers argue—the clause refers to "average moral beliefs of Polish society", especially

[3] "Państwo Prawne w Doświadczeniu Przechodzenia z Polskiej Rzeczypospolitej Ludowej do Rzeczypospolitej Polskiej" (The state of law in the experience of transition from Polish People's Republic to Polish Republic) (1992), 11 *Znak* 23, at 27.

[4] For example, T. Zieliński, "Jako Rzecznik Bronie Litery Prawa" (As Ombudsman I defend the black letter of the law) (1992), 11 *Znak* 11, at 15–17.

values rooted in Christian and European traditions.[5] When understood in more definite legal terms, general clauses may point out some European legal standards and allow them to imbue Polish private law with their content. Although some may perceive such a declaration as too broad an approach to be relevant to legal practitioners, this declaration identifies the axiological horizon, which is an important part of the way in which we normally think of our law. This element becomes more significant at a time of change rather than in a period of non-demanding stability.

3. . . . AND MAKING PLACES FOR THEM

The mechanisms and constructions mentioned above act within the framework of domestic law *sensu stricto*. Polish law is interpreted and understood differently than under communism because the values of law appear to have changed as well as the socio-political context of the state. Another problem is, however, the recognition of a more active role that ratified international law might play in municipal law. At the time of communism—as a general rule—international law did not rank as domestic law unless transformed into an act of municipal law. The ratification of international treaties had no—or at best only little—impact on Polish law and the rights of individuals were affected accordingly. Denying any direct applicability of international law produced a comfortable situation for communist authorities because they could sign main international acts on the one side and refuse to apply their provisions internally on the other. Although Poland was party to the UN Covenant of Civil and Political Rights, to the conventions of the International Labour Organization and a number of other basic acts of international legislation, Poles did not enjoy any of the rights their rulers had formally agreed to accept. Accordingly, the Supreme Court could dismiss an appeal lodged by Solidarity activists against the decision of a lower court, which refused them the possibility to set up an independent trade union. The applicants held that the Polish Trade Union Act of 1982 was inconsistent with both the UN Covenant on Civil and Political Rights (art. 22), and ILO Convention 87. Polish law stipulated that only one trade union could legally exist in one enterprise. Deciding the case, the Court repeated the official view that in the absence of any mechanism transforming international law into municipal rules, ratified treaties were binding on Poland only externally and could not offer any legal basis for a court decision internally.[6] To understand properly what human rights were under communism, it should also be borne in

[5] M. Safian, "Klauzule Generalne w Prawie Cywilnym (przyczynek do dyskusji)" (General clauses in civil law. A contribution to discussion) (1990), 11 *Pa(stwo i Prawo* 48, at 54. A similar view has been expressed by another outstanding civil law professor, Z. Radwański, *Prawo Cywilne—Cześć Ogólna (Civil law—general part)* (Warszawa 1993), at 43.

[6] Judgment of 25 August 1987 (I PRZ 8/87), Orzecznictwo Sadu Najwyższego (Decisions of the Supreme Court) 1987, no. 12, item 199.

mind that the Constitution itself did not afford any remedies in cases where human freedoms were either violated or denied. The Constitution had a special part on rights and freedoms, but this chapter did not operate as a source of individual rights. Constitutional provisions were not directly applicable; citizens might avail themselves of their rights only in the way ordinary statutes provided and the latter differed immensely from the declarations of the Constitution.

Changes started with the collapse of communism (in fact communism was already collapsing as the Round Table negotiations took place between the communists and the opposition). The amendment of 7 April 1989 introduced into the Constitution a rule which gave the president (a new institution which both sides of the negotiations agreed upon) the power to ratify and denounce international treaties, subject to the approval of the Parliament when treaties imposed financial obligations on the State or required changes in municipal legislation. This provision was also a symbolic one and meant a return to the rule of the prewar Constitution of 1921 which was interpreted by the court as having the effect of transforming treaties into domestic law which gave them the same legal force as national legislation. The new approach required clarification and it took Polish courts some time before they elaborated more precise rules.[7] This modification went in parallel with personal changes. New people appeared in courts; people who were previously barred from the judiciary. Professor Adam Strzembosz, who had been expelled from the university and sacked from the Ministry of Justice by communists, became Chief Justice. Professor Andrzej Zoll, whom communist authority had been refusing a professorial nomination for many years, became the President of the Constitutional Tribunal. It must also be stressed that a significant role in the process of change had been played by already existing institutions, especially by the Polish Ombudsman, who could only fully flourish after communism collapsed.

By 1992, the Supreme Court pointed out that since Polish *Sejm* (the lower chamber of Parliament) had adopted a statute authorizing the ratification of an international treaty, and since this treaty has been published in the Official Gazette *(Dziennik Ustaw)*, this has the consequence that the treaty "has been leveled with parliamentary statutes and may be applied by the courts like a statute, with all the consequences resulting therefrom".[8] In other cases the Supreme Court, the Supreme Administration Court and the Constitutional Tribunal has often referred to international law ratified by Poland in order to decide on the application and interpretation of domestic legal provisions. One of the most frequently quoted was that of the European Convention on Human Rights and Fundamental Freedoms. For example, the Constitutional Tribunal

[7] For an overview of approaches of Polish main judicial bodies see W. Czapliński, "International law and Polish municipal law: recent jurisprudence of the Polish supreme judicial organs" (1994), 54 *Zeitschrift für Ausländisches Öffentliches Recht und Völkerrecht*, 871; Z. Kedzia, "The implementation of international human rights agreements in Poland", in *The Relationship between International and Domestic Law* (Dordrecht, Kluwer, 1993), p. 21.

[8] Case III 48/92, Orzecznictwo Sadu Najwyższego. Izba Cywilna (Decisions of the Supreme Court. Civil Division) 1992, no. 10, item 179, at 62.

stated that the ratification of the Convention meant that "all state organs are tied by commitments found therein".[9] It is also worth mentioning that Polish legal doctrine has contributed, in a substantial way, to the transmission of knowledge of the Convention to judicial personnel as well as to the general public. Since the political changes, the number of relevant publications has increased enormously, whereas under communism there were only a few articles written on this issue. These very rare pieces of legal writing were—as two authors qualified them—either an expression of honesty of the researchers or "a manifestation of rebellious attitude, similar to the practice of wearing bright socks or playing jazz under Stalin".[10]

At present, under the new Constitution, which came into force on 17 October 1997, the position of international law has been explicitly defined.[11] Art. 9 reads that Poland internally enforces ratified international rules, and art. 87 states that such rules are one of the recognized sources of domestic law. Moreover, there are three articles introduced specifically in order to facilitate our future membership in the European Union and to clarify the (future) relationship between Polish and European norms. Art. 90 (1) allows that Poland can transfer, on concluding an international treaty, part of its sovereign competence in certain matters to an international organization, or to its organ. In such situation, international treaties will, as a rule, be directly applicable by Polish courts and administrative authorities unless it requires the enactment of a domestic statute (art. 91 (1)). In case of any conflict between a Polish statute and an international act (the European treaties included), priority will be given to the latter (art. 91 (2)). As far as secondary legislation is concerned, it will be applied directly within the Polish legal system and eliminate contradicting municipal rules upon the condition that norms constituting international organizations provide for such applicability of its legislation (art. 91 (3)). It is worth mentioning that all these constitutional provisions were patterned after the corresponding rules within the Dutch Constitution of 1983 (art. 92–94) which was considered the most favorable constitution towards European law amongst member states.

By now, an indispensable role is being played by the practice of the highest judicial and legal bodies of showing lower courts and administrative organs how law may be construed and applied. Judges are encouraged to make use of international law, in particular of the European Convention, during training programs and workshops. They are to make judges aware that the Convention is a living instrument, which must be taken into account in order to render a

[9] Case W 3/93 Orzecznictwo Trybunału Konstytucyjnego (Decisions of the Constitutional Tribunal) 1994, no. I, item 17.

[10] A. Drzemczewski, M. A. Nowicki, "The Impact of the ECHR in Poland: a Shock-taking after Three Years" (1996), 3 *European Human Rights Law Review* 261, at 261–262.

[11] On the provisions of this Constitution regarding the position of international law see A. Wasilkowski, "International Law and International Relations in the New Polish Constitution of 2 April 1997" (1997–1998), 23 *Polish Yearbook of International Law*; S. Biernat, "Constitutional Aspects of Poland's Future Membership in the European Union" (1998), 36 *Archiv des Völkerrechts*, 398.

good decision. The Convention, and the case law of the Strasbourg Court, form standards of dealing with legal issues, not only because a case decided in disregard of these standards may ultimately end up in Strasbourg, but mostly since the standards should be treated as laying down one of the very foundations of the Polish legal order. Accordingly, the highest judicial bodies in Poland have pointed out that the European Convention is an important act to be used for interpretation of domestic law[12] and that it might even offer new legal measures and remedies (and *a fortiori* change the way in which the existing ones are applicable) if the provisions of international treaties have been directly introduced into municipal law or are self-executing.[13]

In every case in which Poland appeared as the defendant in Strasbourg, the point of focus has not directly concerned private law. Proceedings have touched on mostly criminal and procedural matters such as excessive length of proceedings, length of detention on remand and in mental hospitals, refusal to allow an applicant to attend the appeal hearing and dismissal of all requests of hearing evidence. In consequence of the decisions taken by the Commission of Human Rights and the Strasbourg Court, as well as the criticism expressed by legal doctrine of the provisions of Polish penal regulations,[14] there has been a series of changes that have culminated in the enactment of two new codes on criminal law and criminal procedure which came into force 1 September 1998. It does not mean, however, that private law is immune from the impact of the European Convention and the case law resulting therefrom. It would appear that one case, currently pending within the Regional court at Warsaw, may turn out to be a leading and ground-breaking case for legal practice in certain important branches of the civil law and, perhaps, even in broader legal terms. This case ignites a lot of emotions, because it carries a strong political element, but it also makes lawyers, who would pretend to argue on a more neutral legal basis, excited.

[12] See for example resolution of the Constitutional Tribunal of 2 March 1994, case 3/93, Orzecznictwo Trybunału Konstytucyjnego (Decisions of the Constitutional Tribunal) 1994, no. I, at 157–158. The same need was pointed out by the Supreme Court in its recent decisions: in resolution of 20 January 1999, case I KZP 21/98 (the use of evidence obtained from *incognito* witness and the right to defense), "Orzecznictwo Sadu Najwyższego. Izba Karna i Wojskowa" (Decisions of the Supreme Court. Criminal and Military Division) 1999, no. 1–2, item 3; resolution of 15 September 1999, case I KZP 27/99 (State's liability for detention on remand as based on the principle of risk), not yet published.

[13] See for example resolution of Supreme Court of February 19, 1997, case I KZP 37/96, "Orzecznictwo Sadu Najwyższego. Izba Karna i Wojskowa" (Decisions of the Supreme Court. Criminal and Military Division) 1997, no. 3–4, item 21.

[14] Amongst many publications, of special importance were books written by P. Hofmański, *Konwencja Europejska a Prawo Karne (The European Convention and penal law)* (Toruń, 1995); P. Hofmański, *Europejska Konwencja Praw Człowieka i jej Znaczenie dla Prawa Karnego Materialnego, Procesowego i Wykonawczego (European Convention and its significance for substantive, procedural and executive penal law)* (Toruń, 1993); "Europejskie Standardy w Zakresie Kontroli Stosowania Przymusu w Procesie Karnym a Reforma Kodeksu Postepowania Karnego" (European standards for the control of enforcement measures in the criminal process and the reform of Criminal Procedure Code), in *Problemy Kodyfikacji Prawa Karnego (Codification problems of penal law)* (Warszawa, 1993). The author, an outstanding scholar, is now also a judge in the Supreme Court.

The plaintiff in this case is the President of the Republic, Aleksander Kwasniewski, acting as a private person. The defendant is *Życie*, a leading quality newspaper. In August 1997 the paper published a well documented article whose authors stated that in the summer of 1994 Aleksander Kwaśniewski, who at this point was not the president, had spent his holiday in a well known resort at the same time as a Russian citizen, happening to be a high rank former KGB agent, now a businessman. The authors wanted a president's comment on the findings and asked for an interview accordingly. Before the publication appeared, some news about the content of the material broke to the public, so it must also have been known to the future plaintiff. His press office tried to postpone the interview, suggesting that the president was very busy. Having waited for over a week, the newspaper decided to print the article. Once the publication had appeared, the president instituted proceedings for civil libel. He demanded a compensation of 2.5 million zloty, which is the equivalent of over 700,000 US dollars. He presented some evidence that he could not have been in the place he was alleged to have been at the time. To make the political background more understandable, one extra piece of information can be added. Before the election, the plaintiff, who now declares to be the president of all Poles, was the most prominent figure of the post-communist political left. The defendant—on the other hand—is a daily newspaper with strong commitments to the anti-communist Solidarity tradition.

Before the court proceedings started, there had appeared a series of articles and comments written by Polish academics and practicing lawyers who pointed out that damages demanded in civil cases must be evaluated in the light of the European Convention. They referred to the case of *Tolstoy Miloslavsky v. United Kingdom*,[15] which requires compensation to be proportionate and not excessive. In *Tolstoy Miloslavsky*, the Strasbourg Court recognized that a court decision awarding £1,500,000 compensation for libel, committed in a pamphlet, had violated Art. 10 of the Convention. Such an amount was not necessary in a democratic society and did not assure a reasonable relationship of proportionality to the legitimate aim pursued in the proceedings. The Court did not, however, point out what would be reasonable and proportionate. According to some suggestions and practice, a test of proportionality may refer to such elements as the average salary in a particular country or the average damages awarded when more basic goods are violated, especially in cases of death and injury. In Poland, in the latter situation damages are relatively low and under communism any compensation for moral suffering was considered contradictory to the new emerging communist morality. By awarding, in the pending case, any compensation approximate to the plaintiff's demand, Polish courts would risk that their judgement be reviewed by Strasbourg. I hope that they are aware of this risk, not only as a result of the publications preceding and accompanying the proceedings, but mostly because Polish judges have already

[15] 20 *European Human Rights Reports* 1995, 442.

acquired some knowledge about the Convention and its relevance to Polish legal order. Judges in the case must also take into account the fact that if the damages were awarded according to the plaintiff's demand it would mean serious financial problems—and even bankruptcy—of the leading political daily newspaper. This consequence must not be disregarded by the judges, as freedom of the press has been declared one of the most fundamental values which are important for the proper functioning of democratic society, and which are given special protection under the Convention.[16]

4. PREPARING FOR MEMBERSHIP

Having signed the association agreement, Poland has, amongst its other duties, been obliged to approximate its law to the provisions of European law and legislation. It must be borne in mind, first, that approximation does not equal harmonisation, which is required only of the member states. Secondly, the association agreement points out some areas which are specifically covered by the obligation of approximation. Those areas are as follows: customs law, company law, banking law, accounting and taxation of commercial units, intellectual property, protection of workers at the workplace, financial services, principles of competition law, consumer protection, indirect taxation, and rules concerning technological standards, transportation and the environment (art. 69). The agreement requires Poland to take any necessary steps to fulfill this obligation and expressly recognises that the approximation of the country's law to that of the Community is the major precondition for Poland's economic integration into the Community (art. 68). The agreement provides also Poland and the Community with a timetable for implementation and envisages a transitory period of a maximum duration of 10 years divided into two successive stages, each in principle lasting five years (art. 6(1)). Further steps in the approximation process have been specified on the basis of the White Book published by the European Commission in 1995.

Simultaneously with the ratification of the association agreement, the Polish Parliament has passed a resolution obliging the government to formulate a detailed program of adjustment measures for the approximation of Polish law with EC law. Already in July 1992, the Legislative Council, a body formed by the Prime Minister with the aim to point out main legislative priorities, concluded following an analysis of about 500 statutes that almost hundred of them should be reformed and 18 entirely repealed to adjust Polish law to the requirements of economic reform. The role to coordinate and develop Polish legal reforms, in a manner supportive of the process of approximation, was assigned to the Office of the Undersecretary of State for European Integration and

[16] For example in *Lingens* v. *Austria*, 8 *European Human Rights Reports* 407, (41; *Observer and Guardian* v. *United Kingdom*, 14 *European Human Rights Reports* 153, (59.

Foreign Economic Assistance which was established in January 1991. Since September 1996 it has existed as the Committee for European Integration.

In 1994 the Polish government decided that each draft of legal acts proposed by the government and its offices should come through a procedure which would determine whether the draft conforms with the requirements set out in the White Book and with EC law in general. This role, under the present law, has been given to the Committee for European Integration. The Committee (and within its structure the Legal Service Department especially) proposes measures for the approximation process and provides opinions when drafts of legal acts involve any "European issue". Giving its advice, the Department refers to European regulations, directives, decisions and case law. Until 1997, it controlled over 1200 acts and found 17 of them inconsistent with EC provisions.[17]

Since 19 March 1999, when Parliament changed its Internal Rules, the monitoring mechanism also applies to the drafts prepared by Parliament. First, to each draft law must be attached the declaration of the draft's authors stating that the proposal is in conformity with Community law. Second, when the draft law is handed over further to the next stages of legislative procedure, parliamentary commissions are obliged to apply for the opinion from the Committee of European Integration. But even before that change parliamentary commissions, as a matter of legislative procedure, might seek, and not rarely actually sought, advice of either the Committee for European Integration or of their own legal experts. At present, however, all legislative proposals and even decisions (amendments introduced by Senate) must be submitted to the Committee. If competent bodies fail to apply for opinions it constitutes a breach of parliamentary procedure. In its expertise on conformity of domestic law with EC provisions, the Committee fulfils the task which is similar to that given to the European Commission and the Luxembourg court within the European Union. Although opinions are not binding, it is very likely that Parliament and its organs will follow them and, accordingly, the (European) quality of new statutes will improve.

An example of how Polish law is changing under the influence of European standards is offered by company law. In 1934, prior to the Second World War, Poland enacted a commercial code, which was considered as one of the best in Europe at that time. Although the communists did not repeal the code in its entirety, they did repeal some important parts considered to be unnecessary or obsolete (on limited partnership, sole traders, legal persons, business disposal and traders' accounts). Only provisions on partnerships, limited liability and joint stock companies had survived, but they were scarcely used. With the collapse of the old regime, traditional commercial instruments have been

[17] M. Górka, "Realizacja Białej Ksiegi Komisji Europejskiej w Porzadku Prawnych Przeczpospolitej Polskiej Jako Element Procesu Dostosowania Praw Polskiego do Standardów Unii Europejskiej" (Realization of the European Commission's While Book in Poland's legal system as a factor of adjustment process of the Polish law to the European Union standards), in *Polska w Unii Europejskiej (Poland in the European Union)* (Toruń, 1997), 9, at 11.

revitalised to relinquish direct state involvement in economic activities. Both domestic and foreign subjects have been placed under the same legal framework of the commercial code (earlier foreign investors had to act on the basis of regulations enacted specifically for them).

When foreign authors analysed Polish commercial law in the first years after the political changes, they suggested a series of modifications in order to adjust it to the corresponding European directives.[18] To conform with the First and Second Directive (on company disclosure requirements, and capital formation and maintenance), the law would need an amendment requiring each company to publish in a national newspaper all information which is enclosed in the Polish commercial register as well as an expert's evaluation of non-monetary contributions to subscribed capital. There had to be a number of changes concerning rules on accounting (required by the Fourth, Seventh and Eighth Directives). The Eleventh Directive (on branch offices) would require the removal of the permit requirement and the Proposed Fifth Directive (on corporate governance) implied new rules on mandatory employee participation in supervisory boards. Now, Polish company law has been amended in many parts and satisfies most of the standards expressed in the directives. Accordingly, some authors argue that our company regulations have undergone a sufficient procedural approximation analogous to the process of implementing a directive within a member state.[19]

Other authors, however, would go much further. They advocate a draft law on commercial companies, which would take a more substantive approach, namely in respect of incorporation of EC company law into Polish law. The draft law they prepared introduces new forms of commercial activity and rearranges the existing ones. What these authors mean by EC company law is not limited to the very scope of the European directives on commercial companies, but it also covers developments in commercial laws of the main continental legal systems. In consequence the drafters want to introduce, for example, a command joint stock company capable of issuing non-voting preferred shares. These shares do not entitle their shareholder to vote or otherwise participate in the management of the company, but as they are publicly tradable they might accommodate a wider range of investors. Other constructions of the Draft Law would contribute to corporate governance, to the protection of minority shareholders and creditors of the company, and also to clarifying rules on disclosure.[20]

The controversy over the regulations on commercial companies is a good example of how far the Poles are willing to go to be in Europe, and the fact that

[18] See, for example, C. Brzezinski, "The EC-Poland Association Agreement: Harmonization of an Aspiring Member State's Company Law" (1993), 34 *Harvard International Law Journal* 105.

[19] M. Safjan, J. Okolski, J. Modrzejewski, J. Brol, J. Krauss, W. Opalski, M. Modrzejewska, "Stanowsisko w Sprawie Projektu Ustawy—Prawo Spółek handlowych" (An opinion on the draft of Act on Commercial Companies) (1998), 152 *Rzeczpospolita*.

[20] The whole project with the accompanying explaining report was published in 1998, as special issue 1–2 *Studia Prawnicze*.

they are not simply here because they are less skilful or they lack imagination. When someone has an obsolete device he may try to amend it, risking, however, that he will have to repeatedly invest in continuous reparations. A better solution is often to buy a new device and to replace the old one, especially when there is no affection for the latter. There exists, however, an inherent danger when we are using European law. European law consists mostly of directives, which formulate aims to be obtained in particular legal domestic systems. Directives set out standards that all the member states must follow, but the way these states will pursue and achieve the standards depends on the logic, *mentalit(* or the style in which a particular national law operates. Moreover, integration by means of directives is not holistic but compartmentalised, centered on some aspects, fragments, and is—as Jürgen Basedow named it—pointillistic.[21]

The scenario of "integration by directives" presupposes the existence of a law that is changing under the influence of a directive. Directives as such are not designed to create a comprehensive regulation, or even a coherent code. If we, however, think of directives as wonderful instruments which would one day, somehow, magically fit together we may make a serious mistake and not see the wood and trees for the forest. The Poles seem to overestimate the role of directives and expect too much from the application of their guiding provisions. While they are directive-oriented, the Poles seem to disregard the Civil Code of 1964. This approach also explains why the Poles have been postponing the enactment of a new civil code. They seem to say: "Let specific statutes patterned after directives do their work first, and only then will we be able to decide what might be thorough regulation of a general character". United Europe may offer us directives, but if Europe presently provided us with a European code of private law, the Poles—I guess—would be among its most convinced admirers. In comparison with the Civil Code of 1964, the situation of the Commercial Code was different. The successful revival of the whole body of the Commercial Code was possible because the code itself fulfilled the task of reforming Polish economic life, it generated a significant new case law as well as an accumulation of European directives. Accordingly, a far reaching Europeanisation must indeed raise serious doubts.

In this article I have tried to outline the phenomenon of power of aspiration and sketch some structural reasons suggesting why the Poles are so open and eager to accept European rules and standards. In finishing what I have written, I would like to stress that the phenomenon in question will not be everlasting. When an aspiring country becomes a member country we notice another phenomenon emerging. It may be called simply power of membership. Poland is a nation of 40 million people and it will be a demanding member. The change I mentioned is just under way, as far as the Council of Europe is concerned.

[21] "A Common Contract Law for the Common Market" (1996), 33 *Common Market Law Review* 1169, at 1178.

Recently, this European institution has agreed to amend the Convention on Transfrontier Television by introducing a special arbitration procedure designed for cases where broadcasting activity is undertaken from abroad with the aim to circumvent legal requirements, especially for licence, existing in domestic law (delocation practices).[22] Polish insistence on these changes was motivated by the fact that big foreign television companies, such as RTL-7 or HBO, transmit their programs to Poland from abroad to the detriment of the television companies which conform with the provisions of Polish broadcasting law. Although the arbitration procedure, which is designed to settle emerging conflicts amicably, is not a perfect solution (it consists of a series of necessary steps lasting several months and does not end up in a binding decision), its introduction is evidence that Poland has discovered the power of membership.

[22] Art. 24 bis as introduced by art. 30 of the Protocol Amending the European Convention on Transfrontier Television (ETS no. 171). The Protocol was signed 9 September 1998 and has been opened for acceptance since 1 October 1998.

Index

Topics, names and cases are only included in this index when discussed in the text, not simply when referred to briefly